Changing Dimensions in Economic Development

REVIEW BOARD

Changing Dimensions in Economic Development: Theories and Empirics

EDITED BY

DEBASHIS MAZUMDAR
The Heritage College, India

AND

RAJIB BHATTACHARYYA
Goenka College of Commerce and Business Administration, India

emerald PUBLISHING

United Kingdom – North America – Japan – India – Malaysia – China

Emerald Publishing Limited
Emerald Publishing, Floor 5, Northspring, 21-23 Wellington Street, Leeds LS1 4DL.

First edition 2026

British Library Cataloguing in Publication Data
A catalogue record for this book is available from the British Library

ISBN: 978-1-83708-385-5 (Print)
ISBN: 978-1-83708-384-8 (Online)
ISBN: 978-1-83708-386-2 (Epub)

INVESTOR IN PEOPLE

Contents

About the Editors

Debashis Mazumdar is now serving at The Heritage College, Kolkata, West Bengal, India, as Professor and HOD in the Department of Economics. He has been teaching Economics both at UG and PG levels for the last 42 years. He completed his PG study in Economics from Jadavpur University, Kolkata; MPhil in Economics from the University of Calcutta; and done his PhD from Rabindra Bharati University, Kolkata. He has served Sudhiranjan Lahiri Mahavidyalaya, Nadia and Bangabasi College, Kolkata. He has also served Nababullygunj Mahavidyalaya (as Visiting Faculty at the PG (Commerce)). He was also an empaneled research guide for PhD scholars at Vidyasagar University, Medinipur, West Bengal, India, and two scholars have been awarded a PhD degree under his guidance. He has authored/co-authored about 40 text books in Economics (some of which are the prescribed text books at the UG level of Calcutta University), contributed about 65 research articles in national and international journals and edited three conference volumes. He has also worked as Reviewer of Book Proposals and as a member of the Editorial Board in reputed publishing houses like IGI Global (USA), Emerald (UK), Routledge, etc. His research areas consist of international trade, green marketing, rural development, etc.

Rajib Bhattacharyya is Associate Professor (WBES-A), in the Department of Economics, Goenka College of Commerce and Business Administration, Kolkata, India. He obtained his bachelor's degree in Economics from St Xavier's College, Kolkata, and his master's degree in Economics, from the University of Calcutta. He did his MPhil and PhD in Economics, both from the University of Calcutta. He has 22 years of teaching experience at the UG and PG levels. His fields of interest are international trade, finance, Indian economic development, and women empowerment. He has contributed a good number of articles in reputed national and international journals/books, viz., IGI Global (USA), Emerald (UK), Taylor & Francis, and Springer. He has delivered invited lectures in many UGC-sponsored seminars/webinars/conferences. He has also worked as a member of the editorial board of various national- and international-level journals. He had been conferred the best paper award in an international seminar on 'Recent Trends and Perspectives in Economics' in January 2016. He has served as Invited Reviewer in *Indian Economic Journal* (Sage), *Foreign Trade Review* (Sage), *Journal of Asian and African Studies* (Sage), and *International Journal of ICT Research and Development in Africa* (IGI Global). He also has the experience of guiding PhD students (https://orcid.org/0000-0003-1117-6338).

About the Contributors

Margaret Antonicelli, PhD, is Research Fellow at the IULM University of Milan, Statistical Consultant at the Libera Università of Bolzano, and Lecturer of Social Statistic. She has published her work in national and international journals such as *Corporate Governance*, *Social Indicators Research* and *Encyclopedia of Quality of Life and Well-Being Research.*

Asis Kumar Banerjee obtained his MA degree in Economics from the University of Calcutta in 1969 and his PhD in Economics from Johns Hopkins University, Baltimore, Maryland, USA, in 1976. At various stages of his career, he was associated with Presidency College, Kolkata, Indian Statistical Institute, New Delhi, and University of California, Riverside, California, USA. His publications include articles in leading academic journals of international repute. He also acted as Vice-Chancellor, University of Calcutta, and as Professor of Economics (Department of Economics) at the University of Calcutta.

Kaushiki Banerjee is presently working as Assistant Professor of Economics at Barasat Government College, and Research Scholar, Department of Economics, Jadavpur University, India. She was UGC-NET Junior Research Fellow. Her research interests include gender, health, environment, and econometrics. She has made paper presentations in national/international conferences and publications in journals/edited volumes.

Mainak Bhattacharjee is Assistant Professor in Department of Economics at Loreto College, Kolkata, India. He has obtained PhD, MPhil, and MA degrees in Economics from the Jadavpur University. His area of research interest includes macroeconomics, development economics, international trade, and public economics. He has published many research articles with reputed journals and in edited volumes, as well as text books on microeconomics and macroeconomics for the UG level of study in Economics.

Santanu Bhattacharya is Research Scholar in the Department of Economics at Sidho-Kanho-Birsha University, Purulia, India. His doctoral research focuses on cross-country income inequality. Additionally, he has authored several publications on topics such as health economics and female labour force participation.

Santanu Bisai is Associate Professor in Sidho-Kanho-Birsha University, Purulia, India. His research focuses on microfinance, labour, and inequality. He has published more than 25 articles in national and international journals including Springer, Sage, Emerald, and others. One research scholar has been awarded a PhD under his supervision.

Atreyee Sinha Chakraborty is Associate Professor and also Associate Dean of Academics and Programme Co-ordinator of International Business Economics and Finance at Gokhale Institute of Politics and Economics, Pune, India. Her research interests are international trade. Her secondary focus area is the economics of discrimination. She has published sixteen research papers and has also published six book chapters in various books and edited volumes.

Debashis Chakraborty is Professor at Department of Economics, IIFT Kolkata. His research interests include international trade, environmental sustainability, and economic development. For the last decade, he is Editorial Board Member of *Foreign Trade Review* (Sage).

Bidisha Chatterjee is Assistant Professor of Department of Economics, St Xavier's College, Burdwan, West Bengal. She has completed PhD from University of Burdwan, and her research area focuses on climate change and energy economics. Her teaching area includes microeconomics, macroeconomics, development, and environmental economics.

Dyuti Chatterjee is Assistant Professor of Economics in St Xavier's University. She did her PhD from the University of Calcutta and has nearly 15 years of teaching experience. She is actively involved in research and has several research papers to her credit.

Nilendu Chatterjee, PhD, is Assistant Professor in the Department of Economics, Bankim Sardar College, West Bengal, India. He has research interest in resource economics, general equilibrium, and development economics. He has published a number of research articles in several international journals of economics including *Quality and Quantity*, *Journal of Development Review*, *International Journal of Sustainable Economies Management*, *Economic Affairs*, and *Foreign Trade Review* (https://orcid.org/0000-0002-8570-0262).

Bibek Ray Chaudhuri is Professor of Economics at Indian Institute of Foreign Trade (IIFT), Kolkata, India. He did his PhD in Economics from JNU, New Delhi, India. He is Visiting Fellow at School of Environment, Education and Development (SEED), the University of Manchester, UK. He has published his works in journals like *Journal of Business Research* (Elsevier), *Market Intelligence and Planning* (Emerald), *Journal of Political Marketing* (Taylor and Francis), *Journal of Industrial Statistics*, and *Journal of Asian Business Studies* (Emerald). He was a recipient of the prestigious 'Japanese Award for Outstanding Research on Development'.

J. K. Das is Professor, Dean, and Convener of PhD RAC of Commerce at the University of Calcutta. He is also Chairperson of the UG Board of Studies in Commerce. Previously, he held various academic and administrative positions, published over 100 research papers, and delivered more than 300 invited lectures.

Pinaki Das is Professor and Former Head, Department of Economics, Vidyasagar University. He has 19 years of teaching experience at UG and PG levels. He has led five major research projects funded by Department of Science and Technology (DST), University Grants Commission (UGC) and Indian Council of Social Science Research (ICSSR). He has published more than 77 research papers in internationally reputed journals from Springer Nature, Routledge, Sage, etc. He has guided 18 research scholars and authored 7 books.

Soovankar Das is University Grants Commission-National Eligibility Test-Junior Research Fellow (UGC-NET-JRF) PhD Scholar in the Department of Economics, University of Calcutta, India. He has also served as Guest Faculty in the Department of Economics, The Heritage College, Kolkata, India.

Souvik Dasgupta is Assistant Professor in the Department of Economics at Sidho-Kanho-Birsha University, Purulia, India, with over 11 years of PG teaching experience. His research focuses on development economics, particularly health, education, and poverty. He has published in international journals and books, contributing to the field's advancement.

Utpal Kumar De, Professor of Economics, North-Eastern Hill University, Shillong, India, has been teaching for the last 31 years at the PG level. His research interests are in agricultural economics, climate change, adaptation, applied econometrics, and empowerment of women. Besides completing six research projects, he has published 182 research articles in various reputed international and Indian journals as well as edited volumes. He was a keynote speaker or invited speaker in India and abroad and so far guided 19 PhD scholars.

Martina De Anna is PhD candidate at the Department of Economics and Business of the University of Genoa. His research interests focus on sustainable transport, public transport, and urban development.

Mousumi Dutta is Professor in the Department of Economics at Presidency University, Kolkata. She has obtained PhD, MSc, and BSc degrees in Economics from Calcutta University, and MPhil in Economics from Jadavpur University. She has recently finished two international projects, funded by The International Growth Center and London School of Economics. Her areas of interest includes application of econometrics to development issues, in health, gender, and environment.

Swati Dutta holds a master's degree from Burdwan University. She is currently serving as District Nutrition Consultant in the Office of the District Magistrate, Purulia, under UNICEF project. She has published four articles focused on child health and nutrition. Her most recent work was published by Wolters Kluwer.

Richardson Kojo Edeme is Associate Professor in the Department of Economics at Dennis Osadebay University, Asaba, Nigeria. He is equally Research Fellow, Institute of Business Research, University of Economics Ho Chi Minh City, Vietnam. He has published widely in public expenditure policy, trade policy, governance, and environmental sustainability-related areas.

Tommaso Filì is PhD candidate in Marine Science and Technology at the Italian Center of Excellence for Logistics, Transport and Infrastructure (CIELI) of the University of Genoa, and Subject Matter Expert in Applied Economics at the same university. His research interests focus on sustainable yachting, superyacht industry, and urban development.

Antonio Gattulli is Export Manager of Bio Organica Italia. He obtained a PG master's degree in Economic Security, Geopolitics, and Intelligence from SIOI – Italian Society for International Organisation. He is specialised in the field of organic production and healthy food and has contributed to several scientific publications in the field of economics and statistics.

Elisa Gerbasi is PhD student at University LUM Giuseppe Degennaro, Italy. Her main research interests are accounting and business administration, particularly regarding corporate social responsibility and business and human rights.

Tusar Kanti Ghorai is State-Aided College Teacher-I, Department of Commerce, Uluberia College, affiliated to University of Calcutta. He is pursuing PhD in Commerce from Vidyasagar University. He has eight years of teaching experience at UG levels. He has published five research papers in journals and edited books.

Arpita Ghose is Professor-Economics, Chair Professor (Honorary), Planning and Development Unit (PDU), Jadavpur University (JU, NITI-Aayog), Government of India/Former Dean, Faculty of Arts, JU. A PhD from Indian Statistical Institute, Kolkata, she authored/edited books, published research papers in international/national journals/edited volumes. She collaborated on research projects with NITI-Aayog, Government of India, eminent national/international funding institutes. She chaired workshops/conferences. She supervised PhD students, and her research areas are econometrics, macroeconomics, studies on productivity, efficiency, and economies of the social sector.

Uttam Haldar is Assistant Professor of Economics and HOD, Serampore Girls' College, West Bengal, India. He has long teaching experience. His research area includes food and nutrition security, health, education, livelihoods and labour economics, agricultural economics, and environment economics. He has contributed a good number of articles in reputed national and international journals/ edited volume (indexed in Scopus, Web of Science, UGC care) (https://orcid.org/0000-0001-5741-9222).

Zakir Husain is Professor in the Department of Economics at Presidency University, Kolkata. He has obtained PhD and MSc degrees in Economics from Calcutta University. He has been actively engaged in UG teaching (since 1994) and in PG teaching (since 1998). He is currently supervising doctoral research on mental health in India, climate change, and children. In research, his focus has been on applying econometric methods to areas like health, gender, education, and ageing.

Enrico Ivaldi is Associate Professor at IULM University, Milan, and PhD in Applied Economics. He serves on editorial boards and scientific committees, with affiliations in Italy, Argentina, and the Vatican. Author of 70+ publications, his research focuses on social indicators, inequalities, deprivation, and sustainable urban development.

M. Zakir Saadullah Khan, Professor of Economics, Comilla University, Bangladesh, holds a PhD (Jahangirnagar University, Bangladesh), MA in International Business Economics (University of Konstanz, Germany), and MSS and BSS (Hons) in Economics (University of Dhaka, Bangladesh). With 31+ years' experience, he has 80+ research outputs on energy economics, international economics, and economics of Fourth Industrial Revolution (4IR), contributing significantly to economic research and policy discourse in Bangladesh.

Rajeshwari Kumari has an MSc in Economics from the University of Warwick and working as a Senior Associate in Deloitte, UK. Specifically, she has experience in socio-economic impact assessments, energy regulation, and technology, media, and telecommunication (TMT) regulation. She has built expertise across economic research, economic regulation, economic modelling, price control financial frameworks, and cost allocation.

Jagabandhu Mandal is Assistant Professor and Head, Department of Economics, Subarnarekha Mahavidyalaya affiliated to Vidyasagar University. He has 10 years of teaching experience at UG levels. He was working as Project Fellow and Research Assistant of four research projects under UGC-SAP DRS Project, ICSSR Major Research Project, DEC Sponsored Research Project, Department of Minority Affairs, Government of West Bengal.

Ilaria Mastrorocco is PhD candidate at University LUM Giuseppe Degennaro, Italy. Her main research interests are accounting and business administration, particularly regarding corporate social responsibility; environmental, social, and governance ratings; and business and human rights.

Rishabh Mukherjee is MSc Economics graduate from the University of Warwick, UK. He works as Tax and Public Policy Consultant with EY, India. He has delivered actionable insights to various state governments through detailed analysis of the states' fiscal health. He has also performed in-depth evaluations of Government of India policy frameworks.

Enrico Musso is Full Professor of Applied Economics at the University of Genoa and Director of the Italian Centre of Excellence on Logistics, Transport and Infrastructure. He also serves as Editor in Chief of the *International Journal of Transport Economics*.

Tiziano Pavanini is Research Fellow at the Department of Architecture and Urbanism of the Politecnico di Milano. He specialises in transport economics, with a focus on public transport, sustainable urban mobility, mobility as a service, and the mobility of the elderly.

Swapan-Kumar Pradhan is Principal Statistical Analyst at the Bank for International Settlements, which he joined in 2003. Previously, he held various roles in the Statistics Department of the Reserve Bank of India. He holds a master's degree in Statistics and a PhD in Financial Economics from the University of Calcutta.

Ankita Rajgarhia is Assistant Professor in the Department of Economics at The Heritage College, Kolkata. She has obtained her PhD degree in Economics from Presidency University, Kolkata. She has completed her MSc in Economics from Teri University, Delhi, and her BA in Economics from Lady Shri Ram College for Women, Delhi. Her area of research interest includes development economics, game theory, and econometrics.

Michele Rubino, PhD, is Full Professor of Accounting at University LUM Giuseppe Degennaro, Italy. His main research interests include corporate sustainability reporting, human rights, environmental, social and governance rating, accounting information systems, entrepreneurship, digitalisation, and internationalisation. He has published numerous articles and serves on the editorial boards of several international journals.

Madhurima Saha is currently working in the Department of Economics of South Calcutta Girls' College under the University of Calcutta as Whole-time Lecturer. She is also attached with Gargi Memorial Institute of Technology under MAKAUT as Visiting Faculty of Economics. She has many publications in reputed and UGC Care journals.

Jhumur Sengupta is Assistant Professor of Economics at Dinabandhu Andrews College, Kolkata, India. She got her master's (2000) and MPhil (2003) in Economics from Jawaharlal Nehru University, New Delhi. She completed her PhD (2009) at the University of Calcutta. Her area of research includes quantitative techniques and data analysis.

Soumyen Sikdar is Retired Professor, Indian Institute of Management, Calcutta. He was awarded PhD (Economics) from University of Minnesota, USA. He has served as Visiting Faculty in University of Minnesota, USA; Osaka University, Japan; Shenzhen University, China; Presidency College, Calcutta; IGIDR, Mumbai; Burdwan University; and University of Calcutta. He has contributed to many national and international journals of repute and has also published several valuable books from Oxford, Springer, and others.

Kinnori Sinha is Research Scholar at the Indian Institute of Foreign Trade, Kolkata, under the UGC-JRF National Scholarship Scheme. Her research focuses on environmental economics and sustainable development with emphasis on Indian policymaking.

Foreword

This edited volume, a careful and insightful examination of the changing dimensions of development economics, offers a rich tapestry of insights into the theoretical and practical aspects of development dynamics, and it tries to explore the complexities of socio-economic development both at the macro and micro levels. Most of the chapters included in this volume are the outcome of papers presented in an international conference on this theme organised by The Heritage College, Kolkata, India, in collaboration with Ramakrishna Mission Vidyamandira, Belur, Howrah, India.

The chapters in the present volume provide an excellent example of the vibrant research initiatives which are currently taking place in the field of development economics. These chapters discuss not only the need for moving beyond GDP estimate for reflecting the well-being of the society but also touches upon a wide range of thought-provoking topics such as 'Balancing Growth, Equity, and Environment'; 'Enhancing Sustainability Reporting and the Role of Digitalisation'; 'Role of Institutional Quality in Attracting Foreign Portfolio Investment'; 'Problem of Bipolarity in the Process of Economic Development'; 'An Analysis of Cross-country Variation in Environmental Policymaking Path'; 'Regional Integration in Trade – A Game-theoretic Exploration'; and 'Growth vis-à-vis Development: Sign of Convergence or Divergence', providing country-level experiences and delving into in-depth analysis using econometric and statistical tools wherever needed. The authors of these chapters have demonstrated a keen understanding of the specific issues and analysed them with rigour and clarity. The empirical evidence and its prudent presentation are really appealing, and the conclusions drawn therefrom are well supported by sound analytical overtone. The chapter on 'Structural Transformation and Trends in Informality – With Special Reference to India' resonates with the fundamental principles of sound economic reasoning, emphasising the gravity of informalisation in the labour market. In a similar way, the interesting chapter on 'Economic Progress of India: An Assessment Through the Lens of Financial Development Index' provides a comparison among BRICS and six other major Asian countries in terms of this index, and this analysis would serve as a valuable benchmark for future researchers and policymakers as well. Some of the scarcely touched areas of development economics have also been dealt with in some of the chapters of this volume, for example, the authors of the chapter 'Social Dimensions of Human Development: Trends of Union Dissolution in India' have used an exploratory analysis to throw some new lights upon an important issue of the development dynamics. Different other important socio-economic problems which have important bearing upon the development dynamics in a society have also been reflected in some chapters such as 'Association Between Maternal Issues and Malnutrition of the Children of Tribal and Non-tribal Categories in Purulia District of West Bengal, India'; 'Social Discrimination and Inclusive Development in India: An Empirical Analysis'; 'Women SHGs in India: Their Sustainability in Near Future'; 'Impact of Alcohol Ban on Crime and Regional Development in India: The Case of Bihar'; and so on, using diverse methodologies and case studies to explore the complexities of economic development at the regional level.

This book does an excellent job of presenting issues that are at the forefront of the debate on development economics. The authors of the chapters are engaged in thoughtful debates, challenging the existing paradigms and offering fresh perspectives on long-standing issues. This precious collection of research papers can definitely be considered as a valuable resource for students, scholars, and policymakers alike, providing them a strong platform for critical thinking and innovative ideas about the future course of development economics. The editors deserve special acclamation for doing their job so meticulously.

Dr Madhusudan Mohanty
Former Adviser, Emerging Market Economies
Bank for International Settlements, Basel, Switzerland
Email: madhu.mohanty2304@gmail.com

Preface

Over the last few decades, there have been several twists and turns in the evolution of 'development thinking', and the subject matter of development economics has evolved with greater analytical rigour, and it has touched upon different fronts of economic development in a more dynamic manner. Major criticisms have been raised against using gross domestic product (GDP) as a measure of economic and social welfare, particularly among scholars in the field of environmental economics. New goals of development economics moved beyond the narrow domain of correlating economic development with the quantitative aspects of economic progress and emphasised on human development or a comprehensive qualitative development with a wide focus upon how the poorest people are faring out of such growth process. While revisiting the challenges of development, several economists suggested for integrating the quality dimensions of economic progress into development approaches. It is also believed that given the interactions between development strategies and policies of different countries in a globalised world, the impact of properly coordinated and appropriately designed combinations of development policies would be greater than the sum of individual parts of these policies. This calls for a more complex and nuanced role of the state to deal with the need for such coordination.

The world is going through a series of unprecedented shocks over the last two decades. Starting with the global financial crisis (2008–2009), recessions caused by the pandemic (2020–2022), the Russia–Ukraine War (2022) and most recently the escalation in the tariff war between the United States and China. Due to the rapid increase in trade tensions and extremely high levels of policy uncertainty, the International Monetary Fund (IMF) has projected a slowdown in global growth to 2.8% in 2025 and 3% in 2026, which is much below the historical average of 3.7% during 2000–2019 (World Economic Outlook, April 2025).

> Global economic growth could slow to 2.3% due to trade tensions, says UN trade agency. (Geneva, April 16, Reuters)

> Various types of institutions, market structures, norms and ideologies influence moves along the frontier and shifts of the frontier, and it provides a simple formalization of the social forces that lead to institutional persistence and those that can trigger institutional change. (Daron Acemoglu, 2025)

In a globalised world, strategic interactions between the goals of different countries and their coordinated actions to attain the development goals can bring more fruitful results. Thus, economic development should be analysed as a highly multifaceted, non-linear, path-dependent, dynamic process involving systematically shifting interaction patterns that require changes in policies and socio-economic institutions over time. The welfarist approach to welfare economics was gradually transformed into a non-welfarist approach. The non-welfarist approach allows treating individual welfare as multidimensional (taking into account the notions of capability, freedom of choice, social justice, etc.). In this sense, several non-monetary indices of economic development such as Human Development Index, Gender Inequality Index, Multidimensional Poverty Index, etc. belong to the family of neo-welfarist evaluations.

Exploring the different dimensions of interdisciplinary research on development economics and its shifting paradigms are essential for devising comprehensive and effective strategies to promote inclusive and sustainable development globally. As we navigate the shifting paradigms within development economics, it is expected to reflect on the transformative power of ideas. The dynamism of this field demands a willingness to challenge established norms, question assumptions, and embrace innovative approaches.

The present book attempts to incorporate a wide range of contemporary issues in international trade and finance that have assumed significance in the aftermath of the corona pandemic. A brief summary of the chapters is given below:

Chapter 1 focuses on measuring true economic progress beyond GDP. It points out that the link between changes in GDP and changes in economic and social well-being is very weak due to a number of factors. Economists have come up with several suggestions and non-monetary indices such as Gross National Happiness (GNH) index, Comprehensive Wealth Index (CWI), Genuine Progress Indicator (GPI), Index of Sustainable Economic Welfare (ISEW), etc. to capture the subjective well-being of the people of a society. It highlights the 'dashboard approach', as suggested by Amartya Sen, Joseph Stiglitz and Jean Fitoussi.

Chapter 2 investigates the sustainable development trajectories of the BRICS countries – Brazil, Russia, India, China and South Africa – and the group's recent members, namely Egypt, the United Arab Emirates, Ethiopia, Iran and Indonesia. The analysis focuses on the three fundamental pillars of sustainability: the social, economic and environmental dimensions, over the period 2000–2022. An interdisciplinary framework, based on a few indicators such as poverty rates and education levels, GDP per capita and unemployment rates in the economic sphere and CO_2 emissions and natural resource use in the environmental sector, enables to judge sustainability performance of these emerging economies.

Chapter 3 attempts to show that the concept of well-being is inextricably linked to the social role that companies play within their ecosystems. To ensure the economic sustainability of their activities, companies must remunerate all factors of production, including risk capital, at market conditions. Territorial well-being, which combines social, environmental and infrastructural factors, has a positive impact on business performance. This study aims to develop two different indicators of well-being. The first measures the well-being that companies create for the community and the second vice versa. The study uses non-linear and non-compensatory synthesis methods with the aim of providing companies with a strategic and operational tool to assess, measure and improve the wealth that the territory generates and preserves.

Chapter 4 describes how digital transformation is reshaping corporate sustainability reporting by improving the way companies collect, process and disclose environmental, social and governance (ESG) data. The adoption of technologies can significantly support the implementation of the double materiality approach required by the European Sustainability Reporting Standards (ESRS). This chapter analyses how digital transformation supports corporate sustainability reporting under the Corporate Sustainability Reporting Directive (CSRD) and ESRS. It aims to analyse how digital technologies improve data quality and transparency and propose a theoretical framework to support materiality assessment and alignment with the sustainable development goals (SDGs).

Chapter 5 explores the moderation effect of institutional quality on the business environment and foreign portfolio investment nexus. The study covered 40 African countries using data from 2005 to 2023, employing the step-wise system-generalised method of moment (SWS-GMM) estimation strategy. Findings indicate that in the absence of institutional quality, ease of doing business and tax incentive had a negative and significant effect on foreign portfolio investment. The interaction of control of corruption with ease of doing business and the interaction of government effectiveness, political stability, regulatory quality and rule of law with ease of doing business had a positive effect on foreign portfolio investment. The study recommends improvement in the quality of institutions so as to attract more foreign portfolio investments towards the attainment of sustainable development in Africa.

Chapter 6 aims to determine that inequality adversely affects economic growth from both the supply and the demand sides in less developed and developing countries. The study points out that the Gini coefficient of the income distribution has been declining in regions like Sub-Saharan Africa and South-East Asia during 1981–2023, while it has increased in India and North America. This dualistic nature of development has furtherer been overshadowed with polarisation of income and wealth in India with the characteristics of considerable intra-group homogeneity and inter-group heterogeneity. It predicts that the sluggish growth in real wages, educated unemployment and the possible adverse impacts of the presently emerging artificial intelligence can lead our economy towards bipolarity.

Chapter 7 tries to describe that though environmental sustainability is crucial for securing long-term welfare, short-term interest may motivate a country to embrace a path tilted towards economic growth. This kind of trade-off between growth and environmental sustainability has been witnessed across countries at different junctures. India, a resource-rich developing country, has undergone paradigm shifts in terms of environmental policymaking. Reviewing international policy framework and annual data on 141 countries from 1990 to 2020, with special emphasis on Indian data and policies, the current analysis concludes that while conscious attempts have been undertaken to avoid the costs associated with growth-led environmental degradation, the journey of the country to tread along a carefully chosen middle path is still on.

Chapter 8 presents a theoretical model that studies the decision-making process of countries regarding the harmonisation of standards within regional trade blocs (RTBs) and regional trade agreements (RTAs). It employs a game-theoretic approach to explore why countries within a RTB may or may not choose to cooperate in forming agreements that standardise measures like sanitary and phytosanitary (SPS) measures and technical barriers to trade (TBT). The application of the trust game framework demonstrates that countries do cooperate and form agreements on standard harmonisation within RTBs, which may not align with traditional Nash equilibrium predictions but can be explained by the iterative and trust-based nature of international trade interactions within a RTB.

Chapter 9 empirically examines the relationship between sectoral composition and economic growth in Bangladesh, employing a comprehensive analysis encompassing both long-run and short-run dynamics using autoregressive distributed lag (ARDL)-bound tests. Findings reveal the significant contributions of various sectors to GDP growth, with manufacturing and agriculture playing pivotal roles. Additionally, the non-tradable service sector emerges as a key driver of economic growth, highlighting the importance of sectoral diversity for sustained development. Inter-sectoral linkages exhibit complex dynamics, with tradable and non-tradable service sectors showing positive connections with most sectors, while manufacturing and non-manufacturing sectors display negative linkages with agriculture.

Chapter 10 is an attempt to enquire into the dynamics of the gap between the developed, developing and less developed parts of the world over the period from 1990 to 2023. The beta-convergence analysis, using dynamic panel data regression, leaves emphatic evidence of conditional convergence, rather than the absolute, implying a case of typical club convergence, where the countries sharing similar conditions in health, education and prevalence of absolute poverty tend to converge in terms of per capita income. Countries are classified into four broad regions, namely, Latin American Caribbean (LAC), Sub-Saharan Africa (SSA), Middle East and North Africa (MENA) and East Asia Pacific (EAP).

Chapter 11 identifies that the problem of rising income inequality in the South Asia region is one of the major obstacles to the development of the continent's economy and so in order to achieve the SDGs (UN, 2015), by 2030, the South Asian countries must address the raising income inequality of the continent. The present study has used time-series data of income inequality (Gini) and per capita GDP of the South Asia region for the period 1960–2020 to forecast income inequality for the time period 2021–2035. Initially, the study has carried out a separate univariate forecasting analysis (autoregressive integrated moving average (ARIMA)) for economic growth.

Chapter 12 attempts to investigate the linkage between the process of structural transformation with the trends in the informal sector, in the global perspective, and highlights the case of India as a special one. It tries to compare India's structural change with that of China in terms of output share between sectors, employment share between sectors and ratio of labour productivities between sectors. It tries to examine the various measures of informality between the advanced economies (AEs) and emerging market and developing economies (EMDEs). It shows that India's transformation is an exception to the standard classical pattern, as the labour share of agriculture declined and services increased, but the share of manufacturing remained stagnant (in contrast to China). Also, the proportion of self-employment is highest in case of India.

Chapter 13 highlights that the aim of SDGs is achieving a decrease in emission through reduction in energy consumption of non-renewable resources and increasing that of the renewable ones in G-20 economies. The study focuses on the performance of absolute beta convergence of G-20 economies with respect to total energy consumption of non-renewable resources and per capita consumption of overall energy from 2000 to 2022. Conditional beta-convergence analysis has also been performed for showing the possibility of convergence when we hold the growth of industrial output constant. The results suggest that there has been a reduction in total energy consumption of non-renewable resources, both absolutely and conditionally.

Chapter 14 contributes to the literature by establishing (i) the adverse impact of both outdoor and indoor air pollution on health status of the rural young females measured by female life expectancy at birth (FLE) (ii) the interaction effect of (a) outdoor air pollution with income growth (negative) and (b) indoor air pollution with female education (positive) on FLE. The positive interaction effect of FLE and proportion of young females on female worker–population ratio (FWPR) suggests that given their health, a greater proportion of young females raises FWPR as being young, they can ignore their poor health caused by air pollution which increases FWPR. This chapter establishes a significant 'inverted U' interaction effect of health and income growth on FWPR.

Chapter 15 elaborates on union dissolution, encompassing divorce and separation, is an integral aspect of social transformation, reflecting shifts in societal norms, gender roles, economic independence and legal frameworks. Factors such as financial independence, domestic conflicts, changing social norms and globalisation have influenced this trend. It varies among religious groups, across all demographics. This chapter focuses on the trends of union dissolution in India and variations in the rates across the major correlates such as state, age and religious categories. The spatial patterns suggest that there is a clear north–south divide. The variations in union dissolution across different age groups suggest that women in the middle age group are the most vulnerable. The variations in union dissolution across different religious groups suggest that the dissolution rates are highest for Christians.

Chapter 16 demonstrates the role of financial development which contributes significantly to financial inclusion, resource allocation efficiency, investment growth and economic resilience. It utilises the IMF's Financial Development Index to compare financial development among BRICS nations and six other major Asian economies. The cross-country analysis shows that, as of 2021, India ranked lowest among the BRICS countries and mid-tier among the Asian economies studied. The findings suggest a need for targeted regulatory measures in India to enhance financial efficiency, strengthen monitoring mechanisms, enforce regulations impartially, and increase in transparency within the financial system.

Chapter 17 attempts to portray the energy mix in India during the recent years and in near future while examining the carbon emission trends over years as well. On the other hand, the study forecasts total primary energy consumption in India till 2050 using both univariate and multivariate forecasting methods. For multivariate forecasting, we have assumed two alternative possibilities for GDP growth: the business-as-usual (BAUS) and the high-growth scenarios. Based on these findings, the study recommends that Indian government policies should emphasise on expanding renewable energy resources and increasing its availability for consumption in major energy consuming sectors like manufacturing industries and households.

Chapter 18 examines the long-term and short-term dynamics between tax revenues and economic growth in India, with a particular focus on the goods and services tax (GST) introduced in 2017. The research employs advanced time series techniques including unit root tests, Johansen cointegration, Granger causality and vector error correction models (VECMs) to explore the relationship between income tax and GDP. Findings confirm a long-run equilibrium with bidirectional causality between the two variables, although short-run causality from income tax to GDP remains marginal. The GST dummy variable is statistically insignificant in the short run, indicating delayed or structural effects.

Chapter 19 tries to understand the association between child malnutrition and maternal issues across tribal and non-tribal households in Purulia district, West Bengal. The study is based on primary data collected by face-to-face interview methods and stratified random sampling procedures. *z*-scores are calculated for anthropometric measures of malnutrition like stunting, wasting, underweight and mother's body mass index (BMI) following World Health Organization (WHO) guidelines. The study found prevalence of malnutrition is higher among children of working mothers compared to non-working mothers and undernourished mothers with low BMI compared to nourished mothers. Child malnutrition decreases with an increase in a mother's education.

Chapter 20 portrays that SDGs call for equality of opportunity and the elimination of any form of discrimination and socio-economic inclusion of all. Social heterogeneity encourages governments in interest group politics, which contradicts the spirit of inclusive development. Using panel data on Indian states, the relationship between social discrimination and public good provision is tested along three measures of diversity: caste, religion and language. The results show that social discrimination along these lines is negatively associated with public good provision. It concludes that social discrimination hampers the economic development of society.

Chapter 21 emphasises on women self-help groups (WSHGs) with the main objective of offering some employment opportunities to women to make them self-reliant. It was thought that financial inclusion would serve the dual purpose of reducing poverty and at the same time empower these women. The study tries to analyse the patterns of within-region (intra-region), across-region (inter-region) and across-state (inter-state) inequalities in WSHG savings for the period

2013–2014 to 2022–2023 using the Theil Index and the Gini coefficient and has portrayed some mixed results. It also examines conditional convergence in the savings of WSHGs for the same period. It finds significant beta (β) and sigma (σ) convergence in WSHG savings over the years.

Chapter 22 discusses about the impact of alcohol ban on crime and regional development in India. It tries to analyse whether the widespread prevalence of crime in the state of Bihar is due to high alcohol consumption. It used a difference-in-difference (DiD) approach with Bihar being the treatment group and other Indian states as the control group. The DiD coefficient was positive and significant, implying that crime, in fact, increased in the state. Subsequent regressions corroborated the robustness of our results. It identified that the absence of alcohol ban in neighbouring states, rampant corruption and poor enforcement of laws as key reasons behind the counterintuitive results.

Chapter 23 aims to examine the age-wise occupational disparity in West Bengal using National Classification of Occupation (NCO) classifications between working age male and female workers by different occupation statuses using the latest Periodic Labour Force Survey data 2022–2023 separately for the rural and urban sectors. An ordered logit model is performed to determine the possible personal and household factors for the participation of different ranks of occupations for separate gender of both the sectors where marital status, number of children and dependency ratio are found to be potential obstacles for the females to engage in high-rank occupations.

Acknowledgements

As editors we have provided our persistent endeavour to develop a theme which happens to be very relevant in the present-day context of 'Development'. Starting from developing the conceptual framework of the theme, selection of papers, reviewing, editing and ultimate publication of the proposed edited book titled *Changing Dimensions in Economic Development: Theories and Empirics*, it has been a unique, insightful and most contemporary compilation. The authors, who made valuable contributions to this comprehensive volume, were academic experts, eminent economists and active researchers in their respective fields within the country and abroad. It is really a matter of pride and delight that we, as editors, got the opportunity to work with this level of authors and hope that we have succeeded in adding considerable value to the existing literature in the process of making this edited volume. We also expect that this volume will have a high market demand not only to the researchers and academicians as an important reference but also to policymakers and social thinkers of the present generation. We really feel proud as editors that the authors of this book have provided immense support, cooperation and extended their whole-hearted cooperation to make this project a successful one. Hence, it would be unjustified if the contributors are not acknowledged for their valuable contributions. We would also like to express our deep gratitude to Dr Soumyen Sikdar, Professor (Retd.), IIM Calcutta, for taking out his valuable time to set the pace in the initial chapter and Dr Asis Banerjee, Former Professor of Economics and Former Vice-Chancellor, University of Calcutta, for his valuable contribution as a very senior and eminent economist. We also extend our heartiest thanks to other academicians and resource persons of the society associated with this project. We would also like to express our deep gratitude to Professor Madhusudan Mohanty for taking out his valuable time to write the foreword for this book. We also extend our heartiest thanks to the reviewers, other academicians and resource persons associated with this project. We express our special thanks to Rev. Swami Mahaprajnananda, Principal, Ramakrishna Mission Vidyamandira, Belur, Howrah, West Bengal, India, for his whole-hearted support and cooperation.

We must thank the entire Emerald Publishing team for their able and insightful guidance and support at every stage of this edited volume. Second, we express our deep gratitude to eminent academicians like Dr Achin Chakraborty, Professor of Economics and Former Director, IDSK; Dr Saibal Kar, Professor of Economics (RBI Chair Professor), CSSSC; Dr Zakir Saadullah Khan, Professor, Department of Economics, Comilla University, Bangladesh; Dr Kakali Mukhopadhyay,

Professor, Department of Natural Resource Sciences, McGill University, Montreal, Canada; Dr Abhiroop Mukhopadhyay, Professor, Economics and Planning Unit, Indian Statistical Institute, Delhi; Dr Rudrarup Mukherjee, Associate Professor, Department of Economics, Royal Thimphu College, Bhutan; Dr Shiva Raj Adhikari, Professor of Economics, Central Department of Economics, Tribhuvan University, Nepal; Dr Rohit Azad, Faculty member, Centre for Economics Studies and Planning, JNU, Delhi; Mr Swapan-Kumar Pradhan, Principal Statistical Analyst, Monetary and Economic Department, International Banking and Financial Statistics, Basel, Switzerland; Dr Jayanta Kumar Seal, Professor, Indian Institute of Foreign Trade, Kolkata; Dr Arindam Gupta, Professor, Department of Commerce, Vidyasagar University, West Bengal; Dr Tanupa Chakraborty, Professor, Department of Commerce, University of Calcutta; Dr Sukanta Bhattacharya, Associate Professor, Department of Economics, University of Calcutta; and Dr Soheli Ghose, Assistant Professor and Dean, Department of Commerce (Evening), St. Xavier's College, Kolkata.

We would also like to extend our thanks to Prof. Amitava Ghose, Former Teacher-in-Charge, The Heritage College; Dr Anup Sinha, Chief Mentor, Heritage Business School; Dr Basab Choudhuri, Director, The Heritage College; Dr Sandip Kumar Paul, Principal, The Heritage College; Dr Achin Chakraborty, Professor of Economics and Former Director, IDSK; Dr Bibek Roy Choudhury, Professor, IIFT, Kolkata; Dr Madhupa Bakshi, Dean, Media Science, The Heritage Academy; Dr Rimu Choudhuri, Professor, Heritage Business School; Dr Debkumar Chakrabarti, Associate Professor, Department of Economics, Ramakrishna Mission Vidyamandira, Belur, Howrah, and Convener, Conference Committee; Dr Dipanjan Basu, Former Assistant Professor, Department of Commerce, The Heritage College, and Joint Convenor, Conference Committee; Manas Ranjan Bhowmik, Assistant Professor, Department of Economics, Ramakrishna Mission Vidyamandira, Belur, Howrah, and Joint Convenor, Conference Committee, Puja Putatunda, Assistant Professor, Department of Economics, and Organising Secretary, Seminar Committee. We also express our heartfelt thanks to Shri Pradip Agarwal, CEO, The Heritage Group of Institutions; Dr Amalendu Bhunia, Professor and Vice-Chancellor, Kalyani University, West Bengal.

But above all, we are sincerely grateful to our parents and family members for their cooperation, inspiration and tremendous mental support.

Dr Debashis Mazumdar
Dr Rajib Bhattacharyya
EDITORS

Part A

Growth, Development and New Frontiers

Chapter 1

Measuring Economic Progress: Beyond GDP

Soumyen Sikdar

IIM, Kolkata, India

Abstract

Though the growth in real gross domestic product (GDP) or the growth rate of real per capita GDP of any society is often considered as a good index of economic progress of a society, however, the link between changes in GDP and changes in economic and social well-being is very weak due to a number of factors. Hence, economists and social scientists from time to time have pointed out the need for a proper and comprehensive indicator of well-being of society and is often called as 'Beyond GDP Measurement Agenda'. Economists have come up with several suggestions and non-monetary indices such as Gross National Happiness (GNH) index, Comprehensive Wealth Index (CWI), Genuine Progress Indicator (GPI), Index of Sustainable Economic Welfare (ISEW), etc. to capture the subjective well-being (SWB) of the people. The concept of 'hedonic pricing' was also found to be useful to address the shortcoming of the narrow GDP estimate. Further, the 'dashboard approach', as suggested by Amartya Sen, Joseph Stiglitz and Jean Fitoussi, considered several indicators covering financial, human and natural wealth and inequality in distribution, among other things, for measuring the progress of a society on the path of welfare. However, despite all these efforts, primitive unadjusted GDP continues to be the sole focus of attention of politicians the world over and almost the sole basis for the ranking of nations in social media. This chapter provides

Changing Dimensions in Economic Development: Theories and Empirics, 3–10

Published under exclusive licence by Emerald Publishing Limited
doi:10.1108/978-1-83708-384-820261001

a brief outline of these attempts towards finding out alternatives to the narrow GDP estimate of economic progress of any society.

Keywords: Gross domestic product (GDP); subjective well-being; Gross National Happiness Index; Comprehensive Wealth Index; hedonic pricing; dashboard approach

JEL Codes: E01; I38; C83; Q56; C43; D83

Introduction

GDP is the most well known and most widely used measure to capture an economy's overall performance and its growth over time. Economic well-being of citizens should be the ultimate objective of government policy, but the link between changes in GDP and changes in well-being is very weak due to a number of factors. To list just a few important ones:

(a) It ignores the distribution of income in the country.
(b) It leaves out the value of activities outside the ambit of market transactions.
(c) It fails to adequately account for improvement in the quality of products and services and the introduction of new products (often of better quality).
(d) It includes many items we would all like to have less of and fails to reflect the social costs of many economic activities.

The list can be greatly expanded, but we shall concentrate on (b), (c) and (d) only for reasons of space. Item (a) is hugely important, and there is a vast literature on the welfare consequences of inequality in income and wealth. Work done by Stiglitz and Piketty, among many others, is very informative. We shall not go into the distributional issue here.

Activities confined within the household create great value but are excluded from GDP because the corresponding market prices are often unavailable. Time Use Surveys are increasingly being used now to have information about the quantity and variety of this unpaid work. In such surveys, respondents are asked to explain how they spend a 24-hour period, stating the division of time between paid and unpaid work, hours spent in leisure, sleep, travel, child care and so on. Averages are calculated for different groups – men and women, persons of different ages, employed and unemployed, among others. Private sector equivalent jobs are then used to assign values to the unpaid work part. The method certainly has drawbacks, but it is a significant step forward in the right direction.

The quality dimension is not adequately addressed in national income accounts. This flaw has become very acute recently due particularly to the proliferation of more powerful and faster computers and other technological products. GDP works only with market prices, which often fail to be an adequate index of quality. Worse, for computers and other new technological products, fast pace of quality improvement has gone hand in hand with sharp decline in prices (driven by competition and strong scale economies in production). A $1,000 computer of 2020 is a vastly better product than $1,000 worth of the earlier version, say, a computer produced in 2000. The tremendous improvement in user welfare (real growth of the economy) is very poorly reflected in the statistics. Hence, there remains an urgent need for searching out a true indicator of economic well-being of the people of any society.

Literature Review

Economists from time to time have stepped into the field of research and analysis related to the inadequacy of GDP as an indicator of economic development of any society. Fleurbaey (2009) has critically examined various approaches to the measurement of individual well-being and social welfare which were required for the construction of alternative non-monetary indices to economic progress of a society. After delving into the schools of thought like welfarism, liberalism and perfectionism, the author believes that a full convergence of opinions is not likely to occur soon. Sodhi (2011) emphasised upon the development of an alternative measure for the estimation of economic development giving prime importance to human development. As an alternative to the traditional GDP measure of economic development, Brinkman and Brinkman (2011) developed a Social Progress Index (SPI) giving emphasis on three core factors, viz., basic human needs, foundations of well-being and opportunity. This study has shown that social progress of a society is least correlated with GDP, but opportunity (opportunity for all individuals to reach their full potential) exhibits a significant positive relationship with the SWB of the people. Széll (2011), while arguing for the inadequacy of the GDP indicator, clearly mentioned that the development indicator should take into account the quality of life and working life, particularly the quality labour relations, and not the quantity. Another study undertaken by Bleys (2012) looks into the different classification schemes available in the literature for measuring the quality of life and outlines some of the weaknesses in each of these procedures. This study has indicated an alternative classification scheme based on the notions of well-being, economic welfare and sustainability and shown how this alternative scheme can help the policymakers. The rationale underpinning the Organisation for Economic Co-operation and Development (OECD) Better Life Initiative, as a better alternative to GDP measure, has been reviewed by Boarini and d'Ercole (2013). In a short survey of the four main approaches towards measuring economic well-being, both Hawkins (2014) and Giovannini (2015) have shown that there is no single agreed way of measuring well-being, and hence, it is believed that several social scientists will continue to use real GDP per capita as a measure of social progress despite its widely acknowledged limitations. Peterson (2014) made a critical review of composite well-being indices that account for inequality and pointed out that well-being indices should make further strides to ensure the capture of non-economic inequality in terms of education and health.

Jones and Klenow (2016) proposed a simple summary statistic for the welfare of a country's people, measured as a consumption equivalent and computed its level and growth rate for a diverse set of countries. This study indicated that in most of the developing economies, lower welfare compared to income could be attributed not only to lower expectancy at birth but also to more inequality in income distribution. Benjamin et al. (2017) tried to prepare a personal well-being (PWB) index based on self-reported responses to SWB and stated preference (SP) survey questions, disregarding, however, the problem of interpersonal aggregation of PWB indices into a measure of national well-being.

Stiglitz et al. (2018) argue for a parsimonious dashboard of indicators reflecting the economic development of a society in the truest sense of the term because mere increase of GDP does not reflect an increase in the well-being of most citizens because this narrow growth does not reflect the degradation of the environment and the depletion of natural resources. Hence, such growth process can make the economy and its people more insecure, erode trust upon the existing institutions and society and can open up conflicts and social tensions. Stiglitz (2019) believes that the primary concern for Jones (2016) stressed upon 'Beyond GDP Measurement Agenda' should be to keep the well-being of the common people at the forefront and the factors which determine this well-being, and the government of a country should have budgetary allocations to achieve that objective. Aitken (2019) is also of the opinion that more emphasis should be given to measures that reflect both objective and subjective measures of well-being and measures that better reflect the heterogeneity of peoples' experiences.

The study of Malay (2021) portrays different possibilities of articulation showing alternatives to GDP at the macro level and to financial indicators at the micro level which exist and outlines a framework for a better micro–macro articulation. Bloom et al. (2021) also felt the need for developing a comprehensive indicator of economic well-being of a society taking into consideration the factors like real GDP per capita, healthy life expectancy at birth and an inverse measure of the Gini coefficient as a proxy for an average person's opportunities to benefit from economic progress.

Zoundi et al. (2022) proposed a stock-flow approach, taking into account the inflation-adjusted per capita value of the stocks of human capital, natural capital, social capital, produced capital and financial capital, on the one hand, and the flow of well-being arising out of such stocks, for an inclusive economic development for the G-20 countries. Smith et al. (2022) developed a comprehensive/inclusive wealth (C/IW) index as an alternative to the narrow GDP indicator for assessing the economic development of a society and aims at facilitating the policymakers to take correct policy decisions based on C/IW index. In a similar study, Bizikova et al. (2021, 2024) emphasised upon the concept of comprehensive wealth (CW), including the factors such as healthy ecosystems, strong communities, educated citizens, high-quality buildings and infrastructure and sound financial holdings, and based on these factors, they developed a CWI as an alternative to GDP indicator. The CWI incorporated the sub-indices like human capital index, produced capital index, natural capital index and financial capital index. It was observed that CWI remained higher than the simple GDP level for some countries under study.

Kranke (2025) points out that the decoupling of economic growth from various environmental impacts is practically impossible, and therefore, good economic policies do not aim only for growth, rather they consider economic welfare and climate action equally important. Giving an example from Germany, this chapter points out that the pursuit of a green and inclusive growth strategy followed by the Federal Ministry for Economic Affairs and Climate Action of Germany is clearly a marker of good policy.

Analysis

In this chapter, an exploratory method has been adopted to analyse the loopholes of the existing quantitative measure or the GDP measure of economic progress of any society and tries to delve into the inherent fallacy in adopting this measure as the true indicator of economic well-being of the people in any society.

The concept of 'hedonic pricing' is useful to address this shortcoming. Willingness to pay for the different quality characteristics of a laptop, viz., memory size, weight, processing speed, DVD drives and so on, is derived using various means and then a 'hedonic price index' for the product is constructed. No consumer pays the hedonic price of a laptop or *i*-phone, but deflating the total sales value of laptops by their hedonic price index is a good estimate of the value of real computing power in a given year. One 1996 survey suggested that the neglect of innovation and quality improvements had understated the real US growth by 0.6–1.5 percentage points a year, over a period when measured annual GDP growth was 2%–3% on average (Gordon, 2018).

Any final expenditure is counted in GDP, irrespective of its intrinsic merit or morality. If a nation becomes more belligerent and steps up military spending, national income will go up; more crime can increase GDP via expansion of the police force or enhanced activities of lawyers. Ill health promotes GDP by boosting medical spending; oil spills do the same by necessitating cleanup operations. Floods and earthquakes contribute by triggering construction boom. Some alternatives exclude these 'regrettables' from income accounting. The 'measure of economic welfare' (MEW), as suggested by Nordhaus and Tobin in 1972, can be regarded as an early attempt at modifying GDP to derive a better measure of true progress (Hawkins, 2014). In their measurement, the activities regarded as not directly sources of utility in themselves but 'regrettably necessary inputs' (e.g. expenditure on prisons) were treated as intermediate rather than final products, and hence, expenditure on those inputs were excluded from GDP. On the other hand, the monetary estimates of activities (e.g. leisure, work at home) were added as these estimates were supposed to add value to well-being. The ISEW, developed by Daly and Cobb in 1989, also excluded 'regrettably necessary expenditures' from GDP (Hawkins, 2014).

One crucial omission in GDP calculation is the harmful impact of production on the environment and the stock of exhaustible resources. The monetary value of energy used in production and transportation is counted but not the depletion of finite resources of fossil fuel, coal or lithium. Pollutant released by a factory into a river is ignored, unless somebody spends money to clean it up. Depreciation of physical capital is acknowledged in going from GDP to net domestic product (NDP) but not that of natural capital. The Australia Institute (AI) presented a GPI in 1997, and this was updated in 2000. In the GPI estimate adjustments were made for the inclusion of distribution, household work, and exclusion of defence expenditure, and depreciation of built and natural capital (Hawkins, 2014).

More and more national statistical offices are becoming aware of these serious limitations of traditional GDP, and numerous alternatives have been suggested that will be more comprehensive in capturing social costs and benefits of current production and consumption. We discuss some prominent ones below.

With an initiative of the French government, 'The Commission on the Measurement of Economic Performance and Social Progress' (CMEPSP), headed by Joseph Stiglitz, Amartya Sen and Jean Paul Fitoussi, was formed in 2008, and its objective was to identify the limits of GDP as an indicator of economic performance and social progress of any society. The CMEPSP was of the opinion that emphasis should shift from the measurement of GDP to the measurement of well-being of the common people (Stiglitz et al., 2009).

In 2010, a high-powered committee headed by Amartya Sen, Joseph Stiglitz and Jean Fitoussi suggested a 'dashboard approach', where, instead of a single aggregated number, several indicators covering financial, human and natural wealth and inequality in distribution, among other things, are to be carefully watched and monitored by national governments to measure progress on the path of welfare. ISEW and GPI differ in detail, but adjust GDP upward for unpaid household work and reduced working hours and downward for environmental damage. Some related measures reduce GDP when inequality increases. Revisions can be momentous. For the United States, conventional national income per capita increased fourfold between 1950 and 1995, but GPI per capita actually had a two-fifths drop over the same period. And the United States is by no means alone in suffering this undesirable fate.

'Friends of the Earth' society periodically sets out values of different measures for different countries in its website. Interestingly, the site allows users to re-do the calculations by changing the weights assigned to different components. The weights chosen by a pessimist can reduce even a developed country's ISEW down to zero!

The dashboard approach has been carried the furthest by the Australian Bureau of Statistics in its adoption of Measures of Australia's Progress in 2002 (see www.abs.gov.au). This yearly assessment of whether the citizens' life is getting better includes 15 headline indicators chosen in national consultation.

Canada's Index of Well-being has its origins in focus groups spread across the country. These groups collected answers to fairly simple but important questions: 'What matters to you? What makes your life good?' These provided the basis for the eight 'domains' covered in the index: community vitality, democratic engagement, education, environment, healthy populations, leisure and culture, living standards and time use.

Bhutan has its unique GNH index, based on four pillars: environment, equity, cultural values and good governance. In 2010, the Centre for Bhutan Studies (CBS) released the GNH, with the objective of measuring the progress of a country towards the societal foundations of happiness (Malay, 2021). The GNH index measures performance in nine domains considered to be core aspects of happiness, viz., (i) psychological well-being, (ii) health, (iii) utilisation of time, (iv) education, (v) cultural diversity and resilience, (vi) good governance, (vii) community vitality, (viii) ecological diversity and (ix) living standards. These domains were further subdivided into 33 indicators, based on 124 variables (Malay, 2021).

Investment in 'intangible assets' like brand value, firm reputation and other types of 'organisational capital', knowledge stored in computer data bases, creativity in movies and music are growing at a fabulous pace in post-industrial modern societies. Satisfactory methods of accounting for these items do not exist as of now. The US Bureau of Economic Analysis, with a good track record of statistical innovation in the past, has assigned top priority to the project of tackling this novel form of value in the economy. Some progress has been made in the formation of 'satellite accounts' for intangible statistics.

Conclusion

In our foregoing analysis, we have observed that economists from time to time have stepped into the field of research and analysis related to the inadequacy of GDP as an indicator of economic development of any society. They have come up with alternative suggestions and methods for capturing the SWB of the people in a society. The 'Beyond GDP Measure Agenda' is an indication towards those initiatives. Several non-monetary indices like GNH index, CWI, GPI, ISEW, etc. have been developed over time. The 'dashboard approach', as suggested by Amartya Sen, Joseph Stiglitz and Jean Fitoussi, considered several indicators covering financial, human and natural wealth and inequality in distribution, among other things, for measuring the progress of a society on the path of welfare. All these endeavours are strong indications of a positive change in the right direction.

However, despite all these efforts, the primitive unadjusted GDP or the narrow 'income approach' continues to be the sole focus of attention among the policymakers the world over and has remained almost the sole basis for the ranking of nations even in many official reports made by some international financial institutions. This trend needs to be changed as early as possible. Fortunately, there are some encouraging signs of that change.

References

Aitken, A. (2019). Measuring welfare beyond GDP. *National Institute Economic Review, 249*, R3–R16.

Benjamin, D. J., Cooper, K. B., Heffetz, O., & Kimball, M. (2017). Challenges in constructing a survey-based well-being index. *The American Economic Review, 107*(5), 81–85.

Bizikova, L., Halimatussadiah, A., Smit, R., Bernard, G., St., & Tilahun, M. (Eds.). (2024, May 17). Comprehensive wealth as a pathway beyond GDP. In *Comprehensive wealth report: Moving beyond GDP through comprehensive wealth: Findings for Ethiopia, Indonesia, and Trinidad and Tobago* (pp. 3–6). International Institute for Sustainable Development (IISD).

Bizikova, L., Smith, R., & Zoundi, Z. (2021). Why wealth measures are needed to move beyond GDP. In *Measuring the wealth of nations: A review*. International Institute for Sustainable Development (IISD).

Bleys, B. (2012). Beyond GDP: Classifying alternative measures for progress. *Social Indicators Research, 109*(3), 355–376.

Bloom, D. E., Fan, V. Y., Kufenko, V., Osondu, O., Prettner, K., & Yamey, G. (2021). Going beyond GDP with a parsimonious indicator: Inequality-adjusted healthy lifetime income. *Vienna Yearbook of Population Research, 19*, 127–140.

Boarini, R., & d'Ercole, M. M. (2013). Going beyond GDP: An OECD perspective. *Fiscal Studies, 34*(3), 289–314.

Brinkman, R. L., & Brinkman, J. E. (2011). GDP as a measure of progress and human development: A process of conceptual evolution. *Journal of Economic Issues, 45*(2), 447–456.

Fleurbaey, M. (2009). Beyond GDP: The quest for a measure of social welfare. *Journal of Economic Literature, 47*(4), 1029–1075.

Giovannini, E. (2015). Beyond GDP: Ten years after the first OECD world forum where do we stand? *Rivista Internazionale di ScienzeSociali, 123*(1), 3–15.

Gordon, R. J. (2018). *Why has economic growth slowed when innovation appears to be accelerating?* [Working Paper 24554]. National Bureau of Economic Research.

Hawkins, J. (2014). The four approaches to measuring wellbeing. In A. Podger & D. Trewin (Eds.), *Measuring and promoting wellbeing: How important is economic growth?* ANU Press.

Jones, C. I. (2016). The facts of economic growth. In *Handbook of macroeconomics* (Vol. 2A, 3–69). Elsevier B.V.

Jones, C. I., & Klenow, P. J. (2016). Beyond GDP? Welfare across countries and time. *The American Economic Review, 106*(9), 2426–2457.

Kranke, M. (2025). From good to bad? The contested desirability of economic growth. In I. Roberge, H. McKeen-Edwards, & M. Campbell-Verduyn (Eds.), *Ineffective policies: Causes and consequences of bad policy choices* (pp. 31–41). Bristol University Press, Policy Press.

Malay, O. E. (2021). How to articulate beyond GDP and businesses' social and environmental indicators? *Social Indicators Research, 155*(1), 1–25.

Peterson, L. (2014). The measurement of non-economic inequality in well-being indices. *Social Indicators Research, 119*(2), 581–598.

Smith, R., Zoundi, Z., & Bizikova, L. (2022). *Engaging decision-makers in moving beyond GDP and toward wealth*. International Institute for Sustainable Development (IISD). https://www.iisd.org/system/files/2022-01/moving-beyond-gdp-toward-wealth.pdf

Sodhi, J. S. (2011). Beyond GDP: The debate on globalization & development. *Indian Journal of Industrial Relations, 46*(4), 562–570.

Stiglitz, J. (2019). Beyond GDP: It's time for the national accounts to put people first. *Corporate Knights, 18*(1), 28–29.

Stiglitz, J. E., Fitoussi, J.-P., & Durand, M. (2018). *Beyond GDP: Measuring what counts for economic and social performance*. OECD.

Stiglitz, J. E., Sen, A., & Fitoussi, J.-P. (2009). *The measurement of economic performance and social progress revisited*. OFCE. https://ec.europa.eu/eurostat/documents/8131721/8131772/Stiglitz-Sen-Fitoussi-Commission-report.pdf

Széll, G. (2011). Beyond GDP. *Indian Journal of Industrial Relations, 46*(4), 545–552.

Zoundi, Z., Snower, D. J., Smith, R., Miranda, K. L. d., & Bizikova, L. (2022). *Moving beyond GDP: A stock-flow approach to measuring wellbeing for the G20*. International Institute for Sustainable Development (IISD).

Chapter 2

Balancing Growth, Equity and Environment: A Temporal Evaluation of Sustainability in BRICS Economies

Tommaso Filì[a], Martina De Anna[a], Tiziano Pavanini[b], Enrico Ivaldi[c] and Enrico Musso[a,d]

[a]*Department of Economics and Business, University of Genova, Genova, Italy*
[b]*Politecnico di Milano, Milan, Italy*
[c]*Department of Humanistic Studies, IULM University – Faculty of Communication, Milan, Italy*
[d]*CIELI – Italian Centre of Excellence in Logistics, Transport and Infrastructure, University of Genova, Genova, Italy*

Abstract

This research investigates the sustainable development trajectories of the BRICS countries – Brazil, Russia, India, China, and South Africa – and the group's recent members, namely Egypt, the United Arab Emirates, Ethiopia, Iran, and Indonesia. The analysis focuses on the three fundamental pillars of sustainability: the social, economic, and environmental dimensions, over the period 2000–2022. The construction of an interdisciplinary framework, based on a few indicators such as poverty rates and education levels in the field, gross domestic product (GDP) per capita and unemployment rates in the economic sphere, and CO_2 emissions and natural resource use in the environmental sector, enables the research to make a comparative and temporal analysis of the sustainability performance of these emerging economies. Results document diversified patterns of development, with impressive economic progress, pervasive social inequalities, and increasing environmental pressures. Research further points to structural divergence among the initial BRICS members and new entrants to highlight the limits of such economies in combining social inclusion,

Changing Dimensions in Economic Development: Theories and Empirics, 11–23

Published under exclusive licence by Emerald Publishing Limited
doi:10.1108/978-1-83708-384-820261002

protection of the environment, and economic growth. These results form part of the broader literature on sustainable development among the emerging economies and raise critical questions regarding the long-term sustainability of the BRICS model of advancing global sustainability objectives.

Keywords: Sustainable development; BRICS countries; emerging economies; sustainability performance; social; economic; environmental dimensions

JEL Codes: Q01; O57; F63; Q56

1. Introduction

The 1987 United Nations (UN) report, titled 'Our Common Future', signifies the increasing global significance of sustainable development. The report emphasises the importance of addressing present needs while ensuring the conservation of resources for future generations (Nowak & Kobiałka, 2024). This commitment is underscored by the transition from eight millennium development goals (MDGs) to 17 sustainable development goals (SDGs). However, further academic research is required to determine how countries, particularly those in emerging economies such as BRICS countries (Brazil, Russia, India, China, South Africa, Egypt, Ethiopia, Iran, United Arab Emirates, and Indonesia), are performing across economic, social, and environmental dimensions. In order to address this gap, the present work aims to examine the 22-year performance of BRICS economies (2000–2022), using the DP2 (Pena Distance) method in order to assess the temporal evolution of their performance in relation to each of the dimensions of sustainable development. The originality of this work lies in its analysis of the sustainability of countries referred to as 'emerging economies' in an aggregative manner, while considering the existence of significant cultural, geographical, economic, and political differences is crucial to understand their growth patterns.

The extant literature recognises the three dimensions of sustainable development (e.g., Costanza et al., 2016; Dhahri et al., 2021; Featherstone, 2013; Govindan et al., 2020): economic, social, and environmental, which are critical for long-term growth. The nexus between economic sustainability and social and environmental concerns is reflected in the SDGs (Nurramadhani et al., 2024), which promote access to energy, inclusive growth, and sustainable consumption (SDGs 7, 8, 9, 11, 12) among other targets. The concept of social sustainability, as it has evolved since the 1987 UN report (Vallance et al., 2011), emphasises aspects such as equity and poverty reduction, which are covered by various SDGs (1, 2, 3, 4, 5, 10, 16, 17). The concept of environmental sustainability is predicated on the conservation of natural resources while meeting current needs (Goodland, 1995; Morelli, 2011), as evidenced by the SDGs (6, 13, 14, 15) on climate change and ecosystem conservation.

So far, academic research has studied sustainable development in BRICS countries in different ways. Ali et al. (2018) conducted a content analysis to study the adoption of SDGs by the first five BRICS countries (Brazil, Russia, India, Iran, and South Africa) by studying the behaviour of the top 25 multinational companies. Their findings suggest that some key SDGs are missing from the strategic vision of these companies. Furthermore, the authors call for future studies that can include a larger number of countries. This work also aims to address this gap, by examining the sustainable performance of all 10 BRICS countries over time.

A study on the time evolution of the BRICS countries' adoption of the SDGs has already been conducted by Hluszko et al. (2024): in this case, however, the study focused on a systematic literature review of 93 case studies. The results of this work, also focused only to the first five BRICS countries, highlight an increase in scientific publications in China and Brazil from 2016 to 2021 and the main use of five sustainability tools (life cycle assessment, multi-criteria decision-making, cleaner production, material flow cost accounting, and water footprint assessment).

Zaman et al. (2015) studied the four main pillars (economic, environmental, energy, and health) of the so-called green economy of the original five BRICS countries by applying panel cointegration techniques to analyse the relationships between these variables. Their main findings suggest that environmental variables, unlike energy resources, have a negative impact on economic growth in the BRICS countries. Zafar et al. (2023) conducted a study on BRICS countries to assess the interaction between information and communication technologies (ICTs), trade, and tourism, showing that economic growth and tourism are positively correlated with environmental health in the short run, while environmental sustainability is hardly affected by trade. A review of the main green technologies adopted by the first five BRICS countries was conducted by Miranda et al. (2021), Liu (2022) studied the impact of environmental protection regulations, and Barykina et al. (2022) considered energy production as the basis for the sustainable development of these emerging economies.

Our contribution aims to distinguish itself from the existing academic research by analysing the temporal performance (2000–2022) of all 10 BRICS countries (updated to 2025) using a statistical method, to the best of our knowledge, not yet used in the literature: the Pena Distance (DP2). Its characteristics are detailed in the following section.

2. Material and Methods

The data used for this research, which relate to the sustainability performance of the 10 BRICS countries from 2000 to 2022, were extracted from the SDG Transformation Centre database and made available on Kaggle.com. The same database was also used in the preparation of the Sustainable Development Report 2023 by Sachs et al. (2023).

The measurement of sustainable development requires an approach capable of integrating economic, social, and environmental dimensions into a single synthetic indicator. The DP2 method becomes an appropriate choice for this, providing the possibility of combining various indicators with greater discriminant capacity than with other methods, such as principal component analysis (PCA) (Arechavala & Trapero, 2019; Trapero, 1977).

The DP2 method has two main advantages over traditional aggregation techniques. It addresses multicollinearity without losing informational content, unlike PCA, and assigns weights objectively based on each indicator's contribution (Arechavala & Trapero, 2009; Ciacci et al., 2023; Folmer & Heijman, 2005). Moreover, its non-compensatory nature prevents high performance in one dimension from offsetting poor results in others, making it especially suitable for assessing complex issues like sustainable development (Bruzzi et al., 2020; Jiménez-Fernández et al., 2022; Traversa & Ivaldi, 2024).

The construction process of the DP2 index follows a stepwise approach. It begins with the creation of a matrix in which each statistical unit is represented by a set of normalised indicators. The distance calculation is then performed by comparing each unit against a reference value, often represented by the minimum observed value for each indicator (Montero et al., 2010). This allows for the derivation of a quantitative measure that expresses the distance from a less desirable sustainability condition. To ensure comparability across different units and over time, the method includes a standardisation process that adjusts distances based on the variance of the variables (Arechavala et al., 2015).

$$\mathrm{DP2}(j)=\sum_{i=1}^{n}\frac{d_{ij}}{\sigma_i}\left(1-R^2_{i,i-1,i-2,\ldots,1}\right);$$

where:

- $i = 1, \ldots, n$; (variables) and $j = 1, 2, \ldots, m$ (areas).
- $d_{ij}=\left|x_{ij}-x^{*}_{ij}\right|$ is the difference between the value taken by the ith variable in area j and the minimum of the variable in the least desirable theoretical scenario, namely the reference value of matrix X.
- σ_i is the standard deviation of variable i.
- $R^2_{i,i-1,i-2,\ldots,1}$ is the coefficient of multiple linear correlation squared in the linear regression of X_i over $X_{i-1}, X_{i-2}, \ldots, X_1$, and it indicates the part of the variance of X_i explained linearly by variables $X_{i-1}, X_{i-2}, \ldots, X_1$.

This makes sure that each indicator provides only its non-redundant information, preventing the overestimation of highly correlated variables (Ivaldi et al., 2020).

Finally, one of the greatest strengths of the DP2 method is its ability to reconcile spatial and temporal analyses to succeed in monitoring sustainable development longitudinally. This is done by merging information from multiple years into a single data set, where geographic units are comparable both with each other and to the historic path of their performance (Traversa & Ivaldi, 2024). This characteristic enables policymakers to analyse sustainability plans more effectively in the future.

As a result, the outcomes become comparable across both spatial and temporal dimensions (Landi et al., 2018; Norman, 2010):

$$\mathrm{DP2}_{j,k} = \sum_{i=1}^{n}\left[\left(\frac{d_{i,j,k}}{\sigma_i}\right)\left(1 - R^2_{i,i-1,\ldots,1}\right)\right];\ i = 1,2,\ldots,n;\ k = 1,2,\ldots,K$$

Because of these attributes, DP2 is a valuable tool for evaluating sustainable development policies, providing a good analytical foundation for developing public policies and action plans for promoting a balance among economic development, social cohesion, and environmental protection.

3. Results and Discussion

All countries show an upward trend in the DP2 score over time (Fig. 2.1), reflecting overall progress towards sustainability but at varying growth rates between countries. Russia and China lead the charge in this development, China going from 12.38 in 2000 to 16.53 in 2022, while Russia has shown an increasing trend from 13.55 to approximately 15.80, representing improvement across the economic, social, and environmental dimensions of sustainability. India and Brazil have average performance; Brazil starts moderately high (13.47 in 2000) and keeps rising with some ups and downs, while India, starting lower (6.53 in 2000), has consistent growth, reaching over 11 by 2022. Iran, Egypt, and South Africa have slower growth with less dramatic rises than China and Russia. A special case is Ethiopia, which, having started with the lowest DP2 value (2.96 in 2000), demonstrates steady improvement, rising to approximately 7.62 by 2022, indicating very substantial improvements from a very low base. This outcome is in line with the findings of Abdissa et al. (2022) and could be due to the development of local small and medium enterprises (SMEs).

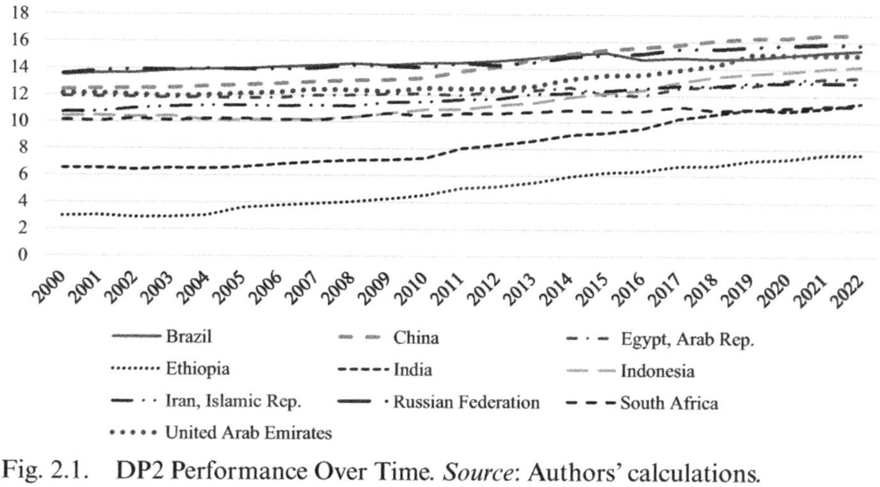

Fig. 2.1. DP2 Performance Over Time. *Source*: Authors' calculations.

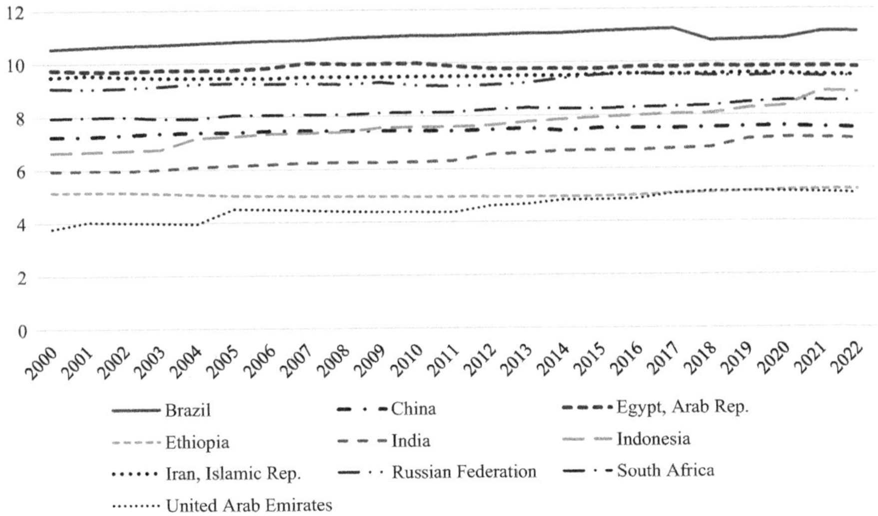

Fig. 2.2. Environmental DP2. *Source*: Authors' calculations.

The environmental DP2 indicator[1] analysis between 2000 and 2022 (Fig. 2.2), related with the UN environmental sustainability goals (SDGs), reveals major differences in the environmental sustainability levels of the countries under review. The analysis focuses on key SDG components such as clean water and sanitation, climate action, life below water, and life on land, highlighting disparities in progress across these critical environmental dimensions.

The environmental DP2 indicator reveals heterogeneous trends among the countries analysed between 2000 and 2022. Brazil, Egypt, Iran, and Russia exhibit relatively high and stable scores, reflecting homogeneous environmental performance and holistic sustainability policies (Salah et al., 2022; Solaymani, 2021; Strielkowski et al., 2021). India and South Africa show consistent improvement, owing to improved environmental policies and management of resources (Leal Filho et al., 2022; Williams, 2024). In contrast, Ethiopia and the United Arab Emirates are ranked lowest, plagued by infrastructural deficits and overexploitation, respectively, despite recent efforts at mitigation (Bhattarai & Yousef, 2025; Wendimu, 2021). China's record steadies after 2008, reflecting policy enforcement limitations (Abbasi et al., 2022), while Indonesia demonstrates average improvement in the face of persistent deforestation issues (Mahendra et al., 2024). Overall, the results highlight unevenness in environmental sustainability, shaped by structural, political, and ecological realities.

[1]An indicator that measures environmental performance in relation to four main goals: (goal 6) clean water and sanitation, (goal 13) climate action, (goal 14) life below water, and (goal 15) life on land.

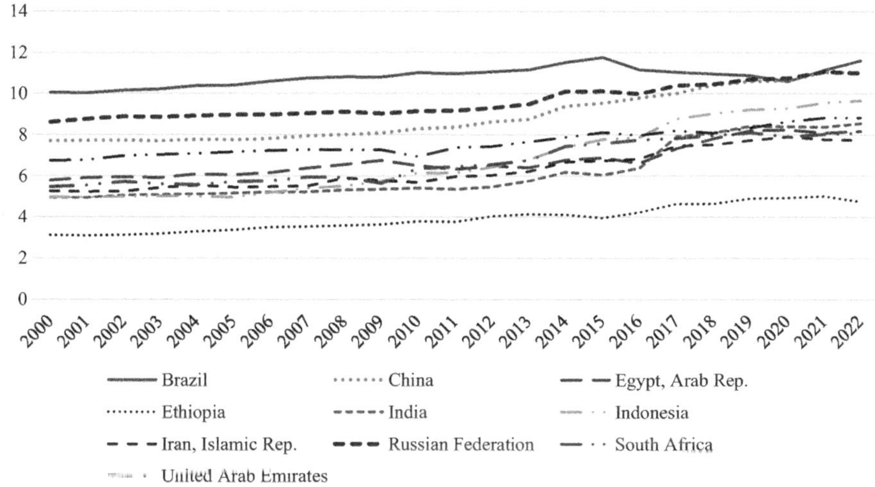

Fig. 2.3. Economic DP2. *Source*: Authors' calculations.

The analysis of the economic DP2 indicator[2] (Fig. 2.3) illustrates the progress of economic performance towards sustainability in 10 countries between 2000 and 2022, according to the UN 2030 Agenda SDGs. The analysis incorporates key economic dimensions such as affordable and clean energy, decent work and economic growth, industry, innovation and infrastructure, sustainable cities and communities, and responsible consumption and production, providing a comprehensive view of sustainable economic development.

The economic DP2 indicator highlights notable disparities in sustainability performance across the countries analysed from 2000 to 2022. Brazil and Russia consistently rank highest, driven by long-term investments in infrastructure and resource management, despite Brazil's temporary recession between 2015 and 2017 (Serbian et al., 2023; Sicsú et al., 2021; Strielkowski et al., 2021). India and South Africa demonstrate steady improvement, supported by innovation and enhanced governance. Conversely, Ethiopia and the United Arab Emirates report the lowest scores, constrained by structural and resource-related challenges (Melaku Belay et al., 2021). China, after rapid early growth, stabilises around mid-level values, potentially reflecting growth maintenance challenges. Indonesia and Egypt show moderate, gradual progress, while Iran records stable growth with limited expansion potential (Wibowo, 2023). These findings underline

[2]An indicator that measures environmental performance in relation to four main goals: (goal 7) affordable and clean energy; (goal 8) decent work and economic growth; (goal 9) industry, innovation, and infrastructure; (goal 11) sustainable cities and communities; and (goal 12) responsible consumption and production.

significant variation in economic sustainability, shaped by national policy frameworks, development stages, and access to resources.

The analysis of the social DP2 indicator[3] (Fig. 2.4) indicates the record of social sustainability performance in 10 countries from 2000 to 2022, based on the UN 2030 Agenda SDGs. The analysis encompasses key social goals such as no poverty, zero hunger, good health and well-being, quality education, gender equality, reduced inequalities, peace, justice and strong institutions, and partnerships for the goals, offering a multidimensional perspective on social progress.

The DP2 social indicator illustrates drastic transformations in social sustainability among countries under study in 2000–2022. Brazil and China exhibit steady development, with Brazil developing from 11.4 to over 12.7 and China from 10.15 to over 13.6, thanks to education and social welfare (Coutinho et al., 2021; Wang et al., 2022). Egypt has steady but limited growth, while Ethiopia has slow and steady improvement but lags well behind on poverty alleviation and education gaps. India and Indonesia show improvement, reflecting more welfare and social infrastructure, though inequality and gender equality are areas of concern (Katoch, 2024). Russia has steady growth, and South Africa has deep-seated issues on poverty and inequality but improves marginally on social scores (Bindman, 2017). The United Arab Emirates is characterised by the highest social DP2 growth due to investments in infrastructure and quality of life (Al Fardan & Marochi, 2021). Overall, the findings highlight the need for

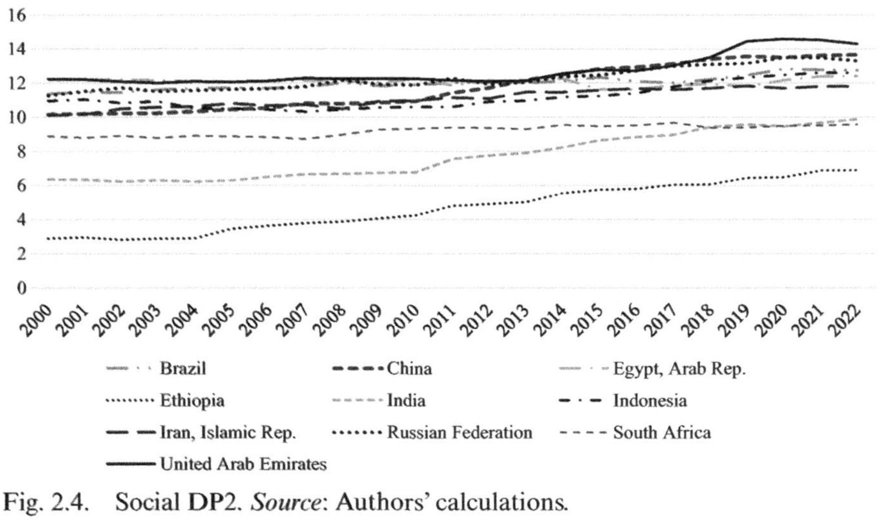

Fig. 2.4. Social DP2. *Source*: Authors' calculations.

[3]An indicator that measures environmental performance in relation to four main goals: (goal 1) no poverty; (goal 2) zero hunger; (goal 3) good health and well-being; (goal 4) quality education; (goal 5) gender equality; (goal 10) reduce inequalities; (goal 16) peace, justice, and strong institutions; and (goal 17) partnerships of the goals.

long-term, cross-cutting policies to address social justice, reduce inequalities, and promote sustainable development in line with the 2030 Agenda.

4. Conclusion

This study examined the sustainable development trajectories of BRICS countries and their new members between 2000 and 2022, considering the economic, social, and environmental dimensions. The main research gap identified concerns the need for a temporal and comparative assessment of the sustainability of these countries, an aspect which has been often overlooked in existing literature.

To address this research gap, we employed the DP2 method, which facilitates the integration and comparison of multidimensional indicators while circumventing challenges related to multicollinearity and the overestimation of weights. The key findings of the research show a general increase in sustainability in all the countries of concern, albeit with glaring disparities. Russia and China have progressed the most, while South Africa and Ethiopia have made lesser progress, particularly in social and environmental sustainability.

The research draws on a list of pioneering theories on economic development to give an eye on BRICS' economic development. Based on Rostow's model of developmental stages, certain nations, such as China and India in this case, appear to have passed the stage of take-off and have reached the mature state of development. There are others, such as Ethiopia, that are just at the starting point of 'preconditions for take-off'. The model provides a useful framework for describing the variance in economic and environmental performance among different countries. The analysis of the DP2 indicator shows that there are gains for some of the BRICS countries towards greater access to basic resources and equity, which is in line with Sen's vision that development is not simply economic progress but also the expansion of human capabilities. Yet our analysis highlights that in countries such as South Africa and Ethiopia, there are still vast inequalities, which indicates that economic growth has not necessarily translated into greater freedom and well-being for all. The DP2 framework adopted in this study aligns with the economist's multidimensional approach, emphasising the need for indicators other than mere economic growth to assess the quality of development. This approach is supported by Stiglitz's theories on the need to quantify well-being over GDP. Drawing on these theories, some policy interventions are proffered as part of our contribution. Stimulating investment in education and health is described as a means of realising inclusive growth and promoting human development, as proposed by Sen (1999). Formulation of focused industrial policies can accelerate the transition from early growth towards more sustainable development, in accordance with Rostow's (1990) model. The application of new sustainability and well-being indicators, as suggested by Stiglitz et al. (2009), is required to guide policymaking towards a trade-off between environmental conservation, social justice, and economic development. These are the critical determinants for sustainable and equitable economic growth in developing countries. The analysis of the BRICS economies also calls for examination of the emerging challenges that are transforming development paradigms across the world. Digitalisation promotes revolutionary impacts in these economies with wide differences. China and India, for instance, have surfed on the digital economy to achieve substantial benefits in their economic indicators. Conversely, countries such as Ethiopia and South Africa are confronted with a severe digital divide, which hinders their social and economic progress. From a global governance viewpoint, the increasing size of the BRICS bloc reflects these economies' growing ambition to reshape global balances. South–South cooperation has also made it possible for the exchange of knowledge and technologies that have increased the sustainability factors of countries such as Russia, while geopolitical conflicts have, in other cases such as Iran, limited the flow of technologies involved in transitioning towards more sustainable models. Recent global shocks revealed vulnerabilities but also differentiated between the resilience capabilities of the BRICS, and while the pandemic slowed down some trends, it accelerated development model innovations as well. All these demands a reinterpretation of the mainstream economic theories: Rostow's model must be re-evaluated in terms of digitalisation, Sen's capabilities approach must include digital access as a core freedom, and Stiglitz's concepts of alternative measures of well-being find expression in multidimensional indices such as the DP2.

DP2 analysis detects a performance gap between original BRICS members and new members. China and Russia show higher progress along sustainability dimensions, in line with earlier development and integration with the world. But countries like Ethiopia and Iran show curtailed developments, particularly in social and environmental aspects, due to structural and geopolitical limitations. The DP2 measure is able to detect these varied development trajectories within the wider BRICS category.

Aside from the contributions of the study, there are limitations that need to be mentioned. For one, aggregate data may not always capture regional variation at the country's level. Second, though secondary data sources are credible, any inaccuracy or discrepancy in the databases can be transmitted to the results. Finally, the DP2 method, as a good tool for synthesis, cannot replace qualitative analyses on the specific policies undertaken by each nation.

For future studies, we suggest several avenues of exploration. First, conducting in-depth analyses at the subnational level could offer a more detailed perspective on the internal dynamics of individual countries. Second, the incorporation of novel indicators, such as those pertaining to governance and technological innovation, could enhance the sustainability framework. Finally, a comparison with other groups of emerging economies would facilitate an assessment of whether the BRICS model represents a singularity or whether there are sustainable development trajectories common to other countries.

References

Abbasi, K. R., Shahbaz, M., Zhang, J., Irfan, M., & Alvarado, R. (2022). Analyze the environmental sustainability factors of China: The role of fossil fuel energy and renewable energy. *Renewable Energy*, *187*, 390–402.

Abdissa, G., Ayalew, A., Dunay, A., & Bálint Illés, C. (2022). Determinants of sustainable growth of SMEs in developing countries: The case of Ethiopia. *Economies, 10*(8), 189.

Al Fardan, M., & Marochi, B. (2021). Implementation of gender policies by the private sector in the UAE: Challenges and opportunities. *Journal for Interdisciplinary Middle Eastern Studies, 7*(2), 127–153.

Ali, I. M. A. (2023). Income inequality, economic growth, and structural changes in Egypt: New insights from quantile cointegration approach. *Economic Change and Restructuring, 56*(1), 379–407.

Ali, S., Hussain, T., Zhang, G., Nurunnabi, M., & Li, B. (2018). The implementation of sustainable development goals in "BRICS" countries. *Sustainability, 10*(7), 2513.

Arechavala, N. S., Espina, P. Z., & Trapero, B. P. (2015). The economic crisis and its effects on the quality of life in the European Union. *Social Indicators Research, 120*, 323–343. https://doi.org/10.1007/s11205-014-0595-9

Arechavala, N. S., & Trapero, B. P. (2009). Synthetic indicators of quality of life in Europe. *Social Indicators Research, 94*, 115–133. https://doi.org/10.1007/s11205-008-9368-z

Arechavala, N. S., & Trapero, B. P. (2019). Measuring deprivation in the European Union with a non-compensatory composite index. *Journal of Applied Statistics, 46*(7), 1243–1259.

Barykina, Y. N., Chernykh, A. G., & Na, B. (2022, February). Energy production as a basis for sustainable development in the BRICS countries. *IOP Conference Series: Earth and Environmental Science, 990*(1), 012016.

Bhattarai, K., & Yousef, M. (Eds.). (2025). Water scarcity and climate change in MENA: Challenges, innovations, and geopolitical impacts. In *The Middle East: Past, present, and future* (pp. 105–136). Springer Nature Switzerland.

Bindman, E. (2017). *Social rights in Russia: From imperfect past to uncertain future*. Routledge.

Bruzzi, C., Ivaldi, E., & Landi, S. (2020). Non-compensatory aggregation method to measure social and material deprivation in an urban area: Relationship with premature mortality. *The European Journal of Health Economics, 21*, 381–396. https://doi.org/10.1007/s10198-019-01139-x

Ciacci, A., Ivaldi, E., Mangano, S., & Ugolini, G. M. (2023). Environment, logistics and infrastructure: The three dimensions of influence of Italian coastal tourism. *Journal of Sustainable Tourism, 31*(7), 1583–1607. https://doi.org/10.1080/09669582.2022.2089294

Costanza, R., Daly, L., Fioramonti, L., Giovannini, E., Kubiszewski, I., Fogh Mortensen, L., Pickett, K. E., Vala Ragnarsdottir, K., De Vogli, R., & Wilkinson, R. (2016). Modelling and measuring sustainable wellbeing in connection with the UN Sustainable Development Goals. *Ecological Economics* 130, 350–355.

Coutinho, R. Z., Montalvo, A. V., Weitzman, A., & Marteleto, L. J. (2021). Zika virus public health crisis and the perpetuation of gender inequality in Brazil. *Reproductive Health, 18*, 1–21.

Dhahri, S., Slimani, S., & Omri, A. (2021). Behavioral entrepreneurship for achieving the sustainable development goals. *Technological Forecasting and Social Change, 165*, 120561.

Featherstone, D. (2013). The contested politics of climate change and the crisis of neoliberalism. *ACME: An International Journal for Critical Geographies, 12*(1), 44–64.

Folmer, H., & Heijman, W. (2005). Multi-dimensional regional inequality as an alternative allocation mechanism for EU Structural Funds remittances: The case of Spain and Hungary. *The Annals of Regional Science, 39*, 337–352. https://doi.org/10.1007/s00168-004-0222-9

Govindan, K., Rajeev, A., Padhi, S. S., & Pati, R. K. (2020). Supply chain sustainability and performance of firms: A meta-analysis of the literature. *Transportation Research Part E: Logistics and Transportation Review*, *137*, 101923.

Goodland, R. (1995). The concept of environmental sustainability. Annual *Review of Ecology and systematics, 26,* 1–24.

Hluszko, C., Huarachi, D. A. R., Ulloa, M. I. C., Salvador, R., Puglieri, F. N., & de Francisco, A. C. (2024). How do the BRICS approach sustainable concerns? A sys tematic literature review. *Environmental Development, 52,* 101075. https://doi.org/10.1016/j.envdev.2024.101075

Ivaldi, E., Penco, L., Isola, G., & Musso, E. (2020). Smart sustainable cities and the urban knowledge-based economy: A NUTS3 level analysis. *Social Indicators Research*, *150*, 45–72. https://doi.org/10.1007/s11205-020-02274-2

Jiménez-Fernández, E., Sánchez, A., & Ortega-Pérez, M. (2022). Dealing with weighting schemes in composite indicators: An unsupervised distance-machine learning proposal for quantitative data. *Socio-Economic Planning Sciences*, *83*, 101339. https://doi.org/10.1016/j.seps.2021.101339

Katoch, O. R. (2024). Tackling child malnutrition and food security: Assessing progress, challenges, and policies in achieving SDG 2 in India. *Nutrition & Food Science*, *54*(2), 349–365.

Landi, S., Ivaldi, E., & Testi, A. (2018). Measuring change over time in socio-economic deprivation and health in an urban context: The case study of Genoa. *Social Indicators Research 139*, 745–785. https://doi.org/10.1007/s11205-017-1720-3

Leal Filho, W., Totin, E., Franke, J. A., Andrew, S. M., Abubakar, I. R., Azadi, H., Nunn, P. D., Ouweneel, B., Williams, P. A., Simpson, N. P., & Global Adaptation Mapping Initiative Team. (2022). Understanding responses to climate-related water scarcity in Africa. *Science of the Total Environment*, *806*, 150420.

Liu, M. (2022). Environmental sustainability impact of environmental protection regulations on the BRICS countries. *Journal of Environmental and Public Health*, *2022*(1), 4626387.

Mahendra, J. R., Aldyan, R. A., & Emovwodo, S. O. (2024). Examining Indonesian government policies in tackling deforestation: Balancing economy and environment. *Journal of Law, Environmental and Justice*, *2*(1), 42–62.

Melaku Belay, S., Tilahun, S., Yehualaw, M., Matos, J., Sousa, H., & Workneh, E. T. (2021). Analysis of cost overrun and schedule delays of infrastructure projects in low income economies: Case studies in Ethiopia. *Advances in Civil Engineering*, *2021*(1), 4991204.

Miranda, I. T. P., Moletta, J., Pedroso, B., Pilatti, L. A., & Picinin, C. T. (2021). A review on green technology practices at BRICS countries: Brazil, Russia, India, China, and South Africa. *Sage Open*, *11*(2), 21582440211013780.

Montero, J. M., Chasco, C., & Larraz, B. (2010). Building an environmental quality index for a big city: A spatial interpolation approach combined with a distance indicator. *Journal of Geographical Systems*, *12*, 435–459. https://doi.org/10.1007/s10109-010-0108-6

Morelli, U. (2011). *Mente e paesaggio: una teoria della vivibilità*. Bollati Boringhieri.

Norman, P. (2010). Identifying change over time in small area socio-economic deprivation. *Applied Spatial Analysis and Policy*, *3*(2–3), 107–138.

Nowak, A., & Kobiałka, A. (2024). The significance of organic farming in the European Union from the perspective of sustainable development. *Economics and Environment*, *88*(1), 1–15.

Nurramadhani, A., Riandi, R., Permanasari, A., & Suwarma, I. R. (2024). Low-carbon food consumption for solving climate change mitigation: Literature review with bibliometric and simple calculation application for cultivating sustainability consciousness in facing sustainable development goals (SDGs). *Indonesian Journal of Science and Technology*, *9*(2), 261–286.

Rostow, W. W. (1990). *The stages of economic growth: A non-communist manifesto*. Cambridge University Press.

Sachs, J. D., Lafortune, G., Fuller, G., & Drumm, E. (2023). *Sustainable development report 2023: Implementing the SDG stimulus*. SDSN. Retrieved March 25, 2024, from https://policycommons.net/artifacts/4445283/2023-sustainable-development-report/5242513/

Salah, S. I., Eltaweel, M., & Abeykoon, C. (2022). Towards a sustainable energy future for Egypt: A systematic review of renewable energy sources, technologies, challenges, and recommendations. *Cleaner Engineering and Technology*, *8*, 100497.

Sen, A. (1999). *Development as freedom*. Oxford University Press.

Serbian, O., Izmailova, D., Mashkin, A., & Glagoleva, S. (2023). Assessment of the reliability of the development of infrastructure projects on transport in the Russian Federation. *Transportation Research Procedia*, *68*, 50–59.

Sicsú, J., de Melo Modenesi, A., & Pimentel, D. (2021). Severe recession with inflation: The case of Brazil. *Journal of Post Keynesian Economics*, *44*(1), 89–111.

Solaymani, S. (2021). A review on energy and renewable energy policies in Iran. *Sustainability*, *13*, 7328.

Stiglitz, J. E., Sen, A., & Fitoussi, J. P. (2009). *The measurement of economic performance and social progress revisited* (Vol. 33, pp. 1–63). OFCE.

Strielkowski, W., Sherstobitova, A., Rovny, P., & Evteeva, T. (2021). Increasing energy efficiency and modernization of energy systems in Russia: A review. *Energies*, *14*(11), 3164.

Trapero, J. P. B. (1977). *Problemas de la medición del bienestar y conceptos afines (Una aplicación al caso español)*. INE.

Traversa, S., & Ivaldi, E. (2024). eGovernment implementation in Italy. Regional index for NRRP goals evaluation. *Social Indicators Research*, *178*(3), 1125–1144. https://doi.org/10.1007/s11205-024-03361-4

Vallance, S., Perkins, H. C., & Dixon, J. E. (2011). What is social sustainability? A clarification of concepts. *Geoforum*, *42*(3), 342–348.

Wang, Q., Niu, G., Gan, X., & Cai, Q. (2022). Green returns to education: Does education affect pro-environmental attitudes and behaviors in China? *PLoS One*, *17*(2), e0263383.

Wendimu, G. Y. (2021). The challenges and prospects of Ethiopian agriculture. *Cogent Food & Agriculture*, *7*(1), 1923619.

Wibowo, A. (2023, October). Global economic challenges for Indonesia: Equitable development for sustainable prosperity. *Prosiding Seminar Teknologi, Akuntansi, Bisnis, Ekonomi, Dan Komunitas*, *3*, 23–40.

Williams, A. (2024). Environmental pollution in India: Issues and solutions. *African Journal of Biological Sciences*, *6*, 22–27.

Zaman, K., bin Abdullah, A., Khan, A., bin Mohd Nasir, M. R., Hamzah, T. A. A. T., & Hussain, S. (2016). Dynamic linkages among energy consumption, environment, health and wealth in BRICS countries: Green growth key to sustainable development. *Renewable and Sustainable Energy Reviews*, *56*, 1263–1271.

Zafar, S. Z., Zhilin, Q., Mabrouk, F., Ramirez-Asis, E., M Alzoubi, H., Hishan, S. S., & Michel, M. (2023). Empirical linkages between ICT, tourism, and trade towards sustainable environment: Evidence from BRICS countries. *Economic research-Ekonomska istraživanja*, *36*(2), 2127417.

Zarzosa, P. (1996). Aproximación a la medición del bienestar social. Idoneidad del indicador sintético "Distancia-P (2)" (Aplicación al caso español). *Cuadernos de Economía: Spanish Journal of Economics and Finance*, *24*(68), 139–163.

Chapter 3

Companies and Territories: Building Metrics and Indices to Assess Mutual Well-being

Margaret Antonicelli[a], *Michele Rubino*[b], *Ilaria Mastrorocco*[b], *Elisa Gerbasi*[b] *and Antonio Gattulli*[c]

[a]*University IULM, Italy*
[b]*University LUM, Italy*
[c]*Bio Organica Italia S.r.l., Italy*

Abstract

The concept of well-being is inextricably linked to the social role that companies play within their ecosystems. To ensure the economic sustainability of their activities, companies must remunerate all factors of production, including risk capital, at market conditions, while producing goods and services that characterise daily life. Accounting and management theory recognises that corporate objectives cannot be reduced to the interests of specific stakeholder groups. The economic and social dimensions of organisations are inextricably intertwined, as economic coordination serves to satisfy human needs. It is obvious that the economic function of organisations is inextricably linked to their social role. At the same time, it should be noted that the territory itself generates well-being by providing companies with resources, services and a supportive environment. Territorial well-being, which combines social, environmental and infrastructural factors, has a positive impact on business performance. This study aims to develop two different indicators of well-being. The first measures the well-being that companies create for the community and the second vice versa. The methodology used in this study involves the initialisation of elementary indicators, which are then divided into domains and synthesised. These domains are then synthesised into a single indicator. The study

Changing Dimensions in Economic Development: Theories and Empirics, 25–36

Published under exclusive licence by Emerald Publishing Limited
doi:10.1108/978-1-83708-384-820261003

uses non-linear and non-compensatory synthesis methods with the aim of providing companies with a strategic and operational tool to assess, measure and improve the wealth that the territory generates and preserves.

Keywords: Corporate well-being; community well-being; sustainability; value creation; indicators

JEL Codes: C13; M14; Q01; Q56

1. Introduction

Sustainability has become a central concept on the global agenda, encompassing environmental, social and economic dimensions (Colglazier, 2015). Originally focused on environmental concerns, it has evolved into a holistic paradigm that promotes balanced growth that fulfils the needs of the present without compromising those of future generations.

In this context, companies are increasingly committed to sustainability, not only to fulfil the expectations of their stakeholders but also to meet legal requirements. The institutionalisation of corporate sustainability has led to a shift from voluntary initiatives to mandatory frameworks, particularly under the influence of European directives (Rubino & Mastrorocco, 2025). Reporting practices have matured into structured and standardised tools to assess both the scope and quality of sustainability-related information (Rubino et al., 2024). This development has been supported by international standards such as the Global Reporting Initiative (GRI), the Sustainability Accounting Standards Board (SASB) and the Task Force on Climate-related Financial Disclosures (TCFD), as well as regulatory frameworks such as the Non-Financial Reporting Directive (NFRD) and the Corporate Sustainability Reporting Directive (CSRD).

Companies' sustainability commitments are now regularly communicated via various reporting tools such as sustainability reports, integrated reports (IR) and non-financial statements. In this scenario, academic and professional literature has mainly focused on the assessment of corporate sustainability performance and disclosure, often neglecting the societal impacts and the concepts and dimensions of well-being that companies can generate in local communities. This conventional approach overlooks how corporate sustainability efforts translate into tangible improvements in community well-being, potentially limiting the effectiveness of sustainability initiatives in addressing local social needs (Węziak-Białowolska et al., 2018).

However, the concept of well-being can also be viewed from another perspective, namely that the area itself creates added value for companies. Today, gross domestic product (GDP) is considered an outdated and inadequate measure to assess the well-being of a nation or region. In response, policymakers have introduced more comprehensive frameworks, such as equitable and sustainable well-being, which are aligned with the United Nations (UN) sustainable development goals (SDGs) to promote a more holistic understanding of social progress. However, there is still a lack of frameworks or indicators that measure well-being and the value that territories create for companies.

The aim of this study is therefore to identify the key dimensions in order to develop two different indicators: one that measures the well-being that companies create for local communities and another that captures the well-being that territories create for the companies operating there.

2. The Relevant Dimensions of the Corporate Well-being Contribution Index (CWCI)

Despite the increasing focus on corporate sustainability performance and disclosure, there is little evidence of how these efforts translate into tangible improvements in community well-being at a local level (Hummel & Schlick, 2016). In this context, it is important to recognise that companies can have a profound impact on the well-being of the communities in which they operate, for various stakeholders such as employees, consumers, suppliers and local residents. Business decisions affect working conditions, healthcare, employee training and job security, the environment and the raising of public funds through taxation. These diverse impacts emphasise the important role that companies play in shaping social well-being and highlight their responsibility to consider the interests of the community in both operational and strategic decisions.

A company's contribution to well-being is inextricably linked to its social role within the community in which it operates. To ensure their survival, companies must remunerate all factors of production, including risk capital, fairly and in line with the market. They also provide a significant proportion of the goods and services that society consumes on a daily basis and therefore occupy a central position in social life. The economic, social and environmental responsibilities of a company are closely linked and underline the understanding that companies exist primarily to fulfil human needs. Therefore, the economic logic underlying business operations essentially supports the social purpose of the company (Delmas & Durand, 2018).

In light of this, the CWCI can be constructed by identifying for each stakeholder category (Parmar et al., 2010) the relevant dimensions that help to assess the company's potential contribution to the overall well-being of the community and area, as described below.

(1) *Employees*. Companies can significantly influence the well-being of their employees. Ensuring health, safety and appropriate working conditions is crucial as it has a direct impact on the physical health, motivation and productivity of employees (Page & Vella-Brodrick, 2009). Equally important are work–life balance and promoting a high-quality working environment, as these factors strongly influence job satisfaction, personal well-being and mental health. Promoting diversity, equality and inclusion (DEI) in the workplace fosters a sense of fairness and belonging among employees and increases creativity and organisational effectiveness. In addition, continuous training,

skills development and the active involvement of employees strengthen their professional growth and sense of contribution, while respect for human rights emphasises companies' ethical commitment to their employees (Charalampous et al., 2019).

This dimension comprises a total of 34 indicators, which are distributed across the following five analytical pillars: (1) health, safety and working conditions; (2) work–life balance, well-being and quality of the working environment; (3) DEI; (4) training, skills development, involvement and participation; and (5) protection and promotion of human rights.

(2) *Local community*. One of the most important aspects is the company's ability to generate local economic impact, which is crucial for promoting employment opportunities, economic stability and sustainable local development. Active community involvement and open dialogue are critical as they ensure alignment with local needs and priorities and foster stronger relationships based on trust. Companies also make a meaningful contribution through initiatives aimed at social, educational and cultural support, promoting community cohesion, integration and collective identity. Finally, promoting health initiatives and improving the overall quality of life in the community demonstrates corporate responsibility for improving community well-being and resilience (Bellandi, 2001).

This dimension comprises a total of 20 indicators, which are distributed across the following four analytical pillars: (1) local economic impact; (2) participation and dialogue with the territory; (3) social, educational and cultural support and territorial cohesion; and (4) community health and quality of life.

(3) *Environment*. This dimension reflects the direct role of companies in tackling pressing global environmental problems. Combating climate change and reducing emissions are crucial, as there is an urgent need to maintain the ecological balance and reduce climate-related risks. Sustainable management of natural resources is also crucial as it safeguards resources for future generations and ensures long-term ecological stability. The introduction of circular economy practices and efficient waste management underlines the company's commitment to minimising its environmental impact. Furthermore, the protection of biodiversity and ecosystems is fundamental, as environmental health and overall human well-being are closely linked (Dasgupta, 2001).

This dimension comprises a total of 16 indicators, which are distributed across the four analytical pillars: (1) climate change and global emissions; (2) sustainable management of natural resources; (3) circular economy and waste management; and (4) biodiversity and ecosystems.

(4) *Customers/consumers*. The quality, safety and reliability of products and services are essential for consumer trust and loyalty. Ethical practices,

transparency and the promotion of consumer awareness strengthen the trusting relationships that are crucial for the sustainable success of companies. Protecting privacy and personal data is also critical and reflects the ethical responsibility and compliance requirements necessary to maintain consumer trust. Finally, sustainable innovation of products and processes recognises changing consumer preferences and ensures the company's market relevance and competitiveness in a sustainability-driven economy (Sirgy & Lee, 2008).

This dimension comprises a total of 21 indicators, which are distributed across the following five analytical pillars: (1) quality, product and service safety; (2) customer satisfaction and loyalty; (3) ethics, transparency and consumer awareness; (4) privacy and personal data protection; and (5) sustainable product/process innovation.

(5) *Suppliers*. Ensuring social and environmental sustainability and respect for human rights throughout the supply chain emphasises the responsibility of companies beyond their direct business activities. Appropriate economic conditions and fair contractual practices are critical to maintaining productive, long-term supplier relationships and promoting economic fairness. Promoting local supply chains and supporting supplier development contributes significantly to local economic resilience and overall sustainability. Transparency, anti-corruption practices and collaboration throughout the supply chain build trust, mitigate risk and improve overall supply chain stability (Menon, 2012).

This dimension comprises a total of 24 indicators, which are distributed across the following four analytical pillars: (1) sustainability and respect for human rights in the supply chain; (2) economic fairness and contractual conditions; (3) promotion of the local supply chain and support for supplier growth; (4) transparency, corruption prevention along the supply chain.

(6) *Shareholders/investors*. Focus on transparent financial and Environmental, social and governance (ESG) reporting, which is essential for informed decision-making and investor confidence. Effective sustainable corporate governance and sound risk management ensure the long-term stability and resilience of the company. Financial stability and sustainable, long-term performance are key dimensions as they guarantee continuous value creation and returns for investors. Adherence to high standards of corporate ethics and regulatory compliance protects against reputational risk and potential liabilities. In addition, creating shared, long-term value aligns investors' financial objectives with broader societal benefits, while responsible investor engagement promotes strategic alignment, trust and transparency (La porta et al., 2000).

This dimension comprises a total of 21 indicators, which are distributed across the following six analytical pillars: (1) ESG reporting; (2) sustainable governance and risk management; (3) financial stability and sustainable long-term performance; (4) business ethics and regulatory compliance; (5) long-term creation of shared value; (6) responsible investor engagement.

Collectively, these six dimensions provide a solid basis for assessing and understanding how organisations can meaningfully contribute to the well-being of all stakeholders (Kumar & Ramachandran, 2021).

3. A Composite Metric for Evaluating Social Value Creation for Enterprises

The relationship between a company and its territory is bidirectional: while the company contributes to the development and vitality of the local environment, it also receives resources, support and legitimacy from it. When considering the concept of well-being, it is therefore important to take into account both sides of this exchange, not only the value that the company creates for the territory but also the conditions that the territory offers for the company's operations and growth. This two-way dynamic emphasises the need for a more integrated and place-based approach to assessing the well-being that companies receive from the local community.

In recent decades, a growing body of research has highlighted increasing concerns about the limitations of GDP as a comprehensive measure of development (Afonso & Jalles, 2016). This criticism has led to the development of multidimensional indicators that provide a more adaptable framework and are able to capture the complex interplay between economic, social and environmental factors. These indicators include the Social Performance Index (SPI) and the Social Productivity Index (SoPI), which have emerged as alternative tools for assessing social well-being and regional socio-economic dynamics.

Building on these innovative contributions, we propose the creation of a coherent metric: the Integrated Index of Social Progress and Territorial Productivity (IISP-TP). This index aims to assess the extent to which local communities foster conditions that support not only their own well-being but also that of the companies operating in their territory. IISP-TP offers two main components that form a single systematic structure.

The SoC's SPI comprises four analytical pillars: Basic Human Rights, Foundations of Well-being, Opportunity and Employability (Antonicelli & Rubino, 2023), which include objective and subjective measures such as hospitalisation, schooling, environmental cleanliness, personal safety and digital literacy and marketable skills development. The index is technically structured as follows:

(a) The Basic Human Rights Index (BHRI)[1] comprises 12 indicators addressing nutrition, shelter, medical care, water and sanitation and personal safety.

[1]Basic Human Rights Index (BHRI) is composed of 12 indicators. The domains are nutrition and basic medical care, water and sanitation, shelter and personal safety. The indicators include access to basic nutrition; access to essential medical services, child mortality rate, access to clean drinking water, access to sanitation facilities, homelessness rate or access to adequate housing, overcrowding in housing units, crime rate/homicide rate, prevalence of gender-based violence, access to emergency and first-aid services, immunisation coverage and maternal health service access.

(b) The Foundation of Well-being Index (FWI)[2] includes 12 indicators such as access to basic knowledge, information and communication technologies, health and wellness and environmental quality.
(c) The Opportunity Index (OI)[3] also includes 12 indicators measuring access to advanced education, inclusiveness, personal rights and freedom of choice.
(d) The Employability Index (EI),[4] more directly tied to labour market readiness and enterprise dynamics, is based on 25 indicators covering areas such as professional development, working conditions, in-company training, compensation structures, digital and soft skills and company policies.

The SoPI evaluates the social productivity or 'social fertility' of the regions based on their infrastructural and cultural productivity value (Antonicelli & Urbani, 2023). The Multidisciplinary Institute of the Model and Theory of Territory Dynamics of the Economics and Humanities Department of the Faculty of Social Sciences at Italy's University of Siena developed the Sistema Locale

[2]The Foundation of Well-being Index (FWI) is composed of 12 indicators. The domains are access to basic knowledge, access to Information and communication, health and well-being and environmental quality. The indicators include adult literacy rate, primary school enrolment rate, secondary school completion rate, broadband or internet penetration rate, mobile phone usage per capita, life expectancy at birth, self-reported general health status, prevalence of chronic illnesses (e.g., diabetes, cardiovascular diseases), PM2.5 air pollution concentration, water quality index, urban green space per inhabitant and public health expenditure per capita.

[3]The Opportunity Index (OI) includes 12 indicators. The domains are personal rights, personal freedom and choice, inclusiveness and access to advanced education. The indicators include political and civil liberties score; freedom of expression index; gender equality index; LGBTQ+ inclusivity rating; representation of ethnic/religious minorities in public life; university-level education access rate; tertiary education enrolment rate; inclusiveness in governance and public institutions; disability access compliance; religious freedom indicators; legal recognition of same-sex unions/marriages; youth not in education, employment or training (NEET rate).

[4]The Employability Index (EI) includes 25 indicators. The domains are professional development, compensation, work environment, digital skills and corporate policies. The indicators include general employment rate, unemployment rate, average gross salary, gender pay gap, availability of performance-based bonuses, employee work–life balance index, share of employees participating in in-company training, participation in lifelong learning or adult education, percentage of employees with certified digital competencies, average hours of digital skills training per year, internal career advancement opportunities, employee turnover rate, employee satisfaction levels (via surveys), workplace health and safety programmes, average weekly working hours, access to remote/hybrid work options, availability of paid parental leave, presence of diversity and inclusion policies, investment in professional development resources, organisational culture rating, share of formal contracts among employed population, coverage of occupational health services, prevalence of temporary or precarious employment, frequency of labour disputes; possession of corporate social responsibility (CSR) or ESG certifications.

Territoriale model (Local territorial system) (SLoT) model which states that society, economy and territory develop interdependently. The so-called basin includes:

(a) The Socio-cultural Content Index (Milieu Index),[5] measuring infrastructural conditions at a region-specific level that have endured over a longer period and demographic characteristics such as dependency ratios, birth rates and educational achievement indicators like literacy rates at the school level, as well as the region's informational infrastructure, which includes broadband, 5G and fibre coverage.
(b) The Performance Index, measuring civic participation, entrepreneurial activity, innovation, governance responsibility and ecological responsibility. Key indicators are the number of new and active businesses, employment in research and innovation industries, voluntary activities and electoral participation.

The IISP-TP integrating two marking domains of integration lets us view social indicators as not only measures of a society's well-being but also as valuable aids for comprehending and improving business settings. Asserts that populations and territories do not merely host enterprises. Instead, these actors collaboratively construct the socio-institutional frameworks and infrastructure that facilitate entrepreneurialism, labour, productivity sustained and enduring competitive edge (Zazzaro, 2010).

This integrated index encapsulates the social robust verticals that serve as the foundation for civic engagement, demonstrating reciprocal advantage. In practical terms, the IISP-TP is positioned to emerge as a powerful strategic analytic framework with context responsive socio-territorial ecosystem development agility internationally framed for investors and corporate strategists focused on resilient skill sets and socio-territorial goals which determine investment efficacy areas enabling cross-regional and city comparative benchmarking while aligned with modern sustainable development policies enabling driven governance performance evaluation.

4. Methodological Approach

To operationalise the two indices (CWCI and IISP-TP), we adopt the Adjusted Mazziotta–Pareto Index (AMPI) methodology. This method suits best on

[5]The Milieu Index includes 20 indicators. The domains are demographic structure and infrastructure and digital access. The indicators include structural dependency ratio; employment rate; overall fixed broadband take-up; at least 100 Mbps fixed broadband take-up; at least 1 Gbps take-up; fast broadband Next generation access (broadband networks) (NGA) coverage; fixed very high capacity network (VHCN) coverage; FTTP coverage (fibre to the premises); 5G spectrum readiness; 5G coverage; mobile broadband take-up; broadband price index; number of museums, libraries, cinemas, theatres; number of nurseries and kindergartens; number of primary schools; number of junior high schools; number of high schools; literacy rate; school dropout rate; and graduation rate.

account of the great variance of the elementary indicators that comprise the index, which are heterogeneous in terms of their measurement units, statistical distributions and conceptual scales. These indicators, such as broadband penetration rates, civic engagement, infrastructure access, employment, digital skills and environmental factors, cannot be summed up by compensatory or simple linear aggregation processes.

The AMPI is a non-compensatory aggregate index method devised by Mazziotta and Pareto (2013, 2016). With respect to internal unbalances, the index is partially penalised within the indicator standardisation process. The index is tailored for multidimensional contexts, which require comparability, like spatial benchmarking, socio-economic diagnostics and multi-domain policy design.

The standard Mazziotta–Pareto Index (MPI) for unit *j* is defined as:

$$MPI_j = M_{zj} \pm S_{zj} * CV_{zj}$$

where:

- MPI_j: Mean of the standardised indicators (z-scores) for unit j.
- S_{zj}: Standard deviation of the z-scores.
- CV_{zj}: Coefficient of variation.
- The '+' sign is used when all indicators are positively oriented (higher = better), and '−' when indicators are negative or mixed.

To ensure comparability across time and units, the AMPI is used, which involves normalisation and penalty adjustment.

To ensure temporal comparability and normalisation across different datasets, the AMPI is used. The AMPI relies on transforming each indicator via:

$$x_{ij}^{*} = 100 \pm \left(\frac{x_{ij} - \overline{x_i}}{s_i} \cdot k \right)$$

- x^*_{ij}: Normalised value of indicator i for unit j.
- x_{ij}: Raw value of indicator i for unit j.
- x_i: Mean of indicator i.
- $\overline{s_i}$: Standard deviation of indicator i.
- k: A scale constant, usually set at 10.
- The sign is '+' for positive indicators and '−' for negative indicators.

The AMPI is then computed as:

$$MPI_j = M_j \pm S_j * CV_j$$

where M_j, S_j and CV_j are calculated on the normalised indicators.

Using the AMPI technique, the construction of the two indices follows a logical series of steps, each of which aims to ensure that the composite index captures, respectively, the company's stakeholder dimension and the subtleties, strata and socio-territorial productivity of the region. This begins with the selection of indicators belonging to each of the six dimensions of the CWCI and to the two main components of the index, that is, the SPI and the SoPI. These indicators are relevant on both, empirical and theoretical constructs with regard to the two dimensions of well-being.

The first step after identifying the indicators is to determine their directionality, that is, whether each variable gets better (e.g. worker satisfaction, literacy rate, broadband coverage) or worse (e.g. unemployment rate, pollution, percentage of recycled materials). This ensures that all indicators point in the same direction, which is essential for meaningful aggregation.

Selecting the AMPI approach to compute the two indices is a decision that is both technical and ideological at once. In dealing with a large set of indicators, each with its own range, sociological meaning, and unit, there is a need for uniformity, equity, and interpretability. AMPI does exactly this. AMPI mitigates the chance of scoring high in one indicator area of each index, for example, in infrastructure or digital access, while having no or low scores in education, civic participation or environmental quality sub-indicators through its processes. By normalising all indicators and mitigating the effect of skewed internal value ratios, AMPI maintains equilibrium. In this way, the method respects the interplay between different aspects of the two dimensions of well-being.

This is of particular importance both for the CWCI as an indicator of the well-being that the company transfers to the territory and for the IISP-TP as a composite indicator designed to take into account the well-being of the population and the quality of the socio-infrastructural environment following the entrepreneurial activity at the geographical level. The interdependence of the idiopathic characteristics of areas means that linear relationships are more subtle and complex and therefore non-linear.

Following this, the raw data undergo a normalisation process. Instead of simple min-max scaling, the AMPI method applies a transformation that centres each indicator around a mean value of 100, with variability scaled by a constant (typically 10). This approach not only makes the indicators dimensionless and comparable but also preserves their relative distribution. Importantly, this normalisation accounts for the natural heterogeneity of the indicators – some expressed in percentages, others in absolute values or indices – and thus avoids the distortion that often arises in traditional standardisation techniques.

After normalisation, the indicators are grouped into their respective sub-indices: for the SPI domain, these include Basic Human Rights, Foundations of Well-being, Opportunity, and Employability; for the SoPI domain, the Milieu Index and the Performance Index. For the CWCI, the indicators are grouped into the six stakeholder specific sub-indices. Within each of these sub-indices, the normalised scores are aggregated to produce an intermediate score for each territorial unit.

However, AMPI does not stop at simple aggregation. To ensure that each well-being dimension is not unjustly rewarded if they excel in one area while underperforming in another, a penalty function is applied. This penalty is based on the internal variability of scores within each domain. In practice, the final score is reduced in proportion to the inconsistency or imbalance between indicators. This reflects the idea that sustainable and inclusive development requires well-rounded rather than uneven performance.

Finally, the penalised sub-index scores are combined to form the overall CWCI and IISP-TP scores. This final step may involve equal or differentiated weighting, depending on the analytical priorities of the study. The result is a robust, interpretable and policy-relevant index that captures both the quality of life provided by a territory and its capacity to sustain and enhance economic activity through socially fertile conditions.

The AMPI method captures this interdependence by focusing on balance rather than punishing excellence in a singular domain. Consequently, the CWCI and IISP-TP are elevated beyond a simple ranking system; it transforms into a strategic and diagnostic framework that illustrates strengths and weaknesses. It serves as a critical glimpse for assessing where key value-for-money investments and interventions should be deployed by policymakers, businesses and communities. In a world where enduring territorial development is ever more centred on sustainable resilience and inclusion, the methodological rigour offered by AMPI enhances the credibility and trustworthiness of the CWCI and IISP-TP as a guide for action.

5. Conclusion

One key feature of the indicator system is its ability to offer a well-rounded view of well-being. By analysing various levels, individual indicators, domains and sub-domains, it captures a wide range of economic, social, environmental, institutional and health-related aspects, allowing for a comprehensive and detailed understanding of territorial development.

The AMPI plays a crucial role in strengthening the framework's methodology. It's specifically designed to aggregate diverse indicators, ensuring statistical consistency by standardising values and applying penalties for any internal imbalances. This non-compensatory method prevents strong performance in one area from overshadowing weaknesses in another, maintaining the integrity of the overall score. It also allows for comparisons across regions, helping to pinpoint disparities, vulnerabilities and key areas for policy action.

In addition to assessing the impacts that companies have in their regions, the index also sheds light on the supportive conditions that these regions provide for businesses. This two-way perspective is vital: companies aren't just standalone entities; they're part of interconnected ecosystems that influence one another. By acknowledging and measuring this mutual relationship, the IISP-TP and CWCI become a valuable tool for shaping place-based policies and investment strategies. Ultimately, it promotes more sustainable and inclusive value creation for both businesses and the communities they serve.

References

Afonso, A., & Jalles, J. T. (2016). Economic performance, government size, and institutional quality. *Empirica, 43*(1), 83–109.

Antonicelli, M., & Rubino, M. (2023). Social performance index. In Maggino, F. (Ed.), *Encyclopedia of quality of life and well-being research* (pp. 6648–6650). Springer.

Antonicelli, M., & Urbani, S. (2023). Social productivity index. In Maggino, F. (Ed.), *Encyclopedia of quality of life and well-being research* (pp. 6648–6650). Springer.

Bellandi, M. (2001). Local development and embedded large firms. *Entrepreneurship & Regional Development*, *13*(3), 189–210.

Charalampous, M., Grant, C. A., Tramontano, C., & Michailidis, E. (2019). Systematically reviewing remote e-workers' well-being at work: A multidimensional approach. *European Journal of Work and Organizational Psychology*, *28*(1), 51–73.

Colglazier, W. (2015). Sustainable development agenda: 2030. *Science*, *349*(6252), 1048–1050.

Dasgupta, P. (2001). *Human well-being and the natural environment*. OUP Oxford.

Delmas, M. A., & Durand, R. (2018). Measuring business impacts on well-being: A goal oriented approach. In *Measuring the impacts of business on well-being and sustainability*. (pp. 1–14) OECD.

Hummel, K., & Schlick, C. (2016). The relationship between sustainability performance and sustainability disclosure – Reconciling voluntary disclosure theory and legitimacy theory. *Journal of Accounting and Public Policy*, *35*(5), 455–476.

Kumar, V., & Ramachandran, D. (2021). Developing firms' growth approaches as a multidimensional decision to enhance key stakeholders' wellbeing. *International Journal of Research in Marketing*, *38*(2), 402–424.

La Porta, R., Lopez-de-Silanes, F., Shleifer, A., & Vishny, R. (2000). Investor protection and corporate governance. *Journal of Financial Economics*, *58*(1–2), 3–27.

Mazziotta, M., & Pareto, A. (2013). A synthetic indicator of quality of development: The case of the Italian regions. *Social Indicators Research*, *114*(1), 121–137.

Mazziotta, M., & Pareto, A. (2016). On a generalized non-compensatory composite index for measuring socio-economic phenomena. *Social Indicators Research*, *127*, 983–1003.

Menon, S. T. (2012). Human resource practices, supply chain performance, and wellbeing. *International Journal of Manpower*, *33*(7), 769–785.

Page, K. M., & Vella-Brodrick, D. A. (2009). The 'what', 'why' and 'how' of employee well-being: A new model. *Social Indicators Research*, *90*, 441–458.

Parmar, B. L., Freeman, R. E., Harrison, J. S., Wicks, A. C., Purnell, L., & De Colle, S. (2010). Stakeholder theory: The state of the art. *The Academy of Management Annals*, *4*(1), 403–445.

Rubino, M., & Mastrorocco, I. (2025). Exploring the influence of board structure and composition on respect for human rights. *Social Responsibility Journal*, *21*(2), 301–319.

Rubino, M., Mastrorocco, I., & Garegnani, G. M. (2024). The influence of market and institutional factors on ESG rating disagreement. *Corporate Social Responsibility and Environmental Management*, *31*(5), 3916–3926.

Sirgy, M. J., & Lee, D. J. (2008). Well-being marketing: An ethical business philosophy for consumer goods firms. *Journal of Business Ethics*, *77*, 377–403.

Węziak-Białowolska, D., Koosed, T., Leon, C., & McNeely, E. (2018). *Measuring the impacts of business on well-being and sustainability*. OECD.

Zazzaro, A. (2010). Reti d'imprese e territorio. Tra vincoli e nuove opportunità dopo la crisi. *Economia Politica, Journal of Analytical and Institutional Economics*, *27*(3), 663–690.

Chapter 4

Digital Technologies and Sustainability Reporting in the European Context: A Theoretical Framework

Michele Rubino, Ilaria Mastrorocco and Elisa Gerbasi

University LUM Giuseppe Degennaro, Casamassima, Italy

Abstract

The digital transformation is reshaping corporate sustainability reporting by improving the way companies collect, process and disclose environmental, social and governance (ESG) data. As regulatory requirements and stakeholder expectations evolve, digital technologies are playing an increasingly important role in improving data collection and management processes for sustainability reporting. The adoption of technologies such as big data analytics, artificial intelligence (AI), machine learning (ML), blockchain and internet of things (IoT) is transforming the management of ESG data. These tools improve the automation, accuracy and optimisation of sustainability reporting processes and enable companies to generate reliable, comparable and standardised information for decision-making and strategic planning. Digital technologies can significantly support the implementation of the double-materiality approach required by the European Sustainability Reporting Standards (ESRS). This approach requires companies to consider both financial materiality, which focuses on the impact of sustainability issues on financial performance, and impact materiality, which looks at the broader impact of the company's activities on society and the environment. By improving data accuracy, consistency and reliability, digitalisation facilitates the effective identification, processing and reporting of sustainability information, improves compliance with evolving regulatory requirements and promotes accountability. This

Changing Dimensions in Economic Development: Theories and Empirics, 37–49

Published under exclusive licence by Emerald Publishing Limited
doi:10.1108/978-1-83708-384-820261004

chapter analyses how digital transformation supports corporate sustainability reporting under the Corporate Sustainability Reporting Directive (CSRD) and ESRS. It aims to analyse how digital technologies improve data quality and transparency and proposes a theoretical framework to support materiality assessment and alignment with the sustainable development goals (SDGs).

Keywords: Sustainability reporting; digital technologies; ESRS; SDGs; CSRD; regulatory compliance

JEL Codes: L86; M41; O33; Q56

1. Introduction

In recent years, sustainability has emerged as a key determinant of corporate competitiveness, requiring firms across different industries to incorporate ESG principles into their strategic framework. The adoption of the SDGs by the United Nations in 2015 and the signing of the Paris Agreement on climate change in the same year marked a decisive turning point in global sustainability efforts. These initiatives have raised awareness of environmental and social challenges and emphasised the need for companies to commit to sustainable practices.

Over the past decade, European companies have been encouraged to integrate ESG considerations into their business operations, not only as a compliance measure but also to increase their legitimacy and build stakeholder trust (Camilleri, 2015). Aligning business strategies with sustainability principles has become essential to securing investments and ensuring long-term resilience.

A defining moment in corporate sustainability reporting was the introduction of the Non-Financial Reporting Directive (NFRD) in 2014, which mandates large companies to disclose non-financial information in their annual reports. However, as concerns about sustainability grew and demand for standardised ESG data increased, the European Union (EU) sought to expand and refine its regulatory framework. This led to the adoption of the CSRD in 2022, which significantly expands sustainability reporting obligations. Unlike the NFRD, which primarily applies to large public interest entities, the CSRD extends disclosure requirements to a wider range of companies, including those listed on regulated markets (Rubino, 2020; Rubino & Mastrorocco, 2025). The CSRD represents a fundamental shift in corporate transparency, sustainability and accountability (Hristov & Searcy, 2025). It requires companies to provide detailed, standardised and comprehensive ESG disclosures to ensure that investors, policymakers and the public have access to reliable and comparable sustainability data. This shift goes beyond voluntary ESG commitments and embeds sustainability as a core component of corporate governance.

Under the framework of the European Green Deal, the CSRD requires compliance with the ESRS, a comprehensive system designed to improve the coherence and quality of sustainability reporting. The ESRS encompass a broad spectrum of sustainability topics, including climate change, human rights and anti-corruption. Sector-specific reporting standards are currently being developed to further refine the disclosure requirements and provide customised guidelines for different industries. The main objective of the ESRS is to enhance the transparency, consistency and reliability of companies' sustainability disclosures, thereby facilitating investors and stakeholders in evaluating and comparing companies' ESG performance more effectively (Miettinen, 2024). The CSRD and ESRS introduce more stringent sustainability disclosure requirements that mark a shift towards greater corporate accountability and alignment with long-term sustainability goals. This evolving regulatory framework emphasises the increasing role of sustainability in shaping corporate strategy and strengthening competitive position in both the European and global economy.

The interpretation and implementation of sustainability principles varies considerably between companies and is influenced by industry characteristics and internal factors. These differences characterise the way in which companies translate their sustainability goals into concrete measures. Effective implementation requires the support of various tools, including business process re-engineering, the development of sustainable products and digital technologies (Broccardo et al., 2023). The integration of digital technologies plays a crucial role in improving sustainability performance. These technologies facilitate the collection, processing and analysis of sustainability-related data and enable the identification of necessary organisational changes, the improvement of companies' planning processes to better align them with the requirements of industrial sustainability and the support of experimentation with innovative business models (Rubino et al., 2023).

The increasing importance of corporate sustainability, which is further emphasised by the expansion of regulations such as the CSRD and the ESRS, has highlighted the need for more effective and transparent sustainability reporting. In this context, digital transformation emerges as a crucial factor as it provides advanced tools to streamline reporting processes, improve data accuracy and improve corporate accountability. Technologies such as big data analytics, blockchain and AI can support real-time monitoring, ensure consistency in ESG reporting and enable data-driven decision-making (Olanrewaju et al., 2024).

This chapter aims to analyse the role of digital technologies in improving the quality, efficiency and transparency of corporate sustainability reporting. It shows how tools such as AI, big data, blockchain and IoT are changing the processes of data collection, management and communication (Rella et al., 2024). It also explores the interaction between digitalisation and the European regulatory framework, focusing on the CSRD, the ESRS and double materiality to understand how digital tools facilitate compliance. Finally, this chapter proposes a conceptual framework that explores how digitalisation can drive more effective sustainability reporting and contribute to the achievement of the SDGs.

This chapter is structured as follows: Section 2 outlines the methodological approach adopted to develop the conceptual framework. Section 3 provides an overview of the theoretical background on the role of digital technologies in improving sustainability reporting. Section 4 discusses the integration of digitalisation within the European regulatory context, focusing on data quality and compliance. Section 5 examines the principle of double materiality introduced by the CSRD and implemented through the ESRS. Section 6 explores how digital innovation acts as a strategic enabler for materiality assessment and alignment with the SDGs. Section 7 outlines a theoretical framework on how digital technologies support sustainability reporting and enable alignment with the SDGs. Finally, Section 8 presents concluding reflections and identifies avenues for future research.

2. Methodological Approach

This chapter adopts a qualitative theoretical methodology based on the analysis of peer-reviewed academic literature and EU regulatory documents, such as the CSRD and ESRS. The objective is to synthesise the current state of knowledge and extract key implications for corporate sustainability reporting. The research is based on a narrative review of academic sources and regulatory materials to assess how digital technologies are currently being used or can be strategically deployed to improve ESG disclosure. Rather than conducting empirical tests, this approach allows for the construction of a conceptual model that connects digital innovation to regulatory compliance, materiality assessments and alignment with the SDGs.

A graphical theoretical framework is proposed to illustrate the positive advantages of digital technologies in data management and relationship with stakeholders, which in turn enable improvements in double-materiality assessment and SDGs alignment, within the context of the European regulatory framework.

3. Theoretical Background: Digital Technologies for Enhancing Sustainability Reporting

The digital transformation of sustainability reporting is reshaping how companies collect, process and disclose ESG data, improving overall accuracy, efficiency and transparency. As regulatory requirements become more stringent and stakeholder expectations evolve, digital technologies are becoming increasingly important to provide the real-time and consistent insights that are essential for effective sustainability management.

Digitalisation, defined as the integration of advanced digital tools into business processes, plays a crucial role in improving the automation, accuracy and optimisation of ESG data management (Cortese & Rubino, 2022; Mondejar et al., 2021). The introduction of big data analytics, AI and ML enables companies to efficiently process large and complex datasets and overcome the ongoing challenges related to data reliability, standardisation and regulatory compliance. This technological development is transforming ESG reporting from a static, compliance-focused process into a dynamic, data-driven system in which sustainability information serves not only for compliance but also for strategic decision-making and long-term value creation (Walton et al., 2024). To achieve accurate, consistent and compliant sustainability reporting, companies need to effectively collect, interpret and manage large amounts of ESG data from various sources. However, the complexity of sustainability metrics, which span areas such as carbon emissions, resource efficiency, social responsibility and corporate governance, poses significant challenges for companies seeking to adapt to evolving reporting standards. Without robust data management systems, companies risk producing inconsistent and inaccurate reports that compromise both compliance and stakeholder trust.

The adoption of advanced technological solutions enables companies to improve the efficiency, accuracy and effectiveness of their sustainability reporting systems and ESG data management processes. Modern information systems have thus evolved from mere tools to strategic enablers capable of managing the complexity of organisations and promoting long-term, sustainable value creation. To take full advantage of these benefits, organisations should use new technologies strategically to improve their information systems, recognising that technological advances only lead to positive results if they are implemented effectively (Rubino & Vitolla, 2014). AI and ML platforms are increasingly being used to automate reporting processes, detect inconsistencies and generate predictive insights, enabling a more strategic, data-driven approach to sustainability management. Blockchain technology also presents valuable potential solutions for ensuring data integrity and promoting transparency. By providing tamper-proof and decentralised records, blockchain minimises the risk of data manipulation and greenwashing, thus strengthening corporate accountability and the credibility of regulators. Similarly, IoT-enabled monitoring systems improve the ability to track energy consumption, carbon emissions and supply chain sustainability in real time, enabling a shift from periodic compliance reporting to continuous, dynamic sustainability management (Wang et al., 2018).

By improving data accuracy, process efficiency and real-time monitoring, these technological innovations enable companies to go beyond mere compliance and take a more transparent, accountable and strategically integrated approach to sustainability. Their integration into corporate reporting ensures that sustainability commitments are effectively met and translated into measurable environmental and social impact, reinforcing sustainability as a core element of long-term corporate strategy.

New digital solutions facilitate the immediate identification of significant ESG-related risks and opportunities across the corporate value chain, increasing the transparency of information and minimising the risks associated with data bias. These advances promote the effective application of the double-materiality approach and closely align business practices with the SDGs.

Several authors have highlighted the benefits of integrating digital technologies into sustainability reporting practices. However, in the European context, the specific implications of the CSRD, the ESRS and the principle of double materiality have not yet been thoroughly investigated. In particular, the role of digital technologies in enabling and operationalising these regulatory innovations remains underexplored in the current academic literature.

4. Digitalisation and Sustainability Reporting in Europe: Data Quality and Regulatory Compliance

The incorporation of digital technologies into management accounting and sustainability reporting represents a transformative change in corporate disclosure practices and presents both opportunities and challenges (Abdelhalim, 2024). As organisations increasingly rely on advanced digital tools to improve reporting processes, the large volume, variety and rapid expansion of data have heightened concerns about data quality (Rikhardsson & Yigitbasioglu, 2017).

While digitalisation promises improved accuracy and efficiency in managing ESG data, the question remains whether improved data quality effectively supports the broader objectives of reporting. Addressing these challenges requires the integration of digitised processes and skills that can improve the understanding and management of critical aspects such as data structures, accuracy, governance, security and cleansing (Arkhipova et al., 2024; Möller et al., 2020). The development of robust digital frameworks and competences is essential to ensure that sustainability reporting processes are both reliable and compliant with evolving regulatory standards.

The CSRD significantly expands the number of companies forced to sustainability reporting obligations and introduces more detailed requirements. These new requirements include reporting in accordance with the ESRS, the inclusion of sustainability-related information in the management report, obtaining external assurance and the use of digital labelling of published information. In response to the growing complexity and scope of sustainability disclosures required by the CSRD, the European Commission has introduced standardised digital frameworks designed to improve the coherence, transparency, accessibility, credibility and verifiability of corporate sustainability reporting.

In order to operationalise these objectives, the European Financial Reporting Advisory Group (EFRAG) created an eXtensible Business Reporting Language (XBRL) taxonomy explicitly designed to facilitate compliance with the ESRS requirements under the CSRD. The XBRL taxonomy uses standardised digital tags for sustainability-related information, making ESG data machine-readable and easy to interpret by regulators, investors and other stakeholders. This structured digital format enables automated processing, validation and improved traceability, significantly reducing inconsistencies in reporting and improving comparability between companies (Seele, 2016).

However, the effectiveness of digital initiatives such as the XBRL taxonomy depends largely on the quality, coherence and reliability of the underlying data. Ensuring high-quality ESG data is therefore critical to meeting evolving regulatory standards and achieving broader sustainability goals. Nevertheless, the implementation of digitalised reporting processes remains a challenge, as gaps in data quality and inconsistencies can undermine the credibility of disclosures. Addressing these challenges necessitates not only technological advancements but also the implementation of robust data governance frameworks to ensure data integrity and credibility throughout the reporting process.

The ongoing digitalisation of sustainability reporting in Europe offers considerable opportunities to improve the quality of ESG reporting, increase transparency and support stakeholder decision-making due to the rapid pace of technological development.

5. Double Materiality According to the CSRD: Improving the Relevance and Reliability of Sustainability Reporting

The CSRD introduces a comprehensive framework that aims to improve corporate accountability and transparency by requiring companies to report on both the impact of their activities on sustainability issues and the impact of sustainability factors on their financial performance (Hristov & Searcy, 2025). This dual reporting requirement is implemented through the ESRS, which provides the necessary technical framework to ensure the consistency and reliability of corporate disclosures. While compliance with these standards is mandatory, the principle of double materiality plays a crucial role in defining the scope of the information reported.

The principle of double materiality requires companies to evaluate and disclose information from two different but interrelated perspectives: financial materiality and impact materiality. Financial materiality concerns the extent to which sustainability-related issues affect a company's financial performance, whereas impact materiality refers to the broader environmental and social consequences arising from the company's operations. This comprehensive approach aims to ensure that sustainability reporting is not only focused on compliance but also truly addresses stakeholder concerns and society's expectations. In practice, companies must disclose all material sustainability information identified through this double-materiality assessment, while non-material data are excluded from reporting. This process has become a fundamental aspect of corporate sustainability reporting and highlights the importance of adopting structured and digitised systems for capturing ESG data to ensure accuracy, accountability and alignment with evolving regulatory requirements. The introduction of the double-materiality framework offers the potential to significantly improve the clarity, relevance and transparency of sustainability information. By explicitly requiring companies to consider material topics from both a financial and an impact perspective, this model promotes a more comprehensive and reliable reporting system that provides greater value to stakeholders who rely on this information in their decision-making.

The process of assessing materiality under the ESRS generally comprises two stages. First, companies are required to identify material sustainability issues, including those relating to ESG aspects. Second, they must determine the specific disclosure requirements and data points associated with each material topic. According to the ESRS, information is considered material if its exclusion or inaccurate representation could materially distort a reasonable investor's overall assessment of the company's sustainability performance. However, the criteria for defining the materiality of information that has an impact on the environment remain somewhat unclear, as the concept of 'significance of information' needs to be further explored. This lack of clarity could lead to inconsistent implementation of materiality assessments, which would undermine the effectiveness of the reporting framework.

In addition, the broad scope of disclosures required under the ESRS raises concerns about potential data quality issues and greenwashing (Mezzanotte, 2024). To effectively address these challenges, organisations must implement comprehensive data collection, processing and validation systems aimed at ensuring that the disclosed information is precise, dependable and verifiable. Integrating digital technologies into this process could increase the credibility and relevance of sustainability information and ensure that it effectively aligns with both the expectations of regulators and the needs of stakeholders.

6. Digital Innovation as a Strategic Enabler for Double-materiality Assessment and SDG Alignment

In recent years, globalisation, increased competition, operational efficiency, automation of business processes and shorter delivery times have redefined the strategic priorities of traditional companies. At the same time, the increased focus on sustainable development has brought new complexities and stricter reporting standards, prompting organisations to adopt advanced technological solutions and revise established management practices.

Sustainability reporting has changed significantly, increasingly driven by regulatory frameworks such as the ESRS, which require comprehensive disclosure based on a double-materiality perspective. The concept of materiality itself is constantly evolving, primarily due to the exponential increase in data and rapid technological progress in the information age (Kuh et al., 2020). Consequently, ensuring the credibility, transparency and reliability of sustainability reports has become a critical objective for companies and stakeholders, especially given the diverse data sources required for rigorous assessments. The data for such assessments often come from various internal and external channels, including community and individual behaviour surveys, environmental metrics derived from IoT devices, geographic and digital media information and operational and financial records (Garst et al., 2022). This complexity significantly increases the risk of inaccuracies and inconsistencies in the reported information.

The integration of advanced digital technologies into sustainability management and reporting has proven to be a promising approach to overcoming these challenges. The use of big data analytics, AI, ML and automated document analysis tools can significantly improve the accuracy, efficiency and reliability of materiality assessments (Zhang & Zhang, 2024). By systematically analysing different streams of information in real time, these technological solutions facilitate the identification of patterns, trends and anomalies in large datasets, significantly improving the accuracy and completeness of financial materiality and impact assessments. As a result, digital technologies enable a more dynamic, accurate and timely assessment process that improves the quality and compliance of corporate ESG reporting.

In addition, digital technologies promise significant potential to address the persistent problem of greenwashing, which remains a critical issue directly related to the ambiguity of materiality assessments. Several studies have highlighted that unclear and inconsistent materiality assessment standards can enable selective or misleading corporate disclosures, undermining stakeholder trust and compromising the perceived credibility and completeness of ESG reports (Zharfpeykan, 2021).

In this context, digital technologies offer effective solutions by reducing subjective judgement through standardised and automated evaluation processes. In particular, technologies such as ML algorithms enable robust and impartial analysis of ESG data, minimise discretionary interpretation and ensure greater transparency (Del Vitto et al., 2023). In addition, blockchain technologies introduce secure and verifiable datasets that significantly reduce the scope for data manipulation and misinformation, thus providing stakeholders with reliable and trustworthy sustainability information. Therefore, the strategic integration of digital technologies is an important opportunity for organisations to effectively manage the complexity associated with the double-materiality assessment. By improving the reliability, transparency and objectivity of ESG disclosures, organisations can better align their sustainability reporting with the evolving regulatory requirements of the ESRS and increase stakeholder confidence. Improved data management systems and robust reporting frameworks supported by digitalisation actively contribute to drive broader sustainability goals. As companies play a central role in achieving the SDGs, the use of digital tools serves as a powerful catalyst for the simultaneous achievement of interconnected sustainability targets.

7. Digital Technologies and Sustainability Reporting: A Theoretical Framework

In light of the discussion in this chapter, we have developed a theoretical framework that illustrates how digital technologies play a fundamental role in data collection, management and communication (Fig. 4.1). These are key aspects that support organisations in conducting effective dual materiality assessments and aligning their strategies with the SDGs by 2030.

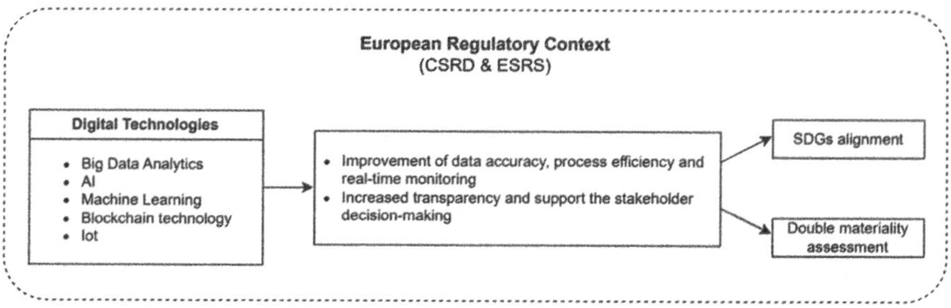

Fig. 4.1. Theoretical Framework. *Source*: Authors' own work.

This framework is embedded in the evolving European regulatory context, primarily shaped by the CSRD and the ESRS, which collectively represent a paradigm shift in sustainability governance. Within this regulatory architecture, digital technologies are emerging not only as operational tools but also as catalysts for systemic transformation. These technologies enable organisations to improve the granularity, accuracy and timeliness of sustainability-related data. Such improvements are not only functional but also strategic, as they significantly enhance the organisation's ability for real-time monitoring, process optimisation and evidence-based decision-making. Furthermore, by promoting transparency and accountability, these tools directly contribute to increasing stakeholder trust.

The framework emphasises two interrelated outcomes of this transformation. First, the ability of organisations to align their business models with the SDGs becomes more tangible and measurable. Second, digital technologies provide the analytical basis for implementing the principle of double materiality, capturing both the financial impact of sustainability risks and the broader socio-environmental impact of corporate activities. Ultimately, the model frames digital transformation as a core enabler of a new paradigm of sustainability management. Rather than being a marginal or technical adjustment, digitalisation is presented as a strategic asset that enables organisations to meet increasing regulatory requirements while advancing their sustainability efforts (Rubino et al., 2020). By linking regulatory requirements with technological capabilities, the framework outlines a clear pathway for organisations to improve the quality and reliability of their sustainability information, streamline internal decision-making processes and strengthen their accountability to stakeholders. In this way, digital technologies become the foundation for promoting data-driven, transparent and impact-oriented business practices in the evolving European sustainability landscape.

8. Conclusion

This study examined the contribution of digital transformation to improving sustainability reporting and emphasised how emerging technologies are significantly improving the quality, credibility and transparency of ESG information. The implementation of CSRD alongside the ESRS represents a substantial advancement towards greater corporate accountability and deeper integration of sustainability principles within European business frameworks. The objective of this study is to provide a comprehensive overview of digital sustainability reporting practices, offering a foundational basis that can assist organisations in developing effective strategies for integrating digital tools into their sustainability reporting processes.

From a theoretical perspective, this research emphasises the need for a holistic and integrative approach that strategically links sustainability and digital innovation. It highlights the crucial role of the double-materiality principle in shaping companies' strategic priorities, serving as a conceptual bridge between organisational impact and financial relevance (Lozano, 2015).

In practice, companies need to invest resources in developing robust digital infrastructures and specialised capabilities to ensure comprehensive and compliant ESG data collection, processing and dissemination. As a result, digital transformation is moving beyond mere compliance to become a strategic driver of competitive differentiation and sustainable long-term value creation.

This chapter contributes to the expanding literature on digital sustainability reporting by proposing a theoretical framework that integrates digital technologies with the evolving European regulatory context, in particular the CSRD and the ESRS. It advances scientific understanding by illustrating how digital tools can improve the quality, traceability and strategic relevance of sustainability reports. To the best of our knowledge, the specific impact of digital technologies on the double-materiality assessment process as defined by the ESRS has not yet been systematically addressed in the academic literature. This chapter fills this gap by highlighting the mechanisms through which digitalisation can support more robust and data-driven assessments of both financial and impact materiality. Furthermore, it highlights how these developments contribute to align sustainability reporting practices with the SDGs, thus positioning digital innovation as a critical enabler of compliance and long-term corporate accountability.

By combining technological, regulatory and strategic perspectives, this chapter offers a novel contribution that can be useful for both academic research and managerial practice, especially in the face of increasing regulatory complexity and stakeholder expectations.

For small- and medium-sized enterprises (SMEs), the extension of reporting obligations, accelerated by the Omnibus proposal,[1] represents both a major challenge and a strategic opportunity. Despite the constraints associated with limited resources and technical expertise, SMEs can benefit significantly from adopting digital technologies to navigate the complex regulatory landscape efficiently. Investing in digital tools for sustainability management not only simplifies regulatory compliance but also fosters strategic innovation that improves SMEs' responsiveness and competitive position in a dynamic market environment.

This chapter represents a first step towards understanding the overlap between digital transformation, legal frameworks and sustainability reporting. Future research could investigate the mechanisms by which SMEs can effectively overcome economic, technical and organisational barriers to digital innovation. In addition, empirical assessments of the effectiveness of European policies in supporting SMEs' digital transformation could provide valuable insights into the refinement of supportive frameworks and targeted incentives. Quantitative analyses examining correlations between digital transformation maturity, ESG performance and financial outcomes could further enrich this discourse by empirically validating the strategic benefits of integrating digital sustainability practices. Finally, additional research that addresses the long-term operational and strategic implications of double materiality could deepen comprehension of its influence on corporate decision-making processes and sustainable value creation.

---

[1]Proposal for a Directive of the European Parliament and of the Council amending Directives (EU) 2022/2464.

References

Abdelhalim, A. M. (2024). How management accounting practices integrate with big data analytics and its impact on corporate sustainability. *Journal of Financial Reporting and Accounting*, *22*(2), 416–432.

Arkhipova, D., Montemari, M., Mio, C., & Marasca, S. (2024). Digital technologies and the evolution of the management accounting profession: A grounded theory literature review. *Meditari Accountancy Research*, *32*(7), 35–64.

Broccardo, L., Truant, E., & Dana, L. P. (2023). The interlink between digitalization, sustainability, and performance: An Italian context. *Journal of Business Research*, *158*, 1–9.

Camilleri, M. A. (2015). Environmental, social and governance disclosures in Europe. *Sustainability Accounting, Management and Policy Journal*, *6*(2), 224–242.

Cortese, D., & Rubino, M. (2022). Information integration, connectivity, and readability of integrated reports: A literature review. In L. Cinquini & F. De Luca (Eds.), *Non-financial disclosure and integrated reporting: Theoretical framework and empirical evidence* (pp. 253–266). Springer.

Del Vitto, A., Marazzina, D., & Stocco, D. (2023). ESG ratings explainability through machine learning techniques. *Annals of Operations Research*, 1–30.

Garst, J., Maas, K., & Suijs, J. (2022). Materiality assessment is an art, not a science: Selecting ESG topics for sustainability reports. *California Management Review*, *65*(1), 64–90.

Hristov, I., & Searcy, C. (2025). Integrating sustainability with corporate governance: A framework to implement the corporate sustainability reporting directive through a balanced scorecard. *Management Decision*, *63*(2), 443–467.

Kuh, T., Shepley, A., Bala, G., & Flowers, M. (2020). *Dynamic materiality: Measuring what matters* (pp. 1–18). SSRN.

Lozano, R. (2015). A holistic perspective on corporate sustainability drivers. *Corporate Social Responsibility and Environmental Management*, *22*(1), 32–44.

Mezzanotte, F. E. (2024). Examining the reasons for impact materiality in EU corporate sustainability reporting. *European Business Law Review*, *35*(7), 925–946.

Miettinen, M. (2024). Are materiality determination practices evolving in the wake of increasing legislation on sustainability reporting? Findings from EU pharmaceutical companies' reports. *International Journal of Law and Management*, *66*(3), 363–392.

Möller, K., Schäffer, U., & Verbeeten, F. (2020). Digitalization in management accounting and control: An editorial. *Journal of Management Control*, *31*(1), 1–8.

Mondejar, M. E., Avtar, R., Diaz, H. L. B., Dubey, R. K., Esteban, J., Gómez-Morales, A., She, Q., & Garcia-Segura, S. (2021). Digitalization to achieve sustainable development goals: Steps towards a smart green planet. *Science of The Total Environment*, *794*, 1–20.

Olanrewaju, O. I. K., Daramola, G. O., & Babayeju, O. A. (2024). Harnessing big data analytics to revolutionize ESG reporting in clean energy initiatives. *World Journal of Advanced Research and Reviews*, *22*(3), 574–585.

Rella, A., Rubino, M., Raimo, N., & Vitolla, F. (2024). Does the digitalization of municipalities affect the efficiency of universities? An Italian case study using DEA and Malmquist index approaches. *Technology in Society*, *77*, 1–13.

Rikhardsson, P., & Yigitbasioglu, O. (2017, May). *Business Intelligence in management accounting research: Current status and future focus* [Conference presentation]. Presented at the 40th Annual Congress European Accounting Association.

Rubino, M. (2020). *La disclosure sui rischi nell'informativa non finanziaria: Evidenze empiriche nel contesto europeo*. EGEA.

Rubino, M., Maggino, F., & Antonicelli, M. (2023). Measuring human IT agility and firms' digitalization using POSET: Evidence from Italy. *International Journal of Quality & Reliability Management*, *41*(1), 127–149.

Rubino, M., & Mastrorocco, I. (2025). The impact of green innovation on corporate social behaviour: Longitudinal analysing of the mixed effects on stakeholder relationships. *European Journal of Innovation Management*, 1–25.

Rubino, M., & Vitolla, F. (2014). Corporate governance and the information system: How a framework for IT governance supports ERM. *Corporate Governance*, *14*(3), 320–338.

Rubino, M., Vitolla, F., & Raimo, N., (2020). Il processo di digitalizzazione aziendale e la digital transformation. In R. Lombardi, M. S. Chiucchi, & D. Mancini (Eds.), *Smart technologies, digitalizzazione e capitale intellettuale* (pp. 54–57). FrancoAngeli.

Seele, P. (2016). Digitally unified reporting: How XBRL-based real-time transparency helps in combining integrated sustainability reporting and performance control. *Journal of Cleaner Production*, *136*, 65–77.

Walton, S., Gehricke, S., & Hazelhurst, T. (2024). Enhancing climate decision making: Insights from early adopters of climate risk disclosure. *Policy Quarterly*, *20*(4), 103 111.

Wang, W., Yang, H., Zhang, Y., & Xu, J. (2018). IoT-enabled real-time energy efficiency optimisation method for energy-intensive manufacturing enterprises. *International Journal of Computer Integrated Manufacturing*, *31*(4–5), 362–379.

Zhang, A. Y., & Zhang, J. H. (2024). Renovation in environmental, social and governance (ESG) research: The application of machine learning. *Asian Review of Accounting*, *32*(4), 554–572.

Zharfpeykan, R. (2021). Representative account or greenwashing? Voluntary sustainability reports in Australia's mining/metals and financial services industries. *Business Strategy and the Environment*, *30*(4), 2209–2223.

Chapter 5

How Does Institutional Quality Moderate the Business Environment in the Attraction of Foreign Portfolio Investment into Africa?

Richardson Kojo Edeme

Department of Economics, Dennis Osadebay University, Asaba, Nigeria

Abstract

The essence of this study was to ascertain the moderation effect of institutional quality on the business environment and foreign portfolio investment (FPI) nexus. The study covered 40 African countries using data from 2005 to 2023, employing the step-wise system-generalised method of moment (SWS-GMM) estimation strategy. Findings indicated that in the absence of institutional quality, ease of doing business had a negative and significant effect on FPI. Tax incentives had a negative and significant effect on FPI. The interaction of control of corruption with ease of doing business had a positive effect on FPI. Similarly, the interaction of government effectiveness, political stability, regulatory quality and rule of law with ease of doing business had a positive effect on FPI. Contrarily, the interaction of voice and accountability with ease of doing business had a negative effect on FPI. Our result highlights the importance of strong institutions in the attraction of FPI into Africa. The study recommends improvement in the quality of institutions so as to attract more FPI towards the attainment of sustainable development in Africa.

Keywords: Business environment; ease of doing business; tax incentive; foreign portfolio investment; institutional quality

JEL Codes: C23; C33; O13; 056; H25

Changing Dimensions in Economic Development: Theories and Empirics, 51–66

Published under exclusive licence by Emerald Publishing Limited
doi:10.1108/978-1-83708-384-820261005

1. Introduction

In Africa, attraction of foreign portfolio investment (FPI) is considered a major trigger meant to generate productive investments to stimulate economic growth and development, attain Agenda 2063, due to lack of domestic productive resources. One of the assured means in the transformational recovery and to lift an economy towards the attainment of sustainable development is to attract FPI (United Nations Conference on Trade and Development [UNCTAD] 2019, 2023; World Bank, 2013). FPI is a component of foreign investment which comprises transfer of financial assets, stocks or cash usually from foreign countries. Such investment inflow which comes in different components is meant to benefit the host country (Calderon et al., 2019; United Nations Conference on Trade and Development (UNCTAD), 2016).

Over the years, apart from fostering ease of doing business, several African countries have anchored on tax incentives as a mechanism to attract FPI and triggered by tax incentives (Appiah-Kubi et al., 2021; Haider et al., 2016; Zee et al., 2002). In spite of these efforts, the level of FPI inflows has been fragile and erratic. For instance, World Bank (2025) data indicate that FPI as a net balance of payment in Nigeria was $502.2 billion, $309.1 billion and $386.5 billion; Rwanda, $79.5 billion, $199.9 billion and $61.2 billion; Kenya $370,022,862.2, $425,131,377.9 and $225.2 billion; Morocco, $327.7 billion, $118.4 billion and $103.2 billion; Zambia, $223.5 billion, $53.1 billion and $100.1 billion in 2017, 2019 and 2021, respectively. UNCTAD (2024) further reported that for the past two decades, Africa received the lowest FPI inflows when compared to other regions of the world.

While several studies have acknowledged the positive effect of a conducive business environment in enhancing foreign investment, the concern among researchers and policymakers is on governance factors and how such influence FPI. Several researchers including (Al-karasneh et al., 2021; Bada, 2016; Baghebo & Apere, 2014; Baldwin et al., 2014; Mangal & Liu, 2020; Mlambo, 2022; Nguyen & Dang, 2022; Obuobi et al., 2022; Walio & Oludayo, 2020) have acknowledge the role of FPI in accentuating economic growth. More recently, the role of institutional quality in enhancing foreign investment has taken centre stage in economic development discourse. The renewed interest on intuitional quality in accentuating FPI is further reinforced by recent efforts to achieve African Agenda 2063 which lay emphasis on the benefit of foreign capital in stimulating sustainable economic development. For African countries, FPI offers opportunities for the acquisition of investments needed to build resilience to transform and lift the economy. Masron and Abdullah (2010), Masron and Nor (2013), World Bank (2016), Layla et al. (2020), Williamson (2000), Appiah-Kubi et al. (2020) and Huynh et al. (2020) articulate that creating a conducive business environment is unlikely to boost foreign investment unless supported by improved intuitional quality. It can therefore be argued that although a conducive business environment is necessary, it may be insufficient to attract FPI in African countries.

Business environment and institutional quality affects foreign investment through various channels. Countries with stronger and conducive business and efficient international trade laws attract more foreign investment. Quality institutions reduce risks and uncertainties associated, creating a more attractive and stable environment for foreign investors. Stronger institutional quality encourages foreign investment. Countries with quality governance ensure transparency and accountability to improve profit and boost investment confidence. Quality institutions encourage technological innovation and attract foreign investment (Contractor et al., 2020). Quality institutions create a conducive business environment which attracts foreign investment and trade openness. The attraction of FPI is influenced by several factors which can be grouped into economic, institutional and socioeconomic factors. However, perusal of literature reveals that so far studies have concentrated on the effect of factors such as economic growth, market size, exchange rate, interest rate, inflation and quality of institution on FPI. Less attention has been given on the effect of economic factors such as conducive business environment and institutional quality on FPI, especially in Africa. Although Ojong et al. (2017), Caixe and Krauter (2014), Masron and Abdullah (2010), Masron and Nor (2013) and Agyei et al. (2022) aver that besides creating a conducive business environment, institutional quality plays a great role on the attraction of FPI into a country, a clear-cut relationship between business environment, intuitional quality and FPI attraction in developing countries of Africa. Besides, some studies have also found that tax incentives have a positive influence on FPI, especially in countries with weak financial market potentials. Enunciated that tax incentives and ease of doing business are crucial in deepening foreign investment in countries well complemented with good governance. Moreover, researchers such as Sabir et al. (2019), Makoni (2018) and Agyei et al. (2022), inter alia, have examined the effect of one or few institutional quality on foreign investment this study focused on the role of array of institutional quality indicators (voice and accountability, government effectiveness, political stability, control of corruption, regulatory quality and rule of law).

This chapter contributes to knowledge by ascertaining the moderation effect of institutional quality on the business environment and FPI nexus. The study covered 40 African countries using data from 2005 to 2023, employing the SWS-GMM estimation strategy.

The remaining part of this chapter is as follows: Section 2 presents the theoretical and empirical literature, Section 3 the methodology, Section 4 results and discussion and Section 5 conclusion.

2. Theoretical and Empirical Literature Review

In the foreign investment discourse, notable theories that have emerged are situated within international investment economics and macroeconomic variables. One school of thought is of the view that investment in financial resources and other components emanates from the developing and emerging economies to the less developed ones, with the intention of making higher returns in the long run. Such investment activities are mostly made possible through portfolio diversification. Foreign investment from developed and emerging economies is not only influenced by economic and political risk factors but also institutional factors. Another theory worthy of discussion in this paper is the ownership, land international theory ascribed to Dunning (1977). The theory hypothesised that foreign investment is driven by three factors: the competitive advantage which offers a country to possess market supply, level of adaptation of the acquired assets and value addition created and location considering the value-adding activities across national boundaries. The theory also reinforces the importance of the structural characteristics like quality institution and tariff in international trade transactions. The Williamson theory laid emphasis on the role of quality of institutions in the quest to further enhance information asymmetries and reduce the risks associated with foreign investments. The hierarchy of the institution theory hypothesises that the ability of a country to attract foreign investments is majorly determined by economic institutions, which are further influenced by existing political institutions. Intuitively, in deciding an investment destination, apart from the business environment, investors also consider the quality of the institution possessed by a country or region.

Providing empirical evidence, the Organization for Economic Corporation and Development (OECD, 2007b) found that corporate tax was an effective that determined the size and quality of foreign capital inflows into an economy. This is in tandem with the finding of previous studies like Atobrah (2015) and Al-Smadi (2018). Desai and Dharmapala (2002) opine that reduction in corporate tax rates had a positive effect on foreign direct investment inflows. Oyerogba et al. (2024) articulated that tax incentives had a positive effect on foreign investment.

Klemm and Parys (2012) stimulates foreign investment in relation to the manufacturing firms in Nigeria. The finding indicated that lower tax rates and longer tax holidays had a positive effect on foreign direct investment. The effectiveness of tax incentives in enhancing foreign investments should be accompanied with accountability and transparency. The study by Hintošová et al. (2016) depicted that business environment had a positive and significant effect on foreign direct investment inflows in Visegrad countries. Rashid and Khalid (2017) and Ogundipe et al. (2019) found that economic growth, population growth, exchange, inflation and foreign debt had a negative and significant effect on FPI inflows.

In a study of developed and developing economies Sabir et al. (2019) highlighted the importance of strong regulatory institutions in stimulating FPI inflows. Su et al. (2021) examined the role of institutional quality on FPI. It was found that rule of law, high regulatory framework and political stability had a positive effect on foreign investments. Lysandron et al. (2016) analysed the influence of governance institutions on different types of foreign investments in developed countries. It was reported that public governance institutions had a positive effect on FPI with private governance institutions having further positive effect on the governance institution and FPI relationship. Wu et al. (2012) found that countries with good governance had the lowest foreign direct investment relative to the quantum of foreign investments, despite the large stock market size. Makoni (2018) found that institutional quality engendered both foreign direct investment and FPI inflows, especially where there is nonexistence of a well-developed financial system.

Agyei et al.'s (2022) study was on the effect of institutional quality on FPI in Sub-Saharan African (SSA) countries. The findings indicated that transparency and accountability, ethical behaviour, effective corporate boards and well-regulated security markets had a positive effect on FPI. Chen and Jiang (2023) aver that institutional quality had a positive effect on foreign direct investment inflows. The moderation effect result indicated that institutional quality attracted foreign direct investment inflows through increase in trade openness, infrastructural development and technological innovation. Appiah-Kubi et al. (2021) found that rule of law, control of corruption, voice and accountability are more likely to attract more FPI. A similar result was reported by Zühal and Yalta (2017), Li et al. (2023) in the case of developing countries and Nubong and Ntuli (2024) in the case of Southern African development community.

From the literature review, apart from the fact that existing studies reported mixed outcomes, limited studies have linked business environment, institutional quality and FPI, especially in Africa. The perceived gap is filled by this study.

3. Methodology

3.1. Methodological Framework and Specification of Models

The study examined how intuitional quality moderates the business environment in the attraction of FPI. Theoretical discussions have indicated that foreign investment is influenced by several factors. The Dunning (1977) theorem which guides the model specification of this study shows the importance of economic, business and non-economic factors in influencing foreign investment. The theory opines that taxation, cost of doing business and other structural features like quality of institutions are paramount in attracting foreign investment. From the empirical literature, the relationship between foreign investments and economic, business and non-economic factors is of the form:

$$\mathrm{FRI}_{it} = F(\mathrm{ECO}_{it} + \mathrm{BUS}_{it} + \mathrm{NECO}_{it}) \tag{1}$$

where FRI_{it} = foreign investment into a particular country and period, ECO_{it} = existing economic factors available, BUS_{it} = business factors, NECO_{it} = non-economic factors.

Masron and Abdullah (2010), Masron and Nor (2013), Layla et al. (2020) and Appiah-Kubi et al. (2021) noted that apart from economic and business factors, institutional quality plays a significant role in securing foreign investment. Accordingly, the model linking business environment, institutional quality and FPI can be stated in its general form as:

$$\phi_{it} = \sum \gamma j = P_{yi,\,t-j} + \varsigma_{it}\varphi_i + \beta_i + \gamma_t + \varepsilon_{it} \tag{2}$$

where ϕ_{it} = dependent variable, ς_{it} = vector of independent (explanatory) variables, ϕ_{it} = vector of estimates, and ε_{it} = error term with its usual properties. In line with the variables under consideration in this study, Equation (2) is re-parameterised and modified in the next section in relation to the objective of our study.

3.2. Empirical Model Specification

The first objective of this study is to examine the effect of the business environment (ease of doing business and tax incentive) on FPI. Drawing inspiration from

Makoni (2018) and Agyei et al. (2022), Equation (2) is expanded to accommodate the variables under consideration as:

$$\begin{aligned} \mathrm{l\_nFPI}_{it} = \mathrm{l\_n}\varsigma + \eta \mathrm{l\_nFPI}_{it-1} + \phi_1 \mathrm{l\_nEDBUS}_{it} + \phi_2 \mathrm{l\_nTAXV}_{it} \\ + \mathrm{INSQ}_{1t}\phi_{3i} + \phi_3 \mathrm{l\_nEXR}_{it} + \phi_4 \mathrm{INF}_{it} + \lambda_i + \beta_t + E_{it} \end{aligned} \tag{3}$$

where FPI is the foreign portfolio investment (net portfolio investment, balance of payment (BOP) current US$), EDBUS is ease of doing business (composite index of ease of doing business), TAXV is tax incentive (corporate tax rate, total tax contribution, percentage of total profit), EXR is exchange rate (official exchange rate, local currency unit (LCU) per U$, period average), and INF is inflation (consumer price, annual percentage).

The second objective of the study is to examine the moderation effect of institutional quality on the business environment and FPI nexus. The model is specified as:

$$\begin{aligned} \mathrm{l\_nFPI}_{it} = \mathrm{l\_n}\varsigma + \eta \mathrm{logFPI}_{it-1} + \phi_1 \mathrm{l\_nDBUS}_{it} * \mathrm{INSQ}_{1t}\phi_{3i} + \phi_2 \mathrm{lnEXR}_{it} \\ + \phi_3 \mathrm{INF}_{it} + \lambda_i + \beta_t + E_{it} \end{aligned} \tag{4}$$

where INSQ is intuitional quality (measured by government effectiveness, control of corruption, political stability and absence of violence, rule of law, voice and accountability and regulatory quality). Other variables are as previously defined.

In both Equation (3) and Equation (4), the dependent variable is FPI, while the key explanatory variables are ease of doing business, tax incentives and institutional quality indicators. The different indicators were included in the model to ensure robustness of result. Ease of doing business was measured with a single index that encompasses starting a business, dealing with construction permit, registering property, enforcing contract, paying taxes, resolving insolvency, access to credit and electricity, trading across international boundaries and protecting minority investors. Literature supports this measure as more appropriate and suitable. The tax incentive is measured by corporate tax. The tax incentive is expected to have a positive effect on FPI. The tax rate determines returns to be derived from foreign investments. By implication, higher tax rate lowers returns on investment and flattens FPI. Exchange rate and inflation rate are control variables to account for the effect of other macroeconomic variables. Both variables are expected to have a depressing effect on FPI due to uncertainty they create in determining profit.

This study covered 40 countries (see the Appendix of this chapter for the list of the countries). These countries are among the countries that received the largest amount of foreign capital inflows into SSA countries in the last two decades. Besides, these countries have showcased improvement in overall institutional quality in the last two decades. Another factor that influenced the choice of the countries was availability of data on the variables for the study period. The study period covered an 18-year period, 2005–2023. Data for the study were generated from World Bank (2025) and World Bank Governance Indicators (2025).

3.3. Estimation Strategy

Most often, lagged dependent variables may be correlated with the error disturbance term, conducting the empirical estimation for this study with the static panel model adopting the fixed effect model (FEM) and random effect (REM) approach yields spurious and misleading results. To overcome this, the SWS-GMM was adopted as the estimation strategy. SWS-GMM estimation is preferred in order to overcome the potential issue of non-stationary in the data and further extended by Arellano and Bond (1991), Arellano and Bover (1995) and Caixe and Krauter (2014). Blundell and Bond (1998) observed that SWS-GMM produces unbiased estimates with decreased precision in relation to the lagged dependent variable. More importantly, the SWS-GMM resolves the problems of endogeneity inherent in the models using the moment's condition. For the appropriateness of SWS-GMM, the presence of autocorrelation among the variables was determined with the Hansen *J*-test for instrumental validity test, while the second order autocorrelation (AR2) in the first difference error was conducted using the Arellano–Bond test.

4. Results and Discussion

4.1. Descriptive Summary Statistics

For a peep into the initial behaviour of the variables used for empirical analysis, the descriptive summary statistics was conducted. Table 5.1 presents descriptive summary statistics.

Table 5.1. Descriptive Summary Statistics.

Variable	Mean	SD	Minimum	Maximum
l_FPI	8.890	1.219	0.079	9.012
EDBUS	3.197	2.901	0.112	2.791
INF	18.111	5.979	2.143	27.435
l_EXR	418.09	3.421	589.34	79.567
TAXV	4.028	6.197	−18.918	57.877
Gvt eff	28.208	20.964	0.948	84.135
Co of crp	31.282	21.702	0.529	91.827
Regqlty	30.235	19.106	0.481	86.058
R of law	29.954	19.904	0.469	82.587
Vc & Ac	31.5	18.807	1.478	75.481
Pol stab	32.553	21.88	0.476	90.566

Source: Author's computation.

In Table 5.1, the average FPI inflow was U$8.890 billion and standard deviation (SD) 1.219. The lowest and highest values were U$0.08 billion and U$9.012, respectively. The average value for ease of doing business and tax incentive stood at 3.19 and 4.03, respectively. Going by the SD of the various institutional quality indicators, it is reflective that the quality of institutions in African countries is generally weak. Also, the average exchange rate was 418 and SD of 3.421. The mean for inflationary rate was 18.11 and SD of 5.98. In the next section, we present the result of the effect of ease of doing business and tax incentive on FPI.

In Table 5.2, the result shows that in the absence of institutional quality, ease of doing business had a negative and significant effect on FPI. As indicated, increase in the quality ease of doing business depressed FPI by about 0.030%. The result contradicts a previous study like Hintošová et al. (2016) that the business environment had a positive effect on foreign direct investment inflows. Also, the tax incentive had a negative and significant effect on FPI. This implies that tax incentive discouraged FPI in Africa. In Africa, the existing corporate tax rate is not conducive to attract the much-needed foreign investment to complement domestic investment to engender foreign investment sustainable growth and development. Our result contradicts the findings by Oyerogba et al. (2024) and Klemm and Parys (2009) that tax incentive had a positive effect on foreign investment.

The following section presents the result of the interaction effect of institutional quality indicators with ease of doing business on foreign portfolio inflow.

In Table 5.3, the result depicts that the interaction of control of corruption with ease of doing business had a positive effect on FPI. Similarly, the interaction of government effectiveness, political stability, regulatory quality and rule of law with ease of doing business had a positive effect on FPI. Contrarily, the interaction of voice and accountability with ease of doing business had a negative effect on FPI. Our result highlights the importance of strong regulatory institutions in the attraction of FPI into Africa. Our result is in tandem with the finding of previous studies like Su et al. (2021), Agyei et al. (2022) and Chen and Jiang (2023) that rule of law, high regulatory framework, control of corruption, voice and accountability, political stability had a positive effect on foreign investment. Moreover, the result indicated that exchange rate and inflation had a positive effect on FPI. This is contrary to the findings by Rashid and Khalid (2017) and Ogundipe et al. (2019) that exchange and inflation had a negative effect on foreign direct investment.

5. Concluding Remarks

The essence of this study was to ascertain the moderation effect of institutional quality on the business environment and FPI nexus. The study covered 40 countries with data from 2005 to 2023. The SWS-GMM estimation strategy was employed for the empirical estimation of the models. Findings indicated that in the absence of institutional quality, ease of doing business had a negative and significant effect on FPI. Additionally, the tax incentive had a negative and significant effect on FPI. The interaction of control of corruption with ease of doing business had a

Table 5.2. Effect of Ease of Doing Business and Tax Incentive on FPI

	(1)	(2)	(3)	(4)	(5)	(6)
Variables	**FPI**	**FPI**	**FPI**	**FPI**	**FPI**	**FPI**
l_EDBUS	−0.030**	−0.032**	−0.037**	−0.062**	−0.027**	−0.039**
	(0.0734)	(0.0711)	(0.0751)	(0.0725)	(0.0686)	(0.0749)
L_EXR	1.588***	0.995***	0.997**	1.562***	1.297***	1.563***
	(0.404)	(0.471)	(0.426)	(0.440)	(0.445)	(0.467)
INF	0.248***	0.247***	0.206***	0.252***	0.237***	0.250***
	(0.0337)	(0.0316)	(0.0334)	(0.0326)	(0.0352)	(0.0345)
l_TAXV	−0.0535*	−0.0681*	−0.0496*	−0.0142*	−0.0732*	−0.0298
	(0.0345)	(0.0405)	(0.0332)	(0.0455)	(0.0403)	(0.0446)
Constant	37.29***	41.06***	39.31***	39.43***	40.24***	36.92***
	(5.215)	(5.407)	(6.088)	(5.482)	(5.303)	(5.653)
AR2	0.287	0.249	0.228	0.323	0.255	0.299
Hansen *J*	0.282	0.339	0.393	0.343	0.375	0.254
Observations	629	629	629	629	629	629

Source: Author's computation.
$^{***}p < 0.01$, $^{**}p < 0.05$, $^{*}p < 0.1$.

Table 5.3. Result of the SWS-GMM Estimate: Interactive Effect of Institutional Quality Indicators With Ease of Doing Business on Foreign Portfolio Inflow.

	(1)	(2)	(3)	(4)	(5)	(6)
Variables	**FPI**	**FPI**	**FPI**	**FPI**	**FPI**	**FPI**
_FPI	0.030***	0.084***	0.061***	0.014***	0.084***	0.040***
	(0.0514)	(0.0525)	(0.0586)	(0.0495)	(0.0487)	(0.0507)
l_EDBUS	−0.118***	−0.133***	−0.0854***	−0.127***	−0.129***	−0.133***
	(0.0188)	(0.0200)	(0.0155)	(0.0249)	(0.0202)	(0.0213)
l_EXR	0.399**	0.439*	0.740**	0.417**	0.553**	0.687***
	(0.189)	(0.222)	(0.321)	(0.183)	(0.217)	(0.213)
INF	0.104***	0.116***	0.113***	0.105***	0.102***	0.112***
	(0.0243)	(0.0249)	(0.0276)	(0.0231)	(0.0233)	(0.0231)
TAXV	−0.0171	−0.0214	−0.0441*	−0.0170	−0.0370	−0.0277
	(0.0197)	(0.0279)	(0.0242)	(0.0247)	(0.0246)	(0.0208)
Con of crp	0.272***					
	(0.0660)					
C of C * EDBUS	0.0021***					
	(0.0005)					
Gvt eff		0.344***				
		(0.0795)				
Gvt eff * EDBUS		0.0027***				
		(0.0007)				
Pol stab			−0.0620			
			(0.0704)			

Pol stab* EDBUS			0.00017 (0.0005)			
Reg qlty				0.351*** (0.0915)		
Reg qlty * EDBUS				0.0027*** (0.0003)		
R of law					0.336*** (0.0760)	
R of law * EDBUS					0.0024*** (0.0007)	
Vc & Ac						−0.353*** (0.0751)
Vc & Ac * EDBUS						−0.0026*** (0.0006)
Constant	30.94*** (5.730)	35.36*** (5.971)	35.28*** (6.343)	33.29*** (6.423)	34.60*** (5.669)	32.78*** (5.886)
AR2	0.123	0.127	0.128	0.126	0.119	0.108
Hansen *J*	0.122	0.091	0.085	0.134	0.181	0.174
Observations	629	629	629	629	629	629

Source: Author's computation.
***$p < 0.01$, **$p < 0.05$, *$p < 0.1$.

positive effect on FPI. Similarly, the interaction of government effectiveness, political stability, regulatory quality and rule of law with ease of doing business had a positive effect on FPI. Contrarily, the interaction of voice and accountability with ease of doing business had a negative effect on FPI. Our result highlights the importance of strong institutions in the attraction of FPI into Africa. The study recommends improvement in the quality of institutions so as to attract more FPI towards the attainment of sustainable development in Africa.

References

Agyei, S. K., Obuobi, N. K., Isshaq, M. Z., Abeka, M. J., Gatsi, J. G., Boateng, E., & Amoah, E. K. (2022). Country-level corporate governance and foreign portfolio investments in Sub-Saharan Africa: The moderating role of institutional quality. *Cogent Economics & Finance*, *10*(1), 2106636-210. https://doi.org/10.1080/23322039.2022.2106636

Al-karasneh, H., Bataineh, A., Hayajneh, O., & Khodirat, O. (2021). Does foreign portfolio investment improve the economic growth of Jordan? *Accounting*, *7*(7), 1669–1674.

Al-Smadi, M. O. (2018). Determinants of foreign portfolio investment: The case of Jordan. *Investment Management and Financial Innovations*, *15*(1), 328–336. https://doi.org/10.21511/imfi.15(1).2018.27

Appiah-Kubi, S. N. K., Malec, K., Maitah, M., Kutin, S. B., Pánková, L., Phiri, J., & Zaganjori, O. (2020). The impact of corporate governance structures on foreign direct investment: A case study of West African countries. *Sustainability*, *12*(9), 1–15. https://doi.org/10.3390/su12093715

Appiah-Kubi, S. N. K., Malec, K., Phiri, J., Maitah, M., Gebeltová, Z., Smutka, L., Blazek, V., Maitah, K., & Sirohi, J. (2021). Impact of tax incentives on foreign direct investment: Evidence from Africa. *Sustainability*, *13*(15), 8661. https://doi.org/10.3390/SU13158661

Arellano, M., & Bond, S. (1991). Some tests of specification for panel data: Monte Carlo evidence and an application to employment equations. *Review of Economic Studies*, *58*(2), 277–297. https://doi.org/10.2307/2297968

Arellano, M., & Bover, O. (1995). Another look at the instrumental variable estimation of error-components models. *Journal of Econometrics*, *68*(1), 29–51. https://doi.org/10.1016/0304-4076(94)01642

Atobrah, R. (2015). *Determinants of foreign portfolio investment: Evidence from Sub-Saharan Africa* [Master's thesis]. Södertörns University.

Bada, O. T. (2016). Empirical evaluation of the effect of foreign portfolio investment on Nigerian economic growth. *International Journal of Comparative Studies in International Relations and Development*, *4*(1), 162–274.

Baghebo, M., & Apere, T. O. (2014). Foreign portfolio investment and economic growth in Nigeria. *International Journal of Business and Social Science*, *5*(11), 108–115.

Baldwin, R., Black, J., & O'Leary, G. (2014). Risk regulation and transnationality: Institutional accountability as a driver of innovation. *Transnational Environmental Law*, *3*(2), 373–390. https://doi.org/10.1017/S2047102514000120

Blundell, R., & Bond, S. (1998). Initial conditions and moments restrictions in dynamic panel data models. *Journal of Econometrics*, *87*(0), 115–143, http://dx.doi.org/10.1016/S0304-4076(98)00009-8

Caixe, D. F., & Krauter, E. (2014). The relation between corporate governance and market value: Mitigating endogeneity problems. *Brazilian Business Review*, *11*(1), 90–110. https://doi.org/10.15728/bbr.2014.11.1.5

Calderon, C., Chuhan-Pole, P., & Kubota, M. (2019). *Capital inflows to Sub-Saharan Africa: On a different path*. https://blogs.worldbank.org/developmenttalk/capital-inflows-sub-saharan-africa-different-path

Chen, F., & Jiang, G. (2023). The impact of institutional quality on foreign direct investment, empirical analysis based on mediating and moderating effects. *Economic Research*, *36*(2). https://doi.org/10.1080/1331677X.2022.2134903

Contractor, F. J., Dangol, R., Nuruzzaman, N., & Raghunath, S. (2020). How do country regulations and business environment impact foreign direct investment (FDI) inflows? *International Business Review*, *29*(2), 101640. https://doi.org/10.1016/j.ibusrev.2019.101640

Dunning, J. H. (1977). Trade, location of economic activity and the MNE: A search for an eclectic approach. In B. Ohlin, H. Per-Over, & P. M. Wijkman (Eds.), *The international allocation of economic activity* (pp. 395–418). Palgrave Macmillan. https://doi.org/10.1007/978-1-349-03196-2_38

Haider, M. A., Khan, M. A., & Abdulahi, E. (2016). Determinants of foreign portfolio investment and its effects on China. *International Journal of Economics and Finance*, *8*(12), 143–150. https://doi.org/10.5539/ijef.v8n12p143

Hintošová, A. B., Kubíková, Z., & Ručinský, R. (2016). Does quality of business environment influence foreign direct investment inflows? A case of Central European countries. *Central European Journal of Management*, *3*(1), 5–13. https://doi.org/10.5817/cejm2016-1-1

Huynh, C. M., Nguyen, V.H.T., Nguyen, H.B., & Nguyen, P.C. (2020). One-way effect or multiple-way causality: foreign direct investment, institutional quality and shadow economy? *International Economics and Economic Policy*, *17*(1), 219–239.

Klemm, A., & Parys, S. (2012). Empirical evidence on the effects of tax incentives. *International Tax and Public Finance*, *19*(3), 393–423.

Layla, F., Majumder, S.C., Appiah, B.K., Martial, A.A., Randolphe, K.G., & Obamb, C.C. (2020). A panel dynamic analysis on inward FDI and institutional quality in South Asia and South East Asia. *Asian Economic and Financial Review*, *10*(6), 654–669.

Li, C., Tanna, S., & Nissah, B. (2023). The effect of institutions on the foreign direct investment-growth nexus: What matters most? *The World Economy*, *46*(7), 1999–2031. https://doi.org/10.1111/twec.13349

Lysandron, P., Solomon, O. H., & Goda, T. (2016). The differential impact of public and private governance institutions on the different modes of foreign investments. *International Review of Applied Economics*, *30*(6), 729–746. https://doi.org/10.1080/02692171.2016.1208737

Makoni, P. L. R. (2018). FDI, FPI and institutional quality-evidence from African countries. *Academy of Accounting and Financial Studies Journal*, *22*(5), 1–13.

Mangal, T. K., & Liu, D. Y. (2020). The impact of economic freedom on foreign portfolio investments: The case of the Caricom single market and economy. *International Journal of Research in Business and Social Science*, *9*(2), 213–222.

Masron, T.A. & Abdullah, H. (2010). Institutional quality as a determinant for FDI inflows: evidence from ASEAN. *World Journal of Management*, *2*(3), 115–128.

Masron, T.A., & Nor, E. (2013). FDI in ASEAN-8: Does institutional quality matter? *Applied Economics Letters*, *20*(2), 186–189.

Mlambo, C. (2022). The impact of international portfolio investment on economic growth: The case of selected African states. *International Journal of Research in Business and Social Science*, *11*(10), 151–159. https://doi.org/10.20525/ijrbs.v11i10.2240

Nguyen, Q. K., & Dang, V. C. (2022). Does the country's institutional quality enhance the role of risk governance in preventing bank risk? *Applied Economics Letters*, *30*(6), 850–853. https://doi.org/10.1080/13504851.2022.2026868

Nubong, G., & Ntuli, L. (2024). Institutions as a determinant of foreign direct investment inflows into the Southern African development community. *BRICS Journal of Economics*, *5*(3), 179–199. https://doi.org/10.3897/brics-econ.5.e120855

Obuobi, N. K., Gatsi, J. G., Appiah, M. O., Kawor, S., Amoah, E. K., & Abeka, M. J. (2022). Trade liberalization policies and foreign direct investment inflows in Africa: Evidence from new measures of trade liberalization. *The Journal of International Trade & Economic Development, 31*(3), 394–409. https://doi.org/10.1080/09638199.2021.1983009

Ogundipe, A. A., Alabi, J., Asaleye, A. J., & Ogundipe, O. M. (2019). Exchange rate volatility and foreign portfolio investment in Nigeria. *Investment Management & Financial Innovations, 16*(3), 241. https://doi.org/10.21511/imfi.16(3).2019.22

Ojong, C. M., Anthony, O., & Arikpo, O. F. (2017). Impact of capital market on foreign portfolio investment in Nigeria. *International Journal of Recent Advances in Multidisciplinary Research, 4*(7), 2668–2677.

Organisation for Economic Cooperation and Development (OECD). (2007a). *Tax effects on foreign direct investment: Recent evidence and policy analysis* (Tax Policy Study No. 17). Organisation for Economic Cooperation and Development.

Organisation for Economic Cooperation and Development (OECD). (2007b). *Tax incentives for Investment – A global perspective: Experiences in MENA and non-MENA countries*. OECD.

Oyerogba, E. O., Alamu, J. A., Olugbenro, S. K., & Sangodare, T. O. (2024). Tax incentives and foreign direct investment: Evidence from Nigeria listed manufacturing firms. *Journal of Tax Reform, 10*(2), 355–380.

Rashid, A., & Khalid, A. (2017). The impact of exchange-rate uncertainty on foreign portfolio investment in Pakistan. *NUML International Journal of Business & Management, 12*(2), 88–102.

Rueda-Sabatar, E. (2000). Corporate governance: And the bargaining power of developing countries to attract foreign investment. *Corporate Governance: An International Review, 8*(2), 117–124. https://doi.org/10.1111/1467-8683.00189

Sabir, S., Rafique, A., & Abbas, K. (2019). Institutions and FDI: Evidence from developed and developing countries. *Financial Innovation, 5*(8), 1–14. https://doi.org/10.1186/s40854-019-0123-7

Su, C. W., Sun, T., Ahmad, S., & Mirza, N. (2021). Does institutional quality and remittances inflow crowd-in private investment to avoid Dutch disease? A case for emerging seven (E7) economies. *Resources Policy, 72*, 102111.

United Nations Conference on Trade and Development (UNCTAD). (2016). World investment report 2016: Investor nationality: Policy challenges. *United Nations, 23*(3), 10–36. https://doi.org/10.18356/44d1623d-en

United Nations Conference on Trade and Development (UNCTAD). (2019). *World investment report: Special economic zones*. United Nations.

United Nations Conference on Trade and Development (UNCTAD). (2023). *World investment report 2023: Investment in sustainable energy for all*. https://unctad.org/system/files/official-document/wir2023_overview_en.pdf

United Nations Conference on Trade and Development (UNCTAD). (2024). World investment report 2024: Investment facilitation and digital government. https://unctad.org/system/files/official-document/wir2024_en.pdf

Walio, O. T., & Oludayo, A. E. (2020). Dynamic effects of foreign portfolio investment on economic growth in Nigeria. *Financial Markets, Institutions and Risks, 4*(3), 5–12. https://doi.org/10.21272/fmir.4(3).5-12.2020

Williamson, O. E. (2000). The new institutional economics: Taking stock, looking ahead. *Journal of Economic Literature, 38*(3), 595–613. https://doi.org/10.1257/jel.38.3.59

World Bank. (2013). *The World Bank annual report 2013*. World Bank. http://hdl.handle.net/10986/16091

World Bank. (2016). *Doing business 2016: Measuring regulatory quality and efficiency*. World Bank Group. https://doi.org/10.1596/978-1-4648-0667-4

World Bank. (2025). *World governance indicators*. World Bank. https://databank.worldbank.org/source/worldwide-governance-indicators

Wu, J., Shaomin, L., & Selover, D. (2012). Foreign direct investment vs foreign portfolio investment: The effect of governance environment. *Management and International Review*, *52*(5), 643–670.

Zee, H. H., Stotsky, J. G., & Ley, E. (2002). Tax incentives for business investment: A primer for policy makers in developing countries. *World Development*, *30*(9), 1497–1516. https://doi.org/10.1016/S0305-750X(02)00050-5

Zühal, K., & Yalta, Y. (2017). Relationship between institutional factors and FDI flows in developing countries: New evidence from dynamic panel estimation. *Economies*, *5*(2), 1–10.

Appendix: Countries Included in the Study

Algeria, Angola, Benin, Botswana, Burkina Faso, Cape Verde, Cameroon, Comoros, Chad, Central African Republic, Congo Democratic, Cote d'Ivoire, Egypt, Equatorial Guinea, Gabon, Ghana, Guinea, Guinea-Bissau, Kenya, Libya, Lesotho, Madagascar, Mali, Malawi, Mauritania, Morocco, Mozambique, Namibia, Niger, Nigeria, Rwanda, Senegal, Sierra Leone, South Africa, Seychelles, Uganda, Zambia, and Zimbabwe

Chapter 6

From Dual Towards Bipolar? Some Recent Trends in the Indian Economy and Their Implications for Development Theory and Policy

Asis Kumar Banerjee[a] *and Debashis Mazumdar*[b]

[a]*University of Calcutta, Kolkata, India*
[b]*The Heritage College, Kolkata, India*

Abstract

Though economic growth sometimes gets prime importance in the development policy of some less developed and developing countries, it has been observed that inequality adversely affects economic growth from both the supply and the demand sides in such economies. On the supply side, inequalities of income and wealth (particularly the latter) create imperfections in the credit market. If an economy is demand constrained, an increase in inequality will make matters even worse as the richer section of the people has a lower propensity to consume than the poor. Though the Gini coefficient of income distribution has been declining in regions like Sub-Saharan Africa and South-East Asia during 1981–2023, it has increased in India and North America. This dualistic nature of development has further been overshadowed with polarisation of income and wealth in India with the characteristics of considerable intra-group homogeneity and inter-group heterogeneity. Sluggish growth in real wages, educated unemployment, and the possible adverse impacts of the presently emerging artificial intelligence (AI) can lead our economy towards bipolarity, and our economy is in danger of being divided into two parts with no interconnection working through labour reallocation from the backward

Changing Dimensions in Economic Development: Theories and Empirics, 67–77

doi:10.1108/978-1-83708-384-820261006

to the advanced sector. Needless to say, that would be the end of the idea of development because a developing economy, by definition, means a dual economy with a *shrinking* backward sector.

Keywords: Gini coefficient; income inequality; wealth inequality; economic growth; dualistic development; polarisation

JEL Codes: D31; O15; O40; P25; J41

Introduction

After the Second World War, all newly independent countries including India focused on the task of economic development. It was emphasised that all citizens should have the right to adequate means of livelihood. This objective necessitated an increase in per capita incomes and, therefore, an increase in the growth rates of these economies. Many of these countries were also aware of the need to ensure that the fruits of economic growth reached all sections of their populations. India went one step ahead and enshrined this distribution objective in the Constitution. The Directive Principles of State Policy required that the state shall direct its policy towards ensuring that 'the ownership and control of the material resources of the community are so distributed as best to subserve the common good' and that 'operation of the economic system does not result in the concentration of wealth and means of production to the common detriment' (Article 39, Clauses (b) and (c) of the Constitution of India).

By the early 1980s, however, it was realised that in pursuing the twin objectives of economic growth *and* equality of the income and wealth distributions, India had not succeeded in achieving either. In 1983, the Gini coefficient of the *monthly per capita consumption expenditure* (MPCE) distribution in India was 0.321. It is seen that while the value of Gini coefficient of the *income* distribution decreased from 0.458 in 1961 to 0.401 in 1981, it has increased continuously since then to 0.629 in 2017 (Fig. 6.1). At the global level, such an increasing trend in Gini coefficient (reflecting inequality in the distribution of pre-tax national income) is observed in North America (Fig. 6.2). However, along with the global average Gini, this Gini coefficient for regions like Sub-Saharan Africa and South-East Asia indicated a declining trend during 1980–2023 (Fig. 6.2).

On the other hand, the record of economic growth was also not anything to proud of. In the 1970s, the average annual growth rate of gross domestic product (GDP) in India was less than 3%. It was derisively described as the 'Hindu rate of economic growth'. As a result, there was only a paltry increase in the average standard of living in the country.

There was a difference of opinion among economists over whether the economic policies of the country required a massive reorientation. Some economists were of the opinion that it had been a mistake not to make economic growth the overriding objective of economic policy. This was not only because a broad-based

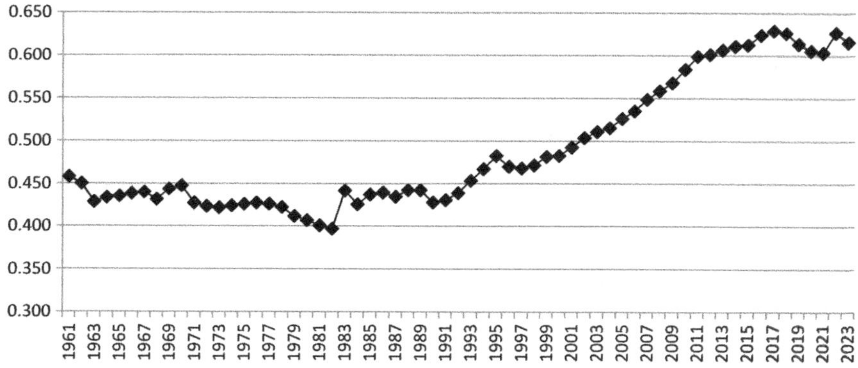

Fig. 6.1. Figure Showing the Gini Coefficient of Pre-tax National Income in India During 1961–2023. *Source*: World Inequality Database, https://wid.world/data/.

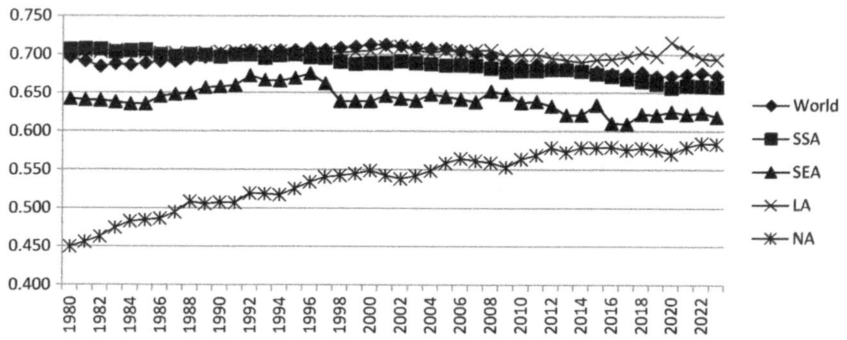

Fig. 6.2. Figure Showing the Gini Coefficient of Pre-tax National Income in Some Regions of the World During 1961–2023. *Source*: World Inequality Database, https://wid.world/data/.

increase in the standard of living of the masses was not possible without a significant increase in per capita income but also because even the *equity* objective required economic growth. Because the income redistribution programmes of the government needed resources at the hands of the government which can ultimately only come from tax revenue, and such resources would continue to be limited until the tax base improved significantly.

Moreover, growth is driven by investment. Since public investment is limited by the availability of resources at the hands of the government, private investment needs to be encouraged. This type of argument was at the root of the drive towards liberalisation and privatisation in the Indian economy that began in the 1980s and, as is well-known, picked up momentum after the reforms initiated in 1991. Caution, however, was sounded by many other economists who pointed out that while economic growth was certainly *necessary*, it was not a *sufficient* condition for a speedy and broad-based development of the economy.

So far as actual governmental policy formulation was concerned, the 'privatisers' won out. However, today in hindsight, it seems that both sides (rather than just one of them) of this policy debate of the 1980s seem to have been vindicated at least partly. The economic reforms certainly bore fruit so far as the GDP growth rate was concerned. The average annual growth rates in the 1980s, 1990s and the 2000s were 5.3%, 5.7% and 7.3%, respectively. The contrast with the 'Hindu rate of growth' is, indeed, striking.

We should recall, however, that economic growth is only the *instrument* that is to be used to achieve the broad-based and equitable growth of standard of living that is the central objective of economic policies enshrined in the constitution. Behind the undoubtedly creditable growth performance of the Indian economy lie a number of fault lines that we can ignore only to our great peril and that have already started sounding alarm bells.

One major fault line, as is well known by now, relates to inequality. Inequality of the distribution of MPCE which, as we have said above, was already quite high in the early 1980s rose even higher in the following decades. The Gini coefficient of MPCE rose to 35.7 in 2011–2012. A recent report on Household Consumption Survey, however, shows a slight decline in the Gini coefficient of MPCE across major Indian states during 2022–2024 (Table 6.1).

Some authors have expressed the opinion that these estimates are biased *upward*. These authors refer to some other estimates that seem to indicate that income Gini in India is not only relatively low but has lately been decreasing. A careful look, however, reveals that the methodologies followed by these authors are flawed (Bakshi et al., 2012).

Inequality of *wealth* is much harder to estimate. The best available estimates, however, again point towards increasing inequality in the post-reforms decades, particularly in the present century. According to Credit Suisse (2022), the Gini coefficient of the wealth distribution increased continuously between 2000 and 2020 from 74.6 to 82.3. The World Inequality Database also reports a continuous increase in this measure of inequality from 0.60 in 1981 to 0.76 in 2023.

We must conclude that while growth has increased per capita income quite rapidly, the resulting increase in the tax base has not been utilised for the purpose

Table 6.1. Gini Coefficient of Consumption Expenditure in India During 2011–2024.

Sector	**Gini Coefficient of Consumption Expenditure**		
	2011–2012	**2022–2023**	**2023–2024**
Rural	0.283	0.266	0.237
Urban	0.363	0.314	0.284

Sources: Survey on Household Consumption Expenditure (2023–2024), National Sample Survey (NSS) Report No. 592, Ministry of Statistics & Programme Implementation (MoSPI), Government of India.

of ensuring equity. At this point, one may ask: why should one be concerned with the issue of inequality? Is it just a matter of one's ethical values? Our own concern with this matter has been driven more by economic considerations than by ethical ones. It turns out that the two objectives of economic policy, growth and equity, are not entirely unrelated after all. The following three points need to be noted in this connection.

First, it has been known for quite some time that in a developing economy, inequality adversely affects economic growth from both the supply and the demand sides. On the supply side, inequalities of income and wealth (particularly the latter) create imperfections in the credit market. In the long run, this adversely affects not only the accumulation of physical capital but also that of human capital by denying people access to educational and health facilities. This has been established both theoretically (for instance, Banerjee & Newman, 1993; Galor & Zeira, 1993; Loury, 1981) and empirically in the context of *developing* economies (for instance, Barro, 2000).

Second, the deleterious effect of inequality on growth is even more obvious from the demand side. If an economy is demand constrained, an increase in inequality will make matters even worse. Since the rich have a lower propensity to consume than the poor, a rise in income and wealth inequalities will obviously reduce aggregate consumption and, therefore, aggregate demand. Thus, a single-minded pursuit of economic growth would be self-defeating in the long run if, simultaneously, there is an increase in inequality of income and wealth and if the economy in question is a developing one.

Third, inequality also has undesirable *short-run* effects. Recent research has established that inequality exacerbates *business cycles*. A more unequal economy would face more violent fluctuations of output and income levels (see Bilbie et al., 2023). Both the amplitude and the periodicity of business cycles would tend to increase.

Issue of Polarisation

We now wish to draw attention to another type of trend in the Indian economy whose implications do not seem to have attracted enough attention. It is not only inequality but also *polarisation* that has tended *to increase*. Intuitively, a polarised economy is one that consists of a small number of groups of individuals where there is considerable *intra-group homogeneity* and *inter-group heterogeneity* (Esteban & Ray, 1994). Logically, it is quite possible that inequality increases but polarisation decreases (or vice versa). Examples are easily constructed. Consider, for instance, an economy with six individuals and with an aggregate income of 21 rupees. Consider two situations, situation X where the income distribution is (1, 2, 3, 4, 5, 6) and situation Y where it is (2, 2, 2, 5, 5, 5).

In going from X to Y, we have transferred one unit of income from individual 3 to individual 1 and have also transferred one unit from individual 6 to individual 4. These are progressive (or Pigou-Dalton) income transfers. Therefore, Y is a less unequal distribution of income than X. Obviously, however, Y is *more* (rather than less) polarised than X. In Y, there are just two groups of people (individuals

1, 2, 3) and (individuals 4, 5, 6). There is perfect homogeneity within the groups in situation *Y*. Heterogeneity between them, however, remains the same as in *X* if we measure heterogeneity by the ratio of the average incomes of the two groups. A polarised economy with just two groups is called a *bipolar economy*.

Thus, despite some similarities, the notions of inequality and polarisation are actually quite different. It is, of course, possible to construct examples where inequality and polarisation move in the same direction.

It is widely agreed that polarisation is bad for economic growth, that is, that an increase in polarisation reduces the rate of economic growth. Economists point towards the social tensions caused by polarisation (Esteban & Ray, 1994).

A number of measures of polarisation have been suggested in the literature. For reviews see, for instance, Duclos and Taptue (2015) and Chakravarty (2009). By using some of these measures, it has now been shown that over the past few decades, the Indian economy has witnessed not only an increase in income and wealth *inequality* but also income and wealth *polarisation*. For trends up to around 2004–2005, see Motiram and Sarma (2014).

The trend has continued into the later years. Many observers believe that the Indian economy has long displayed the signs of bipolarisation with the rich and the poor constituting the vast majority of the population and the middle class being relatively small in size. Before the Covid pandemic, the Indian middle class comprised roughly 10 crore people. The Covid cut it by about a third, thus accentuating the trend. In contrast, China, whose total population is now less than that of India, had, on the eve of the pandemic, a middle class that was about five times as large. Moreover, the pandemic does not seem to have made much of a dent in this figure (www.pewresearch.org/short-reads/2021/03/18).

Many private sector producers in India, too, seem to be of the opinion that the trend towards polarisation has been a major cause of the failure of demand to pick up fast in the post-Covid era. For instance, as late as in October, 2024, the CEO of Nestle India spoke about the 'shrinking' middle class of India as the cause behind the poor performance of the food and beverages sector in the second quarter of the 2023–2024.

The causes behind rising inequality and polarisation in India can be explained as follows:

(a) *Sluggish growth in real wages*: The rate of growth of real wage in India is low in comparison to that of labour productivity. Average annual growth rate of real wages between 2014–2015 and 2021–2022 was less than 1%. (In manufacturing, it was just 0.3%.) However, the growth rate of labour productivity has been quite impressive over the last few decades. Between 1992 and 2021, it was 4.4%. The creditable performance of labour productivity has been described as a result of economic reforms. Even if that is so, the sluggish growth of real wages indicates where the benefits of these reforms have gone.
(b) *Educated unemployment*: On the other hand, there has been little improvement in the picture of employment, especially in the matter of employment of *educated* workers (which is the type of employment that is most important for middle-class workers). While the overall unemployment rate in India

is roughly the same as in most other emerging economies, this is of little consolation since this excludes hidden unemployment. To be physically alive, one must accept any job, no matter how ill-paid it is. That is why the overall unemployment rate is relatively low. A clearer picture emerges if we focus on the educated unemployed. As per the *India Employment Report 2024* Institute of Human Development (IHD)/International Labour Organisation (ILO), the percentage of people with secondary (or higher) education in the unemployed population rose dramatically from 35.2 in 2000 to 65.7 in 2022.

In a sense, however, citing such data begs the question since they lead to the question: what explains slow wage growth and rapid rise in educated unemployment? The nature of technological progress (TP) in India in recent decades has played a key role here. In the capital-abundant and labour-scarce Western economies, TP has always been labour saving. The same, however, has also been the trend in India. To some extent, there has been a mindless imitation of the West. But there have been economic factors too. The digital revolution (DR) has led to a steep fall in the relative prices of investment goods, providing an incentive to substitute capital for labour.

In this connection, we should also note a vital difference between DR that began in the 1990s and the great technological transformations of the historical past such as the one behind the Industrial Revolution (IR). IR not only greatly speeded up the rates of economic growth of the Western countries but also led to vast increases in *aggregate employment* in these economies. While some old livelihoods were destroyed, the advent of the new industries more than made up for this (in some cases with a time lag). For instance, the automobile industry killed off the occupation of the makers and the drivers of hackney carriage but created employment in the automobile factories and the jobs of cab drivers. Similarly, the number of new jobs created in the weaving and knitting mills greatly exceeded that of jobs destroyed in the handicrafts that produced yarn and clothes in the earlier era.

The labour market effect of DR, however, was quite different. While labour productivity and, therefore, the rate of economic growth surged, employment lagged behind, giving rise to the popular phrase ‘jobless growth’.

Emergence of AI

At this point, we must mention the spectre of yet another kind of TP which has now appeared on the horizon viz. AI. While AI is a continuation of DR from the point of view of technology, most observers believe that its labour market impact is going to be somewhat different. The older DR that was based on the type of computers that we use today did not hurt the middle class very much. Its negative effect was concentrated at the lower ends of the salary ladder. The main effect of this was on the degree of *inequality* of the income distribution.

The novelty of AI is the creation of ‘intelligent’ machines. This will replace not only manpower but also human brainpower. The kind of jobs that will face extinction are precisely the one that is the mainstay of the middle class. What effect this will have on *inequality* is not clear. What will happen to *polarisation* is quite clear: it will sharpen.

Implications for Development Theory

The increasing trends in inequality and polarisation in India that we have discussed above are going to have important implications for the theory of development economics. As is well known, this theory was born out of the aspirations of the nations that got their independence from colonial rule after the Second World War. The mainstream theories of those times such as short-run macroeconomic theory (which concentrated on the explanation of business cycles or the aggregative theories of economic growth) were not of much relevance for these newly independent countries whose main problem was to transform themselves from less developed economies into developed ones.

It was noted that a typical developing country was not a one-sector economy. Rather, it had two sectors. There was a large low-productivity and stagnant sector, typically depending on traditional agriculture where production depended only on labour (and a fixed amount of land) and a small dynamic sector comprising industries where production required both capital and labour inputs. It was Lewis (1954) who brought this notion of a 'dual economy' into focus.

In the Lewis model, there was a competitive wage in industry, while in agriculture, there was surplus labour so that marginal productivity was virtually zero, and the wage rate was determined by the equal-sharing principles of traditional societies rather than by marginal productivity.

On the other hand, there was the possibility of expanding the industrial sector. Initially, the capital necessary for the purpose could be provided by tapping the 'hidden rural savings' frittered away in luxury consumption of the rural rich. Labour supply to the industrial sector can be arranged by reallocating labour from the backward sector. Note that such reallocation would not involve any loss of agricultural output since labour's marginal productivity in that sector is zero. Assuming that capitalists did not consume more than an insignificant part of their output, this would generate enough investible resources to permit rapid capital accumulation in the advanced sector.

This will go on until surplus labour in the backward sector is exhausted. At that point, the economy ceases to be a dual one. The agricultural wage rate will then start increasing and catch up with the industrial wage.

Later contributions added many new features to this basic Lewis model. An important extension was the one due to Fei and Ranis (1961, 1964) who emphasised output market duality as well. It is this theory of the dual economy that is the core of what is called the theory of development economics. What is important for our purposes is to note that the entire edifice of this theory is built on the assumption that labour is a crucial factor of production in the industrial sector.

Now, the profound implication of AI is that it would tend to invalidate this most basic assumption of the theory. The magnitude of these implications is by far larger than that of the DR of the past few decades. While DR reduced labour demand, there was a lower bound to the process because computers did not substitute human brainpower.

Today, for the first time in history, *complete* automation is threatening to become a real possibility. The danger is one of bipolarity rather than duality. The economy is in danger of being divided into two parts with no interconnection working through labour reallocation from the backward to the advanced sector. Needless to say, that would be the end of the idea of development because a developing economy, by definition, means a dual economy with a *shrinking* backward sector.

Some economists have discounted the possibility of *complete* automation. They point out that a similar earlier apprehension about the increasing inequality has been belied in practice. Inequality may be increasing but nobody expects it to reach the extreme point where literally all of the income and wealth of the country goes to a few billionaires and everybody else gets zero. The reason is easy to see. On the supply side, as long as production requires *some* labour, workers must be paid *something*. On the demand side, too, it needs to be ensured that workers must have *some* purchasing power. Otherwise, who are to buy the produced goods?

These economists point out that while it is true that, unlike the old-fashioned DR, AI will make labour input in the production process technologically superfluous, the demand-side reason for continued use of some human labour will continue to be in force. Since the industrial producers themselves consume only an insignificant proportion of the total industrial production, they will face an insurmountable demand deficiency problem if they aim for complete automation.

This view contains an element of truth. In fact, this is the reason why bipolarity is a long-run (rather than an imminent) possibility. However, some of the effects of this long-run trend need to be noted. Industrial producers have started formulating their own strategies for dealing with the problem in their own way. A distinction is made between goods and services demanded by the middle class and the poor, on the one hand, and, on the other hand, those that are demanded by the affluent or can be exported. Production of the former type of commodities is discouraged while that of the latter is pursued with enthusiasm. The distinction is often made within the same industry. For instance, in 2024, the production of affordable housing in India fell by as much as 43% while that of luxury housing rose by as much as 53% (see www.aninews.in). There is a similar trend within the automobile industry and in a host of other lines of production such as jewellery, tourism and the fast-moving consumer goods (FMCG) sector, etc. Exports also have received considerably more emphasis than before.

Such strategies may, for some time, keep up the growth rate of GDP of the economy as a whole at respectable levels. It is open to doubt, however, how long luxury consumption can continue to be a source of enduring growth and to what extent exports can be the saviour for the Indian economy in today's world (see Banerjee (2024) for a discussion of these issues). More importantly, recall that the main issue is not the growth rate per se but whether fast growth leads to development in the broad sense in which we are using the term here.

Can Economic Policy Help?

Needless to say, the fearsome possibility of complete bipolarity can only be the end stage of the ongoing process of shrinkage of the middle class. The more immediately relevant question is: Can the general trend of increasing inequality and polarisation be reversed? The experience of at least some of the other countries of the world indicates that there is no logical reason why the answer has to be in the negative. Economic policies can certainly help. What matters is the social and political willingness to formulate and implement such policies. One of the areas where urgent action is obviously required is the containment of the problem of unemployment, especially among the youth and the educated.

We have already cited some estimates of the rate of unemployment among the educated. The picture of unemployment among the youth is similar.

The current rate of youth unemployment in India is 15.8% (PFLS 2022–2023). As per ILO statistics, India occupies the 92nd position in a ranking of 202 countries in a decreasing order of this rate. In other words, there are 110 countries where the rate is lower. In about 40 of them, it is only half of what it is in India or even less. For instance, it is 6.1% in Vietnam, 4.1% in Japan and 3% in Cuba.

The case of Vietnam is particularly remarkable since, like India, Vietnam is also now one of the fastest growing economies of the world. Thus, high GDP growth does not necessarily have to be achieved at the cost of a shrinking middle class.

Therefore, policy planners should take a good look at some of the good practices in this regard that are being followed in some of the other countries of the world. What is needed is a careful consideration of whether or how much of them can be adapted to the Indian context. Needless to say, we also need to be innovative, finding our own ways of dealing with the matter.

Even a cursory attempt to do so reveals that the government has to play a crucial role in this context. Apart from the obvious and well-known importance of public investment in the social sectors, the government also seems to have a role in emphasising the right kind of economic reforms in the private sector. For instance, there is more to labour law reforms than simply to make it easier for employers to lay off workers. There is also the matter of letting labour enjoy the fruits of rising labour productivity.

It was Bertrand Russell who, many years ago, foresaw that technical progress would at some stage make unemployment the overriding socio-economic issue. He suggested a reduction in the daily working hours as a means of avoiding retrenchment, reminding us that at one stage workers had to work for 16 (or more) hours a day. It was labour movements that forced the employers to adopt the eight-hour working day in the United States. There is no evidence that this lowered the growth rate of the US economy. Quite the contrary.

Needless to say, the basic issue is not the length of the working day. Rather, it is how to ensure equitable growth. Our central message is: do embrace TP but ensure that the resulting increase in labour productivity translates into broad-based development rather than into rising unemployment.

References

Bakshi, A., Ramachandran, V. K., Rawal, V., & Swaminathan, M. (2012). *Household income surveys in India: Lacunae and illustrations from village surveys* [Paper presentation]. Paper presented at the 32nd General Conference of the International Association for Research in Income and Wealth, Boston. Retrieved September 13, 2022, from www.iariw.org

Banerjee, A. K. (2024). *Inequality, economic growth and business decision-making*. Routledge.

Banerjee, A. V., & Newman, A. F. (1993). Occupational choice and the process of Development. *Journal of Political Economy*, *101*, 274–298.

Barro, R. J. (2000). Inequality and growth in a panel of countries. *Journal of Economic Growth*, *5*, 5–32.

Bilbie, F. O., Primiceri, G., & Tambalotti, A. (2023). *Inequality and business cycles* [Working Paper No. 31729]. National Bureau of Economic Research.

Chakravarty, S. R. (2009). *Inequality, polarization and poverty: Advances in distributional analysis*. Springer.

Credit Suisse. (2022). *Global wealth report 2022*. Credit Suisse Research Institute.

Duclos, J.-Y., & Taptue, A.-M. (2015). Polarization. In A. B. Atkinson & F. Bourguignon (Eds.), *Handbook of income distribution* (Vol. 2, pp. 301–358). Elselvier.

Esteban, J.-M., & Ray, D. (1994). On the measurement of polarization. *Econometrica*, *62*, 819–851.

Fei, J. C. H., & Ranis, G. (1961). A theory of economic development. *American Economic Review*, *51*, 533–565.

Fei, J. C. H., & Ranis, G. (1964). *Development of the labour surplus economy: Theory and policy*. Richard Irwin.

Galor, O., & Zeira, J. (1993). Income distribution and macroeconomics. *Review of Economic Studies*, *60*, 35–52.

Lewis, W. A. (1954). Economic development with unlimited supply of labour. *Manchester School*, *22*, 139–191.

Loury, G. (1981). Intergenerational transfers and the distribution of earnings. *Econometrica*, *49*, 843–867.

Motiram, S., & Sarma, N. (2014). Polarization, inequality and growth: The Indian experience. *Oxford Development Studies*, *42*, 297–318.

PFLS. (2022–2023). *Periodic Labour Force Survey Report, July, 2022-June, 2023*. National Sample Survey Office, Ministry of Statistics and Programme Implementation, Government of India.

Chapter 7

Dancing to the Growth Tunes? An Analysis of Cross-country Variation in Environmental Policymaking Path with Special Reference to India

Kinnori Sinha, Debashis Chakraborty and Bibek Ray Chaudhuri

Indian Institute of Foreign Trade (IIFT), Kolkata Campus, India

Abstract

Under the United Nations (UN) forums since 1972, a series of discussions have been conducted to secure sustainable growth at the global canvas, which culminated into the sustainable development goals (SDGs) and the Paris Climate Deal (2015). While environmental sustainability is crucial for securing long-term welfare, short-term interest may motivate a country to embrace a path tilted towards economic growth. This kind of trade-off between growth and environmental sustainability has been witnessed across countries at different junctures. India, a resource-rich developing country, has undergone paradigm shifts in terms of environmental policymaking at times while witnessing cyclical movements on the economic front. Reviewing international policy framework and annual data on 141 countries from 1990 to 2020, with special emphasis on Indian data and policies, the current analysis concludes that while conscious attempts have been undertaken to avoid the costs associated with growth-led environmental degradation, the journey of the country to tread along a carefully chosen middle path is still on.

Keywords: India; environmental policy; sustainability; economic growth; policy reforms; trade-off

JEL Codes: C23; Q01; Q50; Q56; Q58

Changing Dimensions in Economic Development: Theories and Empirics, 79–92

doi:10.1108/978-1-83708-384-820261007

1. Introduction

The environment can be defined as the surroundings in which any living creature operates as an integral part of the prevailing ecosystem. When the ecological equilibrium is disturbed, massive efforts are required to bring it back to the original scenario, both at micro and macro levels. In addition, disruption of this equilibrium can lead to enormous economic consequences with global ramifications (Auffhammer, 2019). However, competition among countries for securing higher growth and prevalence of conflicting interests often result in continuation of policies that lead to environmental degradation and climate change. The failure of World Trade Organization (WTO) member countries to finalise the actionable subsidy categories that lead to illegal, unreported, and unregulated (IUU) fishing, even after two-decade-long intense negotiations, is a case in point (Rickard, 2022).

It is held by a branch of literature that a rise in income level would eventually lead to growing demand for a better environment in a country, thus ensuring better conservation practices (Stern, 1998). The underlying philosophy is that income-oriented considerations alone fail to measure economic development, which in turn shapes a society's perception towards protection of the environment (Stern et al., 1996). Sometimes, policy myopia may influence the short-term choice of a country, favouring economic growth opportunities over environmental sustainability. The concept of sustainable development, raised in the Brundtland Commission's report (1987), stressed the role of several emerging issues (e.g., population pressure, modernisation, deforestation, climate change) in this wider context (UN, 2015).

Being *homo-economicus* or *economic man* as per the treatise of John Stuart Mill, every man intends to maximise personal benefit, that is, welfare. The conflict arises when the welfare of the society is at loggerheads with the individual's welfare, due to potential disagreements among various stakeholders. Nonetheless, such conflicts might be addressed with the help of policy instruments, for example, taxation and subsidies (Pigou, 1920). Thus, existence of a strong governance-enhancing body with effective laws and policies, that would proactively and effectively ensure the convergence of individual preferences with national interests, is of utmost importance.

The trade-off between economic growth and environmental sustainability has been extensively documented by existing literature in the form of the Environmental Kuznets Curve (EKC) hypothesis (Grossman & Krueger, 1991). The EKC phenomenon underlines that while economic growth is positively related to environmental degradation/pollution up to a critical income level, beyond that stage, the relationship may turn negative (Dinda, 2004). The development patterns of many developed as well as developing countries support this contention (Mukherjee & Chakraborty, 2015a).

Considering this evolving perspective, the current chapter is arranged along the following lines. The international deliberations to secure sustainable development and lower environmental vulnerability are briefly noted first, followed by a preliminary correlation analysis of 141 nations, with emphasis on India.

A discussion on the environmental policymaking framework in India followed by the growth–sustainability trade-off in the context of the Indian growth experience is discussed next, based on which the concluding remarks are drawn.

2. Methodology

The current chapter discusses international deliberations and India's environmental policymaking framework to achieve sustainable development. A preliminary discussion on the growth–sustainability trade-off has been done by studying annual data on 141 nations spanning from 1990 to 2020 and examining the correlation between CO_2 emissions per capita and gross domestic product per capita (GDPPC) (Grossman & Krueger, 1991; Shafik & Bandopadhyay, 1992), keeping in mind other variables like the rule of law index, education index, health index, urban population, and trade that might influence the relationship, along with a graphical analysis of the much-celebrated EKC. A similar analysis has been done on annual Indian data from 1990 to 2020, as a case study.

The regression equation of the EKC has been considered for correlation analysis with various control variables taken from the existing literature.

$$CO_{2it} = \beta_0 + \beta_1 GDPPC_{it} + \beta_2 GDPPC_{it}^2 + \gamma_{it}\left[\text{Rule of law} + \text{Education} + \text{Health} + \text{Urbanisation} + \text{Trade}\right] + \varepsilon_{it}$$

where:
i = country.
t = year.
CO_2 = total CO_2 emission per capita including Land-use change and forestry (LUCF).
GDPPC = gross domestic product per capita at constant prices (2015 US$).
Rule of law index = captures the extent of confidence that agents have in rule and law.
Education index = component of Human Development Index.
Health index = component of Human Development Index.
Urbanisation = urban Urban population as a percentage of total population.
Trade = trade as a percentage of GDP.

3. Global Policymaking on Environmental Sustainability

After the Second World War, given the need for reconstruction, growth considerations dominated the thought process and actions of many countries for more than two decades. Subsequently, the need to responsibly tread along the growth path was acknowledged during the late 1960s. For instance, the Environmental Protection Agency (EPA) was set up in the United States in 1970, to protect human health, on one hand, and the environment, on the other hand. The UN Conference on Environment and Sustainable Development in 1972 was the first international forum where countries formally acknowledged this responsibility and agreed upon 26 principles on development and the environment to fulfil this goal. The journey to protect the global 'common' led to inception of the UN Environment Programme (UNEP) in 1972, thus creating the ground for several milestones, for example, the Rio Earth Summit (1992), Kyoto Protocol (1997), World Summit on Sustainable Development (WSSD, 2002), and Paris Agreement (2015) in the future.

In 1979, the First World Climate Conference (WCC-1) was held, which attempted to analyse and assess the existing knowledge regarding climate change-related concerns and carefully chalked out a plan to use resources that would meet sustainability goals (International Commission on Radiological Protection (ICRP), 2020). The resulting deliberations set the stage for formation of the World Climate Programme (1979), the World Climate Research Programme (1980), and the Intergovernmental Panel on Climate Change (IPCC, 1988). The concerns over depletion of the ozone layer, which posed a major threat to human lives, were acknowledged, and subsequently addressed in the Vienna Convention (1985), leading to formation of universally accepted norms in 2009. With approval from 197 countries, the Vienna Convention also aimed to reduce global chlorofluorocarbon production, which successfully led to adoption of the Montreal Protocol (1987). In 1987, the World Commission on Environment and Development (WCED) report proposed a definition of sustainable development, keeping in mind the requirements of people and nations across the development spectrum, which emerged as a basis for subsequent deliberations (Brundtland, 1987).

The sustainability narrative received further boost after the Earth Summit held in Rio de Janeiro (1992), where participation by all the world leaders brought about a radical change in the attitude and behaviour to deal with climate change-related concerns. The summit was quite impactful as it led to agreement on many important principles across the globe, for example, the Rio Declaration on Environment and Development, the Convention on Biological Diversity (CBD), and the UN Framework Convention on Climate Change (UNFCCC) in 1992, the UN Convention to Combat Desertification (UNCCD) in 1994, and so on. In recognition of the development dimension postulated by the EKC hypothesis, financial help in the form of grants from developed to developing nations was proposed to facilitate actions combatting climate change through the Global Environmental Facility (GEF). The First Conference of Parties (COP 1) held in Berlin (1995) started negotiations for introducing compliance requirements for the developed nations to reduce carbon emissions. Acknowledgement of the development-centric disparity across countries in harmful greenhouse gas (GHG) emissions led to the establishment of a strong forum, setting legally binding obligations for clean development mechanisms within the Kyoto Protocol in 1997 (COP 3). The protocol underlined the role of common, yet differentiated, responsibilities for countries while focusing on controlling the emissions of several GHGs.

During the mid-1990s, after the inception of the WTO, while member countries reduced tariff barriers, it was feared that continuation of weak environmental standards might provide some countries unfair advantages in export markets ('race to the bottom' hypothesis). These geographic disparities in environmental policymaking led to the imposition of environmental standard-induced trade restrictions, on one hand, and acted as catalysts in initiating discussions on the introduction of border trade measures, on the other hand (Sheldon, 2006). In the 21st century, while the role of securing a sustainable future by addressing the emerging concerns (e.g., loss of biodiversity, ozone layer depletion, global warming) was not diluted, recurrence of economic downturns (e.g., sub-prime crisis, eurozone crisis) complicated the negotiation process. The Millennium Summit in 2000 reshaped the concept of sustainable development by setting eight millennium development goals (MDGs) for the UN member nations. The WSSD at Johannesburg in 2002, focusing on issues like preserving resources, addressing the demand for food and water, meeting economic and energy requirements, also played a key role in the ongoing process.

Nevertheless, the US strategic decision to not participate in the Kyoto Protocol significantly compromised the global collaboration to counter the climate change effects (Hovi et al., 2010). Conversely, many developing countries cautiously treaded the negotiation rounds, fearing a potential compromise on their future growth path, particularly owing to anticipated stricter compliance requirements, on one hand, and absence of clear agreements on issues relating to local capacity-building, on the other hand (Murdiyarso, 2004). It was often feared, particularly in developing countries, that compliance with multilateral environmental norms in the absence of technology transfer and appropriate support mechanisms may improve sustainability only at the cost of economic growth. Premonition on certainty of such a growth–sustainability trade-off often discouraged developing countries from committing at the UN forums (Parikh & Parikh, 2004). Due to the prevalence of such growth consideration led to differences, while the Copenhagen Summit (COP 15, 2009) proposed containing temperature rise at 2°C, the actual success remained limited, given the legally non-binding nature of the recommendations.

The first legally binding agreement in two decades was finally reached during COP 21 (Paris Agreement, 2015), where 174 nations agreed to limit temperature rise to below 2°C or even 1.5°C. The agreement duly recognised the existing and potential GHG emissions and climate change-related concerns in both developed and developing countries. With promise of upgraded technology transfer and financial support to the developing nations, the accord aimed at battling climate change consequences more effectively (Brandi, 2017). A new set of global goals (popularly known as the SDGs) was also designed that aimed at achieving sustainable economic growth with more environment-friendly actions. The continued disparities in SDG compliance across countries, however, continue to underline the crucial role of growth-led considerations (Marti & Cervelló-Royo, 2023).

Apart from the UN forums, the WTO has also shown concerns regarding environmental conservation, for example, restraining subsidised fishing in international waters, to curb the consequent depletion of ocean resources. Since the Doha Mandate (2001), the subsequent WTO ministerial meetings have conducted negotiations regarding the prohibition of subsidies offered to the fisheries sector, to reduce IUU fishing in international waters. However, despite signing an Agreement on Fisheries Subsidies in 2022, the negotiations have so far failed to agree on the coverage of harmful subsidies, for prohibition in all the member countries (Chaisse et al., 2024). The failure underlines the rift in strategic growth considerations, expected benefits from stricter discipline on environmentally sensitive subsidies, and value of enhanced sustainability among the member countries.

4. Environment–Growth Nexus: Empirical Evidence

The literature identifies CO_2 emissions as one of the major GHGs that exacerbate the growing environmental concerns, and GDPPC (at constant prices) has been considered an indicator of economic growth. However, the growth–environment relationship is rather complex and influenced by many factors. Stages of growth (Rostow, 1959) and development accomplished by a nation play a pivotal role in shaping the outlook of the nation towards sustainable development involving environmental concerns as well.

In Fig. 7.1, panel data comprising information from 141 nations categorised as high-income, upper-middle-income, lower-middle-income, and low-income countries (according to the World Bank) have been analysed. The data span over 30 years, from 1990 to 2020. To understand the relationship between CO_2 emissions per capita, GDPPC, and the square of GDPPC, a graphical representation of the data has been created, which exhibits an inverse U-shaped curve. This inverse U-shaped curve confirms the existence of the EKC, which asserts that during the initial stage of economic growth, environmental degradation occurs rapidly; however, as a nation progresses, environmental degradation declines (Grossman & Krueger, 1991).

The EKC has offered hope to many economists and policymakers, suggesting that with long-term economic growth and development, environmental degradation may decrease. Nonetheless, this claim has been debated by many, leading to

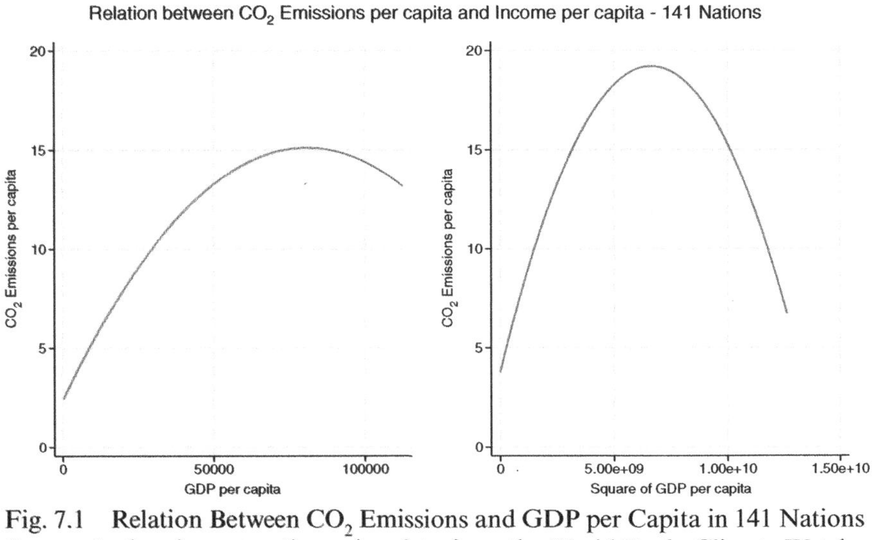

Fig. 7.1 Relation Between CO_2 Emissions and GDP per Capita in 141 Nations
Source: Authors' construction using data from the World Bank, Climate Watch and the Global Data Lab.

opposing conclusions. Varying outcomes of EKC from region to region might be due to different indicators used and various econometric methods applied to evaluate the relationship (Stern et al., 1996). EKC essentially establishes a long-run relationship between environmental degradation and economic growth. The conflicting conclusion regarding the validity of EKC across the globe might stem from the short-run fluctuations and shocks in an economy as well.

Political institutions (Bhattarai & Hammig, 2001; Olsson, 2007) play a crucial role in shaping a nation's policies and outlook. It has been suggested that strong governance often leads to improved efforts towards environmental conservation (Fan et al., 2022). Education and awareness (Balaguer & Cantavella, 2018) among the populace also positively influence environmental conservation. Conversely, urbanisation, industrialisation, and trade can adversely impact environmental conservation.

Though EKC remains one of the most celebrated theories, few other theories illuminate the complex relationship between economic growth and environmental degradation. For instance, the forest transition theory (Mather, 1992, 2007) and the resource curse hypothesis (Sachs & Warner, 2001) stand out among others.

Forest Transition Theory (1992) suggests that urbanisation, modernisation, and trade may reduce environmental degradation by alleviating pressure on forests and natural resources, allowing these resources time to regenerate. This phenomenon has often been observed in developed nations. The 'resource curse hypothesis' (2001) posits that an abundance of natural resources in a nation can lead to greater environmental degradation and lower levels of development, as it may foster complacency in seeking alternative income-generating methods. Motivated by these contradictions in the existing literature and theories, the current study examines the correlation between the aforementioned factors and environmental degradation.

In Table 7.1, out of 141 nations, 48 have been classified as high-income countries, 40 as upper-middle-income countries, 36 as lower-middle-income countries, and 17 as low-income countries, as per World Bank. To examine the relationship between environmental conservation and economic growth, CO_2 emissions per capita (Climate Watch) have been used as the indicator of environmental degradation, while GDPPC at constant prices (World Bank) has served as the indicator of economic growth. Additional factors influencing this relationship include the rule of law index (World Bank), the education and health components of Human development index (HDI) (Global Data Lab), urban population as % of total population (World Bank), and trade % of GDP (World Bank).

Table 7.1 indicates a positive relationship between all variables and CO_2 emissions per capita. To verify the existence of the EKC, the square of GDPPC has been also analysed, revealing a strong correlation with GDPPC, which suggests that multicollinearity could be a concern. According to the literature, an increase in the rule of law, health, and education indices should reduce CO_2 emissions. However, country-level heterogeneity in terms of the level of growth and development attained may account for these results and warrants further investigation.

India, categorised as a lower-middle-income country (World Bank) and one of the fastest-growing nations globally, presents an ideal case study for examining the relationship. Consequently, a correlation matrix has been created using

Table 7.1. Correlation Matrix.

Data on 141 Countries – 1990–2020								
	CO_2 Emission	**Log GDPPC**	**Log $GDPPC^2$**	**Rule of Law Index**	**Health Index**	**Education Index**	**Urban Population**	**Trade (% of GDP)**
CO_2 emission	1.00							
Log GDPPC	0.52	1.00						
Log $GDPPC^2$	0.52	1.00	1.00					
Rule of law index	0.38	0.82	0.82	1.00				
Health index	0.32	0.84	0.84	0.68	1.00			
Education index	0.35	0.84	0.84	0.69	0.82	1.00		
Urban population	0.45	0.82	0.82	0.58	0.71	0.71	1.00	
Trade (% of GDP)	0.24	0.35	0.35	0.33	0.30	0.33	0.26	1.00

Source: Authors' construction using data from the World Bank, Climate Watch Data, Global Data Lab.

Table 7.2. Correlation Matrix.

	Indian Data From 1990 to 2020							
	CO_2 Emission	**Log GDPPC**	**Log GDPPC^2**	**Rule of Law Index**	**Health Index**	**Education Index**	**Urban Population**	**Trade (% of GDP)**
CO_2 emission	1.00							
Log GDPPC	0.99	1.00						
Log GDPPC^2	0.99	1.00	1.00					
Rule of law index	(−)0.86	(−)0.80	(−)0.80	1.00				
Health index	0.99	0.99	0.99	(−)0.83	1.00			
Education index	0.98	0.98	0.98	(−)0.83	0.99	1.00		
Urban population	0.97	0.99	0.99	(−)0.79	0.99	0.98	1.00	
Trade (% of GDP)	0.63	0.56	0.56	(−)0.66	0.58	0.61	0.51	1.00

Source: Authors' construction using data from the World Bank, Climate Watch Data, Global Data Lab.

annual Indian data from 1990 to 2020 in Table 7.2. Interestingly, it has been found that India exhibits a negative relationship between the rule of law index and CO_2 emissions, suggesting that as governance improves, CO_2 emissions decline. However, anomalies related to education and health indices persist, suggesting policymakers tread carefully while balancing economic development and growth along with environmental conservation.

Contrary to popular belief, the correlation between CO_2 emissions and the rule of law index from a global perspective is positive, whereas, for India, the negative relationship suggests that India's governing bodies have been trying to address the environmental issues efficiently, nudging us to delve further into the paradigm shift in Indian policymaking.

5. Environmental Governance in India

As the current challenges of rising population, and the resulting conflicting interests among users, were absent during the pre-colonial period, environmental considerations mostly centred around forests and water bodies. Forests were seen as a primary source of natural resources, food, and shelter as well as an obstacle during wartime (Pouchepadass, 1995). The rising population and the associated consequences in the colonial period led to some legislative interventions. For the smooth functioning of the *Imperial Forest Department* established in 1864, the first *Forest Act* (1865) was passed. The primary purpose of the Act was to define property rights over forest lands. The loopholes in the provisions, however, soon came to surface, and the *Indian Forest Act* (1878) was subsequently passed (Guha, 1990). Although the provisions created wildlife sanctuaries and national parks, the monetisation of the forest produce (e.g., timber) and game (hunting) was given more priority than protecting wildlife (Pouchepadass, 1995). Focus on wider benefits, for example, construction of railways, which also facilitated transport of coals and timbers, led to further deforestation (Das, 2011). Amendments in *Indian Forest Act* (1927) maintained the process of defining ownership rights of forest land, leading to a conflict between the bureaucracy and forest dwellers, by disrupting the age-old symbiotic relationship of the latter group with forest areas.

In the early days of the post-independence period, the primary policy focus centred around poverty alleviation and environmental orientation was not prominent. *Indian Forest Policy* (1952), which aimed at increasing the forest cover, can be viewed as a simple extension of the colonial regime. The category 'forest' came under *State* list, as a result of which regional variation in subsequent forest cover depletion needs to be viewed through the prism of local economic undercurrents. The period indeed witnessed the introduction of several provisions with direct and indirect consequences on environmental governance, for example, the *Factories Act* (1948), the *River Boards Act* (1956), and the *Mines and Minerals (Regulation and Development) Act* (1957) were introduced (Sankar, 1998). Conversely, the environment was not a consideration under the *Atomic Energy Act* (1962) and the *Insecticides Act* (1968), which underlined the dominance of growth targets in the policy space.

After India's participation at the UN Conference at Stockholm (1972) as a signatory member, the sustainability narrative emerged in subsequent environmental policymaking. Conservation of biodiversity and wildlife received attention through the *Wildlife Protection Act* (1972) and the *Forest Conservation Act* (1980). Acknowledging the holistic nature of the environment and the need for protection of natural resources, the *Water (Prevention and Control of Pollution) Act* (1974), the *Air (Prevention and Control of Pollution) Act* (1981), and *National Forest Policy* (1988) were introduced. After the Bhopal Gas Tragedy (1984), the environmental laws were particularly re-visited to protect the environment and people. Apart from the immediate passing of the *Environment Protection Act* (1986), the *Biodiversity Protection Act* (2002) and *Scheduled Tribes and Other Traditional Forest Dwellers Act* (2006) were some of the landmark acts and policies introduced in the subsequent period.

In 1991, India adopted the New Economic Policy with the motive to liberalise, privatise, and globalise the economy and embarked on a journey to achieve rapid economic growth. Being a resource-abundant country, soon India became a popular destination for foreign investors. Thus, the need to conserve the environment was now felt more than ever. Consequently, the *Ozone-depleting Substances (Regulation and Control) Rules* of 2000, the *Energy Conservation Act* (2001), and the *Biodiversity Act* (2002) were laid down. The introduction of National Environment Policy (NEP) in 2006, periodic modifications in *Bharat Stage* regulations to curb vehicular pollution, and Central Pollution Control Board (CPCB) monitoring mechanisms are some other instances of positive interventions. In concurrence with the Rio Summit (1992), the *National Green Tribunal Act* of 2010 was implemented to ensure judicial resolution of environmental damage-related disputes (Antony, 2001; Jilani, 2017). The *Compensatory Afforestation Fund Act* of 2016 was designed to make the industrial sector accountable for any harm and thus to compensate the state government (90% of Compensatory afforestation fund (CAF) money) and the central government (10% of CAF money) for the cost of deforestation and damage caused by their actions.

The growing seriousness towards environmental conservation policies in the country has been both internally and externally motivated. Among the internal factors, the growth considerations as well as occurrence of calamities and mass response patterns, playing different dimensions over decades, shaped the outlook towards sustainability (Mukherjee & Chakraborty, 2015b). Among the external factors, multilateral pressure, reputation at international forums, and economic undercurrents remained the prime drivers.

6. Growth–Environment Trade-off in India: Recent Dynamics

During the last two decades, India has maintained a higher growth trajectory vis-à-vis the global average, despite witnessing occasional fluctuations, which has crucially shaped the country's outlook towards the sustainability narrative (Bhowmik & Poddar, 2021). For instance, the country witnessed a relatively modest growth pattern in the post-1991 period, primarily owing to the lower manufacturing efficiency.

From the late 1990s, exports from the service sector increased, and the resulting growth enabled the policymakers to embrace a bolder environmental policy choice, and so some proactive (e.g., the provisions involving forest dwellers) and preventive (e.g., climate action plan, formation of green tribunal) policies were introduced. However, this globalisation drive and domestic growth dynamics, in turn, necessitated greater resource requirements, which put pressure on environmental sustainability as well (Mukherjee & Kathuria, 2006). While environmental compliance remained modest among small industries, the same was often lagging even in some quarters of the formal industrial sector (Sahu, 2010). In addition, the growth momentum led to a massive urbanisation drive where the metropolis and cities expanded to their suburban areas, leading to higher vehicular pollution, felling of trees, etc. The focus on output growth in key sectors rather than addressing pollution and climate change may lead to intensification of brown activities (e.g., mining), with possible consequences on sustainability (Bhattacharji, 2020). However, given the informed awareness on the sustainability front, environmental considerations remain a crucial driver of the policy formulation process.

7. Conclusion

With many international deliberations and global partnerships of nations taking place over the years, efforts at the global level are quite evident to mitigate the ill effects of climate change. However, inequality among the nations in terms of economic growth and development has been causing disturbances in the path of sustainable development at the global level.

The opposing outcomes of the growth–environment trade-off varying from region to region indicate that countries with different economic growth have been able to tackle environmental issues differently. Each country makes a case study exhibiting a unique relationship between economic growth and environmental degradation, resulting in slow progress in mitigating environmental issues globally.

The Indian context discussed in the current analysis reveals that environmental awareness displays a cyclical pattern vis-à-vis the growth dynamics. However, there can be a one-to-one correspondence between the two in the long run. While the progress made by the country so far is appreciable, given the climate change-related consequences already observed in the country, there is no room for complacency. Moreover, the transition in Environmental Performance Index (EPI) for India, which shifted from 120th rank in 2008 to 180th position in 2022 (University of Yale, n.d.) deserves close attention. In addition, the presence of several Indian cities in the poor-to-moderate air quality range in the global scale is another worrying sign (Air Quality Index, n.d.). Maintaining a middle path, like many other nations, balancing growth considerations with sustainability, therefore should remain the priority of Indian policymakers.

References

Air Quality Index. (n.d.). *Live AQI city ranking*. Retrieved April 27, 2024, from https://www.aqi.in/in/real-time-most-polluted-city-ranking

Antony, M. J. (2001). *Landmark judgments on environmental protection*. Indian Social Institute.

Auffhammer, M. (2019). *The (economic) impacts of climate change: Some implications for Asian economies* [Working Paper No. 1051]. Asian Development Bank Institute.

Balaguer, J., & Cantavella, M. (2018). The role of education in the environmental Kuznets curve: Evidence from Australian data. *Energy Economics*, *70*, 289–296.

Bhattacharji, C. (2020). *Atmanirbhar Bharat: Missing a focus on air pollution and climate change* (Policy Brief No. 375). Observer Research Foundation.

Bhattarai, M., & Hammig, M. (2001). Institutions and the environmental Kuznets curve for deforestation: A cross-country analysis for Latin America, Africa, and Asia. *World Development*, *29*(6), 995–1010.

Bhowmik, D., & Poddar, S. (2021). Cyclical and seasonal patterns of India's GDP growth rate through the eyes of Hamilton and Hodrick Prescott filter models. *Asia-Pacific Journal of Management and Technology*, *1*(3), 7–17.

Brandi, C. (2017). *Trade elements in countries' climate contributions under the Paris Agreement*. International Centre for Trade and Sustainable Development (ICTSD).

Brundtland, G. H. (1987). *Our common future: Report of the World Commission on Environment and Development*. United Nations.

Chaisse, J., Chakraborty, D., & Kumar, A. (2024). Sustainable seas? Assessing impact and commitments in WTO fisheries subsidies. *Asian Journal of WTO & Public Health*, *19*(1), 27–65.

Das, P. (2011). Colonialism and the environment in India: Railways and deforestation in 19th century Punjab. *Journal of Asian and African Studies*, *46*(1), 38–53.

Dinda, S. (2004). Environmental Kuznets curve hypothesis: A survey: *Ecological Economics*, *49*(4), 431–455.

Fan, M., Li, M., J., & Shao, S. (2022). Is high natural resource dependence doomed to low carbon emission efficiency? Evidence from 238 cities in China. *Energy Economics*, *115*, 106328.

Grossman, G., & Krueger, A. (1991). *Environmental impacts of a North American free trade agreement* [NBER Working Paper No. 3914]. National Bureau of Economic Research.

Guha, R. (1990). An early environmental debate: The making of 1878 Forest Act. *The Indian Economic and Social History Review*, *27*(1), 65–84.

Hovi, J., Sprinz, D. F., & Bang, G. (2010). Why the United States did not become a party to the Kyoto protocol: German, Norwegian, and US perspectives. *European Journal of International Relations*, *18*(1), 129–150.

International Commission on Radiological Protection. (2020). *Annual report*. ICRP.

Jilani, W. M. (2017). Environmental protection and judicial activism. *Indian Journal of Natural Resources Energy & Environmental Law*, *2*, 1–12.

Mather, A. S. (1992). The forest transition. *Area*, *24*(4), 367–379.

Mather, A. S. (2007). Recent Asian forest transitions in relation to forest-transition theory. *The International Forestry Review*, *9*(1), 491–502.

Marti, L., & Cervelló-Royo, R. (2023). Disparities in sustainable development goals compliance and their association with country risk. *Sustainable Development*, *31*(1), 3038–3051.

Mukherjee, S., & Chakraborty, D. (2015a). *Environmental challenges and governance: Diverse perspectives from Asia*. Routledge.

Mukherjee, S., & Chakraborty, D. (2015b). Walking a thin line between growth and development concerns? Environmental governance in India. In S. Mukherjee & D. Chakraborty (Eds.), *Environmental challenges and governance: Diverse perspectives from Asia* (pp. 49–74). Routledge.

Mukherjee, S., & Kathuria, V. (2006). Is economic growth sustainable? Environmental quality of Indian states after 1991. *International Journal of Sustainable Development*, *9*(1), 38–60.

Murdiyarso, D. (2004). Implications of the Kyoto protocol: Indonesia's perspective. *International Review for Environmental Strategies*, *5*(1), 145–156.

Olsson, O. (2007). Conflict diamonds. *Journal of Development Economics*, *82*(2), 267–286.

Parikh, J., & Parikh, K. (2004). The Kyoto protocol: An Indian perspective. *International Review for Environmental Strategies*, *5*(1), 127–144.

Pigou, A. C. (1920). *The economics of welfare*. Macmillan & Co.

Pouchepadass, J. (1995). Colonialism and environment in India: Comparative perspective. *Economic and Political Weekly*, *30*(33), 2059–2067.

Rickard, S. J. (2022). Interest, institutions and the environment: An examination of fisheries subsidies. *International Studies Quarterly*, *66*(2), 1–14.

Rostow, W. W. (1959). The stages of economic growth. *The Economic History Review*, *12*(1), 1–16. Wiley on behalf of the Economic History Society.

Sachs, J. D., & Warner, A. M. (2001). The curse of natural resources. *European Economic Review*, *45*(4–6), 827–838.

Sahu, P. R. (2010, September 9). No pollution clearance: Vedanta runs 10 units. *Hindustan Times*.

Sankar, U. (1998). *Laws and institutions relating to environmental protection in India* [Occasional Paper]. Madras School of Economics.

Shafik, N., & Bandopadhyay, S. (1992). *Economic growth and environmental quality: Time series and cross-country evidence* [World Bank Policy Research Working Paper No. 904]. World Bank.

Sheldon, I. (2006). Trade and environmental policy: A race to the bottom? *Journal of Agricultural Economics*, *57*(3), 365–392.

Stern, D. I. (1998). Progress on the environmental Kuznets curve? *Environment and Development Economics*, *3*(2), 173–196.

Stern, D. I., Common, M. S., & Barbier, E. B. (1996). Economic growth and environmental degradation: The environmental Kuznets curve and sustainable development. *World Development*, *24*(7), 1151–1160.

United Nations. (2015). *Global sustainable development report*. United Nations.

University of Yale. (n.d.). *Environmental performance index depository*. Retrieved April 21, 2024, from https://epi.yale.edu/epi-results/

Chapter 8

Regional Integration in Trade: A Game-theoretic Exploration

Atreyee Sinha Chakraborty

Gokhale Institute of Politics and Economics, Pune, India

Abstract

This research presents a theoretical model that studies the decision-making process of countries regarding the harmonisation of standards within regional trade blocs (RTBs) and regional trade agreements (RTAs). It employs a game-theoretic approach to explore why countries within a RTB may or may not choose to cooperate in forming agreements that standardise measures like sanitary and phytosanitary (SPS) measures and technical barriers to trade (TBT). The study finds that countries are more likely to harmonise standards and cooperate if the discounted value of long-term gains (sometimes increased consumer surplus over the period) outweighs the short-term losses (sometimes immediate fall in producer surplus) due to harmonisation. The application of the trust game framework demonstrates that countries do cooperate and form agreements on standard harmonisation within RTBs, which may not align with traditional Nash equilibrium predictions but can be explained by the iterative and trust-based nature of international trade interactions within a RTB.

Keywords: Regional trading blocs; free trade agreements; regional cooperation; standard harmonisation; Nash equilibrium; trust game

JEL Codes: F13; F15; C720

Changing Dimensions in Economic Development: Theories and Empirics, 93–105

Published under exclusive licence by Emerald Publishing Limited
doi:10.1108/978-1-83708-384-820261008

1. Introduction

Over the last few decades, the world has witnessed the creation of a large number of RTBs and/or the signing of RTAs in almost every region of the world. The European Union (EU), the Association of South East Asian Nations (ASEAN), the South Asian Association of Regional Cooperation (SARRC), the North American Free Trade Association (NAFTA, presently replaced United States–Mexico–Canada Agreement (USMCA) in 2020), Comprehensive and Progressive Agreement for Trans-Pacific Partnership (CPTPP), European Free Trade Association (EFTA), and the Regional Comprehensive Economic Partnership (RCEP) are a few examples of this trend. Therefore, studying the welfare implications of trading blocs has become very relevant in the present global trade scenario. In Article 24, the architects of the General agreement on tariff and trade (GATT) allowed for free trade areas and customs unions, both being preferential trade agreements (PTAs). The GATT has also over time permitted developing countries a greater latitude to undertake PTAs that fall short of free trade areas and customs unions: the latter two require a commitment to getting internal tariff barriers down to zero, whereas the former permit permanent discriminations at levels other than zero (Bhagwati, 2002). While RTBs and RTAs are believed to increase welfare to countries involved, as it is a movement towards free trade, some economists believe that RTBs and RTAs can have a negative welfare effect on trade volume and world welfare as they control entry decisions, pricing, marketing, etc., which may distort the free flow of trade and the resulting distortion may reduce the welfare. For any country joining or not joining an RTB or signing or not signing of RTA is a strategic question and depends on the perceived gains and losses and the influence of the same on the overall welfare of the country. Most of the studies in this field have discussed the welfare effect from the viewpoint of 'tariff liberalisation', and very few studies have focused on the non-tariff barrier (NTB)-related provisions within RTBs or RTAs. The present research singles out the provision of SPS measures and TBT-related agreements in RTBs or RTAs. Empirically, we find a lot of variations in SPS and TBT-related measures in trade agreements ranging from sticking to national standards (i.e. no agreement related to standard harmonisation among members/signatories) to standard harmonisation towards regional or international standards (Organisation for Economic Co-operation and Development (OECD), 2015). There are also pieces of evidence of contravening the agreements related to standards by one of the signatories. Therefore, it will be interesting to study the determining factors behind the choice of strategy by participating countries and to determine the best responses under different circumstances. This research might be helpful to understand the reason behind the variation in SPS and TBT-related (collectively product standards) provisions across trade agreements. The research also applies the concept of trust game to explain why the frequency of product standard-related trade disputes is lesser among the signatories than the non-signatories.

2. Literature Review

With tariff barriers becoming increasingly less important, regulatory regimes like labour standards and environmental norms as well as product standards and technical regulations are becoming more important determinants of trade. This chapter has singled out export standards (termed as TBTs and SPS measure in the World trade organisation (WTO) context) as one particular domestic regulatory regime and will analyse the provisions related to the same in RTBs or RTAs. The empirical evidence shows differences in export 'standards', that is, the product standards and conformity assessment procedures across countries can greatly influence trade volumes and patterns. As the government of the importing country can set standards based on domestic firms' product characteristics or technology capacity, it can raise foreign exporters' costs to adjust according to these requirements. Moreover, there often exists a great difference in standards across markets, each of which requires an individual compliance cost such as the redesign cost for exporters. Hence, the difference in standards across markets can severely affect a firm's export capacity and the overall volume of trade. RTBs present opportunities for controlling barriers to trade by 'harmonisation' of standards by its inbuilt advantage as the countries of the same region share similar 'geo-climatic and cultural practices' – the preconditions of standard harmonisation. Unfortunately, export standards are most often not an important issue in some RTAs. Fabio (2020) shows although the trade potential offered to RTA signatories seems obstructed by non-discriminatory (multilateral) SPS measures, the entry into force of a trade agreement can help signatories meet stringent standards, further facilitating market access. This is allowed, in particular, by the provision of concrete commitments concerning SPS measures within RTAs, the most promising of which are mutual recognition of standards and the institution of joint SPS committees to implement technical cooperation between signatories on SPS issues. Moving towards these solutions would stimulate trade among countries.

Santeramo and Lamonaca (2022) show in a sample of RTAs in OECD (2011) that almost half of the analysed agreements provide for specific commitments on SPS measures. Within them, we find sufficient variability in specific provisions, 7 out of 48 RTAs harmonise their national measures on the international standards (principle of harmonisation); 8 out of 48 RTAs accept SPS measures of trading partners as equivalent (principles of equivalence); 9 out of 48 RTAs ensure that their SPS measures are adapted to the SPS characteristics of the region of origin and destination of the product (principle of regionalisation); 7 out of 48 RTAs ensure that their SPS measures are based on an assessment of the risks to human, animal, or plant life or health (principle of assessment of risk); 19 out of 48 RTA establish national enquiry points and notify the creation or change of any SPS regulation before they are adopted to ensure transparency (principle of transparency).

The cooperation within the regional trading bloc can take various forms like free trade zones, PTAs, customs unions, harmonisation, or mutual recognition of standards. The trade potential offered to RTA signatories seems obstructed by non-discriminatory (multilateral) SPS measures; the entry into force of a trade agreement can help signatories meet stringent standards, further facilitating market access. This is allowed, in particular, by the provision of concrete commitments concerning SPS measures within RTAs, the most promising of which are mutual recognition of standards. Being part of such deep trade agreements tends to reduce difficulties related to compliance with SPS measures (Murina & Nicita, 2017). Allowing for the harmonisation of domestic and non-tariff policies (Grant, 2013), deep trade agreements provide technical assistance to enhance the competitiveness of signatories operating in markets where the stringency of SPS measures and the costs of compliance are high (Henson & Jaffee, 2008; Hoekman, 2002; Murina & Nicita, 2017).

Harmonisation and mutual recognition of standards can be beneficial and can have a significant positive impact on trade within the signatories of RTA (Wieck & Rudloff, 2020) but may have a negative impact among non-signatories (Grant, 2013). In the present world, we can see different kinds of situations concerning product standards within the RTBs. Overall, while regional trading blocs may aim to harmonise standards and regulations to facilitate trade among member countries, variations in export standards-related agreements can still exist. However, moving towards harmonisation of standards would stimulate trade among countries, but at the same time, a country may defer from harmonisation of standards (even within the RTB) due to the perceived short-run benefit of deferring from the standards. Also, the standard game-theoretic approach predicts that the mutually beneficial free trade (in this case non-differentiated standard) may not be the Nash equilibrium due to unilateral incentive to deviate from the same. At the mutual best response point, countries will go for protectionism (here differential standards), that is, non-cooperation which is a Pareto suboptimal situation. Using prisoners' dilemma, we can see collective action problems arise and deter cooperation under a single-play prisoners' dilemma. However, as both Keohane (1984) and Oye (1986) argue, international trade is an iterated game in which it is unlikely that participants will perceive the end of the game as near. This iterative character of the game leads to a stable, cooperative solution. Grieco (1990) shows that cooperation is unlikely to exist with asymmetric payoffs, even in a repeated prisoner's dilemma. In this context, the present research tries to identify the determining factors for a country to join and retain cooperation (e.g. agreeing to standard harmonisation) in the RTB. Using the framework of Nash equilibrium and extending it towards the trust game (Berg et al., 1995), the study finds the conditions under which members of RTBs cooperate. The free trade always gives the Pareto optimal outcome, and the restrictive trade results into the suboptimal outcomes. But the basic understanding of trade policy shows us that restrictive trade will be the Nash equilibrium, and countries will be caught into the typical prisoner's dilemma while they will behave like 'rational fools'. The only way out from this dilemma is the signing of free trade agreements. But adherence to those agreements also becomes a question when the deviation from those agreements becomes more beneficial for a country at least in the short run.

The study becomes more relevant in the present global economic scenario as very recently the imposition of tariff by the United States on Canada and Mexico violates the terms of the The U.S.-Mexico-Canada agreement (USMCA), which came into effect during 2018–2019. It shows a country under some circumstances may choose to deviate from RTAs or bilateral/multilateral trade agreements.

The present chapter singles out harmonisation and mutual recognition of standards and tries to find out the optimum strategy of participants in a regional trading blocs. Many studies have examined the dynamics of cooperation within RTBs, focusing on factors like trade benefits, tariff rates, political alliances, and economic incentives. However, there may be a gap in research that applies the Nash equilibrium framework and trust game to the context of RTBs, especially concerning how harmonisation and mutual recognition of standards influence cooperation. The present study fulfils this gap by using the Nash equilibrium framework and extending it to the trust game to explore the conditions under which RTB members cooperate. By focusing on the role of harmonisation and mutual recognition of standards, the present study seeks to provide new insights into the strategic behaviour of RTB participants, which has been under explored in the literature.

3. The Model

The author has framed a theoretical model assuming international trade as an interactive game. The model assumes refraining from any kind of agreement can lead to a short-term gain for a non-participating country though leading to a loss in the long term. This is true for all countries. Using the framework, the model finds out what the short-run and long-run equilibrium strategies for a country concerning joining, refraining, or withdrawing from an agreement of standard harmonisation. The model also uses the framework of the trust game to explain why countries cooperate and sustain cooperation in following international harmonised standards even if that's not the Nash equilibrium.

Suppose there is a RTA named R consisting of three countries A, B, and C, where country A is exporting to countries B and C. The importing country imposes varied standards and technical requirements on the goods that are marketed in its market. The standard is quality related and not negative externality linked. We assume complying with standards does not affect consumers' demand for the regulated product. Firm 1 is domiciled in country A, in which it sells q_{1A} units of output, while it exports q_{1B} and $q_{1C,}$ respectively, to country B and country C. We also assume the marginal cost of production (excluding compliance cost) is m which is identical across firms.

Suppose D_{ij} shows the variable compliance cost for the ith firm to export to the jth country market. To comply with the standard, the exporting country (i.e. firm i here) has to bear a fixed set-up cost F_j to enter into export market j and the variable cost D_{ij}, and unless the standards are harmonised, F_j and D_{ij} vary across markets. Firms 2 and 3 are situated in countries B and C, respectively. Let us take the total cost of compliance with the foreign standard as:

$$E_{ij} = D_{ij} + F_j \tag{3.1}$$

3.1. Differentiated Standards

As long as standards in countries B and C are different, country A has to bear the compliance cost separately. The importing or standard-imposing country also has to maintain the same standard for domestic production of the product, but we can assume that the cost of compliance will be lower than that of the exporting country (Sanjuán et al., 2023). We can assume the cost of compliance for countries B and C is zero as the products produced inside the economies already adhere to the standard.

Once countries B and C harmonise the standard to say $\hat{S}$, the welfare level of all the countries will change.

The profit of firm 1 (exporting firm)

$$\pi_1 = (a - bq_{1A})q_{1A} + \{a - b(q_{1B} + q_{2B})\}q_{1B} + \{a - b(q_{1C} + q_{3C})\}q_{1C} \\ -E_{1B}q_{1B} - E_{1C}q_{1C} - m(q_{1A} + q_{1B} + q_{1C}) \quad (3.2)$$

The profit of importing country firms

$$\pi_B = \{a - b(q_{1B} + q_{2B})\}q_{2B} - mq_{2B} \quad (3.3)$$

$$\pi_c = \{a - b(q_{1C} + q_{3C})\}q_{3C} - mq_{3C} \quad (3.4)$$

As assumed and observed empirically, $E_{2B} < E_{1B}$ and $E_{3c} < E_{1C}$

The equilibrium exports are:[1]

$$q_{1B} = \frac{(a - 2E_{1B} - m)}{3b} \quad (3.5)$$

$$q_{1c} = \frac{(a - 2E_{1C} - m)}{3b} \quad (3.6)$$

Total export:

$$q_{1B} + q_{1C} = \frac{\{2a - (2E_{1B} + 2E_{1c}) - 2m\}}{3b} \quad (3.7)$$

However, assuming production technology shows Increasing Returns to Scale (IRS) and the cost function shows the cost of exporting to countries B and C be: $E_{1B} \cdot q_{1B}{}^{0.5}$ and $E_{1C} \cdot q_{1C}{}^{0.5}$, respectively. For simplicity, we are assuming the other part of cost (apart from compliance cost) still shows Constant returns to scale (CRS). The equilibrium outputs are:[2]

$$q_{1B} = \left\{\left((a - m) + \sqrt{(a - m)^2 - (12b^* E_{1B})}\right) / 6b\right\}^2 \quad (3.8)$$

---

[1]Derived in Appendix 1.

[2]Derived in Appendix 2.

$$q_{1C} = \left\{\left(a - m) + \sqrt{(a-m)^2 - (12b^* E_{1C})}\right) / 6b\right\}^2 \quad (3.9)$$

Total export:

$$q_{1B} + q_{1C} = \left(\left\{2(a-m) + \sqrt{(a-m)^2 - 12b^* E_{1B}} + \sqrt{(a-m)^2 - 12b^* E_{1C}}\right\} / 6b.\right)^2 \quad (3.10)$$

3.2. Effect of Harmonisation of Standard

This section examines the impact of standard harmonisation on intra-regional trade. Instead of straightforward assuming upward or downward harmonisation (Chen & Mattoo, 2004), we can assume harmonisation at the average rate of standard that leads to the compliance cost common to both markets.

$$E = (E_{1B} + E_{1C}) / 2 \quad (3.11)$$

Assuming the initial standard in one of the countries (say country B) is more stringent than another (country C), it is upward harmonisation for the latter and downward harmonisation for the former ($E_{1c} < E < E_{1B}$).

The equilibrium exports under CRS,

$$q_{1B} + q_{1C} = \left\{2a - \left(2E_{1B} + 2E_{1c}\right) - 2m\right\} / 3b \quad (3.12)$$

The equilibrium exports under IRS,

$$q_{1B} + q_{1C} = 2\left\{\left\{(a-m) + \sqrt{(a-m)^2 - 6b^*(E_{1B} + E_{1c})} + \right\} / 6b\right\}^2 \quad (3.13)$$

Harmonisation of standards will work as a trade booster when the production technology shows IRS as the firms can reap the benefits of economies of scale.

Lemma 3.1: Harmonisation to average standard will lead to an increase in the import and so as the volume of trade in the region when the production technology shows IRS, whereas it will not affect the volume or trade if the production technology shows CRS.

Proof: Follows from (3.7) and (3.12); (3.10) and (3.13).

Lemma 3.2: Import in the harmonising region increases unambiguously for the country with the most stringent initial standard (country B) as the exporting country can reap the benefits of both the integrated market and reduction in compliance cost, whereas for country C, the effect on import is ambiguous as the exporting country can get the benefit of only the former.

Nevertheless, the import in country C will increase if,[3]

$$E_{1B} < 3E_{1C} \tag{3.14}$$

The above result predicts that if the difference between the initial standards is not sufficiently high, then the import in the country can increase after harmonisation even if it follows upward harmonisation.

3.3. *Effect on Welfare*

The welfare effect of standard harmonisation on an exporting country depends on the effect on the producer's surplus as the consumer surplus of the exporting country remains unchanged with or without harmonisation. The revenue from the export market which has undergone downward adjustment will surely increase unless the demand is highly inelastic.[4] The revenue from the market with upward adjustment will also increase if condition (3.14) is fulfilled and demand is not very inelastic.

For the importing country, for country **B** (downward harmonisation), there will be a larger flow of quantity due to an increase in imports resulting in a fall in price and consumer surplus will rise. Though the fall in price may result in a reduction of profit, the reduction in the cost of compliance even for the domestic firm (due to downward harmonisation) may compensate the same (though the effect may not be very large in magnitude as the cost of compliance for firm 2 (and firm 3) was already lower. So, the ultimate effect on the welfare of country B will depend on the direction and magnitude of change in the producer's surplus. In general, producer's surplus is likely to decrease due to downward harmonisation. For country C (upward harmonisation), there can be an increase in imports if condition (3.14) is fulfilled increasing consumer surplus. However, in that case, producer's surplus may fall due to a fall in price and an increase in compliance cost. So, the ultimate effect will depend on the relative magnitudes.

3.4. *Finding Out the Optimum Strategy*

The standard game-theoretic approach predicts that the mutually beneficial free trade may not be the Nash equilibrium due to unilateral incentive to deviate from the same. At the mutual best response point, countries will go for protectionism, that is, non-cooperation which is a Pareto suboptimal situation. Suppose before harmonisation the welfare situation of countries B and C were (W, W). Assuming both countries have agreed on the harmonisation of standards of n products and to follow a regional or international standard and both can gain in welfare by that. The welfare after harmonisation is $(W + r, W + r)$. Now, if one country

---

[3]Comparing values of q_{1c} before and after harmonisation.

[4]As there will be fall in price in the importing country due to increase quantity from exporting country.

slightly deviates and increases the standard of a product, then it may improve upon the welfare situation by reducing imports resulting in a larger producer's surplus (large enough to outweigh the fall in consumer surplus), and the other country may face a welfare loss due to larger flow of imports resulting in a smaller producer's surplus (small enough to compensate for gain in consumer's surplus). We can express the situation in the following manner:

Assuming $(r - d) < 0$, in Table 8.1, deviation from regional standard becomes the dominant strategy for both countries and hence the Nash equilibrium.

Now, the question is why do the countries stick to the regional standard when there is an incentive to deviate towards differentiated standards. This chapter tries to apply the concept of one-time games and repeated games to explain the same. Given it's a one-shot game, deviation is the dominant strategy for both countries, but as in the case of international trade the interactions are repetitive, deviation may give a short-term gain but a long-term loss. So, each country will decide the strategy depending on present and future gain.

Gain from harmonisation,

$$W + r + ((W + r)/(1 + s)) + ((W + r)/(1 + s)^2) + \dots\dots\dots\dots$$

Gain from deviation,

$$W + r + d + ((W)/(1 + s)) + ((W)/(1 + s)^2) + \dots\dots\dots\dots$$

The optimum strategy for a country will depend upon the discount rate. The lower the discount rate, the higher the chance of harmonisation and vice versa. Apart from the discount rate, if there is a long-run benefit of differentiating standards as differentiated standards lead to the protection of domestic producers leading to import substitution and promotion of domestic industries which has a further positive impact on welfare, then also the country can decide to maintain differentiated standards. In that case, the country may refrain from harmonisation of standards and can go for differentiated standards.

Even if we keep aside the idea of one-shot or repeated interaction, the application of the concept of trust game (Berger et al., 1995) explains the reason why the members of a RTA should go for harmonisation of standards. The element of trust leads to the expectation of repercussion which again results in cooperation,

Table 8.1. Pay-off Matrix.

		Country 2	
		Harmonisation	**Deviation**
Country 1	Harmonisation	$W + r$, $W + r$	$W + r - d$, $W + r + d$
	Deviation	$W + r + d$, $W + r - d$	W, W

that is, sticking to harmonised regional standards. Element of trust is expected to be present more in RTBs for sharing the same geo-climatic and cultural background.

4. Discussion

How the standards impact trade among signatories of RTAs or members of RTBs is an interesting and empirical question. The RTAs provide for specific commitments, whose effect in terms of trade may vary according to the presence of standards and the depth of regulatory cooperation (Grant & Boys, 2012; Lejárraga & Shepherd, 2013). We can see the provision of both regional and national standards (i.e. both harmonised and differentiated standards) within the RTBs, for example, the study conducted by OECD (2015) shows out of 55 sample RTAs, 15% have a specific commitment towards harmonisation. There is evidence of disputes among the signatories of RTAs for contravening the agreed standards, for example, disputes between Canada and the United States regarding the application of safeguard measures by the United States on certain Canadian photovoltaic cells, notwithstanding Canada-United States-Mexico agreement (CUSMA) (Loprespub, 2022). Nevertheless, empirical evidence shows that the number of specific trade concerns raised on standard-related issues is lower for signatories of RTAs. Santeramo and Lamonaca (2022) found that for their sample of RTAs, SPS issues are about four times lower for signatories of RTAs. Overall, 47% of all SPS-specific trade concerns between signatories are reported as being resolved, as compared with 34% of concerns regarding SPS issues between non-signatories. The importance of RTAs has increased many-fold times as in the present global economic scenario where the introduction of the reciprocal tariff policy by the United States is there in place. India is also on her way to talk on the Free trade agreements (FTAs) with trading partners, for example, the United States, EU, the United Kingdom, and New Zealand. So, our discussion on FTAs becomes more relevant as its crucial to find out when a country may deviate from the agreement towards protectionist trade policy.

5. Conclusion

The theoretical framework developed in the research addresses these issues, that is, the reasons behind the differences in optimum responses regarding standard harmonisation among participating countries of RTAs. As the gain (loss) from harmonisation or maintaining differentiated standards will depend on the specific product, cost of production, cost of compliance, and elasticity of demand and supply, the welfare effect of harmonisation will vary across products. Moreover, the short-run and long-run effects of harmonisation will also differ. The present research explains the countries' optimum strategy may be not to harmonise or harmonise the export standards with the RTBs. The application of the concept of trust game (the more the element of trust, the more the chances of cooperation) explains why the members of RTBs may have fewer trade disputes related to standard harmonisation compared to non-members.

References

Berg, J., Dickhaut, J., & McCabe, K. (1995). Trust, reciprocity, and social history. *Games and Economic Behavior*, *10*(1), 122–142. https://dibartolomeo.comunite.it/courses/ee/Berg%20et%20al%201995.pdf

Bhagwati, J. N. (2002). *Free trade today*. Columbia University Press. https://scholarship.law.columbia.edu/books/258

Fabio, S. (2020). *Trade effects of SPS measures in regional trade agreements* [Commissioned papers]. International Agricultural Trade Research Consortium. https://doi.org/10.22004/ag.econ.304053

Grant, J. H. (2013). Is the growth of regionalism as significant as the headlines suggest? Lessons from agricultural trade. *Agricultural Economics*, *44*(1), 93–109. https://doi.org/10.1111/agec.12003

Grant, J., & Boys, K. (2012). Agricultural trade and the GATT/WTO: Does membership make a difference? *American Journal of Agricultural Economics*. *94*, 1–24. https://doi.org/10.1093/ajae/aar087

Grieco, J. (1990). *Cooperation among nations*. Cornell University Press.

Henson, S., & Jaffee, S. (2008). Understanding developing country strategic responses to the enhancement of food safety standards. *The World Economy*, *31*(4), 548–568. https://doi.org/10.1111/j.1467-9701.2008.01095.x

Hoekman, B. (2002). Strengthening the global trade architecture for development: The post Doha agenda. *World Trade Review*, *1*(1), 23–45. https://doi.org/10.1017/S1474745601001046

Keohane, R. O. (1984). *After hegemony: Cooperation and discord in the world political economy*. Princeton University Press.

Lejárraga, I., & Shepherd, B. (2013). *Quantitative evidence on transparency in regional trade agreements. OECD Publishing*. https://doi.org/10.1787/5k450q9v2mg5-en

Loprespub. (2022, July 19). *The Canada–United States–Mexico agreement: State-to-state dispute settlement*. Hill Notes, Quick Reads on Canadian Topics/Dispute Settlement under the USMCA – Congressional Research Service. https://hillnotes.ca/2022/07/19/the-canada-united-states-mexico-agreement-state-to-state-dispute-settlement/

Murina, M., & Nicita, A. (2017). Trading with conditions: The effect of sanitary and phytosanitary measures on the agricultural exports from low-income countries. *The World Economy*, *40*(1), 168–181. https://doi.org/10.1111/twec.12369

OECD. (2011). *Regional trade agreements - Treatment of agriculture*. OECD Food, Agriculture and Fisheries Papers, No. 44. OECD Publishing.

OECD. (2015). *Regional trade agreements and agriculture* [OECD Food, Agriculture and Fisheries Paper No. 79]. OECD Publishing. https://doi.org/10.1787/5js4kg5xjvvf-en

Oye, K. A. (1986). *Cooperation under anarchy*. Princeton University Press.

Sanjuán, A. I., Philippidis, G., Ferrer Pérez, H., & Gracia de Rentería, P. (2023). Empirical insights on the dynamics of SPS trade costs: The role of regulatory convergence and experience in EU dairy trade. *Food Policy*, *119*, 102524. https://doi.org/10.1016/j.foodpol.2023.102524

Santeramo, F. G., & Lamonaca, E. (2022). Standards and regulatory cooperation in regional trade agreements: What the effects on trade? *Applied Economic Perspectives and Policy*, *44*(4), 1682–1701.

Wieck, C., & Rudloff, B. (2020). Bilateral positive integration: Different strategies for regulatory cooperation in the TTIP. In R. Krämer-Hoppe (Eds.), *Positive integration-EU and WTO approaches towards the 'trade and' debate* (pp. 17–34). Springer. https://doi.org/10.1007/978-3-030-46911-1_2

Appendix 1: Production Under Non-harmonised Compliance Cost Which Shows CRS

$$\pi_1 = (a - bq_{1A})q_{1A} + \{a - b(q_{1B} + q_{2B})\}q_{1B} + \{a - b(q_{1C} + q_{3C})\}q_{1C} - E_{1B}q_{1B} - E_{1C}q_{1C} - m(q_{1A} + q_{1B} + q_{1C}) \tag{3.2}$$

$$\pi_B = \{a - b(q_{1B} + q_{2B})\}q_{2B} - mq_{2B} \tag{3.3}$$

$$\pi_c = \{a - b(q_{1C} + q_{3C})\}q_{3C} - mq_{3C} \tag{3.4}$$

Differentiating (3.2) and (3.3) w.r.t. q_{1B} and q_{2B}, respectively, and setting equal to zero First order condition (FOC)

$$\frac{\partial \pi_1}{\partial q_{1B}} = a - 2bq_{1B} - bq_{2B} - E_{1B} - m = 0 \tag{A.1}$$

$$\frac{\partial \pi_B}{\partial q_{2B}} = a - bq_{1B} - 2bq_{2B} - m = 0 \tag{A.2}$$

Solving (A.1) and (A.2),

$$q_{1B} = \frac{(a - 2E_{1B} - m)}{3b} \tag{A.3}$$

Differentiating (3.2) and (3.4) w.r.t. q_{1C} and q_{3C}, respectively, and setting equal to zero (FOC)

$$\frac{\partial \pi_1}{\partial q_{1C}} = a - 2bq_{1C} - bq_{3C} - E_{1C} - m = 0 \tag{A.4}$$

$$\frac{\partial \pi_B}{\partial q_{3C}\cdot} = a - b - q_{1C} - 2bq_{3C} - m = 0 \tag{A.5}$$

Solving (A.1) and (A.2),

$$q_{1c} = \frac{(a - 2E_{1C} - m)}{3b} \tag{A.6}$$

Appendix 2: Production Under Non-harmonised Compliance Cost Which Shows IRS

$$\pi_1(\text{IRS}) = (a - bq_{1A})q_{1A} + \{a - b(q_{1B} + q_{2B})\}q_{1B} + \{a - b(q_{1C} + q_{3C})\}q_{1C} \\ - E_{1B}q_{1B}^{0.5} - E_{1C}q_{1C}^{0.5} - m(q_{1A} + q_{1B} + q_{1C}) \tag{A.7}$$

The profit function for other two firms remains unchanged as the compliance cost is zero for them as per assumption.

Differentiating (A.7) w.r.t. q_{1B} and setting equal to zero (FOC)

$$\frac{\partial \pi_1}{\partial q_{1B}} = a - 2bq_{1B} - bq_{2B} - E_{1B}(0.5)q_{1B}{}^{-0.5} - m = 0 \tag{A.8}$$

Solving (A.8) and (A.2)

$$q_{1B} = \left\{\left((a-m) + \sqrt{(a-m)^2 - (12b^* E_{1B})}\right) / 6b\right\}^2 \tag{A.9}$$

Differentiating (A.7) w.r.t. q_{1C} and setting equal to zero (FOC)

$$\frac{\partial \pi_1}{\partial q_{1C}} = a - 2bq_{1C} - bq_{3C} - E_{1C(-0.05)}q_{1C}^{0.5} - m = 0 \tag{A.10}$$

Solving (A.10) and (A.5)

$$q_{1C} = \left\{\left(a - m) + \sqrt{(a-m)^2 - (12b^* E_{1C})}\right) / 6b\right\}^2 \tag{A.11}$$

Chapter 9

Sectoral Composition and Economic Growth: Evidence From Bangladesh

M. Zakir Saadullah Khan[a] *and Utpal Kumar De*[b]

[a]*Department of Economics, Comilla University, Bangladesh*
[b]*Department of Economics, North-Eastern Hill University (NEHU), India*

Abstract

This study examines the relationship between sectoral composition and economic growth in Bangladesh, employing a comprehensive analysis encompassing both long-run and short-run dynamics. Through statistical techniques including unit root tests, co-integration analysis, and augmented autoregressive distributed lag (ARDL)-bound tests, the study investigates the time series properties of variables and establishes long-run relationships. Findings reveal the significant contributions of various sectors to gross domestic product (GDP) growth, with manufacturing and agriculture playing pivotal roles. Additionally, the non-tradable service sector emerges as a key driver of economic growth, highlighting the importance of sectoral diversity for sustained development. Inter-sectoral linkages exhibit complex dynamics, with tradable and non-tradable service sectors showing positive connections with most sectors, while manufacturing and non-manufacturing sectors display negative linkages with agriculture. The study also examines the indirect effects of sectoral output on GDP growth through mediation by other sectors, emphasising the substantial impact of the non-tradable service sector on overall economic growth. Short-run analysis further corroborates these findings, demonstrating the significant contributions of all sectors to GDP growth. Diagnostic tests confirm the reliability of most inter-sector models, indicating good model fit and reliability. Overall, this study offers valuable insights for policymakers and

Changing Dimensions in Economic Development: Theories and Empirics, 107–128

doi:10.1108/978-1-83708-384-820261009

stakeholders, emphasising the importance of fostering inter-sectoral interconnectedness and efficiency to promote resilient and inclusive economic growth in Bangladesh.

Keywords: Sectoral decomposition; economic growth; shift-share decomposition method; ARDL; mediation model

JEL Codes: C32; E01; E23

Introduction

Bangladesh has sustained remarkable economic growth for over a decade, even amid elevated uncertainty. According to *The Spectator Index 2019*, it stands as one of the fastest-growing economies globally, exhibiting stable economic performance (Nordea, 2020). Since gaining independence in 1971, The economy of Bangladesh has undergone substantial transformation, achieving significant milestones such as poverty reduction and attaining lower-middle-income status in 2015. Notably, it is slated to graduate from the United Nations' (UN) least developed countries list by 2026, demonstrating rapid recovery from the COVID-19 pandemic with GDP growth rates of 6.9% and 7.1% in 2021 and 2022, respectively (The World Bank, 2023).

Despite a track record of growth, the economy of Bangladesh continues to grapple with several socio-economic challenges like unemployment, absolute poverty, and inequality, which have been affecting the efforts of economic transformation. It has been a challenge to manage the economy despite long-term political instability and the influence of global affairs. According to World Bank economists (Baumol et al., 1989; Kuznets, 1963; Rostow, 1971), the economic growth of a country is brought about by changes in the economy's sectoral composition (Linden & Mahmood, 2007), and the shift in the composition of GDP also results in distinct structural changes. The changes in sectoral composition with economic expansion are determined by the respective degrees of elasticity of the sectors (Clark, 1940; Fisher, 1939). However, experiences of changes in sectoral composition with extended GDP over time vary between developed and developing countries (Kaur et al., 2009). Long-run economic progress also depends on policies that encourage resource shifts between sectors, from low-to-high-productivity sectors (Velnampy & Achchuthan, 2013). The process of economic growth in Bangladesh over the period led to a change in sectoral composition – an increase in the share of the industry and service sectors in GDP at the expense of the share of the agriculture sector. On the contrary, transformation of the economic structure might have contributed to the economic growth of Bangladesh, but what 'degree of influence' different sectors has on economic growth (Acemoglu et al., 2012) is an issue of investigation.

The shifting composition of GDP has substantially altered inter-sectoral production and demand linkages (Kaur et al., 2009), underscoring the importance of structural transformation across sectors for policy formulation. Given that each sector's interconnection with the broader economy shapes its influence on growth, policymakers must grasp these dynamics to design policies effectively reallocating resources among sectors, fostering inclusive growth and development (Leal, 2015; Singariya & Naval, 2016). Particularly for emerging economies like Bangladesh, studying sectoral interlinkages is critical as it helps identify and support positive development drivers among sectors, sustain economic growth rates, and address socio-economic challenges. Hence, this study aims to investigate the extent to which various sectors impact Bangladesh's overall economic growth through direct and indirect effects, estimating each sector's contribution to GDP growth both directly and through linkages with other sectors' output growth.

This chapter provides a nuanced analysis of Bangladesh's economy's sectoral composition, focusing on both direct and indirect impacts on GDP growth. Beyond the application of traditional ARDL models, it introduces mediation analysis, a novel approach that reveals how sectoral outputs influence GDP through their linkages with other sectors. This approach provides a holistic understanding of inter-sectoral dynamics, revealing economic dependencies often overlooked in conventional studies. The chapter also applies input–output modelling within a Leontief framework, examining production linkages between sectors, particularly non-tradable services. This combination of mediation analysis, input–output linkages, and direct and indirect sectoral effects offers deeper insights into Bangladesh's economic transformation and provides policy guidance for fostering inter-sectoral efficiencies.

Sectoral Composition and Growth Trends in Bangladesh

Bangladesh's development trajectory exemplifies a departure from absolutes, embracing a strategy of balanced growth (Lewis, 1955; Nurkse, 1953; Rosenstein-Rodan, 1943) as well as unbalanced growth (Hirschman, 1958; Singer, 1958; Streeten, 1959), with a recent shift towards a strategy akin to the Korean model. The initial two decades following independence in 1971 were marked by stagnation, with the average economic growth rate struggling to surpass 4%. However, starting from the 1990s, the growth rate gained momentum, surpassing 6% in the 2000s, exceeding 7% in 2016, and reaching over 8% in 2019. Despite the challenges posed by the pandemic, the economy displayed resilience, achieving a growth rate of 7.1% in 2022.

Table 9.1 delineates the share of six broad sectors – agriculture, manufacturing, non-manufacturing industry, tradable service, non-tradable service, and non-market service sectors – in Bangladesh as per the International Standard Industrial Classification of All Economic Activities (ISIC) Revision 3. The data reveal that the contribution of agriculture to GDP stood at 34.73% in 1976, declined to 28.7% in 1990, further dwindled to 18.38% in 2010, and significantly reduced further to 11.20% in 2022. This consistent decline in share of agriculture was predominantly offset by the manufacturing sector, whose share rose from 8.5% in 1976 to 12% in 1990, 17.2% in 2010, and further to 24.95% in 2022. Additionally, the non-manufacturing industry's share increased from 4.7% in 1976 to

Table 9.1. Sectoral Share to GDP at Constant Prices (Base Year: 2005–2006).

Sector	1976	1980	1990	2000	2010	2020	2022
Agriculture (*a*)	34.73	32.2	28.7	24.6	18.38	13.73	11.2
Manufacturing (*m*)	8.5	10.8	12	14.8	19.2	23.59	24.95
Non-manufacturing industry (*nm*): mining, utilities, and construction	4.7	5.8	8.2	9.9	9.58	11.19	12.61
Tradable services (*t*): transport, storage and communications, financial intermediation, and real estate activities	14.82	19.12	20.07	20.28	20.72	20.58	19.67
Non-tradable services (*nt*): wholesale and retail trade, hotels and restaurants, and other community, social and personal services	34.17	28.28	25.02	24.01	24.67	22.74	21.93
Non-market services (*nk*): public administration and defence, education, health, and social work	3.08	3.8	6.01	6.41	7.45	8.17	9.64

Source: Bangladesh Economic Review and the Bangladesh Bank Time Series Database.

8.2% in 1990, culminating at 12.61% in 2022, with an average growth rate of 2% per decade.

Furthermore, the data indicate that agriculture and the non-tradable service sector were major contributors to GDP during the 1970s and 1980s. But their share gradually declined over time. The diminishing share of these sectors, particularly the rapid decline in share of agriculture, was compensated by the burgeoning manufacturing sector. The manufacturing sector's ascent, from a nominal percentage of GDP, outpaced the share of agriculture by the first decade of the 21st century and nearly matched the highest contributing non-tradable service sector by 2022. Additional sectors mitigating the decrease in agriculture and non-tradable service sectors include non-manufacturing and non-market sectors of the economy. The non-market sector includes activities such as public administration, defence, education, health, and social work, which provide goods and services not intended for market sale or profit generation. Notably, the share of the tradable service sector remained relatively constant over the period. The service sector as a whole emerged as the largest contributor to GDP, maintaining a steady share over time, with a slight increase in the non-market service sector's share at the expense of the non-tradable service sub-sector, while the share of tradable services remained largely unchanged.

Materials and Methods

Conceptual Framework

The shift-share decomposition method serves as a valuable tool in exploring how a country's sectoral composition influences its economic growth. This method aims to dissect the change in an aggregate into structural components, reflecting alterations in the composition of the aggregate and changes within the individual units constituting it (Fagerberg, 2000, p. 400). Considering GDP growth as an aggregate, it can be broken down into components associated with the sectoral composition and growth within different sectors of the economy. Let there be 'i' sectors in the economy, each producing real value-added 'y_i', and the sum of all sector's real value-added making up the real GDP of the economy, denoted as '$y = \sum y_i$'. Economic growth, or the growth of output (g), can be expressed as follows:

$$g = \frac{\Delta y}{y} = \frac{\Sigma \Delta y_i}{\Sigma y_i} = \sum \left[\frac{\Delta y_i}{y_i} \cdot \frac{y_i}{\Sigma y_i} \right] = \sum [g_i . s_i] \tag{1}$$

where 'g_i' represents the real output growth of sector 'i', and 's_i' represents the structural component, indicating the share of sector 'i' output in the aggregate GDP. According to Forster et al. (2019), the effects of these components on GDP growth are termed the 'direct effect', which reflects the sectoral growth (g_i) based on the relative size of the sector (s_i), with larger sectors experiencing more pronounced growth. Additionally, sectors exert 'indirect effects' on GDP growth, representing the influence a sector has on other sectors through linkages in the production of intermediate and investment goods (Forster et al., 2019).

The inter-sector linkages can be depicted by the balance equation of the Leontief input–output model:

$$y_i = \sum y_{ij} \tag{2}$$

where 'y_{ij}' represents the output of sector 'i' used in the production of output in all other 'j' sectors, including the household sector (consumption as final goods). The technical relationship between sectors, denoted by 'a_{ij}', expresses the number of units of output of sector 'i' required to produce one unit of output in sector 'j', and it can be expressed as follows:

$$a_{ij} = \frac{y_{ij}}{y_j}$$

or,

$$y_{ij} = a_{ij} y_j \tag{3}$$

Substituting the value of y_{ij} into Equation (2),

$$y_i = \sum a_{ij} y_j \tag{4}$$

To facilitate the analysis of inter-sector relationships, an implicit assumption of multiplicativity is employed, which allows to represent sectoral outputs in a way that their contributions can be combined multiplicatively rather than additively. This assumption posits that the output of sector i can be thought of as a product of factors that represent the contributions of inputs from all sectors (j).

Under this assumption, the relationship can be approximated as follows:

$$y_i \approx \prod a_{ij} . y_j \tag{5}$$

This formulation suggests that the output of sector i is the product of the technical coefficients a_{ij} and the outputs y_j of other sectors. Thus, by taking the natural logarithm of both sides, the multiplicative relationships can be linearised as:

$$\ln(y_i) = \ln(\prod (a_{ij} . y_j)) \tag{6}$$

Using the property of logarithms that allows the logarithm of a product to be expressed as a sum, Equation (6) can be written as:

$$\ln(y_i) = \sum \left[\ln(a_{ij}) + \ln(y_j) \right] \tag{7}$$

The total differential of the logarithmic value of sector 'i' output, 'y_i', yields the sectoral output growth equation as follows:

$$\mathrm{d}(\ln(y_i) = \sum \left[\mathrm{d}(\ln(a_{ij}) + \mathrm{d}(\ln(y_j) \right]$$

$$\text{or } g_i = \sum \left[\mathrm{d}(\ln(a_{ij}) + g_j \right] \tag{8}$$

Equation (8) elucidates the inter-sector linkages, where the growth of sector 'i' output depends on (i) the growth of all other 'j' sectors outputs (g_j), and (ii) the rate of change in inter-sector technological relationships expressed by '$\mathrm{d}(\ln(a_{ij})$'. These indirect channels illustrate how sectoral growth indirectly influences GDP growth based on a sector's degree of influence in the production of other sectors.

The Model

To empirically examine the contribution of sectoral output to the economic growth of Bangladesh, this study conducts a twofold analysis, involving the estimation of both the 'direct effect' and the 'indirect effect' of changes in sectors (i). In this endeavour, mediation analysis, widely utilised across various academic disciplines, serves as the framework for inferring mechanisms, dissecting the total effects of an independent variable on a dependent variable into 'direct effects' and 'indirect effects' (Vansteelandt & VanderWeele, 2012). The direct effect is defined as the degree to which a change in an exogenous variable produces a change in an endogenous variable without traversing through any other variable(s), while the indirect effect refers to the degree to which a change in an exogenous variable leads to a change in an endogenous variable via an intervening variable or mediator (Turnes & Ernst, 2015).

In this study, the direct effect represents the contribution of sector-*i* output growth to the overall economic growth (*g*), estimated based on the empirical model (9) below. Sector-*i* also contributes to the growth of all other '*j*' sectors' outputs (g_j) that utilise outputs of sector-*i* as inputs, while sector-*j* also contributes to economic growth (*g*). The indirect effect embodies the contribution of sector-*i* output growth to economic growth (*g*) through '*j*' sectors' output growth (g_j), constituting the mediation effects, and is estimated jointly based on empirical models (9) and (10) following the approaches of Judd and Kenny (1981), Sobel (1982), and Baron and Kenny (1986):

$$y = \beta_0 + \beta_i \sum y_i + \beta_j \sum y_j + \mu \tag{9}$$

$$y_i = \alpha_0 + \alpha_j \sum y_j + \varepsilon \tag{10}$$

where 'y_j' denotes the economic size of the contributing sector-*i* and 'y_j' denotes the economic size of the mediation sector-*j* that utilises sector-*i* outputs as inputs. Given inter-sector linkages in production, '$j = i - 1$' in Equation (4), representing the total sectors in the economy, which can be interchangeably used.

According to mediation analysis, the parameters β_j are interpreted as the direct effect and $\alpha_i\beta_j$ as the indirect effect of a unit change in the growth of sector-*i* (exposure) on economic growth, concerning changes in the growth of the mediator sector-*j*, following the product of coefficients approach proposed by Sobel (1982). In the equations, 'μ' and 'ε' denote the stochastic error terms.

To investigate the empirical relationship between sectoral composition and economic growth in Bangladesh, this study classifies the economy into six broad sectors following the ISIC. Therefore,

i,j = {*a* (agriculture), *m* (manufacturing), *nm* (non-manufacturing industries), *t* (tradable services), *nt* (non-tradable services), *nk* (non-market services)} .

The logarithmic transformation of the above functions yields the following empirical econometric models to be evaluated:

$$\ln y = \alpha + \beta_1 \ln y_a + \beta_2 \ln y_m + \beta_3 \ln y_{nm} + \beta_4 \ln y_t + \beta_5 \ln y_{nt} + \beta_6 \ln y_{nk} + \mu \tag{11}$$

$$\ln y_i = \alpha_0 + \alpha_j \sum \ln y_j + \varepsilon \tag{12}$$

where *i*, *j* = {*a*, *m*, *nm*, *t*, *nt*, *nk*}, and *j* excludes *i*-sector.

The Data

Following the ISIC Revision 3, the sectors of Bangladesh in this study are classified into six broad sectors – agriculture (*a*) including forestry and fisheries; manufacturing (*m*); non-manufacturing industry (*nm*) encompassing mining, utilities, and construction; tradable services (*t*) comprising transport, storage and communications, financial intermediation, and real estate activities; non-tradable services (*nt*) involving wholesale and retail trade, hotels and restaurants, and other community, social, and personal services; non-market services (*nk*) encompassing public administration and defence, education, health, and social work.

GDP data are collected from the World Development Indicators (WDI) database,[1] while sectoral GDP data are compiled from various issues of the Bangladesh Economic Review[2] and the Bangladesh Bank time series database spanning the period 1973–2022.[3] All variables in the models are in logarithmic form, and thus, the coefficients of the independent variables provide their respective elasticity values.

The Econometric Methods

The empirical methodology framework for analysing interlinkages between sectors has undergone evolution and expansion over time. Several studies have relied on input–output analysis, following the pioneering work of Chenery and Watanabe (1958) and Hirschman (1958), to examine changes in interlinkages among sectors in production. Econometric methodologies, such as the standard Granger causality tests method, have been employed to identify causal relationships between sectors, while co-integration analysis coupled with error correction modelling (ECM) techniques has been extensively utilised to examine long-run and short-run inter-relationships between sectors. This study employs an econometric modelling exercise using a co-integration test approach, as co-integration tests scrutinise the presence of long-run equilibrium relationships among a set of economic time series variables (Kaur et al., 2009).

Given the nature of the data, the existence of co-integration relationships between variables is examined through three alternative approaches – the Engle–Granger test method proposed by Engle and Granger (1987), the Johansen co-integration test method proposed by Johansen (1988) and subsequently expanded by Johansen and Juselius (1990), and the ARDL co-integration approach or bound test of co-integration approach. The Engle–Granger method is employed

[1]https://databank.worldbank.org/reports.aspx?source=2&country=BGD

[2]https://mof.gov.bd/site/page/44e399b3-d378-41aa-86ff-8c4277eb0990/Bangladesh-Economic-Review-Archive

[3]https://www.google.com/url?sa=t&source=web&rct=j&opi=89978449&url=https://www.bb.org.bd/econdata/time_series_data1972-2023.xlsx&ved=2ahUKEwjZt6zctuyIAxW8XGwGHXtLLRYQFnoECBMQAQ&usg=AOvVaw2QDv_HjAoqmraTBT-BN6oCv

to test for a unique co-integrating relationship, while both the Johansen test and ARDL co-integration test methods can be applied to test for the existence of more than one co-integrating relationship between series that are non-stationary, and to parameterise them into the ECM (Nkoro & Uko, 2016).

The empirical estimation involves a multi-step procedure. The initial step is to test the data series for stationarity since the underlying time series are assumed to be stationary (moving around the mean over time) or at least stationary around a deterministic trend. This study employs the augmented Dickey–Fuller (ADF) unit root test to investigate whether the variables are stationary or not. If the test rejects the null hypothesis of stationarity, indicating non-stationarity of the data series, the analysis proceeds to the second step, which involves co-integration testing.

In an economic model utilising non-stationary time series data, the presence of co-integration between variables indicates the existence of steady-state equilibrium between variables, thus demonstrating long-run relationships. If all underlying data series are non-stationary and integrated of the same order, order one $I(1)$, then Johansen co-integration tests can be applied. However, when the underlying data series used in the model consist of a mix of $I(0)$ and $I(1)$, the ARDL approach to co-integration tests is suggested. If the co-integration tests confirm that the variables of the model are co-integrated, the analysis proceeds to the third step, involving the estimation of the models.

In this step, the appropriate approach is chosen based on the stationarity test results to investigate the interrelationship between the variables in Equations (7) and (8). The ARDL approach is applied if the variables in the model exhibit different orders of integration, while the vector error correction model (VECM) approach is utilised if all the variables are integrated at order one.

Results and Discussion

To investigate the relationship between sectoral composition and economic growth in Bangladesh in the long run, various tests were conducted to examine the time series properties of the variables. These included unit root tests, co-integration analysis, and empirical estimation methods. Here are the key findings and discussions based on the results.

Unit Root Test of the Variables

Table 9.2 presents the results of the ADF unit root tests for the variables of the study. The results indicate that non-manufacturing, tradable services, and non-market services value-added are stationary at the level, while GDP, agriculture, manufacturing, and non-tradable service value-added are stationary at the first difference. This suggests that the order of integration is a mixture of $I(0)$ and $I(1)$, indicating a need to investigate long-run equilibrium relationships using the ARDL-bound test approach.

Table 9.2. ADF Unit Root Tests.

	Level		First Difference		
Variables	**ADF Statistics**	***p*-Value**	**ADF Statistics**	***p*-Value**	***I(d)***
lnGDP	2.483236	1.0000	−4.324792	0.0072	*I*(1)
lnAgri	−1.400815	0.8473	−4.355248	0.0068	*I*(1)
lnManf	0.827628	0.9997	−3.312037	0.0793	*I*(1)
lnN_Manf	−5.378770	0.0003			*I*(0)
lnT_Ser	−4.373240	0.0071			*I*(0)
lnN_Tr Ser	−2.428954	0.3602	−4.068527	0.0145	*I*(1)
lnN_Mkt Ser	−3.507478	0.0525			*I*(0)

Source: Authors' calculation.

The Long-run Co-integration Analysis

The augmented ARDL-bound tests were employed to examine the long-run relationships between GDP and sectoral output, as specified in Equation (9), and inter-sectoral output, as outlined in Equation (10). Prior to this, the determination of the optimal lag length for the ARDL models was conducted using the Schwarz Information Criterion (SIC), which selected a maximum of four lags for all models in the study.

Table 9.3 presents the outcomes of the ARDL-bound test for Equation (9) and each of the six models from Equation (10), with the dependent variables varied individually. The results indicate that the calculated *F*-statistics for all models exceed the upper-bound values at both the 5% and 1% levels of significance, implying the presence of co-integration among the variables in each model. Therefore, the *F*-bound test results confirm the existence of long-run relationships among the variables under examination.

Augmented ARDL Estimates of the Model

To estimate the coefficients representing the long-run relationship between the variables in our models and to draw inferences from these values, we employed the ARDL procedure. Table 9.4 summarises the long-run inter-sector linkages and the relationship between sectoral output and GDP, based on the Bayesian Information Criterion (BIC) selection method with appropriate ARDL models incorporating a 'trend'.

The findings reveal that in the GDP model, the coefficients of sectoral output are statistically significant at the 5% level, indicating that the output of all six sectors (agriculture, manufacturing, non-manufacturing, tradable service, non-tradable service, and non-market service) significantly impacts GDP growth in

Table 9.3. Result of the ARDL Bounding Test

<table>
<tr><th rowspan="3">Equations</th><th colspan="5">Critical Value Bounds of the F-Statistic</th></tr>
<tr><th>Calculated F-Statistics</th><th colspan="2">5%</th><th colspan="2">1%</th></tr>
<tr><th></th><th>I(0) Bound</th><th>I(1) Bound</th><th>I(0) Bound</th><th>I(1) Bound</th></tr>
<tr><td>F_{gdp} (GDP|Agri, Manf, N_Manf, TrSer, N_Tr Ser, N_Mkt Ser)</td><td>5.034</td><td>2.87</td><td>4</td><td>3.6</td><td>4.9</td></tr>
<tr><td>F_{agri} (Agri | Manf, N_Manf, Tr Ser, N_Tr Ser, N_Mkt Ser)</td><td>5.240</td><td rowspan="6">3.12</td><td rowspan="6">4.25</td><td rowspan="6">3.93</td><td rowspan="6">5.23</td></tr>
<tr><td>F_{manf} (Manf|Agri, N_Manf, Tr Ser, N_Tr Ser, N_Mkt Ser)</td><td>6.828</td></tr>
<tr><td>F_{n_manf} (N_Manf|Agri, Manf, Tr Ser, N_Tr Ser, N_Mkt Ser)</td><td>16.818</td></tr>
<tr><td>F_{tr} (Tr Ser|Agri, Manf, N_Manf, N_Tr Ser, N_Mkt Ser)</td><td>15.173</td></tr>
<tr><td>F_{n_tr} (N_TrSer|Agri, Manf, N_Manf, Tr Ser, N_Mkt Ser)</td><td>5.913</td></tr>
<tr><td>F_{n_mkt}(N_MktSer|Agri, Manf, N_Manf, Tr Ser, N_Tr Ser)</td><td>4.886</td></tr>
</table>

Source: Authors' calculation.

the long run. Notably, the manufacturing sector emerges as the most influential contributor to GDP, with a 1% increase in manufacturing output leading to a 0.38% increase in GDP. Following closely, the agriculture sector contributes significantly, with a 1% increase in agricultural output resulting in a 0.21% increase in GDP. Additionally, a 1% increase in non-manufacturing, tradable service, non-tradable service, and non-market service sectors leads to respective increases of 0.05%, 0.065%, 0.16%, and 0.06% in GDP growth during the study period. Among the service sub-sectors, the non-tradable service sector exhibits the highest contribution to GDP, with an output elasticity of 0.16%.

Furthermore, the inter-sector linkages elucidated by the six models indicate intricate relationships among different sectors. For instance, in the agriculture sector model, manufacturing, non-manufacturing, and non-market service sector outputs exhibit long-run negative linkages, while tradable and non-tradable service sector outputs demonstrate positive linkages with agricultural output. Conversely, in the non-market service sector model, only the coefficient of non-manufacturing sector output is statistically significant. Similar patterns of

Table 9.4. Long-run Coefficients From Augmented ARDL Estimates of the Models.

Independent Variables	Dependent Variables						
	lnGDP	lnAgri	lnManf	lnN_Manf	lnTr_Ser	lnN_Tr Ser	lnN_Mkt Ser
ARDL	(1, 0, 4, 2, 0, 0, 3)	(2, 1, 1, 0, 0, 0)	(1, 1, 4, 3, 4, 0)	(4, 0, 3, 4, 2, 0)	(4, 4, 3, 1, 4, 2)	(2, 1, 1, 4, 3, 0)	(1, 0, 3, 4, 0, 4)
lnAgri	0.211* (6.815)		−0.934** (−2.159)	−0.322** (−2.204)	1.637* (5.373)	0.711* (3.829)	0.307 (0.806)
lnManf	0.381* (18.618)	−2.886*** (−1.862)		−0.018 (−0.154)	0.260** (2.395)	0.473* (4.013)	0.254 (1.088)
lnN_Manf	0.051** (2.430)	−0.615* (−2.634)	−3.191* (−3.828)		0.575* (3.316)	1.384* (3.492)	1.971* (2.751)
lnTr_Ser	0.065** (2.089)	0.875* (4.553)	0.820 (1.546)	0.129 (0.678)		−0.690** (−2.070)	−0.273 (−0.526)
lnN_Tr Ser	0.161* (5.732)	0.521* (3.436)	2.629* (4.089)	0.661* (3.496)	−0.760** (−2.504)		−0.467 (−1.290)
lnN_Mkt Ser	0.064* (4.191)	−0.358** (−2.452)	0.891*** (1.854)	0.247 (1.565)	−0.516 (−1.641)	−0.325 (−1.652)	
C	2.630** (10.99)	6.866** (2.603)	1.991 (0.486)	1.572 (0.197)	−1.699 (−1.282)	−2.902 (−1.309)	−5.386 (−1.259)
@ Trend	−0.001 (−0.69)	0.055** (2.381)	0.121* (3.246)	0.034* (3.853)	0.002 (0.119)	−0.057** (−2.419)	−0.072 (−1.720)

Source: Authors' calculation.

Note: Figures in parentheses are *t*-statistics.

*, **, and *** indicate statistical significance at 1%, 5%, and 10% levels, respectively.

significant linkages are observed in the models for the manufacturing, tradable service, and non-tradable service sectors, highlighting the dynamic interactions shaping Bangladesh's economic landscape.

Direct and Indirect Effects of Sectoral Growth on GDP

Table 9.5 elucidates the product of coefficient values representing the contribution of various sectors' output to GDP growth via linkages with other intermediary sectors' output growth. This encapsulates the indirect effects of each sector's output on GDP. Following Sobel's (1982) methodology, these indirect effects are computed as the product of statistically significant coefficients, as outlined in the models of Equations (9) and (10) (Elliott et al., 2017), denoted as $\alpha_j\beta_i$.

The second column of Table 9.4 illustrates the product values of statistically significant coefficients of agriculture output (lnAgri) across different sectoral models derived from Equation (10), alongside the statistically significant coefficients of various sector outputs in the GDP model from Equation (9). This computation corresponds to the product of coefficients found in the second column and third row of Table 9.3. Similarly, the third column of Table 9.4 delineates the product of coefficients from the second column and the fourth row of Table 9.3, portraying the indirect impact of manufacturing sector output (lnManf) on GDP

Table 9.5. Direct and Indirect Effects of Sectoral Output on GDP.

Mediation Sector	**Contributing Sector**					
	lnAgri	**lnManf**	**lnN_Manf**	**lnT_Ser**	**lnN_Tr Ser**	**lnN_Mkt Ser**
lnAgri		−0.061	−0.130	0.185	0.110	−0.076
lnManf	−0.358		−0.122	0.313	1.002	0.340
lnN_Manf	−0.017	−0.001		0.007	0.034	0.013
lnT_Ser	0.107	0.017	0.037		−0.050	−0.034
lnN_Tr Ser	0.114	0.076	0.223	−0.111		−0.052
lnN_Mkt Ser	0.020	0.016	0.126	−0.017	−0.030	
Indirect effects	−0.134 (−0.738)	0.047 (1.038)	0.134 (0.40)	0.376** (1.715)	1.067* (4.151)	0.191 (1.273)
Direct effects	0.211 (6.815)	0.381 (18.618)	0.051 (2.430)	0.065 (2.089)	0.161 (5.732)	0.064 (4.191)
Total effects	0.078	0.429	0.186	0.441	1.228	0.255

Source: Authors' calculation.

Notes: Figures in parentheses of indirect effects present the *z*-statistics using the Sobel test using the delta method and parentheses of direct effects present *t*-statistics.

* and ** indicate statistical significance at 1% and 5% levels, respectively.

across different intermediary sectors. Analogous calculations are conducted for other columns, depicting the indirect effects of respective sector outputs on GDP through diverse intermediary sector outputs.

Judd and Kenny (1981), Sobel (1982), and Baron and Kenny (1986) posited that each α_j and β_i should exhibit statistical significance in Equations (9) and (10). In contrast, Hayes (2017) contends that since the indirect effect is derived as the product of coefficients $\alpha_j\beta_i$, inference should be based on $\alpha_j\beta_i$ rather than individual tests of α_j and β_i. Accordingly, the total indirect effects of various sectors on GDP are calculated as the sum of each sector's respective indirect effect $\alpha_j\beta_i$ (Preacher & Hayes, 2008), represented by the cumulative values in the corresponding column of Table 9.4.

It illustrates the overall indirect impact of each sector on GDP through its connections with other sectors. Remarkably, the agricultural sector's output demonstrates negative indirect effects on GDP, whereas the remaining five sectors exhibit positive indirect effects. Notably, the non-tradable service sector emerges as having the most substantial indirect impact on GDP, with an elasticity value exceeding one, while the other sectors exhibit elasticity values below one.

The figures in parentheses accompanying the total indirect effects denote the significance test statistics, utilising z-statistics as employed by Sobel (1982), Preacher and Hayes (2008), and Turnes and Ernst (2015).

$$z_{ij} = \frac{\sum \alpha_{ji}\beta_{ij}}{\sqrt{\sum[\alpha_{ji}^2 \mathrm{SE}(\beta_{ij})^2 + \beta_{ij}^2 \mathrm{SE}(\alpha_{ji})^2 + 2\sum(\alpha_i\alpha_j \mathrm{SE}(\beta_i\beta_{ij}) + \beta_i\beta_j \mathrm{SE}(\alpha_i\alpha_j)]}} \tag{11}$$

The numerator represents the aggregate of all parallel multi-mediators, that is, the total indirect effect of each sector on GDP growth through other sectors. Meanwhile, the denominator reflects the standard error of the total indirect effect, known as the Sobel test, derived from the multivariate delta method based on a first-order Taylor series approximation (Oehlert, 1992) following Bollen (1987) and Preacher and Hayes (2008).

Since the economy has moved towards industry and services, agriculture's direct contribution to Bangladesh's GDP has probably decreased, as indicated by the negative but negligible coefficient for the sector. Agriculture's share has decreased throughout time, but it may now play a more indirect role by way of linkages with other sectors. The insignificant value of agriculture's direct impact on overall economic growth may also be explained by the sector's slower rate of productivity growth compared to other sectors.

Results indicate that except for the tradable and non-tradable service sectors, the other four sectors do not yield any significant total indirect effects on GDP. Notably, the non-tradable service sector exhibits a significant elasticity value of 1.097, implying that a 1% increase in its output, utilised in other sectors' production as input, results in a 1.097% increase in GDP. Conversely, the insignificant total indirect effects of the other four sectors suggest that, as users of sector output, they do not mediate the effects of a sector on GDP.

The partial regression coefficients (β_i) in Equation (10) signify the direct effect of a sector's output growth on GDP growth, all of which are positively and significantly associated. This implies that all six sectors of the economy contribute significantly and positively to GDP growth. Notably, the manufacturing sector assumes the most prominent role, with an elasticity value of 0.3812, followed by the agricultural sector with an elasticity of 0.2114. Therefore, a 1% increase in manufacturing output results in a 0.38% increase in GDP, while a 1% increase in agricultural output leads to a 0.21% rise.

Analysis of the Short-run Dynamics

Table AI in Appendix delineates the outcomes of the short-run ARDL analysis. The presence of negative signs and values less than one, alongside statistically significant error correction term (ECM_{t-1}) across all models, suggests that any economic shocks experienced are transient, ultimately converging to equilibrium in each scenario. Notably, the speed of adjustment in the overall economy, particularly GDP, is relatively swift. Among the sectors, both the non-manufacturing and agriculture sectors demonstrate a faster convergence to equilibrium compared to the manufacturing sector, tradable service, non-tradable service, and non-market service sectors.

The short-run ARDL findings for GDP align with the long-run results, indicating that all sectors of the economy significantly contribute to GDP growth even in the short term. Specifically, in the short run, the non-tradable service sector significantly impacts all other four sectors, except for the agriculture and non-manufacturing sectors, which only influence the tradable service sector. Additionally, the non-market service sector notably contributes solely to tradable service sector growth. Among the other sectors, agriculture significantly contributes to the growth of the tradable and non-tradable sectors, manufacturing to the tradable and non-market service sectors, and the tradable service sector to manufacturing and non-tradable service sectors in the short run.

Diagnostic Tests of the Models

To evaluate the adequacy and reliability of the estimated ARDL models, diagnostic tests are conducted for seven equations. These tests include the Breusch–Godfrey (B–G) χ^2-test for serial correlation, the Breusch–Pagan–Godfrey (B–P–G) test for heteroscedasticity, the Jarque–Bera test for normality of errors, and the Ramsey Regression equation specification error test (RESET) test for model specifications. *F*-statistics are employed to assess the joint significance of the respective models. To ensure stationary time series, the models are estimated with constant and trend specifications, accounting for the autoregressive process in the time series variables.

Table 9.6 presents the diagnostic test statistics, along with the probability value (*p*-value) in parentheses, for all seven estimated models. It reveals that, except for the GDP growth model, serial correlation exists in all other six inter-sector

Table 9.6. Results of Diagnostic Tests of the Models.

Dep. Var.	B–G Test	B–P–G Test	J–B Test	RESET Test	*F*-Statistics	Model Fitness
lnGDP	**8.419** **(0.015)**	21.76 (0.151)	1.629 (0.443)	2.869 (0.101)	13,322.41 (0.00)	Existence of serial correlation
lnAgri	1.970 (0.3734)	14.153 (0.166)	1.252 (0.535)	1.785 (0.191)	1,693.62 (0.00)	Good fitness
lnManf	2.262 (0.323)	14.996 (0.308)	0.215 (0.898)	1.540 (0.225)	8,407.77 (0.00)	Good fitness
lnN_Manf	2.711 (0.258)	18.340 (0.245)	1.068 (0.586)	0.57 (0.457)	1,371.43 (0.00)	Good fitness
lnT_Ser	2.262 (0.323)	11.755 (0.974)	3.298 (0.192)	3.348 (0.085)	1,972.05 (0.00)	Good fitness
lnN_Tr Ser	1.975 (0.3724)	16.945 (0.458)	0.358 (0.836)	1.021 (0.323)	23,073.64 (0.00)	Good fitness
lnN_Mkt Ser	2.053 (0.358)	19.763 (0.138)	0.15 (0.927)	0.101 (0.753)	1,114.59 (0.00)	Good fitness

Source: Authors' calculation.

Note: Figures in the parentheses represent probability.

models. However, all models exhibit significant *F*-statistic values at a 1% level, indicating their overall significance. Additionally, the estimations for the remaining six models demonstrate good fit regarding serial correlation, heteroskedasticity, normality, and model specifications, thereby being considered well fitted.

Conclusion

The study analysed the relationship between sectoral composition and economic growth in Bangladesh, using statistical techniques like unit root tests, cointegration analysis, and augmented ARDL-bound tests. Results showed that manufacturing and agriculture significantly contributed to GDP growth, with manufacturing having the highest elasticity value. The study also revealed intricate inter-sector linkages, with tradable and non-tradable service sectors having positive relationships with most sectors. The study also highlighted the positive indirect effects of all sectors except agriculture, with the non-tradable service sector having the highest indirect effects.

Compared to earlier research, this study provides a deeper comprehension of the connection between Bangladesh's sectoral composition and economic growth. It focuses on the significance of cross-sectoral relationships, especially the indirect effect of non-tradable services on GDP growth, which has been overlooked in previous studies. Through the use of cutting-edge empirical techniques, such as mediation analysis, the study examines both direct and indirect sectoral contributions, providing a comprehensive understanding of the ways in which different sectors interact. The study also examines long- and short-term dynamics, offering insights into sectoral adjustment following economic shocks. In contrast to the more general approaches suggested by other studies, it also places emphasis on policy proposals aimed to increase sectoral efficiency and inter-connection.

The study provides valuable insights into the sectoral dynamics of Bangladesh's economy, emphasising the necessity of a balanced and diversified sectoral composition for sustained economic growth. Policymakers and stakeholders can leverage these findings to formulate strategies promoting inter-sectoral interconnectedness and efficiency, aiming at promoting a balanced and diversified sectoral composition within the economy. This could involve targeted investments, incentives, or regulatory measures to support the growth of key sectors and enhance inter-sectoral linkages.

Statements and Declarations

Declaration

This is to declare that this chapter has not been published previously (in the form of an abstract or a published lecture or academic thesis) and is not under consideration for publication elsewhere. Its publication is approved by the author and that, if accepted, it will not be published elsewhere in the same form, in English or in any other language, including electronically without the written consent of the copyright holders.

Funding

There is no specific grant received from any agency or sources in the public, commercial, or profit sectors to conduct the study or for this chapter.

Conflicts of Interest/Competing Interests

The authors declare that there is no conflict of interest at all. Additionally, the authors declare that this research was conducted in the absence of any commercial or financial relationships that could be construed as a potential conflict of interest.

References

Acemoglu, D., Carvalho, V. M., Ozdaglar, A., & Tahbaz-Salehi, A. (2012). The network origins of aggregate fluctuations. *Econometrica*, *80*(5), 1977–2016.

Baron, R. M., & Kenny, D. A. (1986). The moderator-mediator variable distinction in social psychological research: Conceptual, strategic and statistical considerations. *Journal of Personality and Social Psychology*, *51*, 1173–1182.

Baumol, W. J., Blackman, S. A. B., & Wolff, E. N. (1989). *Productivity and American leadership: The long view*. MIT Press.

Bollen, K. A. (1987). Total, direct, and indirect effects in structural equation models. *Sociological Methodology*, *17*, 37–69.

Chenery, H. B., & Watanabe, T. (1958). International comparisons of the structure of production. *Econometrica: Journal of the Econometric Society*, *26*(4), 487–521.

Clark, C. (1940). *The conditions of economic progress*. Macmillan and Company Ltd.

Elliott, R. J., Sun, P., & Zhu, T. (2017). The direct and indirect effect of urbanization on energy intensity: A province-level study for China. *Energy*, *123*, 677–692.

Engle, R. F., & Granger, C. W. J. (1987). Co-integration and error-correction: Representation, estimation and testing. *Econometrica*, *55*, 251–276.

Fagerberg, J. (2000). Technological progress, structural change and productivity growth: A comparative study. *Structural Change and Economic Dynamics*, *11*(4), 393–411.

Fisher, A. G. B. (1939). Production, primary, secondary and tertiary. *Economic Record*, *15*(1), 24–38.

Forster, T., Kentikelenis, A. E., Reinsberg, B., Stubbs, T. H., & King, L. P. (2019). How structural adjustment programs affect inequality: A disaggregated analysis of IMF conditionality, 1980–2014. *Social Science Research*, *80*, 83–113.

Hayes, A. F. (2017). *Introduction to mediation, moderation, and conditional process analysis: A regression-based approach* (2nd ed.). Guilford Press.

Hirschman, A. O. (1958). *The strategy of economic development*. Yale University Press. ISBN 0-300-00559-8.

Johansen, S. (1988). Statistical analysis of cointegrating vectors. *Journal of Economic Dynamics and Control*, *12*, 231–254.

Johansen, S., & Juselius, K. (1990). *Some structural hypotheses in a multivariate cointegration analysis of the purchasing power parity and the uncovered interest parity for UK* (No. 90-05). University of Copenhagen.

Judd, C. M., & Kenny, D. A. (1981). Process analysis: Estimating mediation in treatment evaluations. *Evaluation Review*, *5*(5), 602–619.

Kaur, G., Bordoloi, S., & Raj, R. (2009). An empirical investigation of the inter-sectoral linkages in India. *Reserve Bank of India Occasional Papers*, *30*(1), 29–72.

Kuznets, S. (1963). Quantitative aspects of the economic growth of nations: II. Industrial distribution of national product and labor force. *Economic Development and Cultural Change*, *11*(2), 1–80.

Leal, J. (2015). *Key sectors in economic development: A perspective from input-output linkages and cross-sector misallocation* [Working Paper No. 2015-23]. Banco de México.

Lewis, W. A. (1955). *Theory of economic growth*. Allen and Unwin.

Linden, M., & Mahmood, T. (2007). *Long run relationships between sector shares and economic growth: A panel data analysis of the Schengen region*. Economics and Business administration University of Joensuu.

Nkoro, E., & Uko, A. K. (2016). Autoregressive distributed lag (ARDL) cointegration technique: Application and interpretation. *Journal of Statistical and Econometric Methods*, *5*(4), 63–91.

Nordea. (2020). *Bangladesh: Economic and political overview*. Trade Portal, Nordea. https://www.nordeatrade.com/fi/explore-new-market/bangladesh/economical-context?vider_sticky=oui

Nurkse, R. (1953). The problem of currency convertibility today. *Proceedings of the Academy of Political Science*, *25*(3), 61–78.

Oehlert, G. W. (1992). A note on the delta method. *American Statistician*, *46*(1), 27–29.

Preacher, K. J., & Hayes, A. F. (2008). Asymptotic and resampling strategies for assessing and comparing indirect effects in multiple mediator models. *Behavior Research Methods*, *40*(3), 879–891.

Rosenstein-Rodan, P. N. (1943). Problems of industrialisation of eastern and south-eastern Europe. *The Economic Journal*, *53*(210–211), 202–211.

Rostow, W. W. (1971) *The stages of economic growth*. Cambridge University Press.

Singariya, M. R., & Naval, S. C. (2016). An empirical study of inter-sectoral linkages and economic growth in India. *American Journal of Rural Development*, *4*(4), 78–84.

Singer, H. (1958). *The concept of balanced growth and economic development; theory and facts*. University of Texas Conference on Economic Development.

Sobel, M. E. (1982). Asymptotic confidence intervals for indirect effects in structural equation models. In S. Leinhardt (Ed.), *Sociological methodology* (pp. 290–312). American Sociological Association.

Streeten, P. (1959). Unbalanced growth. *Oxford Economic Papers*, *11*(2), 167–190.

The World Bank. (2023). *The World Bank in Bangladesh*. Retrieved December 24, 2023, from https://www.worldbank.org/en/country/bangladesh/overview

Turnes, P. B., & Ernst, R. (2015). Strategies to measure direct and indirect effects in multi-mediator models. *China-USA Business Review*, *14*(10), 504–514.

Vansteelandt, S., & VanderWeele, T. J. (2012). Natural direct and indirect effects on the exposed: Effect decomposition under weaker assumptions. *Biometrics*, *68*(4), 1019–1027. https://doi.org/10.1111/j.1541-0420.2012.01777.x

Velnampy, T., & Achchuthan, S. (2013). Fiscal deficit and economic Growth: A study on Sri Lankan economic perspective. *Developing Country Studies*, *3*, 166–174.

Appendix

Table AI. Short-run Coefficients from Augmented ARDL Estimates of the Models.

Independent Variables	Dependent Variables						
	dlnGDP	dlnAgri	dlnManf	dlnN_Manf	dlnTr_Ser	dlnN_Tr Ser	dlnN_Mkt Ser
ECM_{t-1}	−0.884* (−10.537)	−0.583* (−3.368)	−0.312* (−3.147)	−0.727* (−4.545)	−0.359* (−4.20)	−0.241* (−3.183)	−0.370* (−4.442)
$dlnAgri_t$	0.187* (6.397)		−0.045 (−0.300)	−0.234 (2.738)	0.284* (3.718)	0.070*** (1.919)	0.114 (0.821)
$dlnAgri_{t-1}$		0.038 (0.234)			−0.067 (−0.813)		
$dlnAgri_{t-2}$					0.035 (0.481)		
$dlnAgri_{t-3}$					−0.249* (−3.519)		
$dlnManf_t$	0.267* (10.425)	−0.286 (−0.193)		0.379 (2.432)	0.082 (1.221)	0.228 (1.209)	0.282*** (1.902)
$dlnManf_{t-1}$	−0.045 (−1.268)			0.246 (3.060)	−0.223** (−2.345)		−0.342*** (−1.791)
$dlnManf_{t-2}$	0.039 (1.493)			0.199 (−2.017)	0.192** (2.558)		0.426* (2.989)
$dlnManf_{t-3}$	−0.074* (−4.402)						

$dlnN\_Manf_t$	0.0341	−0.212**	−0.343***	−0.185	−0.101	0.121*	0.442*
	(1.623)	(−2.375)	(−1.815)	(−1.240)	(−1.071)	(4.495)	(2.946)
$dlnN\_Manf_{t-1}$	0.142*		0.198	−0.210		−0.070	0.348**
	(4.449)		(1.123)	(−1.250)		(1.887)	(2.602)
$dlnN\_Manf_{t-2}$			−0.234***	−0.218		0.022	−0.447*
			(−1.718)	(−2.051)		(−1.217)	(−5.027)
$dlnN\_Manf_{t-3}$			0.581*			−0.140	−0.264*
			(5.217)			(0.845)	(−3.496)
$dlnTr\_Ser_t$	0.058**	0.510	0.202	−0.182	0.168	−0.417*	−0.101
	(1.997)	(4.516)	(0.624)	(−0.735)	(1.117)	(−6.337)	(−0.554)
$dlnTr\_Ser_{t-1}$			1.535*	1.242	−0.266**	−0.339	
			(3.355)	(7.245)	(−2.477)	(−5.134)	
$dlnTr\_Ser_{t-2}$			−1.135*	−0.145	−0.294*	0.279*	
			(−3.587)	(−0.755)	(−3.192)	(−3.903)	
$dlnTr\_Ser_{t-3}$				−0.296			
				(−3.157)			
$dlnN\_Tr\ Ser_t$	0.142*	−0.304	1.931 *	0.767***	−0.942*		−0.981*
	(4.215)	(−2.238)	(5.042)	(1.988)	(−8.435)		(−3.710)
$dlnN\_Tr\ Ser_{t-1}$			0.837	0.562***	1.632*	0.217*	1.206*
			(1.645)	(1.814)	(5.943)	(4.432)	(4.608)
$dlnN\_Tr\ Ser_{t-2}$			−1.411		−0.841*		−0.265
			(−3.184)		(−6.045)		(−1.001)

(Continued)

Table AI. (*Continued*)

Independent Variables	Dependent Variables						
	dlnGDP	**dlnAgri**	**dlnManf**	**dlnN_Manf**	**dlnTr_Ser**	**dlnN_Tr Ser**	**dlnN_Mkt Ser**
dlnN_Tr Ser_{t-3}			0.621 (2.888)		0.212** (2.498)		−0.549* (−3.125)
dlnN_Mkt Ser_{t}	0.108* (4.215)	−0.209 (−2.919)	0.278 (2.394)	0.179 (1.582)	−0.087 (−0.936)	−0.078 (−1.652)	
dlnN_Mkt Ser_{t-1}	−0.004 (−0.138)				0.348* (5.127)		
dlnN_Mkt Ser_{t-2}	0.056* (2.985)						

Source: Authors' calculation.
Note: Figures in parentheses are *t*-statistics.
*, **, and *** indicate statistical significance at 1%, 5%, and 10% levels, respectively.

Chapter 10

Growth Vis-à-Vis Development: Are the Countries Converging or Diverging Over Time?

Debashis Mazumdar[a] *and Mainak Bhattacharjee*[b]

[a]*The Heritage College, Kolkata, West Bengal, India*
[b]*Loreto College, Kolkata, West Bengal, India*

Abstract

The persistently large income gap between the developed countries (DCs) of the North and relatively less developed and developing countries (LDDCs) of the South is one of the most notable features of the international community over the last few decades. Different research works in this field have indicated that the average annual growth rate of per capita income (PCI) in LDDCs has been faster compared to that in DCs particularly since early 1990s indicating a sign of convergence in the growth process. However, the absolute gap between the DCs and LDDCs in terms of per capita Gross national product (GNP) has widened over years. In this backdrop, this chapter is an attempt to enquire into the dynamics of the gap between the developed, developing and less developed parts of the world over the period from 1990 to 2023. The beta-convergence analysis, using dynamic panel data regression, leaves emphatic evidence of conditional convergence, rather than the absolute, implying a case of typical club convergence, where the countries sharing similar conditions in health, education and prevalence of absolute poverty tend to converge in terms of PCI. This chapter essentially points out that a mere convergence in the growth rate does not necessarily translate into the narrowing of income and development gap, based on the selected 150 countries across the globe, classified with respect to income level, high, middle and low and four broad regions, namely, Latin American Caribbean (LAC), Sub-Saharan

Changing Dimensions in Economic Development: Theories and Empirics, 129–140

doi:10.1108/978-1-83708-384-820261010

Africa (SSA), Middle East and North Africa (MNA) and East Asia Pacific (EAP), epitomising the developing world.

Keywords: Economic growth; economic development; globalisation; absolute and club convergence; development gap

JEL Codes: O40; O10; F6; O47; O1

1. Introduction

The persistently large income gap between rich countries of the North and relatively poor countries of the South is one of the most notable features of the international community over the last few decades. Even casual observation often suggests the presence of vast differences in living standards across countries. In particular, there is a sharp divide between developed industrialised countries and the less developed or developing countries. The economic difference between the two groups of countries is not merely a difference of wealth. There are also a number of common structural characteristics, such as underdeveloped financial markets, poor infrastructure and a more pervasive role of the government in the economy, which distinguish the former from the latter. Moreover, 'the rich country–poor country' dichotomy extends into the social and political realms as well, with the rich countries generally enjoying greater political stability and social peace.

Just as inequality among the citizens of a country breeds tension and conflict, inequality among the countries of the world constitutes an obstacle to international harmony and understanding. On many international issues, developing countries and DCs form antagonistic blocs. For example, in the negotiations preceding the birth of the World Trade Organization (WTO) in 1995, developing countries vehemently opposed efforts by DCs to open discussions about labour standards. The two blocs also clash regularly over environmental issues, where DCs tend to call for more strict controls, as well as human rights issues. While we should not exaggerate the seriousness of the conflict between the two groups of countries, there is an unmistakable global divide along wealth lines.

Most of the LDDCs have a low PCI base in comparison with the DCs. So, a pertinent question that naturally evolves in the process of economic growth is whether these LDDCs can catch up with the income growth as well as the level of PCI attained by the DCs. The phenomenon of the poor countries catching up with rich countries over time is called 'convergence' in economic jargon. Some economists often argue that though some less developed or developing countries lag behind the DCs in this growth process, there is every possibility of catching up of the higher growth trajectory by the LDDCs in the long run. So, the growth process across nations would show a tendency to converge over time. Such convergence in the growth process is supposed to be made possible through the use of better technology by the LDDCs and a shift of resources from the slow-growth sector to the high-growth sector in an economy. It is also assumed that the marginal productivity of capital in LDDCs would be much higher than that in DCs because the usage of capital in the production process remains at a low level in LDDCs.

There is no doubt that some of the LDDCs have experienced spectacular improvement in their income growth particularly during the last two decades leading to some signs of growth convergence between the DCs and the LDDCs. But despite such convergence in economic growth, there still remain several indications of development divergence between these two groups of nations.

2. Literature Review

During the 1980s, some research papers (Baumol, 1986; Bradford, 1988) aimed at testing whether poor countries tended to grow faster than the rich ones using β-convergence models. This convergence is usually conditional because countries have different structural characteristics (propensity to save, population growth rate, technological progress, etc.). It is conditional on specific policies and institutional arrangements that have proved hard to identify and implement (Rodrik, 2011).

Some seminal works on convergence, viz., β-convergence, have been done during 1990s and afterwards by economists such as Barro (1991), Barro and Sala-i-Martin (1992, 1995), Mankiw et al. (1992), Sala-i-Martin (1996), Verspagen (1995), Islam (1995), Evans (1997), Lee et al. (1998), Bond et al. (2001), Tsangarides (2001), Hoeffler (2002), Lee and McAleer (2004), etc. some of which indicated that economies converged on an average annual rate of 2% closing the gap between present levels of income and balanced growth levels. Some of these studies using panel data find even higher rates of β-convergence. While analysing the evidence of β-convergence in the United States using county-level data covering the period 1970–1998 and containing over 3,000 cross-sectional observations, Young et al. (2008) demonstrated that β-convergence is a necessary but *not* sufficient condition for σ-convergence. This view, however, had already been acknowledged earlier by Barro and Sala-i-Martin (1992).

The importance of β-convergence was emphasised by Friedman (1992) and Quah (1993) since both of them suggested that β-convergence speaks directly as to whether the distribution of income across economies is becoming more equitable or not.

Another study (Sarkar, 1999) shows that the growth pattern during the period 1960–1990 did not show any sign of convergence. A typically poor country in the early 1960s did not experience a higher real growth. Hence, there is no catching up of the standard of living of rich countries by poor countries. This is true for the different regions of the South (Africa, Asia and Latin America) and for the South as a whole.

Similarly, the study made by Berry et al. (2014) shows that during 1960–2009, nation-states in the global system have not evolved significantly closer (or more similar) to one another along a number of dimensions (viz., economic, demographic, knowledge, financial and political). They have found evidence that subcomponents of the global system, both trade blocs and core/periphery components, have become more distant from one another over time without any significant indication of convergence.

While analysing the future course of such convergence, Rodrik (2011) has pointed out that economic growth in the developing nations should not depend on growth in the advanced economies but on the difference in the productivity levels of the two groups of countries (i.e. on the convergence gap). The rate at which the lagging economies catch up is determined by their ability to absorb ideas and knowledge from the technology frontier. However, this convergence process may fail for many reasons. For instance, a combination of exogenous factors and policy circumstances may discourage firms and entrepreneurs in less developed and developing nations from undertaking productivity-enhancing investments. Hence, a special emphasis has been given on pro-active policies of the government that foster structural transformation and spawn new industries for having a sustained process of convergence.

Some studies reveal (Gnangnon, 2019) that the trade policy space exerts a positive and significant effect on transitional convergence, and the greater the trade policy space, the higher is the transitional convergence. The transitional convergence is defined as the catch up of a country's real PCI with the world's average real PCI. This empirical analysis covering 150 countries from 1995 to 2015 shows that although the trade policy space exerts a positive impact on economic growth, this positive effect depends on countries' structural policies.

Another study (Johnson & Papageorgiou, 2020) has examined the record of cross-country growth over the past 50 years and tried to show whether developing countries had made progress on closing the income gap between their PCIs and those in the advanced economies. This study indicates that, as a group, they have not been able to close this gap.

While analysing the real convergence in economic growth in Malta with that of other EU27 economies post-financial crisis, another study (Micallef, 2020) identifies three important lessons for a country's convergence process: (i) the perils associated with rapid growth driven by the accumulation of imbalances; (ii) the need for a flexible adjustment process following an economic shock; and (iii) the European Union (EU) and euro area memberships are no panacea for real convergence, without institutions that are conducive to technological adoption and productivity growth.

Convergence in economic growth could not, however, ensure the convergence in the process of economic development between nations. This process of economic development incorporates various factors which influence the quality of living of the common people in any country (say, pattern of income distribution, health, education, nutritional facilities, etc.).

Some economists are of the opinion that differences in current standards of living are the result of past differences in rates of economic growth. The principal determinant of global inequality then is the extent to which countries converge or diverge from the income levels of the developed world (Frieden, 2001).

Economists like Thirlwall (2006), Ocampo and Vos (2008), Milanovic (2009, 2012), Meier and Rauch (2010) and Todaro and Smith (2012) have addressed this question and explained different aspects of international and global inequalities.

Several reports of the World Bank (2012) and UNDP (2013, 2014) have also dealt with different aspects of global inequality in the process of economic growth and development. The striking contrasts in the global economy and the differences in the initial conditions in the development process of DCs and LDDCs have been indicated in these studies. While explaining the reasons for such development gap, some of these works point to the persistently low levels of technological efficiency as the proximate source of the gap between the rich and poorer countries (Hulten & Isaksson, 2007).

Some studies have clearly indicated that the gap between rich and poor has widened particularly during the era of economic globalisation (Cornia, 2003; Elmawazini & Nwankwo, 2013; OECD, 2008; Ortiz & Cummins, 2011; Sikdar, 2006).Though income inequality is a critical factor in determining other non-income outcomes of human well-being (such as health, nutrition and education), it is not the only factor-driving inequalities in non-income outcomes (Sen, 2003). Research has consistently pointed to the role of institutions (say, inefficient or inadequate service delivery systems), governance failures (such as corruption and absence of the rule of law) and public policy shortcomings (e.g., biases in public expenditure in favour of the privileged class) as key drivers of inequalities in non-income dimensions of material well-being (UNDP, 2013).

3. Objective of the Study

The study is essentially intended to enquiring the relevance of the convergence projection of the neo-classical growth doctrine among the countries in terms of PCI in the long run. Hence, in this chapter, our main objective is to find out whether the growth rates of PCI in the DCs and the LDDCs have converged over time and whether that growth convergence has been accompanied by a substantial reduction in North–South gap in living standards over the last few decades or not.

So, we want to focus our attention to different aspects of 'development divergence' in the backdrop of 'growth convergence'. That is, have the poor countries been catching up with rich countries in recent times? Is such a convergence in the process of economic growth necessarily implies a convergence in the process of economic development across nations? This is an important issue in development economics because the polarisation of the world into two disparate components does not bode well for international peace or prosperity, especially in the long run. Conversely, our objective is to get an answer to the question that can we expect an increasingly more equitable distribution of resources among the nations to contribute substantially towards the formation of a more stable international order? This chapter is but a modest attempt to review these aspects.

4. Data and Methodology

The study is based on secondary data excerpted from World Development Report on 150 countries across the world classified with respect to income as high-income countries (HICs), middle-income countries (MICs), low-income countries (LICs) (as World Bank Nomenclature) and with respect to regions, LAC, SSA, MNA and EAP. Disparity in the annual average growth rate of real gross national income (GNI) per capita has been demonstrated for the period from 1990 to 2021. β-convergence has been performed on the countries included in the groups aforementioned, for the period 1990–2021 on (i) real GNI per capita, (ii) life expectancy at birth, (iii) mean years of schooling, headcount ratio and (iv) inequality indicator (as defined by the ratio of the income share of top 20th percentile to the same for bottom 20th percentile). Conditional β-convergence test has been conducted on (i), having considered (ii), (iii) and (iv) as controls.

5. Inter-group Dynamics in Per Capita Real Gross Domestic Product (GDP) Growth Post-globalisation

We have already stated that convergence in the process of economic growth connotes faster growth in LDDCs than those of DCs. To start with, we have measured the average annual growth rate of real PCI (viz., GNI per capita at 2005 US$ for the period 1960–2013 and at 2015 US$ for the period 2014–2023) for nine different subgroups of economies, viz., the HICs, LICs, developing countries of LAC, SSA, MNA and EAP over the time span 1990–2023. It is observed that while the average annual growth rate of real PCI has shown a declining trend in HICs (Table 10.1), the LIC group has shown significant upturn in their respective PCI growth rates during 1990–2013, and these growth rates during 2000–2013 have been higher than those achieved by the HIC group. Such an upward trend in PCI growth is also observed for subgroups LAC, SSA, MNA and EAP during 1990–2013. In fact, all these subgroups indicated a higher growth rate of PCI compared to that of the HIC group during 2000–2013 (Table 10.1). However, during 2014–2023, the PCI growth in subgroups like MNA and Less developed country (LDC) remained higher than that of HICs.

A close look at the deviations of the PCI growth rate of each subgroup of economies from that of the HIC group indicates that these growth rates are divergent in nature, that is, the growth rate of PCI in the HIC group surpassed the same attained by the other subgroups such as LAC and Low middle income

Table 10.1. Average Annual Growth Rate of Real PCI in Different Subgroups of Economies During 1990–2023.

Period	Average Annual Growth Rate (%) of Real PCI						
	HIC	LAC	LIC	SSA	MIC	MNA	EAP
1990–2000	1.93*	1.4*	0.23	−2.0	1.86*	1.39*	7.15*
2000–2013	1.0*	2.3*	3.3*	2.56*	4.71*	3.28*	8.39*
2014–2023	0.46**	−0.33***	0.2	−0.33*	0.94*	0.63**	2.16*

Sources: World Development Indicators (2015, 2023), World Bank (compiled by the authors).
***, ** and * significant at 1%, 5% and 10% levels, respectively.

Table 10.2. Inter-group Deviations in PCI Growth During 1990–2023.

Deviation in PCI Growth	1990–2000	2001–2013	2014–2023
PCIHIC − PCILAC	−0.53	−1.3	0.94
PCIHIC − PCILIC	−1.7	−2.3	1.89
PCIHIC − PCISSA	−3.93	−1.56	1.05
PCIHIC − PCIMNA	−0.54	−2.28	−0.04
PCIHIC − PCIEAP	5.22	−7.39	1.34
PCIHIC − PCIMIC	−0.4	−3.23	1.28

Source: Compiled by the authors based on Table 10.1.

country (LMC) during 1960–1970 (Table 10.2). While a positive difference implies such divergent nature in this growth process, a negative difference would imply a convergence in this process. Let the average annual growth rate in real PCI in the HIC group be denoted by G_{HIC} and that of any other subgroup (say, non-HIC group) be denoted by G_{NHIC}. Now, a convergence in this growth requires that $(G_{\text{HIC}} - G_{\text{NHIC}}) < 0$. Here, we can assume that if $|G_{\text{HIC}} - G_{\text{NHIC}}| > 1$, that would signify a strong convergence while $0 < |G_{\text{HIC}} - G_{\text{NHIC}}| < 1$ would signify a weak convergence. According to this criterion, there have been indications of divergence during 1990–2000 (except for the EAP group) (Table 10.2). However, there are signs of strong convergence in six non-HIC subgroups during 2000–2013. Nonetheless, the period from 2014 to 2023 saw a reversal of converging dynamics for the subgroups, except, MNA.

6. Absolute and Conditional Convergence Test

This section presents the standard *b*-convergence tests to look into if the countries happened to converge with each other in per capita GNI (at purchasing power parity [ppp] $) within and across the income and regional groups considered in the present study over the period from 1990 to 2023. The evidence of absolute or conditional convergence is to be traced in the persistence of inter-group variation of PCI among the countries which in turn resonates with the disparity among the countries in achievement of economic development as indicated by life expectancy at birth, education and poverty incidence. Further, it will help bring into glare the possibility of income and regional bias in the inter-country difference in economic development as what remains as predominant snag upon sustainable development all around the globe. The present line of study thus consists in dynamic fixed-effect panel data regression analysis, with log-transformed per capita GNI as the dependent variable, while independent variables being one-period lagged-dependent variable, life expectancy at birth, mean years of schooling, headcount ratio and seven dummy variables (three for income groups, namely, high, middle and low, and four for the regional groups, namely, LAC, MNA, SSA and EAP, as articulated in the following table). However, in order to rule out the possibility of inconsistency and multi-collinearity in regression, the aforementioned regression has been specified with dependent and independent variable in differenced form and the dummy variables, of which, however, only two out of the three and three out of the four, have been included. Here, to elicit the evidence of conditional convergence vis-à-vis absolute, within and between the income groups and regional groups, we have estimated the above-mentioned dynamic panel data model in four distinct ones as delineated in Table 10.3. As emergent, from Model 1, there had been significant divergence in per capita GNI among counties within and between the groups (with respect to income and region) over the period from 1990 to 2023, since the coefficient of lagged per capita GNI is positive and statistically significant. Moreover, the positive coefficient of dummy I_1 indicates a widening gap between HICs, on the one hand, and MICs and LICs, on the other hand. While the negative coefficient of dummy I_2 leaves a much striking implication that while the gap between the MICs and the LICs had narrowed over the specified period of time, yet the MICs might have escalated their difference from the high-income counterparts. Alternatively, it indicates that MICs have had their gap from HICs being widened up, yet they might have worsened off relative to the LICs. This is much to note in this regard, in as much as it

Table 10.3. Test of Absolute and Conditional Convergence.

Independent Variable	**Model 1**	**Model 2**	**Model 3**	**Model 4**
Intercept	1.006*	1.0045**	0.01645**	0.1561
Lagged per capita GNI	1.0213**	−0.0129***	1.0559*	−0.1491***
First differenced life expectancy at birth	–	1.0096**	–	0.1172***
First differenced mean years of schooling	–	0.0346**	–	0.2086***
First differenced headcount ratio	–	(−)0.1952**	–	−0.0602***
I_1 (dummy for high-income group)	0.0619**	0.0054**	–	–
I_2 (dummy for middle-income group)	(−)0.0235**	−0.0162**	–	–
R_1 (dummy for LAC)	–	–	0.0113***	0.0019**
R_2 (dummy for SSA)	–	–	−0.0109***	0.0026**
R_3 (dummy for MNA)	–	–	−0.0241**	−0.0005**
F-statistic	25.6123**	67.4578***	71.2783**	77.8043***

Source: Authors' computation from World Bank Data.

***, ** and * indicate significance at 1%, 5% and 10% levels, respectively.

resonates closely with the missing middle phenomenon where the contraction in the middle layer makes it almost indistinguishable from the bottom layer. Moving forward to Model 2, the negative coefficient of lagged per capita GNI indicates countries that had been catching up or had come closer to one another are those which share a more or less a similar or comparable profile in terms of health condition, educational attainment and persistence of poverty and point the case of conditional convergence among them. The coefficients of other health, education and poverty indicators are intuitive, and these together imply that the degree of convergence being directly related to life expectancy at birth, mean years of schooling, while indirectly with headcount ratio. The smaller magnitudes of the coefficients of the income dummies suggest that the average income gap between HICs and others had been relatively low after having controlled for the difference in health, education and so between MICs and LICs. This apart, there is a much clear evidence of club convergence, especially among the HICs. The other two models, namely Model 4 and Model 5, reverberate the same picture as revealed by the previous model.

Comparing between the estimates of the coefficient of lagged per capita GNI of Model 4 and Model 5, it becomes clear that developing countries in terms of health, education and poverty conditions tended to converge and while those which are dissimilar had been divergent. Moreover, the case of club convergence may be elicited for the regional country groups, LAC and SSA.

6. Conclusion

This study shows that there remains a definite indication of conditional β-convergence in the growth rate of per capita GNI across different groups of nations over the period 1990–2023 which implies that the average annual growth rates of real PCI in less developed and developing nations have been higher than that achieved by the developed nations during that period. Thus, higher growth rates of PCI in LICs and lower MICs in comparison with those of HICs can substantially bring down the income disparities between countries that can augur well for the world economic development in the long run.

However, despite such indications of growth convergence, there still remain areas of development divergence between the LICs and HICs. These divergences become evident in the form of international and global inequality in the distribution of income, uneven outcomes in education, health and nutrition between those groups of nations and a divergence in terms of human development index over the last few decades. Hence, we need a suitable policy frame both at the global and local levels that can suitably reduce this dichotomy in near future. The supply-side approach to growth economics put greater emphasis on higher economic growth as an effective policy parameter. In that approach, it is believed that growth would automatically 'trickle down' and benefit a greater part of the common people in a society. However, economists opposing such a view find that higher economic growth cannot guarantee higher well-being for the common people in a country characterised by highly unequal distribution of income-generating assets.

Thus, a policy debate is often triggered by such conflicting approaches to growth dynamics.

For instance, while Amartya Sen (1999) believes that India should invest more in its social infrastructure to boost the productivity of its people and thereby raise growth, Jagdish Bhagwati argues that only a focus on economic growth can generate enough resources required for investing in social sector schemes (Bhagwati & Panagariya, 2013). Investing in health and education to improve human capabilities is central to Sen's scheme of economic development. According to Amartya Sen, if the government policy fails to boost up such investments, inequality will widen, and the growth process itself will be affected. In his own words,

> Growth of GNP or of individual incomes, can, of course, be very important as means to expanding freedoms enjoyed by the members of the society. But freedoms depend also on other determinants, such as social and economic arrangements (for example, facilities for education and health care) as well as political and civil rights (for example, the liberty to participate in public discussion and scrutiny). Development requires the removal of major sources of dependency: poverty as well as tyranny, poor economic opportunities as well as systematic social deprivation, neglect of public facilities as well as intolerance or over activity of repressive states. (Sen, 1999, pp. 1–2)

Thus, it is much imperative that the policymakers should strive for some feasible channels through which pro-growth factors can be made pro-developmental.

References

Barro, R. J. (1991). Economic growth in a cross-section of countries. *Quarterly Journal of Economics, 106*(2), 407–444.

Barro, R. J., & Sala-i-Martin, X. (1992). Convergence. *Journal of Political Economy, 100*(2), 223–251.

Barro, R. J., & Sala-i-Martin, X. (1995). Convergence across states and regions. *Brookings Papers on Economic Activity, 1*, 107–182.

Baumol, W. J. (1986). Productivity growth, convergence, and welfare: What the long-run data show. *American Economic Review, 76*(5), 1072–1085.

Berry, H., Guillen, M. F., & Hendi, A. S. (2014). Is there convergence across countries? A spatial approach. *Journal of International Business Studies, 45*, 387–404. https://doi.org/10.1057/jibs.2013.72

Bhagwati, J., & Panagariya, A. (2013). *Why growth matters: How economic growth in India reduced poverty and the lessons for other developing countries*. Public Affairs.

Bond, S. R., Hoeffler, A., & Temple, J. R.W. (2001). *Estimation of empirical growth models* [Discussion Paper No. 3048]. CEPR.

Bradford, D. J. (1988). Productivity growth, convergence, and welfare: Comment. *American Economic Review, 78*(5), 1138–1154.

Cornia, G. A. (2003). *The impact of liberalization and globalization on income inequality in developing and transitional economies* [Working Paper No. 14]. International Labour Office.

Elmawazini, K., & Nwankwo, S. (2013). Globalization and income gap between rich and poor nations. *Economic Issues, 18*(2), 19–40. http://www.economicissues.org.uk/Files/2013/213Elmawazini.pdf

Evans, P. (1997). How fast do economies converge? *Review of Economics and Statistics, 36*, 219–25.

Frieden, J. (2001). Inequality, causes and possible futures. *International Social Science Review, 2*(1), 33–40. http://scholar.harvard.edu/files/jfrieden/files/nequalitiesfutures_0.pdf

Friedman, M. (1992). Do old fallacies ever die? *Journal of Economics Literature, 30*, 2129–2132.

Gnangnon, S. K. (2019, October). Does multilateral trade liberalization help reduce poverty in developing countries? Oxford Development Studies, *47*(4), 435–451.

Hoeffler, A. (2002). The augmented Solow model and the African growth debate. *Oxford Bulletin of Economics and Statistics, 64*(2), 135–158.

Hulten, C. R., & Isaksson, A. (2007). *Why development levels differ: The sources of differential economic growth in a panel of high and low income countries*. https://www.unido.org/fileadmin/user_media/Publications/Pub_free/Why_development_levels_differ.pdf

Islam, N. (1995). Growth empirics: A panel data approach. *Quarterly Journal of Economics, 110*(4), 1127–1170.

Johnson, P., & Papageorgiou, C. (2020, March). What remains of cross-country convergence? *Journal of Economic Literature, 58*(1), 129–175.

Lee, K., Pesaran, M. H., & Smith, R. (1998). Growth empirics: A panel data approach – A comment. *Quarterly Journal of Economics, CXIII*, 319–323.

Lee, K. L., & McAleer, M. (2004). Convergence and catching up in ASEAN: A comparative analysis. *Applied Economics, 36*(2), 137–153.

Mankiw, N. G., Romer, D. H., & Weil, D. N. (1992). A contribution to the empirics of economic growth. *Quarterly Journal of Economics, 107*, 407–437.

Meier, G. M., & Rauch, J. E. (2010). *Leading issues in economic development* (8th ed., pp. 127–131). Oxford.

Micallef, B. (2020). Real convergence in Malta and in the EU countries after the financial crisis. *Journal of Economic Integration, 35*(2), 215–239. https://www.jstor.org/stable/26917202

Milanovic, B. (2009). Global inequality and the global inequality extraction ratio: The story of the past two centuries (Policy Research Working Paper 5044). World Bank.

Milanovic, B. (2012). Global inequality recalculated and updated: The effect of new PPP estimates on global inequality and 2005 estimates. *Journal of Economic Inequality, 10*, 1–18.

Ocampo, J. A., & Vos, R. (Eds.). (2008). *Uneven economic development*. Orient Longman.

OECD. (2008). *Growing unequal? Income distribution and poverty in OECD countries*. OECD Publishing. http://www.oecd.org/els/soc/41494435.pdf

Ortiz, I., & Cummins, M. (2011). *Global inequality: Beyond the bottom billion: A rapid review of income distribution in 141 countries*. UNICEF. http://www.unicef.org/socialpolicy/files/Global_Inequality.pdf

Quah, D. T. (1993). Galton's fallacy and the convergence hypothesis. *Scandinavian Journal of Economics, 95*, 427–443.

Rodrik, D. (2011). *The future of economic convergence* [NBER Working Paper No. 17400, pp. 1–49]. National Bureau of Economic Research.

Sala-i-Martin, X. (1996). Regional cohesion: Evidence and theories of regional growth and convergence. *European Economic Review, 40*, 1325–1352.

Sarkar, P. (1999). Theory of convergence and real income divergence 1950–92. *Economic and Political Weekly, 34*(8), 500–504. http://www.jstor.org/stable/4407680

Sen, A. (1999). *Development as freedom*. Oxford University Press.
Sen, A. (2003). Development as capability expansion. In S. Fukuda-Parr & A. K. Shiva Kumar (Eds.), *Readings in human development*. Oxford University Press.
Sikdar, S. (2006). *Contemporary issues in globalization – An introduction to theory & policy in India* (2nd ed., pp. 194–197). Oxford University Press.
Thirlwall, A. P. (2006). *Growth and development with special reference to developing economies* (8th ed., pp. 23–30, 54–63). Palgrave Macmillan.
Tsangarides, C. G. (2001). On cross country growth and convergence: Evidence from Africa and OECD countries. *Journal of African Economies*, *10*(4), 355–389.
Todaro, M. P., & Smith, S. C. (2012). *Economic development* (10th ed., pp. 39–40, 71–78). Pearson.
UNDP. (2013). *Humanity divided: Confronting inequality in developing countries*. United Nations Development Programme Bureau for Development Policy.
UNDP. (2014). *Human development report*. UNDP.
Verspagen, B. (1995). Convergence in the global economy. A broad historical viewpoint. *Structural Change and Economic Dynamics*, *6*(2), 143–165.
World Bank. (2012). *Inequality in focus* (Vol. 1, No.1). World Bank. http://siteresources.worldbank.org/EXTPOVERTY/Resources/Inequality_in_Focus_April2012. pdf
Young, A. T., Higgins, M. J., & Levy, D. (2008). Sigma convergence versus beta convergence: Evidence from U.S. county-level data, *Journal of Money, Credit and Banking*, *40*(5), 1083–1093.

Chapter 11

Forecasting of Income Inequality in the South Asian Region: An ARIMA Model with Exogeneous Variable

Santanu Bhattacharya and Souvik Dasgupta

Department of Economics, Sidho-Kanho-Birsha University, Purulia, India

Abstract

The central topic of an ongoing argument among philosophers, economists, and policymakers around the globe has been the distribution of income. It is a significant economic concern because it affects social cohesion, economic growth, and overall quality of life. The problem of rising income inequality in the South Asian region is one of the major obstacles to the development of the continent's economy. In order to achieve the sustainable development goals (United Nations, 2015) by 2030, the South Asian countries must address the raising income inequality of the continent. This puts an importance on the exercise of forecasting income inequality for the South Asian region. The present study has used time-series data of income inequality (Gini) and per capita gross domestic product (GDP) of the South Asian region for the period 1960–2020 to forecast income inequality for the time period 2021 to 2035. Initially, the study has carried out a separate univariate forecasting analysis (autoregressive integrated moving average (ARIMA)) for economic growth. On the basis of these projected values of economic growth, a bivariate forecasting analysis of income inequality by the AutoRegressive Integrated Moving Average with eXogenous (ARIMAX) variables is then performed. Results of the study suggest that income inequality will show some positive regular significant growth in South Asia during the period 2021–2035.

Keywords: Income inequality; South Asia; forecasting; auto-ARIMA; ARIMAX

JEL Codes: C22; C53; D63

Changing Dimensions in Economic Development: Theories and Empirics, 141–154

doi:10.1108/978-1-83708-384-820261011

1. Introduction

The central topic of an ongoing argument among philosophers, economists, and policymakers around the globe has been the distribution of income. Income inequality pertains to the disparate allocation of income among individuals or groups within a society. It is a significant economic concern because it affects social cohesion, economic growth, and overall quality of life. One of the most prevalent metrics for gauging income inequality is the Gini coefficient (or Gini index). The Gini coefficient is a statistical measure that represents the distribution of income or wealth within a population. It ranges from 0 to 1 (or 0 to 100 when expressed as a percentage), where 0 denotes perfect equality (everyone receives an equal share of income) and 1 (or 100) signifies perfect inequality (one individual receives all the income, leaving none for others). The study of economic development and income inequality has a long theoretical history that began with Ricardo. However, the systematic study of income distribution by size at different stages of development began only after World War II. It was initiated by the Nobel Prize winner in economics, Simon Kuznets. The subsequent study of Simon Kuznets found that economic development and income inequality have an inverted U-shaped relationship, with relative income inequality increasing in the early stages and decreasing in the later stages of development. A number of empirical studies supported his seminal work (Anser et al., 2020; Deyshappriya, 2017; Lee & Lee, 2018). Income inequality-related issues were included in the UN's 17 sustainable development goals established in 2015, the challenges of closing the income gap between upper- and lower-income groups remain considerable, and remedial policies remain largely ineffective. According to the United Nations World Economic Forum (2022), the richest 10% of the global population receive 52% of the total global income, while the poorest 50% receive only 8.5%.

The World Bank has classified the countries under seven broad regions: (1) East Asia and Pacific, (2) Europe and Central Asia, (3) Latin America and Caribbean, (4) Middle East and North Africa, (5) North America, (6) South Asia, and (7) Sub-Saharan Africa. Out of these seven regions, South Asia is considered to be the second most populous region in the world. The region consists of a total of eight countries namely Afghanistan, Bangladesh, Bhutan, India, the Maldives, Nepal, Pakistan, and Sri Lanka. During the last three decades, the region has experienced considerable growth along with increasing income inequality. The problem of rising income inequality in South Asia is one of the major obstacles to development of the continent's economy. In order to achieve the sustainable development goals (UN, 2015) by 2030, the South Asian countries must address the intensifying income inequality of the continent. This puts an importance on the exercise of forecasting income inequality for the region.

The present study attempts to forecast income inequality of the South Asian region considering its economic growth projections for the upcoming 15 years. Such an analysis will highlight the nature of income inequality the region will face during the upcoming decades, which will further be helpful in implementing proper policy for the region. The rest of this chapter is organised as follows: The next section provides a brief overview of relevant studies followed by objectives of study in the section thereafter. The data and econometric methodology applied in the present work are narrated in Section 4. The empirical findings[1] and analysis are presented in Section 5. Finally, we conclude and discuss some probable policy implications of the study in Section 6.

2. Literature Review

The classical school of economic thought posits that there exists a positive correlation between income inequality and economic growth. Advocates of this perspective, such as Adam Smith and David Ricardo, argued that an unequal distribution of income that favours capitalists could stimulate savings and investment, thereby fostering economic expansion. Smith, in his seminal work of 1776, emphasised the pivotal role of capital accumulation in driving economic growth. According to Smith, if capitalists, as key agents of capital accumulation, garner a larger share of national income, this would lead to increased capital accumulation and, consequently, higher economic growth. Similarly, David Ricardo, a successor to Smith in the classical tradition, echoed these sentiments in his works, notably in 1821. Ricardo extended Smith's arguments by developing a theory of land rent and formulating the principle of comparative advantage. Through these frameworks, Ricardo justified his stance on income distribution, positing that a distribution favouring capitalists could incentivise productive activities, leading to enhanced economic growth.

The origins of income inequality theories can be traced back to early 20th-century hypotheses that sought to establish a correlation between income distribution and the spectrum of individual capabilities (Mincer, 1958). This foundational approach was epitomised by Moore (1911), who posited that 'industrial acumen – encompassing general sagacity and vigor – adheres to a normal or Gaussian distribution'. This premise led to the rationalisation of wage disparities as a natural consequence of heterogeneous human aptitudes, a perspective that gained significant traction in early economic thought Schumpeter (1916) initially garnered acclaim for advancing this paradigm, which seemed to offer a straightforward explanation for the observed variations in income. However, the apparent elegance of this theory belied its underlying complexities and limitations. As empirical evidence accumulated, the logical frailties of this simplistic model became increasingly apparent, ultimately precipitating its repudiation within academic circles. A pivotal challenge to this theory came from Pigou (2017), who proffered a compelling counterargument based on empirical observations. Pigou noted that real-world income distributions consistently aligned with Pareto's law rather than the Gaussian model predicted by the ability-based hypothesis. This discrepancy engendered a profound paradox: How could one reconcile the putative normal distribution of abilities with the markedly skewed distribution of income observed in society? Pigou's widely accepted resolution to this conundrum posited the existence of intervening factors that obfuscate the direct relationship

[1]All results and diagrams are derived in the R-studio (4.3.1) software.

between ability and income. This nuanced perspective acknowledged the role of ability in income determination while recognising the complex interplay of various socioeconomic factors that influence financial outcomes. Such factors might include education, social connections, inherited wealth, market structures, and systemic inequalities, among others.

A large number of empirical studies have been conducted in the field of income inequality, but only a few studies have dealt with forecasting of income inequality. We have briefly reviewed the underlying studies explaining future projections of income inequality and growth–inequality nexus-related issues. Kuznets (1955) introduced the concept of the Kuznets curve, hypothesising an inverted U-shaped relationship between economic growth and income inequality. His theory suggested that inequality increases during the early stages of economic development but eventually decreases as economies mature and develop more inclusive institutions. Kaldor (1960) and Kalecki (1971) provided foundational insights into the role of economic policies in shaping income distribution and growth. Kaldor's discussion on the Radcliffe Report emphasised the importance of monetary and fiscal policies in maintaining economic stability, while Kalecki's analysis of class struggle highlighted the impact of power dynamics on national income distribution. Galor and Zeira (1993) provided a theoretical framework linking income distribution to macroeconomic outcomes. They proposed that imperfect capital markets and unequal access to education can create a persistent inequality trap, where the poor remain unable to invest in human capital, thus perpetuating economic disparities. Alesina and Perotti (1996) explored the link between income distribution and political instability, proposing that greater income inequality can lead to increased political unrest, which subsequently hampers investment. Their findings suggested a cyclical relationship where political instability and low investment exacerbate income inequality, creating a vicious cycle detrimental to economic stability and growth. De La Croix and Doepke (2003) investigated how differential fertility rates affect inequality and economic growth. They argued that higher fertility rates among lower-income groups can perpetuate income inequality across generations, as these families tend to invest less in education and human capital. Their model underscores the role of family planning and education policies in addressing long-term income disparities. The seminal work by Banerjee and Duflo (2003) examined the nuanced relationship between inequality and growth. They argued that the impact of inequality on growth is context dependent, varying across different stages of development and institutional frameworks. Their empirical analysis indicated that while some level of inequality may incentivise investment and growth, excessive inequality can undermine economic performance by limiting access to education and capital for the poorer segments of society.

Deyshappriya (2017) examined the impact of various macroeconomic factors on income inequality in Asian countries. His study identified key drivers of inequality, including economic growth, inflation, and government spending. The findings highlighted the complex interplay between these factors and suggested targeted policy measures to reduce inequality in the region. Sulaiman et al. (2017) investigated the long-term relationship between income inequality and economic growth in Malaysia, providing empirical evidence that supported the existence of a Kuznets curve in a developing country context. Their findings indicated that targeted policies to promote inclusive growth are essential for reducing inequality. Lee and Lee (2018) explored the relationship between human capital and income inequality in the Asia Pacific region. Their study showed that higher levels of education and skills can reduce income inequality by improving employment opportunities and wages for lower-income individuals. Chong and Ka (2019) focused on forecasting income inequality using demographic projections. They emphasised the importance of considering demographic trends, such as ageing populations and changes in household composition, in predicting future income distribution patterns. Their findings suggested that demographic shifts can significantly influence the trajectory of income inequality over time. Anser et al. (2020) delved into the dynamic interrelationships among poverty, inequality, crime, and social expenditures across 16 countries. Using a two-step Generalised method of moments (GMM) estimation, they demonstrated how high levels of inequality and poverty contributed to higher crime rates, while social expenditures play a crucial role in mitigating these adverse effects. This study highlighted the importance of policy interventions in breaking the link between inequality and social issues. Hamilton (2020) did a comprehensive study of time-series analysis, including methods such as ARIMA models, which were crucial for forecasting economic variables like income inequality. His work provided the statistical foundation necessary for rigorous economic forecasting and analysis. Suparmono (2021) forecasted the impact of the COVID-19 pandemic on income distribution, highlighting how economic shocks can exacerbate existing inequalities. His study underscored the need for responsive policy measures to mitigate the adverse effects of such crises on vulnerable populations.

To our knowledge, the present study will be the first of its kind which deal with the forecasting-related issues of income inequality under consideration of projected economic growth at the regional level.

3. Research Objective

The objective of the present study is to forecast the income inequality of the South Asian region considering economic growth as an exogenous variable. Figs. 11.1 and 11.2 illustrate the nature of economic growth and income inequality in the South Asian region during 1960 to 2020, respectively. During the time period, the region has experienced considerable economic growth. However, the income inequality has irregularly decreased during the period of 1950–1975. But after 1975, the income inequality started to increase and still it is continuing. In addition to this, it is important to highlight that the Gini coefficient was near about 50 by the beginning of the last decade, which is considered extremely high in terms of absolute values. There was a slight decrease in income inequality in the year 2020, but it is still too early to draw any conclusion about whether or not income inequality will decrease in the decades to come. It is therefore important to forecast the income inequality in South Asia over the next one or two decades considering the projections of economic growth for the upcoming period.

Economic growth as an exogenous variable is crucial in forecasting income inequality because it influences income distribution without being directly affected by inequality in the short run. It impacts wage structures, job creation, and capital accumulation, often benefiting skilled workers more. Growth also affects government revenues, enabling redistribution policies that can reduce or worsen inequality. The Kuznets curve suggests that inequality first rises with growth before eventually declining. Overall, economic growth shapes inequality through structural changes, labour market shifts, and policy responses.

4. Data and Methodology

The present study forecasts income inequality of the South Asian region for the time period 2021–2035 using Auto-ARIMA and Auto-ARIMAX models. It has used time-series data on income inequality (measured by Gini coefficient) and per capita GDP of the region for the time period 1960–2020. Gini coefficient data are collected from the World Income Inequality Database, whereas per capita GDP (constant 2015 US$) data are collected from the World Development Indicator, World Bank. The variables used in the study, viz., income inequality, per capita GDP, and its natural logarithm, are denoted as Gini, Per Capita gross domestic product (PCGDP), and Natural logarithm of Per Capita gross domestic product (LNPCGDP), respectively (see Tables 11.1–11.4 and Figs. 11.1–11.6).

Table 11.1. Summary Statistics.

	Mean	Maximum	Minimum	SD	Skew	Kurto	J-B	Probability	Observations
Gini	48.63	51.51	45.27	1.75	−0.07	1.86	3.89	0.14	61
LNPCGDP	6.46	7.52	5.79	0.53	0.56	2.04	5.56	0.06	61

Source: Authors' own calculation.

Table 11.2. Unit Root Test (ADF Test).

	Gini (1960–2020)	LNPCGDP (1960–2020)	
	Level	Level	First Difference
t-statistic	−3.5157	−1.5339	−4.7635
p-value	0.04	0.76	0.01
Lag order	4	3	3

Source: Authors' own calculation.

Table 11.3. Results of Estimated Forecasting Models.

LNPCGDP Series (1960–2020), ARIMA (0, 2, 1)				
	AR1	**AR2**	**MA1**	**MA2**
Coefficients			−0.8831	
Standard error			0.066	
$Sigma^2$ = 0.2706	Log likelihood = −45.42	AIC = −256.6	BIC = −252.45	AICC = −256.39
Gini ~ LNPCGDP (1960–2020), ARIMAX (1, 0, 0)				
	AR1	Intercept	LNPCGDP	
Coefficients	0.6454	29.9238	2.9027	
Standard error	0.1042	2.1614	0.3327	
$Sigma^2$ = 0.2706	Log likelihood = −45.42	AIC = 98.84	BIC = 107.29	AICC = 99.56

Source: Authors' own calculation.

Table 11.4. Ljung–Box Test.

	ARIMA (0, 2, 1)	**ARIMAX (1, 0, 0)**
Q^*	6.91	11.03
df	9	9
p-value	0.6461	0.27
Lags	10	10

Source: Authors' own calculation.

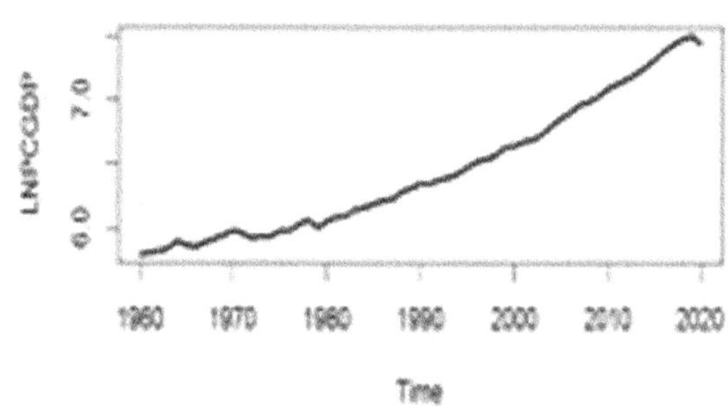

Fig. 11.1. Patterns of Economic Growth (1950–2020) in the South Asian Region. *Source*: Authors' own calculation.

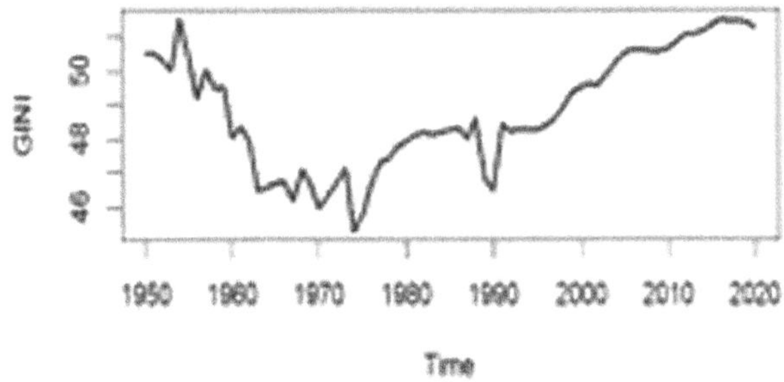

Fig. 11.2. Patterns of Income Inequality (1950–2020) in the South Asian Region. *Source*: Authors' own calculation.

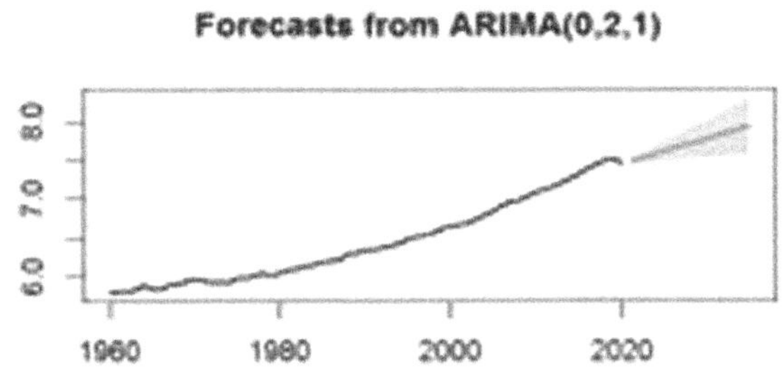

Fig. 11.3. Forecasting of Economic Growth for the Period 2021–2035 by ARIMA Model. *Source*: Authors' own calculation.

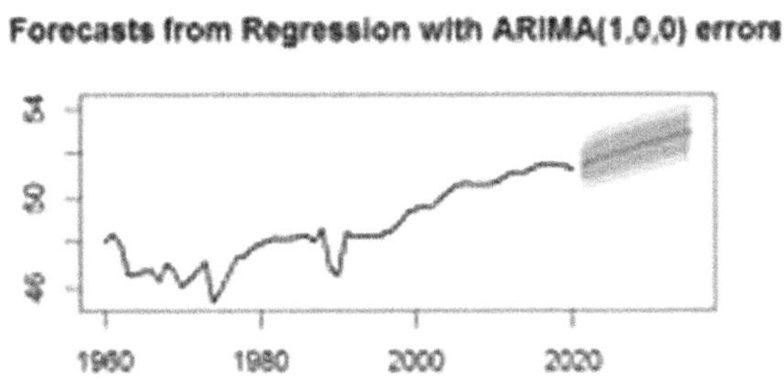

Fig. 11.4. Forecasting of Economic Growth for the Period 2021–2035 by ARIMAX Model. *Source*: Authors' own calculation.

The ARIMA model[2] is a univariate model in which future values of the dependent variable are predicted based on the past lags of dependent variable and

[2]Box and Jenkins (1976) introduced the ARIMA model, which is why it is known in the literature as the Box–Jenkins method.

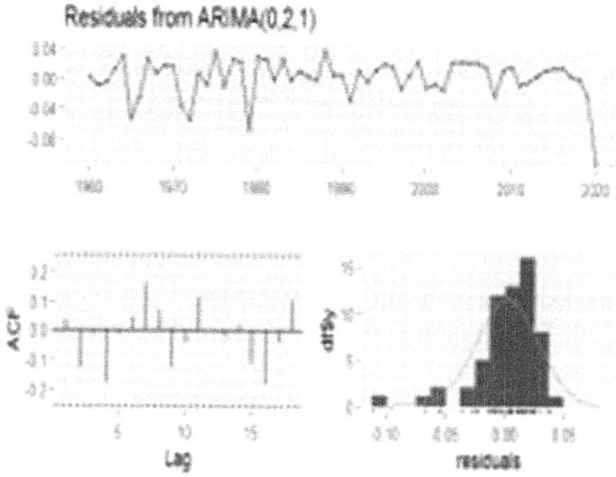

Fig. 11.5. Model Diagnostics Test for ARIMA (0, 2, 1). *Source*: Authors' own calculation.

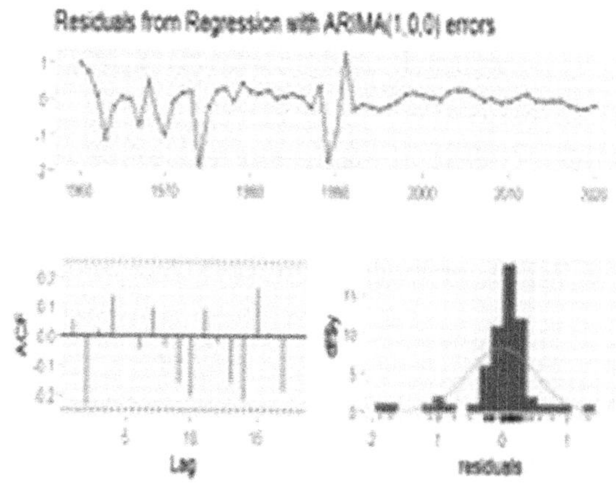

Fig. 11.6. Model Diagnostics Test for ARIMAX (1, 0, 0). *Source*: Authors' own calculation.

error term. The ARIMA model can be used even for non-stationary time series. The general form of the ARIMA (p, D, q) model is defined as

$$\Delta^D Y_t = \beta_0 + \sum_{i=1}^{p} \beta_i \Delta^D Y_{t-i} + \mu_t - \sum_{j=1}^{q} \alpha_j \mu_{t-j}$$

where Y_t denotes the level of income inequality at time t; Y_{t-i} is $(t-i)$ time-lagged value of income inequality ($i = 1 \ldots \ldots p$); μ_t is a series of random errors, with mean zero and constant variance; μ_{t-j} is $t - i$, ($j = 1 \ldots \ldots q$) time periods that are incorporated; and $\Delta^D Y_t$ is the Dth differenced time series.

The ARIMAX model is used for a bivariate or multivariate analysis in which predicted values are estimated based on regressor(s) along with the previous lags of the dependent variable and error term. The ARIMAX model is also known as ARIMA with an exogenous variable. The ARIMAX (p, D, q) model is given as follows:

$$\Delta^D Y_t = \gamma X_t + \beta_0 + \sum_{i=1}^{p} \beta_i \Delta^D Y_{t-i} + \mu_t - \sum_{j=1}^{q} \alpha_j \mu_{t-j}$$

Using the backshift operators, the ARIMAX model can be specified as (Peter & Silvia, 2012; Suharsono et al., 2015; Tamuke et al., 2018):

$$\phi(\beta)\Delta^D Y_t = \beta X_t + \theta(\beta)\mu_t$$

$$\Rightarrow \Delta^D Y_t = \frac{\beta}{\phi(\beta)} X_t + \frac{\theta(\beta)}{\phi(\beta)} \mu_t$$

where

$$\phi(\beta) = 1 - \phi_1 \beta^1 - \phi_2 \beta^2 - \ldots - \phi_p \beta^p$$

$$\theta(\beta) = 1 - \theta_1 \beta^1 - \theta_2 \beta^2 - \ldots - \theta_q \beta^q$$

We note that autoregressive coefficients get mixed up with both the covariates and the error term. Regression models with ARIMA errors are defined as:

$$\Delta^D Y_t = \beta X_t + \eta_t$$

$$\text{Here, } \eta_t : \sum_{i=1}^{p} \beta_i \Delta^D Y_{t-i} + \mu_t - \sum_{j=1}^{q} \alpha_j \mu_{t-j}$$

While estimating ARIMA and ARIMAX models we need to provide the values of $\{p, D, q\}$ by differencing to eliminate non-stationarity. However, optimal values of $\{p, D, q\}$ are generated itself in case of Auto-ARIMA and Auto-ARIMAX models which are based on Hyndman–Khandakar algorithm. Optimal values imply the values which are most suitable for the existing dataset to make better forecasting. In the present study Auto-ARIMA and Auto-ARIMAX models are fitted for forecasting income inequality of the South Asian region. The appropriate or best-fitted ARIMA and ARIMAX forecasting models are selected based on the minimisation of Akaike's information criterion (AIC), Bayesian information criterion (BIC), and corrected Akaike's information criterion (AICC). These are calculated as (Tylkowski & Hojan, 2019):

$$\text{AIC}(p,q) = -2\ln(\text{LL}) + 2(p+q+k+1)$$

$$\text{AICC}(p,q) = -2\ln(\text{LL}) + \frac{2(p+q+k+1)n}{n-p-q-k-2}$$

$$\text{BIC}(p,q) = -2\ln(\text{LL}) + (p+q+k+1)\log(n) \tag{xii}$$

where *p*: Auto regressive (model) (AR) parameter, *q*: Moving average (model) (MA) parameter, *k*: number of model parameters, *n*: sample size, and LL: log likelihood.

5. Results and Discussions

The descriptive results of the present study are presented in Table 11.1. During the period 1950–2020, on an average, the absolute value of Gini coefficient for the region of South Asia is 48.63 with a standard deviation of 1.75. It has been found that the maximum and minimum Gini coefficient values during this period are 51.51 and 45.27, respectively. During 1950–2020, the distribution of Gini series for the region is found to be negatively skewed and platykurtic. On the other hand, the mean value of LNPCGDP is 6.46, with a standard deviation of 0.53. The maximum and minimum values of LNPCGDP during this period are 7.52 and 5.79, respectively. A positive skewed and platykurtic distribution is observed for the LNPCGDP series of the region.

Table 11.2 summarises the stationarity test results of two data series. A stochastic process is said to be stationary if its mean and variance are constant over time, and the value of covariance between any two time periods depends only on the distance (or, gap) between the two time periods and not the actual time with which the covariance is computed. The study has used Augmented Dickey Fuller (ADF) unit root test to check the stationary of the two variables, viz., Gini and LNPCGDP. The unit root test results suggest that Gini is stationary at a level while LNPCGDP is stationary at the first difference.

The Auto-ARIMAX model is mainly based on the Hyndman–Khandakar algorithm, which combines unit root tests Kwiatkowski-Phillips-Schmidt-Shin (test) (KPSS), the minimisation of information criteria, and the maximum likelihood method to determine the best-fitting model for the data. Initially, the study has carried out a separate univariate forecasting analysis (ARIMA) of LNPCGDP for the period 1960–2020. On the basis of these projected values of LNPCGDP, a bivariate forecasting (ARIMAX) analysis of income inequality is performed for the period 1960–2020. The following ARIMA and ARIMAX models are selected on the basis of minimised AIC, BIC, and AICC values. Results of the estimated forecasting models are presented in Table 11.3. In the case of the LNPCGDP series (1960–2020), the best-fitted model is the ARIMA (0, 2, 1), in which the MA1 term has a negative influence on the LNPCGDP. It is found that the model ARIMAX (1, 0, 0) is the best-fitted model for the Gini with the LNPCGDP series (1960–2020). In this case, the study has found that the explanatory variable LNPCGDP has a positive impact on the Gini coefficient.

Residual diagnostic tests and the over fitting procedure are used here to determine the goodness of fit of the fitted models to the original time series. Results of the diagnostic tests are presented in Table 11.4. The figures 11.5 and 11.6 suggest that the residuals of the fitted models, ARIMA (0, 2, 1) and ARIMAX (1, 0, 0), follow normal distribution, are independently distributed, and have constant mean at zero. The insignificant results of Box–Ljung test give evidence that residuals represent white noise.

After the identification and adequacy check of the ARIMA (0, 2, 1) and ARIMAX (1, 0, 0) models, they have been used to forecast the income inequality considering economic growth projections in South Asia for the period of 2021–2035. Forecasted values of the fitted model are given in Figs. 11.3 and 11.4, respectively. From the result, the study has found that income inequality will show some positive regular significant growth in South Asia during the period 2021–2035.

6. Conclusion and Policy Implications

The present study tries to forecast income inequality considering the economic growth projections in the South Asian region for the period of 2021–2035. Auto-ARIMA and Auto-ARIMAX models are fitted for forecasting analysis which is based on the Hyndman–Khandakar algorithm. Forecasting analysis is executed based on the minimisation of AIC, BIC, and AICC values. In case of univariate forecasting analysis of economic growth, the ARIMA (0, 2, 1) model has been found to be fitted best. On the basis of the forecasted values of economic growth from the model ARIMA (0, 2, 1), the study has fitted the ARIMAX (1, 0, 0) model to forecast income inequality considering economic growth projections for the period 2021–2035. The ARIMAX (1, 0, 0) model suggests that income inequality will show some positive regular significant growth in South Asia during the period 2021–2035. This study sheds light on the impending income inequality challenges facing the South Asian region in the coming decades. Understanding these dynamics is crucial for devising effective policy interventions. The study underscores that while the economic growth trajectory of South Asia is expected to ascend in the upcoming decade, this surge is likely to exacerbate income inequality within the region. Hence, it is imperative to formulate policies that can mitigate the escalating trend of income inequality and promote more equitable economic development.

Beyond the factors examined in this study, a wide array of additional variables can play a crucial role in shaping growth. While the current findings hold significance within the scope of the stated hypothesis, it is important to recognise that the trajectory of growth may also be affected by other influential drivers that were not considered in this analysis. These overlooked factors may interact in complex ways, underscoring the need for a more comprehensive approach that captures the full range of dynamics influencing growth patterns.

References

Alesina, A., & Perotti, R. (1996). Income distribution, political instability, and investment. *European Economic Review*, *40*(6), 1203–1228.

Anser, M. K., Yousaf, Z., Nassani, A. A., Alotaibi, S. M., Kabbani, A., & Zaman, K. (2020). Dynamic linkages between poverty, inequality, crime, and social expenditures in a panel of 16 countries: Two-step GMM estimates. *Journal of Economic Structures*, *9*, 1–25.

Banerjee, A. V., & Duflo, E. (2003). Inequality and growth: What can the data say? *Journal of Economic Growth*, *8*, 267–299.

Box, G. E. P., & Jenkins, G. M. (1976). *Time series analysis: Forecasting and control* (Rev. ed.). Holden-Day.

Chong, T. T. L., & Ka, Y. T. (2019). *Forecasting income inequality with demographic projections (MPRA Paper No. 99160)*. University Library of Munich.

De La Croix, D., & Doepke, M. (2003). Inequality and growth: Why differential fertility matters. *American Economic Review*, *93*(4), 1091–1113.

Deyshappriya, N. P. R. (2017). *Impact of macroeconomic factors on income inequality and income distribution in Asian countries, ADBI Working Paper, No. 696*. Asian Development Bank Institute (ADBI).

Galor, O., & Zeira, J. (1993). Income distribution and macroeconomics. *The Review of Economic Studies*, *60*(1), 35–52.

Hamilton, J. D. (2020). *Time series analysis*. Princeton University Press.

Kaldor, N. (1960). The Radcliffe report. *The Review of Economics and Statistics*, *42*(1), 14–19.

Kalecki, M. (1971). Class struggle and the distribution of national income. *Kyklos*, *24*(1), 1–9.

Kuznets, S. (1955). Economic growth and income inequality. *The American Economic Review*, *45*(1), 1–28.

Lee, J. W., & Lee, H. (2018). Human capital and income inequality. *Journal of the Asia Pacific Economy*, *23*(4), 554–583.

Mincer, J. (1958). Investment in human capital and personal income distribution. *Journal of Political Economy*, *66*(4), 281–302.

Moore, H. L. (1911). *Laws of wages: An essay in statistical economics*. Macmillan.

Peter, Ď., & Silvia, P. (2012, September). ARIMA vs. ARIMAX – Which approach is better to analyze and forecast macroeconomic time series. In *Proceedings of 30th international conference mathematical methods in economics* (Vol. 2, pp. 136–140). Karviná.

Pigou, A. (2017). *The economics of welfare*. Routledge.

Schumpeter, J. A. (1916). Das Grundprinzip der Verteilungstheorie. *Archiv für Sozialwissenschaft und Sozialpolitik*, *42*, 1–88.

Suharsono, A., Suhartono, S., Masyitha, A., & Anuravega, A. (2015). Time series regression and ARIMAX for forecasting currency flow at Bank Indonesia in Sulawesi region. In N. Ahmad, J. Zulkepli, A. Ibrahim, N. Aziz, & S. Abdul-Rahman (Eds.), *Innovation and analytics conference and exhibition IACE 2015: Proceedings of the 2nd innovation and analytics conference and exhibition article 050025 (AIP conference proceedings; Vol. 1691)*. American Institute of Physics Inc.

Sulaiman, N. F. C., Yussof, I., Zaidi, M. A. S., & Sulaiman, N. (2017). Long run relationship between income inequality and economic growth: Evidence from Malaysia. *International Journal of Academic Research in Business and Social Sciences*, *7*(6), 2222–6990.

Suparmono, S. (2021). Forecasting the inequality of income distribution in consequence of the Covid-19 pandemic. *Jurnal Ekonomi Pembangunan*, *19*(1), 27–38.

Tamuke, E., Jackson, E. A., & Sillah, A. (2018). Forecasting inflation in Sierra Leone using ARIMA and ARIMAX: A comparative evaluation. Model building and analysis team. *Theoretical and Practical Research in Economic Fields*, *9*(1), 63–74.

Tylkowski, J., & Hojan, M. (2019). Time decomposition and short-term forecasting of hydrometeorological conditions in the south baltic coastal zone of Poland. *Geosciences*, *9*(2), 68.

United Nations. (2015). *World economic situation and prospects 2015*.

World Economic Forum. (2022). *Annual report 2021–2022*.

Chapter 12

Structural Transformation and Trends in Informality: With Special Reference to India

Rajib Bhattacharyya

Goenka College of Commerce and Business Administration, Kolkata, India

Abstract

The historical perspectives of structural transformation dates back to the famous contributions of W. W. Lewis (1954), Robert Solow (1956), Simon Kuznets (1966) and many others who interpreted it as a gradual process of sustained transformation from low productive agriculture to high-productive industry and later on to services through increase in per capita income (PCI) and a betterment in working environment or alternatively by a shift towards the proportion engaged in regular wage or salaried work, as opposed to casual wage work or self-employment. But this pattern of structural transformation has not followed the same pattern across countries. The present study seeks to make an in-depth analysis of its various forms and interpretations. In this context, the study attempts to make a comparative analysis of India's structural change with that of China in terms of output share between sectors, employment share between sectors and ratio of labour productivities between sectors. In recent times, the persistent growth of the informal economy has been inextricably linked with structural transformation. So, the study tries to examine the various measures of informality between the advanced economies (AEs) and emerging market and developing economies (EMDEs). India's transformation is an exception to the standard classical pattern, as the labour share of agriculture declined and services increased, but the share of manufacturing remained stagnant (in contrast to China). Also, the proportion of self-employment is highest in case of India as compared to any of the selected

Changing Dimensions in Economic Development: Theories and Empirics, 155–171

Published under exclusive licence by Emerald Publishing Limited
doi:10.1108/978-1-83708-384-820261012

EMDEs and AEs, and both demand- and supply-side factors resulted in the rising trends of informal labour in India.

Keywords: Structural transformation; informal labour market; self-employment; labour productivity; measures of informality

JEL Codes: F16; O17

1. Introduction

Structural transformation is a gradual process of sectoral shift from low productive economic activity to high-productive modern activity. It implies a movement of surplus labour from agricultural and other informal economic activities to higher productive industry and services or the non-farm sector. Hence, a successful structural transformation should lead to sustained increase in PCI, increase in the bargaining power of workers, raising labour share of income and improvement in working conditions. Historically, the relationship between growth and structural change encircles three inter-related but distinct phenomena:

(a) Kuznets Process (Kuznets, 1955) – points towards an invariable accompaniment of growth in developed countries, which is the shift away from agriculture initially to manufacturing and then to services (transfer of labour from agriculture to higher value-added activities in the non-farm economy), a process usually referred to as industrialisation and urbanisation.
(b) Solow Process (Solow, 1956) – refers to enhancement of output through the incentives to save, accumulate physical and human capital (which implies endogenising technological change).
(c) Lewis Process (Lewis, 1954; Ranis & Fei, 1961) – refers to the migration of labour from the low-productive subsistence sector to the high-profit-oriented technologically advanced modern sector. So, the dual economy model focuses on inter-sectoral relationships and flows.

All the above theories provide commentary perspectives to growth and structural change. In the Solow model, as poor nations suffer from deficiency of physical and human capital, the returns to capital accumulation is high and economic convergence is feasible. In the Lewis type, dual economy model growth can be achieved by transferring low-productive rural farmers into urban modern industries where productivity is much higher. But this guides us towards important challenges to development: (i) ensuring rapid resource transfer to the modern sector, that is, challenge of 'structural transformation', and (ii) accumulation of skills and broad institutional capabilities for generation of sustained growth, that is, challenge of 'fundamentals' (Rodrik, 2013). The three processes (mentioned above) may result in a cycle of growth with structural change if they can be mutually reinforcing. This materialises if labour productivity rises simultaneously in both the modern industrial and rural subsistence sectors, leading to increased income and demand for industrial goods as well as services (assuming that the labour absorption does not reduce the employment intensity in the modern sector). This further raises productivity due to labour reallocation in favour of higher productive sectors. The story of successful structural transformation is more or less – the increase in labour productivity through reallocation of surplus labour, increase in bargaining strength, labour share and improved working conditions – in both early developed and newly industrialised developed nations.

Growth is a necessary but not a sufficient condition for structural change. The possibilities of a low-level equilibrium or a vicious cycle cannot be ruled out. If growth is restricted to the industrial sector only and/or intensifies the use of more capital, productivity of the majority of workers remains low, and both income and demand expands slowly. Labour reallocation is stalled, and so wages and working conditions do not improve. Nayyar (2019) pointed out two discernible phases of structural change in India: (i) 1950–1980 – modest structural change with manufacturing replacing agriculture and (ii) 1980–2010 – service sector-led growth (partly due to construction and not due to manufacturing). Mehrotra and Parida (2021) identified the role of both demand and supply factors for stalled structural transformation in spite of growth due to falling labour force participation (LFP) and alarming rise in open unemployment, which may have a serious adverse impact on demographic dividend in the long run. Also, labour productivity can be enhanced via technical change without labour reallocation, and so growth may occur without structural change.

2. Literature Survey

An enormous body of literature has developed to examine both the theoretical and empirical analyses of structural change and informal labour market separately. But very few have tried to establish the interlinkages between the two as development progresses. Kuznets (1966) has shown how over time the share of agriculture declines and the shares of the industrial and services sectors increase. His analysis shows 10 nations (the United Kingdom, France, Germany, the Netherlands, Norway, Sweden, Italy, Canada, Japan and Russia) have lower shares of the services sector compared to the industrial sector, whereas two countries, that is,, the United States and Australia, have recorded higher shares of the services sector than the industrial sector. Deepak (2019) analysed structural change in 14 Asian nations over the period 1970–2016 and found that some countries (like South Korea, Taiwan, Singapore, China, Malaysia and Indonesia) have followed a standard pattern but others (like India, Turkey, Thailand, Philippines, Pakistan, Sri Lanka, Bangladesh and Vietnam) are exceptions to the rule. Rodrik (2013) and Ghose (2020) have tried to explain the theoretical perspectives behind these structural changes. Elgin et al. (2021) provide a detailed description of the various interpretations and measures of informality and its empirical database.

Ulyssea (2020) reviews the economic literature on informality, its causes, and its consequences for development which includes structural models that integrate both micro and macro effects. Schneider and Enste (2000), Schneider et al. (2010) and Medina and Schneider (2018) concentrated on the development of the shadow economy. Loayza et al. (2005) linked the formal and the informal economy by empirical evidences on the impact of regulation on growth and informality. Perry et al. (2007) tried to demonstrate that the origin of informality lies in the involuntary exclusion principle. Falco and Haywood (2016) and Günther and Launov (2012) were in favour of greater independence and freedom and flexible regulatory compliance as the origin of informality. Kanbur (2009) and Kanbur and Keen (2015) identified wilful non-compliance, avoiding motivation as the basic cause of informality. Basole (2022) made an extensive study on the Indian economy regarding structural transformation and employment generation where he used five indicators to track changes over time. Singh (2025) in his paper tried to conclude that for India to attain the level of a developed country status, structural transformation requires industrialisation. Ghatak et al. (2024) in their study have reached a conclusion that during the period since 2017–2018, the 'quantity' of employment has grown, but this is mainly due to increase in self-employment or casual workers, portraying a fall in quality of job creation.

3. Objective of the Study and Methodology

The present study seeks to make an in-depth analysis of the fundamental theoretical foundations of the structural change from the historical perspective and its various forms of interpretations. It tries to analyse whether the pattern of structural change found in India follows the traditional classical pattern or does it deviate from it. In this context, it attempts to make a comparison of India's structural change with its biggest competitor as an emerging market, that is, China. The comparison is based on three major macroeconomic indicators of structural change: output share between sectors, employment share between sectors and ratio of labour productivities between sectors. Then, the study tries to relate the issue of structural change to informality, focusing on various interpretations, origins and measures of informality. The measures of informality are addressed with a comparative analysis of selected AEs and EMDEs. Finally, we focus on India as a case study for this. The whole analysis is based on secondary data available from (i) Economic Transformation Database (ETD) (https://www.wider.unu.edu/project/etd---economic-transformation-database); (ii) Groningen Growth and Development Centre (GGDC, Faculty of Economics and Business, https://www.rug.nl/ggdc/structuralchange/etd/), 10-Sector Database for China; (iii) National Sample Survey Office (NSSO) Surveys of Employment and Unemployment and Central Statistical Organisation (CSO) National Accounts Statistics for India; (iv) CEPR Discussion Paper 16497, Centre for Economic Policy Research, London; and (v) World Development Indicator (WDI, 2024).

4. Structural Change – An Historical Perspective

Analysis of the structural change in various countries of the world from the historical perspective reveals some key insights to development. In case of developed economies of Europe and North America, manufacturing played a crucial role in the initial stages followed by services-led revolution in the later stages. So, a classical pattern of structural change produced reallocation of labour from agriculture to non-agriculture (which includes both manufacturing and services) in the early stages and from both agriculture and manufacturing to services in the later stages. The same pattern of structural change was observed in case of newly industrial nations of East Asia (like Korea, Japan, Taiwan, Malaysia) and currently EMDEs like China and Vietnam. The strong association between this pattern of structural change and economic development may be explained in terms of 'Growth Laws of Kaldor' (Kaldor, 1967). It emphasises three pivotal roles of manufacturing of early stages of development of a nation (Ghose, 2020).

(a) Due to the operation of increasing returns to scale in manufacturing as opposed to decreasing returns to scale in agriculture, labour productivity is higher in manufacturing than agriculture. Increased output and productivity give rise to division and specialisation of jobs, and due to spillover effects of technology and skill, it further induces growth in services.
(b) For nations with low income, the income elasticity of demand for industrial goods is higher than agricultural products. Also, as productivity in manufacturing is higher, the relative price is lower, and this boosts industrial production.
(c) Due to transition of low-skilled labour in the high-productive sector, manufacturing boosts construction and other services. This enhances growth and improves the conditions of workers through higher bargaining strength.

When the economies develop sufficiently based on the initial industry-led growth, things start to change gradually. The income elasticity of demand shifts more to services and away from manufacturing. This is reinforced by the decline in the absorptive capacity of industry which eventually displaces the productivity effect. So, in the matured stages, the services take over as the lead sector and labour get transferred from the agriculture and industry towards services.

5. Does India's Structural Change Contradict the 'Classical Pattern'?

India's structural change is one major exception which defies the classical pattern of growth laws of Kaldor. The reason for this typical nature of structural change can be better understood when we look at the comparison of employment shares and ratios of labour productivity between sectors over time during the period 1955–2010 (Figs. 12.1–12.3).

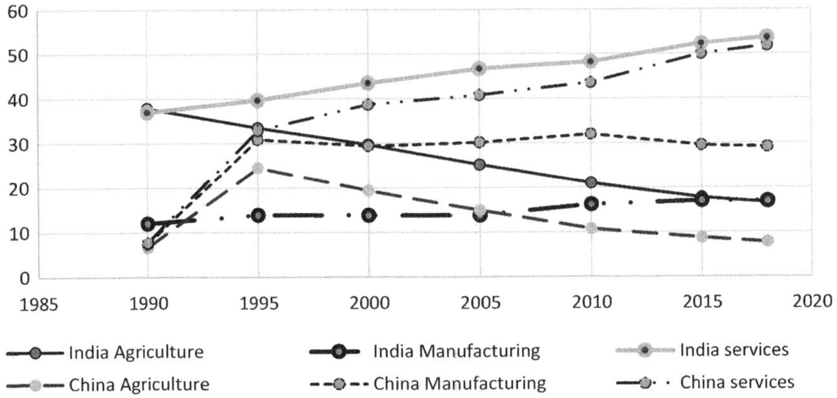

Fig. 12.1. Comparison of Structural Change in India and China: Output Share Between Sectors. *Sources*: Author's construction based on data from (i) ETD (https://www.wider.unu.edu/project/etd---economic-transformation-database); (ii) GGDC, 10-Sector Database for China; and (iii) WDI (2024).

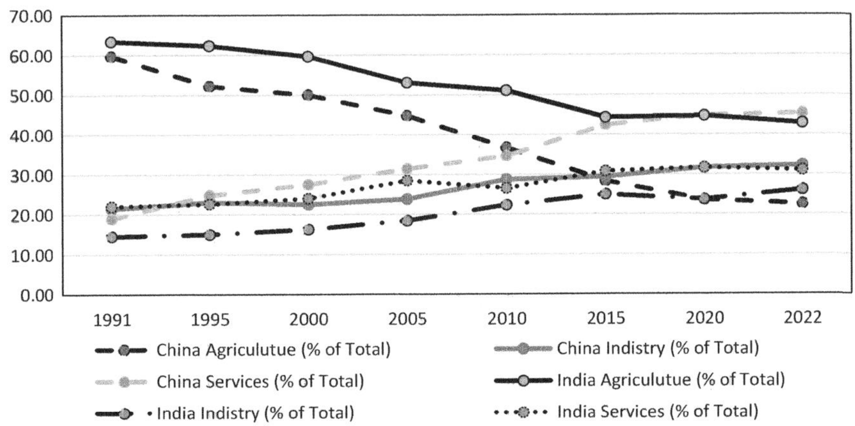

Fig. 12.2. Comparison of Structural Change in India and China: Employment Share Between Sectors. *Sources*: Author's construction based on data from (i) ETD (https://www.wider.unu.edu /project/etd---economic-transformation-database); (ii) GGDC, 10-Sector Database for China; and (iii) WDI (2024).

A few facts surface:

(i) The process of structural transformation has been clearly portrayed in the changing composition of the share of output in value-added in case of both China and India for the period 1990–2018 (as released from the ETD (released on 15 July 2021) (Fig. 12.1).

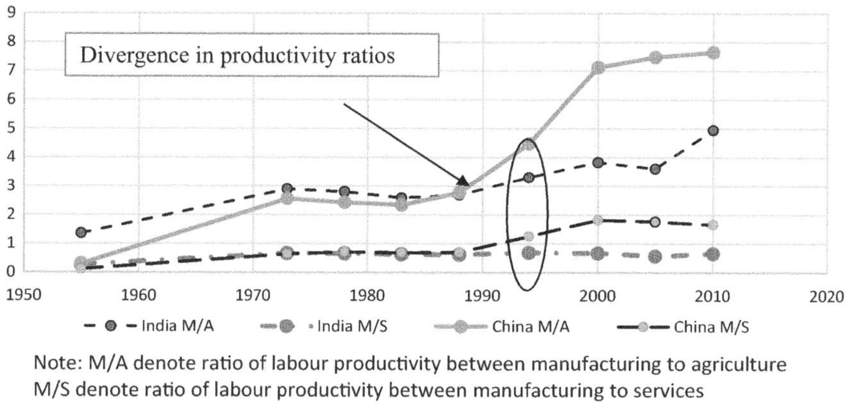

Fig. 12.3. Comparison of Structural Change in India and China: Ratio of Labour Productivities Between Sectors. *Sources*: Author's construction based on data from (i) ETD (https://www.wider.unu.edu /project/etd---economic-transformation-database); (ii) GGDC, 10-Sector Database for China; and (iii) WDI (2024).

(ii) Though in both nations the labour share of agriculture declined and services increased, but in India, the share of manufacturing remained stagnant, while in China, it depicts a sustained rise (Fig. 12.1).
(iii) The pace of structural change was much slower in India than in China. Starting from China's liberalisation (manufacture led growth) since 1978, the period 1978–2010 recorded a sharper fall in agriculture in China than in India (in China 34 while in India 20 percentage points), and considering the period of service sector-led growth in India (2000–2010), the employment share in services in China rose sharply than in India.
(iv) After India's march towards liberalisation, that is, 1994–2010, though in China manufacturing productivity growth continued to rise rapidly as compared to services, it slowed down in case of India (Fig. 12.2).

So, one may conclude that the manufacturing did not play the role of a leading sector in the structural transformation in India (which contradicts the classical pattern of growth laws of Kaldor). It is exceptional in the sense that throughout the entire period 1955–2010, the labour productivity growth in services is higher than that of manufacturing.

6. Structural Change and Informality

While analysing the issue of structural change and productivity growth, in many cases, the matter of informality has often been overlooked, though it has been an important feature in many EMDEs in recent decades (Voskoboynikov, 2017).

There are various complex and multifaceted measures and definitions of the informal economic circumstances of the nation and the characteristics of the workers. According to an estimate of the International Labour Organization (ILO, 2018), about 60% of the total employed workforce (in the age group of 15 years and above) are engaged in the informal sector.

6.1. Various Interpretations of Informality

By the standard definition, activities that are not recorded or are under-recorded are regarded as informal, and participants do not want it to be revealed for various reasons. Formally, one may define informality as market-based and legal production of goods and services that is hidden from public authorities for monetary, regulatory or institutional reasons (Schneider & Enste, 2000; Schneider et al., 2010). Monetary reasons include the avoidance of taxes and social security contributions, regulatory reasons include the avoidance of government bureaucracy or regulatory burdens and institutional reasons include corruption, related often to the poor quality of political institutions and weak rule of law. These factors affect firms and workers' decisions to participate in the formal sector (Perry et al., 2007; Ulyssea, 2020). For the purposes of this chapter, the informal economy involves activities that, if recorded, would contribute to gross domestic product (GDP), and does not cover illegal activities or household production (Medina & Schneider, 2018; Schneider et al., 2010).

6.2. Origins of Informality

Depending on the cause, informality may be broadly categorised into the following five divisions:

(a) *Involuntary Exclusion Principle*: Oppressive entry regulations and deficiency of human capital may exclude some firms and workers to remain outside the formal modern industry (Loayza et al., 2005; Perry et al., 2007).
(b) *Voluntary Exclusion Principle:* There are also situations when firms voluntarily exit for reasons like greater independence and freedom and flexible regulatory compliance (Falco & Haywood, 2016; Günther & Launov, 2012).
(c) *Wilful Non-compliance, Avoiding Motivation and Outside the Regulation System*: Kanbur (2009) and Kanbur and Keen (2015) identified these tendencies as the causes of informality.
(d) *Subsistence Based*: Commonly found in low-income countries with poor technological capabilities for subsistence (Docquier et al., 2017).
(e) *Extensive and Intensive Margin*: In case of extensive margin, informality declines with firm size (as the visibility to the government increases with size or the opportunity cost of operating rises, and hence, there may arise a need to access formal credit). In intensive margin, there is a decline in the average proportion of informal workers within the formal firms when the firm grows bigger (Ulyssea, 2020).

6.3. Measures of Informality

6.3.1. Indirect Measure of Informality

There are two major indirect approaches to estimate the size of the informal sector:

(i) Dynamic general equilibrium (DGE) model-based estimates of informal output (% of official GDP).
(ii) Multiple indicators and multiple causes (MIMIC) model-based estimates of informal output (% of official GDP).

In the DGE-based estimate, the optimisation decision of the households involves decision regarding allocation of labour between formal and informal sectors at each period of time and changes of its allocation over time (Elgin & Oztunali, 2012; Ihrig & Moe, 2004). Compared to other models, the DGE approach is more comprehensive in both country and year coverage. On the other hand, in the MIMIC model (Feige, 2016; Medina & Schneider, 2018; Schneider et al., 2010), structural equations are formulated to calculate the relative size of informal economic activity. The two most advantages of the MIMIC approach are that it incorporates multiple possible causes of informal activity and captures multiple outcome indicators, and hence, it is readily used as a measure of informality across nations over time.

Figs. 12.4–12.7 attempt to make a comparison between the DGE and MIMIC model estimates of the measurement of the informal sector between some selected AEs (the United Kingdom, the United States, France, Japan, Denmark, Norway and Sweden) and EMDEs (China, India, Colombia, Chile, Hungary, Vietnam and Mexico) during the period 1990–2020 using the database provided by Elgin et al. (2021). The DGE estimates are shown in Figs. 12.4 and 12.5, whereas the MIMIC estimates are represented in Figs. 12.6 and 12.7. But barring a few exceptions, more or less similar trends in ranking are observed on the basis of the two estimates in both AEs and EMDEs.

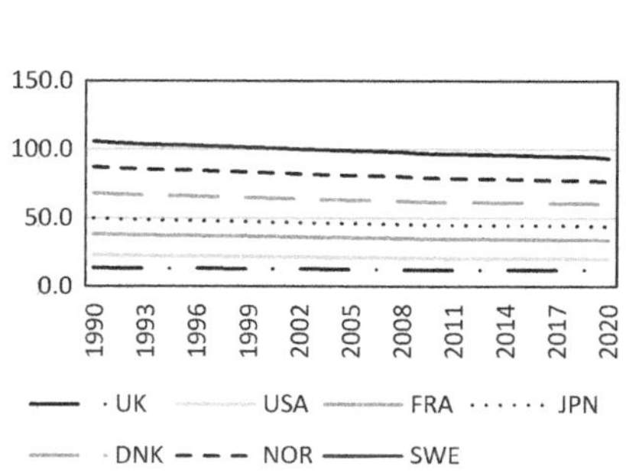

Fig. 12.4. DGE Estimate of Informal Output (as % of Official GDP) in AEs.
Source: Author's construction based on Elgin et al. (2021).

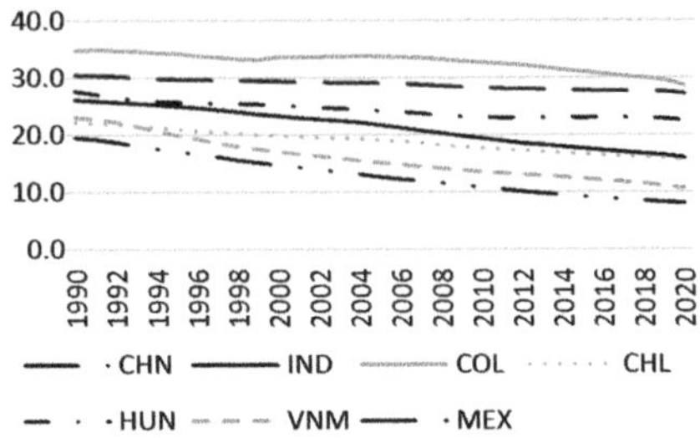

Fig. 12.5. DGE Estimate of Informal Output (as % of Official GDP) in EMDEs. *Source*: Author's construction based on Elgin et al. (2021).

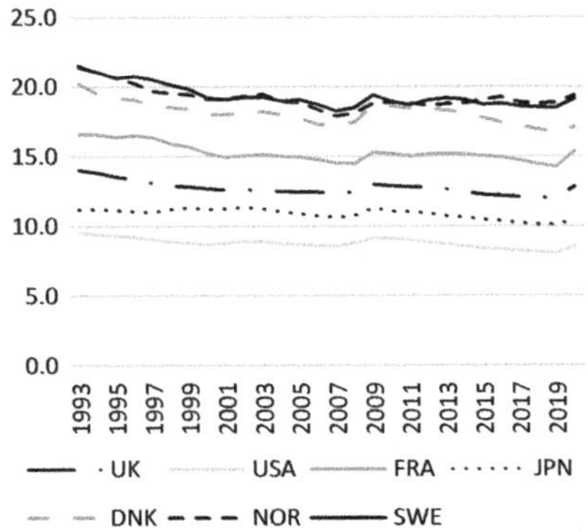

Fig. 12.6. MIMIC Estimate of Informal Output (as % of Official GDP) in AEs. *Source*: Author's construction based on Elgin et al. (2021).

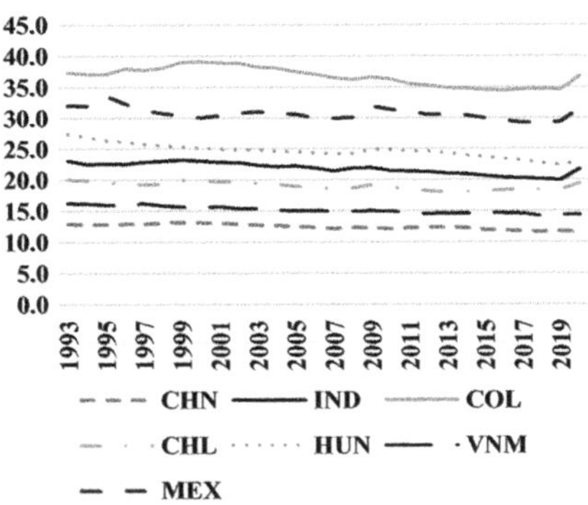

Fig. 12.7. MIMIC Estimate of Informal Output (as % of Official GDP) in EMDEs. *Source*: Author's construction based on Elgin et al. (2021).

6.3.2. Direct Survey Measure of Informality

In this survey-based direct measure, there are four measures: three based on labour estimates and one based on pension coverage.

(i) The commonest form of measure share of self-employment in total employment (named as SEMP) (Porta & Shleifer, 2014; Maloney, 2004). As defined by the 1993 International Classification of Status in Employment, self-employed workers include four sub-categories of jobs, as classified in the World Bank's WDI and by the ILO: employers, own-account workers, members of producers' cooperatives and contributing family workers. Self-employed workers are those who, working on their own account (own-account workers or employers) or with one or a few partners or in a cooperative, hold 'self-employment jobs'.
(ii) Informal employment (% of total employment; ILO; harmonised series).
(iii) Employment outside the formal sector (% of total employment; ILO; harmonised series).
(iv) Labour force with pension (% of labour force).

Figs. 12.8 and 12.9 point out towards a new measure of informality, that is, self-employment (% of total employment). Fig. 12.8 shows the change in self-employment from 1990 to 2020 (figures are taken at a gap of five years). They demonstrate a very important fact that among the seven selected EMDEs, the proportion of self-employment is highest in case of India as compared to any

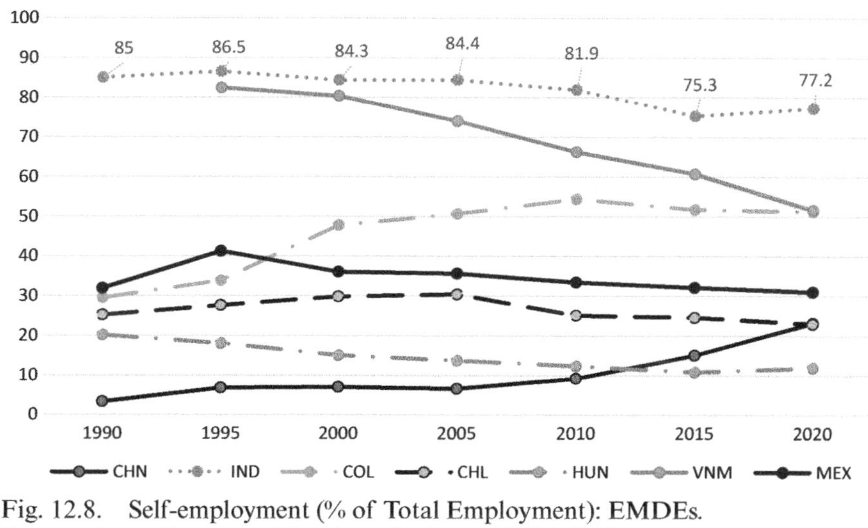

Fig. 12.8. Self-employment (% of Total Employment): EMDEs.
Sources: https://www.worldbank.org/en/research/brief/informal-economy-database; Elgin et al. (2021).

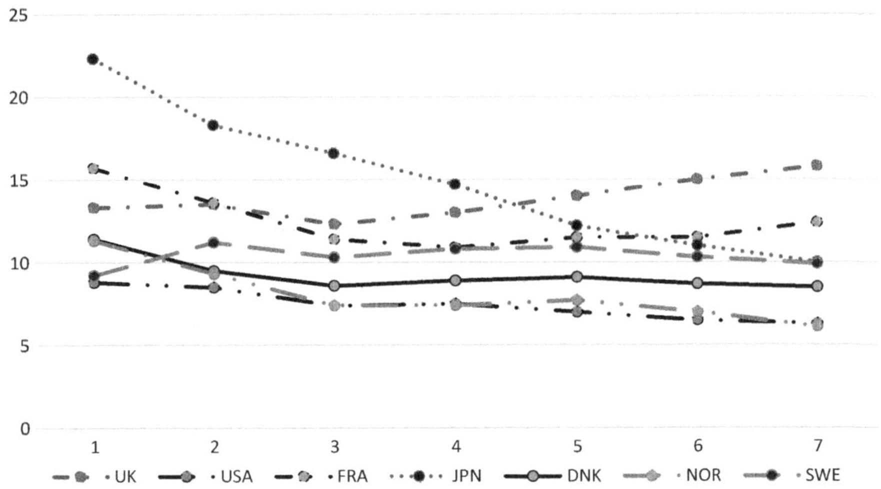

Fig. 12.9. Self-employment (% of Total Employment): AEs.
Sources: https://www.worldbank.org/en/research/brief/informal-economy-database; Elgin et al. (2021).

of the selected EMDEs and AEs. Though it declined after 2010, but still it is more than three-fourths of the total employment in India. No other countries have maintained this high proportion of self-employment other than Vietnam at the beginning of the 1990s. But there was a drastic fall in this percentage, and it now occupies about half of total employment. In sharp contrast to this, the proportion of self-employment as a percentage of total employment is much low in the last three decades, and for most of the selected AEs, it lies within the range 6%–12% in recent years except for Japan which had a comparatively high percentage of self-employed workers among the selected set of AEs in the beginning of 1990s, but there was a sharp fall, and now, it is about 10%. Within the EMDEs, countries like India, China and Colombia are experiencing a rising trend in percentage of self-employed workers, while others like Vietnam, Chile, Hungary and Mexico are experiencing a decreasing trend.

6.4. Growing Informality Trends in India

One of the major aims of achieving inclusive growth in India is to reduce the share of informal employment in total employment. However, with over 90% of the entire workforce being informal (defined as those without any social insurance) and 85% of the non-agricultural workforce being informal. Surplus labour in agriculture is absorbed in unorganised manufacturing in micro-enterprises employing less than 10 workers, where no social insurance was available. Most illiterate are either casual workers or in self-employment usually engaged in low productivity work. People with relatively poor levels of education are absorbed in agriculture, traditional services or construction or unorganised manufacturing (with no social insurance). Stringent and numerous labour laws are applied in the organised registered enterprises, which has resulted in the growth of informal sector labour, and this may be regarded as one of the most important demand side factors contributing to the rapid growth of informal jobs in India. This has been further reinforced by the supply-side factor, that is, deficiency in educational levels due to inadequate investment in schools, higher education and vocational training, which produces workforce employable only at the informal sector.

The share of workers in non-agricultural employment rose much faster than the share in regular wage employment or organised sector. Between 1983 and 2019, the share of the non-farm sector in employment rose 20, but the majority of such jobs were of the informal variety. On net, the share of regular wage work increased less than 3 percentage points and that of the organised sector less than 2 percentage points.

6.5. Plausible Explanations for Sustained Rise of Informality in India

Historically speaking, there were various reasons for the growth and persistence of informality in India's labour force, which were the result of factors affecting both the demand and the supply of labour. Some of the most important reasons are highlighted here (Mehrotra & Giri, 2023).

(i) *Demand side explanation for rise of informality*:

Four different reasons stand out for explaining the growth of informal labour demand in India.

(a) The growth strategy itself is responsible for this pattern of growth in India. Under the Mahalanobis strategy, the Government of India and its Planning Commission in the Second Five Year Plan (1955–1956 to 1959–1960) decided to follow a strategy based on import-substituting industrialisation (ISI), with more emphasis on heavy industry. It was regarded as deliberate initiative towards a state-led capitalism, substituting for the absence of large corporates. As a consequence, surplus labourers from agriculture migrated to the non-agricultural sector in search of jobs. They got inevitably absorbed in traditional services in both rural and urban areas. Those who didn't get the opportunity to work in the organised sector got absorbed in unorganised manufacturing in micro-enterprises employing less than 10 workers, which is devoid of any kind of social insurance cover for informal workers.
(b) The second reason is a result of a direct policy-induced pattern of growth that impacted the demand for labour. The Industrial Policy resolutions implemented by the Government of India initiated a process where manufacture of consumer products of a non-durable nature was being reserved for the small-scale sector. The entry of medium-sized enterprise or large business houses was prohibited from this sector. This backfired and led to the perverse incentives to remain small, with inevitable loss in terms of economies of scale. The small enterprises had no incentive to

grow and absorb more workers in their manufacturing units, thus exacerbating a problem resulting from the heavy industry first strategy of ISI. It was believed that the small-scale sector would use labour-intensive techniques in the production of consumer goods, thus adding to the supply of consumer goods as well as creating employment opportunities for the fast-expanding labour force.

(c) A third factor is related to the numerous and complex labour laws of the central and state governments, impacting absorption of labour in organised manufacturing. The labour laws are much more flexible and less binding which are applicable to the small enterprises. On the contrary, the larger business houses were subjected to stringent and complex labour laws over time, imposed by both the central and state governments, which were aimed at protecting the workers in the organised sector. So, there has been a very slow growth of workers in the organised sector, whereas most of the growth in the non-agricultural unorganised sector were concentrated in micro, small and medium enterprises (MSMEs) with workers lacking coverage of any kind of social security and insurance.

(d) A fourth important reason might be to avoid uncertainty arising from greater volatility in the global market, there has been a tendency of the entrepreneurs in the ancillaries of export-oriented units to employ workers on informal terms so that they can be retrenched without any compensation during a demand slack.

(ii) *Supply-side explanation for increasing informality*:

The driving force of consistent rise in informal sector workers in India is the deficiency in skill and education which is the result of adequate investment in the social sector (viz., education and health). Statistical data provide some support to the statement. National sample survey (NSS) data allow an analysis of the education level of the workforce. Hardly any illiterates have regular salaried jobs. Barely 3% of the workforce has technical education at the tertiary level, and another 7.2% has general academic education at the tertiary level. As recently as 2017–2018, only 2.4% of the workforce has formally acquired any vocational education or training (Mehrotra, 2020).

Periodic labour force survey (PLFS) (2021–2022) shows that out of the entire working age (15+ years) population of 1,021 million, 493 million are in the workforce and the remaining 528 million are out of the workforce. Within the workforce, 211 million are in the agricultural sector and 282 million are in the non-agricultural sector. Within the non-agricultural sector, 112 million are regular wage workers and 170 million are self-employed and casual workers. In the category of self-employed and casual workers, the workers are mostly illiterate and are usually engaged in low productivity work. Within the self-employed, almost half are own-account workers, in contrast to those who work in MSMEs (employing about 2–9 workers). In the total workforce, just over half have education up to the secondary level and half of them are self-employed. But which is more alarming is that nearly three-fourths of those with secondary education, that is, about 75 million actually are in casual work.

If we concentrate on vocational education, less than 5% of the workforce has formal training. However, one interesting point to note is that the probability of getting a regular salary job is higher for those with technical education below the graduate level as well as at the graduate level and above compared to a graduate with only general academic education (Mehrotra, 2016). Hence, the quality of labour force is one of the major reasons for growing informality in India.

However, notable is that technical education below the graduate level as well as at the graduate level and above significantly raises the probability of getting a regular salary job than if you were a graduate with only general academic education (Mehrotra, 2016). So, the workforce with low levels of education is mostly absorbed in the agricultural sector, or those who were not absorbed in agriculture gets the opportunity of working in the informal sector with low-paid unsecured jobs like traditional services or construction or unorganised manufacturing. These informal sector workers are not protected by any kind of social security measures or insurance.

7. Conclusion

The present analysis clearly demonstrates the interlinkages between structural changes and growth of informal sector workers, particularly in the EMDEs as compared to AEs. In case of developed economies of Europe and North America, manufacturing played a crucial role in the initial stages followed by services-led revolution in the later stages. The same pattern of structural change was observed in case of newly industrial nations of East Asia (like Korea, Japan, Taiwan, Malaysia) and currently EMDEs like China and Vietnam. But India's structural transformation does not exhibit the classical pattern of change as share of agriculture declined and services increased, but in India, the share of manufacturing remained stagnant. Hence, the manufacturing sector has not performed the desired role as it played in case of most of AEs. Moreover, there has been a steady rise in the share of the workforce engaged in self-employed and casual wage work which are not protected by any social security or insurance. This suggests that the pattern of economic growth that India has experienced since the 1980s has created non-farm opportunities mainly of an informal nature. So, more attention should be paid to the creation of human capital investment in the planning process which may result in higher productivity, hence higher incomes, and higher margins for employers, who could not grow their enterprises.

References

Basole, A. (2022). Structural transformation and employment generation in India: Past performance and the way forward. *The Indian Journal of Labour Economics*, *65*, 295–320.

Docquier, F., Müller, T., & Naval, J. (2017). Informality and long-run growth. *The Scandinavian Journal of Economics*, *119*(4), 1040–1085.

Elgin, C., & Oztunali, O. (2012). *Shadow economies around the world: Model based estimates*. Working Papers 2012/05. Bogazici University, Department of Economics. https://ideas.repec.org/s/bou/wpaper.html

Elgin, C., Kose, M. A., Ohnsorge, F., & Yu, S. (2021). *Understanding informality* [CEPR Discussion Paper 16497]. Centre for Economic Policy Research.

Falco, P., & Haywood, L. (2016). Entrepreneurship versus joblessness: Explaining the rise in self-employment. *Journal of Development Economics*, *118*(January), 245–265.

Feige, E. L. (2016). Reflections on the meaning and measurement of unobserved economies: What do we really know about the "Shadow Economy"? *Journal of Tax Administration*, *2*(1). https://ssrn.com/abstract=2728060

Ghatak, M., Jha, M., & Singh, J. (2024). *Quantity vs quality: Long-term trends in job creation in the Indian labour market*. The India Forum.

Ghose, A. K. (2020). *Structural transformation of India's economy* [Working Paper WP 01/2020]. IHD.

Günther, I., & Launov, A. (2012). Informal employment in developing countries: Opportunity or last resort? *Journal of Development Economics*, *97*(1), 88–98.

Ihrig, J., & Moe, K. S. (2004). Lurking in the shadows: The informal sector and government policy. *Journal of Development Economics*, *73*(2), 541–557.

ILO. (2018). *Digital labour platforms and the future of Work: Towards decent work in the online world*. International Labour Office.

Kaldor, N. (1967). *Strategic factors in economic development*. Ithaca.

Kanbur, R. (2009). *Conceptualizing informality: Regulation and enforcement* [IZA Discussion Paper 4186]. IZA-Institute of Labor Economics.

Kanbur, R., & Keen, M. (2015, June 15). *Rethinking informality* [Blog]. Voxeu. https://voxeu.org/article/rethinking-informality

Kuznets, S. (1955). Economic growth and income inequality. *The American Economic Review*, *XLV*(1), 1–30.

Kuznets, S. (1966). *Modern economic growth: Rate, structure and spread*. Yale University Press.

Lewis, A. (1954). Economic development with unlimited supplies of labour. *The Manchester School*, *22*(2), 139–191.

Loayza, N. V., Oviedo, A. M., & Servén, L. (2005). *The impact of regulation on growth and informality: Cross-country evidence* (Vol. 3623, pp. 1–20). World Bank Publications.

Maloney, W. F. (2004). Informality revisited. *World Development*, *32*(7), 1159–1178.

Medina, M., & Schneider, F. (2018). *Shadow economies around the world: What did we learn over the last 20 years?* [IMF Working Paper 18/17]. International Monetary Fund.

Mehrotra, S. (2016). *Seizing the demographic dividend - Policies to achieve inclusive growth in India*. Cambridge University Press.

Mehrotra, S. (2020). *Informal employment trends in the Indian economy: Persistent informality, but growing positive development*. ILO working paper, Geneva.

Mehrotra, S., & Giri, T. (2023). Enterprise informality in India: The blind spots in public policy. *The Indian Journal of Labour Economics*, *66*, 687–710. https://doi.org/10.1007/s41027-023-00450-9

Mehrotra, S., & Parida, J. K. (2021). Stalled structural change brings an employment crisis in India. *The Indian Journal of Labour Economics*, *64*, 281–308. https://doi.org/10.1007/s41027-021-00317-x

Nayyar, D. (2019). India's path to structural transformation: An exception and the rule. In C. Monga & J. Yifu Lin (Eds.), *The Oxford Handbook of Structural Transformation* (pp. 465–488). Oxford Handbooks. https://doi.org/10.1093/oxfordhb/9780198793847.013.20

Perry, G. E., Maloney, W. F., Arias, O. S., Fajnzylber, P., Mason, A. D., & Chanduvi, J. S. (2007). *Informality: Exit and exclusion*. World Bank.

Porta, R. L., & Shleifer, A. (2014). Informality and development. *Journal of Economic Perspectives 28*(3), 109–126.

Rannis, G., & Fei, J. C. H. (1961). A theory of economic development. *The American Economic Review*, *51*(4), 533–565. http://www.jstor.org/stable/1812785

Rodrik, D. (2013). *Structural change, fundamentals, and growth: An overview*. Institute for Advanced Study.

Schneider, F., Buehn, A., & Montenegro, C. E. (2010). *Shadow economies all over the world: New estimates for 162 countries from 1999 to 2007* [Policy Research Working Paper 5356]. World Bank.

Schneider, F., & Enste, D. H. (2000). Shadow economies: Size, causes, and consequences. *Journal of Economic Literature*, *38*(1), 77–114.

Singh, L. (2025, April 29). Innovations, structural transformation and employment across space and time. *The Indian Journal of Labour Economics*, *68*, 1–21. https://doi.org/10.1007/s41027-025-00562-4

Solow, R. (1956). A contribution to the theory of economic growth. *The Quarterly Journal of Economics*, *70*, 65–94.

Ulyssea, G. (2020). Informality: Causes and consequences for development. *Annual Reviews of Economics*, *12*, 525–546.

Voskoboynikov, I. B. (2017). *Structural change, expanding informality and labour productivity growth in Russia*. BOFIT Discussion Papers 18/2017. https://ssrn.com/abstract=3080252

World Development Indicator. (2024). *World Bank*. https://databank.worldbank.org/source/world-development-indicators

Chapter 13

Convergence Analysis of Energy Consumption in the G-20 Economies

Nilendu Chatterjee

Department of Economics, Bankim Sardar College, South 24 Parganas, India

Abstract

The present study examines how G-20 countries are progressing towards sustainable development goals (SDGs), focusing on reducing emissions by shifting from non-renewable to renewable energy sources. Given that G-20 economies account for around 85% of global gross domestic product (GDP), 66% of the world's population, and 75% of international trade, their role is crucial in shaping global environmental outcomes. A key tension explored is whether emission reduction can go hand in hand with economic growth, particularly industrial expansion. While nations acknowledge the need for cleaner energy, the practical commitment to this transition remains under scrutiny. To investigate this, the present study analyses data from 2000 to 2022 using three convergence methods – absolute beta convergence is used for assessing whether G-20 countries are reducing non-renewable energy use over time. Conditional beta convergence considers growth of industrial output as an important factor and sees if convergence still holds when this factor is held constant. Sigma convergence is used for checking if the variation in energy use across countries is narrowing. Findings reveal that G-20 countries have, on average, reduced their total non-renewable energy consumption – both in absolute terms and when industrial growth is accounted for. The presence of sigma convergence further suggests that nations are adopting renewable energy in a more uniform way. Hence, while economic growth remains a priority, G-20 countries are showing measurable progress in transitioning towards cleaner energy, indicating a potential alignment between sustainability and development goals.

Changing Dimensions in Economic Development: Theories and Empirics, 173–184

Published under exclusive licence by Emerald Publishing Limited
doi:10.1108/978-1-83708-384-820261013

Keywords: G-20 economies; renewable resources; non-renewable resources; energy consumption; convergence analysis

JEL Codes: C33; C52; C53; P52; Q20; Q30; Q38; Q43; Q47; Q48

1. Introduction

The concept of convergence in economics is traditionally associated with income levels, where poorer economies are expected to catch up with richer ones over time (Solow, 1956). However, the idea of convergence has been extended to other domains, including energy consumption. Convergence analysis, a concept borrowed from economics, refers to the idea that economies with different initial conditions will tend towards similar outcomes over time. In the context of energy consumption, convergence could imply that economies with lower initial energy consumption levels catch up with those with higher levels, leading to a reduction in disparities over time (Chatterjee & Dinda, 2016).

The G-20 economies collectively represent over 80% of global GDP, 75% of global trade, and nearly 60% of the world's population. As global concerns about climate change, energy efficiency, and sustainable development intensify, the energy consumption patterns of these nations have become a key area of focus. While economic growth and industrial development drive energy demand, advancements in renewable energy, energy efficiency, and digital infrastructure are reshaping global energy consumption. This chapter investigates whether disparities in energy consumption across G-20 countries are narrowing (converging) or widening (diverging), and what this means for global sustainability.

Energy consumption is a critical driver of economic growth and development. As the global economy continues to evolve, understanding the patterns and trends in energy consumption among major economies is essential for formulating energy policies and addressing climate change. The G-20 economies, representing the world's largest economies, are particularly important in this context, as they account for a significant share of global energy consumption.

The G-20 economies represent a significant portion of the global economy and energy consumption. Understanding the convergence or divergence of energy consumption patterns within this group is crucial for formulating effective energy policies and mitigating environmental concerns. This chapter examines the existing literature on energy consumption within G-20 nations, focusing on the interplay between trade liberalisation, economic growth, energy types (renewable and non-renewable), and environmental impact (primarily CO_2 emissions). We synthesise findings from multiple studies to assess the degree of convergence and highlight areas of divergence. The analysis considers both long-run and short-run relationships, acknowledging the dynamic nature of energy consumption patterns.

Several studies have explored the relationship between trade liberalisation, and energy consumption (Baek & Kim, 2010; Lu et al., 2019). Baek and Kim (2010) found that trade and income growth positively affected environmental quality in developed G-20 countries but negatively impacted it in developing countries. This suggests a divergence in the environmental consequences of economic growth and trade, depending on the level of development. Conversely, Lu et al. (2019) focused on the positive impact of renewable energy consumption and tourism investments on international tourist arrivals within G-20 members, suggesting a potential pathway towards more sustainable growth in developing economies. However, the study's focus on tourism and renewable energy does not fully address the broader energy consumption patterns and their convergence across the entire G-20.

Convergence in energy consumption refers to the process by which economies with different energy use patterns move towards similar levels of per capita energy consumption over time. This convergence can occur in terms of total energy consumption, energy intensity (energy use per unit of GDP), or the share of renewable energy sources in the energy mix. There are three forms of convergence analysis, in practice – beta convergence, sigma convergence, and club convergence. The concepts of beta, sigma, and club convergence can be applied to the study of energy consumption patterns to gain insights into the dynamics of energy use across regions. For instance, beta convergence can help identify whether developing regions are catching up with developed regions in terms of energy consumption. Sigma convergence can provide insights into whether the variability in energy consumption levels across regions is decreasing over time. Club convergence can help identify whether regions are converging to different energy consumption patterns based on their economic and technological characteristics. Convergence analysis is not limited to per capita energy consumption but can also extend to other dimensions, such as energy efficiency, fuel mix diversification, and renewable energy adoption.

There are two primary types of convergence are discussed below:

Beta convergence: This refers to the catching-up process, where economies with lower per capita energy consumption grow faster than those with higher consumption, leading to a reduction in disparities over time. The coefficient of the initial energy consumption level will indicate the speed of convergence (if negative and significant).

Sigma convergence: This measures the reduction in the dispersion of energy consumption across economies, indicating whether energy use is becoming more uniform.

Conditional beta convergence: This expands on beta convergence by incorporating control variables such as GDP per capita, energy intensity, technological indicators, and policy variables. This allows us to examine convergence after accounting for other influences.

Club convergence: This expresses the convergence of different groups or regions within a broader group to different steady-state levels.

A comparative analysis of beta, sigma, and club convergence is given in Table 13.1.

Table 13.1. Brief Comparison About Three Forms of Convergence.

Criteria	Beta Convergence	Sigma Convergence	Club Convergence
Focus	Catch-up process of regions with lower initial energy consumption	Reduction in the dispersion of energy consumption levels across regions	Convergence of regions to different steady-state levels
Empirical analysis	Measures the speed of convergence	Measures the reduction in variability	Measures convergence to different steady-state levels
Strengths	Provides insights into the catching-up process	Useful for understanding the overall convergence pattern	Captures the diversity in convergence patterns
Weaknesses	Ignores the overall variability in energy consumption levels	Does not provide insights into the catching-up process	Requires prior classification of regions into clubs

Source: Developed by the author.

Different forms of convergence have their specific equations which are given below.

Sigma convergence: Calculation of the standard deviation of per capita energy consumption or other concerned variables across G-20 countries over time.

Beta convergence (absolute): $\Delta\ln(E_{it}) = \alpha + \beta\ln(Ei_0) + \varepsilon_{it}$, where E_{it} is the per capita energy consumption in country i at time t, Ei_0 is the initial per capita energy consumption, and ε_{it} is the error term.

Beta convergence (conditional): $\Delta\ln(E_{it}) = \alpha + \beta\ln(E_{i0}) + \gamma X_{it} + \varepsilon_{it}$, where X_{it} represents a vector of control variables.

The convergence analysis for G-20 economies occupies the centre of discussion for several reasons.

Energy consumption patterns vary significantly across the G-20 economies, reflecting differences in economic structures, population sizes, technological advancements, and energy policies. Convergence analysis refers to the study of whether these energy consumption patterns are becoming more similar over time or diverging. This analysis is essential for addressing global energy challenges, as it provides insights into the trends, opportunities, and barriers that shape energy use across diverse economies.

The G-20 economies account for approximately 80% of global energy consumption and 75% of greenhouse gas emissions, making them central to the global energy transition. As the world strives to meet the goals of the Paris Agreement and achieve a low-carbon future, understanding the dynamics of energy consumption in these economies is crucial.

The global energy transition towards renewable energy sources and reduced carbon emissions requires coordination among G-20 economies. Convergence analysis helps identify whether these economies are moving in a similar direction in terms of energy use and policy implementation. For instance, are developing economies catching up with developed economies in renewable energy adoption? Are energy-intensive industries in all G-20 economies becoming more energy efficient?

The Paris Agreement relies on the collective efforts of G-20 economies to reduce greenhouse gas emissions and limit global warming to well below 2°C. Convergence analysis can help assess whether these economies are aligning their energy consumption patterns with the Agreement's goals. For example, are G-20 economies converging towards lower carbon intensity in their energy mixes? Are they adopting similar strategies to phase out coal and scale up renewable energy?

Energy inequality, both within and across countries, remains a significant challenge. Convergence analysis sheds light on disparities in energy access and consumption, particularly between developed and developing G-20 economies. For example, while some G-20 countries are transitioning to low-carbon energy systems, others continue to rely heavily on fossil fuels due to economic and infrastructural constraints.

Convergence analysis provides valuable insights for policymakers by identifying best practices and barriers to energy transition. For instance, if convergence is observed in renewable energy adoption, it may indicate successful policy frameworks that can be replicated across economies. Conversely, if divergence persists, it may signal the need for targeted interventions or international cooperation to address specific challenges.

2. Literature Review

The concept of convergence in economics was popularised by the work of Barro and Sala-i-Martin (1992), who examined the convergence of income levels across regions and countries. Since then, the concept has been applied to various economic indicators, including energy consumption.

The relationship between energy consumption and economic growth has been a subject of extensive research. The prevailing hypothesis suggests a positive correlation, where increased energy consumption fuels economic expansion (Destek & Okumu, 2018; Rajaguru & Khan, 2021). Destek and Okumu (2018) found a cointegration relationship between biomass energy consumption and economic growth in G-20 countries, with increased consumption leading to higher growth. This supports the energy–growth nexus but is limited to biomass energy and doesn't explore the broader energy mix. Rajaguru and Khan (2021) investigated the diminishing trend of energy intensity and its relationship with growth volatility across 48 countries (including many G-20 members). Their findings suggested that energy intensity is falling, implying a move towards greater sustainability in the production process. However, the study's focus on energy intensity doesn't directly address the convergence of overall energy consumption levels across G-20 economies.

The environmental Kuznets curve (EKC) hypothesis posits an inverted U-shaped relationship between economic growth and environmental degradation, suggesting that environmental quality initially deteriorates with economic development but improves beyond a certain income level (Damrah et al., 2022; Rahman et al., 2022; Zaekhan & Nachrowi, 2015). Zaekhan and Nachrowi (2015) found that GDP per capita is a determinant of CO_2 emissions per capita, consistent with the EKC hypothesis. However, this study only covers the period 2001–2010 and doesn't account for the diverse energy mixes within the G-20. Damrah et al. (2022) examined the role of natural resources in achieving environmental sustainability in nine major oil-producing countries (a subset of the G-20), finding that economic development contributes to increased environmental degradation. Rahman et al. (2022) also explored the EKC hypothesis in the context of tourism and energy mix for the top 10 tourist destinations (again, a subset of the G-20), finding support for the EKC but emphasising the role of renewable energy in improving environmental quality. These studies, while informative, are limited in their scope and don't provide a comprehensive picture of convergence across the entire G-20.

The role of renewable energy sources in achieving environmental sustainability is a critical area of investigation (Gnangoin et al., 2022; Lu et al., 2019; Zaekhan & Nachrowi, 2015). Lu et al. (2019) highlighted the positive effects of renewable energy consumption on international tourist arrivals in G-20 countries, suggesting a potential for sustainable development. Zaekhan and Nachrowi (2015) demonstrated that increased renewable energy consumption per capita reduces CO_2 emissions per capita. Gnangoin et al. (2022) further substantiated this finding, showing that renewable energy consumption and human capital are complementary levers for reducing CO_2 emissions in newly emerging market economies (a subset of the G-20). These studies suggest a potential for convergence towards more sustainable energy mixes, but this remains contingent on various factors including technological advancements, policy support, and economic conditions.

The transition to renewable energy sources also involves technological innovation (Chien et al., 2022; Raihan & Voumik, 2022; Udeagha & Ngepah, 2022). Udeagha and Ngepah (2022) found that green technological innovation improves environmental sustainability in South Africa, suggesting a potential model for other G-20 economies. Raihan and Voumik (2022) similarly showed the positive impact of technological innovation on CO_2 emission reduction in China. Chien et al. (2022) investigated the role of technological innovation and cleaner energy in Association of Southeast Asian Nations (ASEAN) countries (a subset of the G-20), revealing the significant negative impact of renewable energy on carbon emissions and ecological footprints. These studies highlight the importance of technological innovation in facilitating the transition to renewable energy and achieving environmental sustainability, but the extent to which this drives convergence across the G-20 remains an open question.

The studies reviewed employed various econometric techniques, including cointegrated vector autoregression (CVAR) (Baek & Kim, 2010), fully modified ordinary least squares (FMOLS) (Destek & Okumu, 2018; Lu et al., 2019), fixed effect model (FEM) (Zaekhan & Nachrowi, 2015), panel unit root tests and cointegration tests (Destek & Okumu, 2018), and panel quantile regression

(Azam et al., 2022). The choice of methodology influences the results and interpretations. Some studies focused on specific energy sources (e.g., biomass (Destek & Okumu, 2018), renewable (Lu et al., 2019)), while others examined the overall energy mix (Baek & Kim, 2010). The time periods covered also vary significantly, limiting direct comparisons. Many studies are limited to subsets of the G-20 or focus on specific countries, hindering a comprehensive analysis of convergence across the entire group.

Furthermore, the studies often focus on the relationship between energy consumption and economic growth, neglecting the broader socio-political factors that influence energy choices (Eder et al., 2017; Popov & Semyachkov, 2018). Eder et al. (2017) developed a multivariate model to predict motor vehicle rates in Russian regions, highlighting the influence of economic, social, and institutional factors. Popov and Semyachkov (2018) analysed strategic aspects of digital economy development in Organisation for Economic Co-operation and Development (OECD), European Union (EU), and Russia, emphasising the role of information infrastructure and institutional environment in driving digitisation and, by extension, influencing energy consumption patterns. These factors are crucial for understanding the complexities of energy consumption and the potential for convergence across diverse economic and political systems within the G-20.

Based on the synthesised literature, several observations can be made regarding the convergence of energy consumption in G-20 economies. There is evidence of a declining trend in energy intensity in many G-20 countries (Rajaguru & Khan, 2021), suggesting an improvement in energy efficiency. However, this doesn't necessarily imply convergence in overall energy consumption levels. Developed G-20 economies tend to exhibit a positive relationship between trade, economic growth, and environmental quality (Baek & Kim, 2010), while developing economies often experience the opposite (Baek & Kim, 2010). This divergence could be attributed to differences in technological capabilities, institutional frameworks, and environmental regulations.

The adoption of renewable energy sources shows a potential for convergence towards more sustainable energy mixes (Gnangoin et al., 2022; Lu et al., 2019). However, the rate of adoption varies considerably across G-20 countries, influenced by factors such as policy support, technological advancements, and economic incentives. The EKC hypothesis, while supported by some studies (Rahman et al., 2022; Zaekhan & Nachrowi, 2015), doesn't fully explain the complex relationship between economic growth and environmental degradation in the context of diverse energy mixes and development levels. The role of technological innovation in driving the transition to renewable energy and improving environmental quality is evident (Chien et al., 2022; Raihan & Voumik, 2022; Udeagha & Ngepah, 2022), but its impact on convergence remains unclear.

The influence of socio-political factors, such as institutional quality and urbanisation, is often overlooked (Eder et al., 2017; Popov & Semyachkov, 2018). These factors play a significant role in shaping energy policies and consumption patterns, and their impact on convergence needs further investigation. The methodological limitations of existing studies, including varying methodologies, time periods, and geographic scopes, also hinder a definitive assessment of convergence.

Under the given backdrop, one can say that there are ample scopes for further convergence analysis of G-20 economies, regarding different aspects of energy consumption – since there are several key areas of energy consumption which are yet to be researched upon for this important group of economies. This study will look to explore all such aspects and fill up this lacuna.

3. Data, Methodology, and Econometric Analysis

Here, we have considered the data of per capita energy consumption of non-renewable resources (ENER), per capita energy consumption (PCE) – this variable obviously combines both forms of resources – non-renewable and renewable. We have also considered the industrial output (IND) which is measured as the percentage share of industry in the national output or GDP. The data for the first two variables have been collected from the International Energy Agency (IEA), and the data of the industrial output have been collected from the World Development Indicators, World Bank. The dataset covers the period of 2000–2022 which is for above two decades. We have performed absolute beta convergence (β), conditional beta convergence, and sigma convergence (σ).[1] We have used different statistical tools and applied a simple ordinary least square method for conducting the convergence analysis, and we have represented our findings by following the econometric and diagrammatic approach.

We have used the following two equations for conducting the convergence analysis, that is, for performing the beta and sigma convergence analysis.

$$g_{it} = \alpha + \beta \mathrm{EN}_{it-1} + u_{it} \tag{1}$$

$$g_{it} = \alpha + \beta \mathrm{EN}_{it-1} + \gamma \mathrm{IND} + u_{it} \tag{2}$$

We have used Equation (1) for estimating absolute beta convergence and sigma convergence, and the second equation (2) is used for estimating conditional beta convergence. Although we have reported the results of random effects panel regression results here, we have tested all the other panel regression models such as – FEM, Maximum Likelihood Estimation test (MLE), etc. Here, g represents the average growth rate of the concerned variables – ENER and PCE. In both the equations, a specific country or nation is presented by the subscript 'i' and the time period under study is presented by 't'. In Equation (2) IND is the vector of conditional variable. In this case, the subscripts have been used according to the need of the study. All the variables have been converted into their log values for the sake of removing the heterogeneity from the dataset. The random variable 'u_{it}'

[1]We have used the inspection method of Levin-Lin-Chu panel unit root test (LLC), Im-Pesaran-Shin test (IPS), Fisher-Augmented Dickey-Fuller test (ADF), and Fisher-Phillips-Perron (PP) tests for checking the stationarity of the panel dataset, and the tests suggested that all the variables follow $I(0)$.

has the property of zero mean and finite variance, and the variance is independent over time and region.

The conclusion regarding convergence or divergence depends on the sign of β – a positive sign would imply a divergence, whereas a negative sign would confirm the existence of convergence, if and only if these results pass the required statistical tests successfully. The result of the absolute beta convergence is reported in Table 13.2.

From Table 13.2, it is evident that for G-20 economies, there is absolute beta convergence for the two concerned variables – per capita energy consumption and per capita energy consumption from non-renewable resources, for the study period 2000–2022, since the β coefficient is having a negative sign, and it is significant. The speed of convergence for renewable energy uses is 58%, and it is higher than overall per capita consumption of energy which is 47%. These results indicate the fact that economies with lower per capita consumption of energy have been catching up with the faster ones, and the disparity between them has been falling. Even if there is absolute convergence for both ENER and PCE across G-20 economies, the speed of convergence varies across nations – which could be because of several socio-economic reasons. This calls for the test of conditional beta convergence. The report for conditional beta convergence is reported in Table 13.3, where we have hold the industrial output constant.

The above table vividly indicates the existence of conditional beta convergence of both the energy-related variables even when we control for the industrial

Table 13.2. Absolute Beta Convergence: ENER and PCE.

Parameter	**Coefficient (β)**	***t*-Statistic**	**Speed of Convergence (λ)**	R^2
ENER	−0.025***	−2.15	−0.58	0.87
PCE	−0.067***	−3.07	−0.47	0.68
Constant	3.024***	2.04	−0.77	0.60

Source: Author's calculation.
*** denotes significance at 1% level.

Table 13.3. Conditional Beta Convergence.

Parameter	**Coefficient (β)**	***t*-Statistic**	***p*-Value**	**Wald χ^2**	R^2
ENER	−0.020***	−3.90	0.006	32.56***	0.89
PCE	−0.044**	−2.01	0.040	24.66***	0.74
IND	0.15	3.50	0.001		
Constant	2.30	4.20	0.000		

Source: Author's calculation.
*** denotes significance at 1% level; ** denotes significance at 5% level.

output. These two tables give the valuable insight that the G-20 economies have been moving towards a common direction. The conditional beta coefficients for both ENER and PCE are lesser in magnitude than the absolute beta coefficient, suggesting that the industrial output influences convergence. The positive coefficient for the industrial output indicates that higher industrial activity is associated with higher energy consumption.

A more convenient approach of examining convergence on a cross-country basis is by using sigma convergence, that is, whether there is any reduction in the dispersion or trend of variance of energy usage across economies – which indicates to the possible existence or non-existence of a uniform way of consuming energy by these 20 economies. This convergence or divergence can be represented by diagrammatic techniques followed by the level of significance and value of β coefficient by using Equation (1).

Table 13.4 shows that there is the presence of sigma convergence of the two energy-related variables under study as evident from the estimated values of the slopes of the trends of variation of ENER and PCE. These values are −0.07 and −0.22 for ENER and PCE, respectively, and both of these are significant at 5% level. The results are reported in Table 13.4, which establishes the presence of sigma convergence, that is, the intercountry variance in consumption of energy among G-20 economies has been falling over the study period.

4. Conclusion

This study investigates the convergence of per capita energy consumption and energy consumption of non-renewable resources in the G-20 economies for the period of 2000–2022 using absolute beta convergence, conditional beta convergence, and sigma convergence analyses. The results indicate that while absolute convergence is present, the inclusion of the industrial output as a conditioning variable reduces the speed of convergence. Sigma convergence is evident, with decreasing disparities in energy consumption over time. These findings underscore the importance of the industrial output in shaping energy consumption patterns and highlight the need for policies that promote energy efficiency and renewable energy adoption. Future research could extend this analysis to include additional conditioning variables, such as technological progress and energy prices. Here, one can say that the evidence of absolute convergence implies that G-20 economies are moving towards similar levels of per capita energy consumption. This could reflect technological diffusion and shared policy frameworks. The smaller

Table 13.4. Sigma (σ) Convergence.

Variables	Constant	b	F	Adjusted R^2	RMSE
ENER	2.66** (0.02)	−0.07** (0.03)	48.8	0.68	0.60
PCE	3.72** (0.04)	−0.22** (0.05)	56.6	0.71	0.41

Source: Author's calculation.
Note: Root Mean Square Error.
** denotes significance at 5% level.

beta coefficient in the conditional model highlights the role of the industrial output in shaping energy consumption. Economies with higher industrial activity tend to consume more energy, which may slow convergence. The declining standard deviation of energy consumption indicates that disparities among G-20 economies are narrowing. This could be attributed to increased global cooperation on energy policy and the adoption of renewable energy technologies. Regarding policy suggestions one can say that policies aimed at improving energy efficiency, particularly in industrial sectors, can help reduce energy consumption disparities. Again, promoting renewable energy adoption can support convergence while addressing climate change concerns. It can be said that enhanced and continued global cooperation on energy policy can enhance convergence and promote sustainable energy use.

References

Azam, A., Rafiq, M., Shafique, M., & Yuan, J. (2022). *Towards achieving environmental sustainability: The role of nuclear energy, renewable energy, and ICT in the top-five carbon emitting countries*. Frontiers Media. https://doi.org/10.3389/fenrg.2021.804706

Baek, J., & Kim, H. (2010). *Trade liberalization, economic growth, energy consumption and the environment: Time series evidence from g-20 economies*. https://doi.org/10.11644/KIEP.JEAI.2011.15.1.224

Barro, R. J., & Sala-i-Martin, X. (1992). Convergence. *Journal of Political Economy*, *100*(2), 223–251.

Chatterjee, N., & Dinda, S. (2016). Convergence of forest resources in Jangalmahal, West Bengal. In R. C. Das (Ed.), *Handbook of research on global indicators of economic and political convergence* (pp. 511–537). IGI Global. https://doi.org/10.4018/978-1-5225-0215-9.ch022

Chien, F., Hsu, C., Sibghatullah, A., Vu, H. M., Phan, T. T. H., & Tien, N. H. (2022). *The role of technological innovation and cleaner energy towards the environment in ASEAN countries: Proposing a policy for sustainable development goals*. Taylor & Francis. https://doi.org/10.1080/1331677x.2021.2016463

Damrah, S., Atrovi, E., Atyeh, M., & Shawtari, F. A. (2022). *Employing the panel quantile regression approach to examine the role of natural resources in achieving environmental sustainability: Does globalization create some difference?* Multidisciplinary Digital Publishing Institute. https://doi.org/10.3390/math10244795

Destek, M. A. & Okumu, L. (2018). *Biomass energy consumption, economic growth and CO_2 emission in g-20 countries*. https://doi.org/10.18506/anemon.453801

Eder, L., Filimonova, I., Nemov, V., & Provornaya, I. (2017). *Forecasting of energy and petroleum consumption by motor transport in the regions of the Russian federation*. https://doi.org/10.17059/2017-3-18

Gnangoin, T. Y., Kassi, D., Edjoukou, A. J., OuYang, K., & Dai, Y. (2022). Renewable energy, non-renewable energy, economic growth and CO_2 emissions in the newly emerging market economies: The moderating role of human capital. *Frontiers in Environmental Science*, *10*, 1017721. https://doi.org/10.3389/fenvs.2022.1017721

Lu, Z., Gzgr, G., Lau, C. K. M., & Paramati, S. R. (2019). *The dynamic impacts of renewable energy and tourism investments on international tourism: Evidence from the G20 countries*. Vilnius Gediminas Technical University. https://doi.org/10.3846/jbem.2019.10181

Popov, E., & Semyachkov, K. (2018). *Comparative analysis of strategic aspects of development of digital economy*. https://doi.org/10.17072/1994-9960-2018-1-19-36

Rahman, M. H., Voumik, L. C., Islam, M., Halim, M. A., & Esquivias, M. A. (2022). *Economic growth, energy mix, and tourism-induced EKC hypothesis: Evidence from top ten tourist destinations*. Multidisciplinary Digital Publishing Institute. https://doi.org/10.3390/su142416328

Raihan, A., & Voumik, L. C. (2022). *Carbon emission reduction potential of renewable energy, remittance, and technological innovation: Empirical evidence from China*. Global Society of Scientific Research and Researchers. https://doi.org/10.56556/jtie.v1i4.398

Rajaguru, G., & Khan, S. (2021). Causality between energy consumption and economic growth in the presence of growth volatility: Multi-country evidence. *Journal of Risk and Financial Management*, *14*(10), 471. https://doi.org/10.3390/jrfm14100471

Solow, R. M. (1956). A contribution to the theory of economic growth. *Quarterly Journal of Economics*, *70*(1), 65–94.

Udeagha, M. C. & Ngepah, N. (2022). *Dynamic ARDL simulations effects of fiscal decentralization, green technological innovation, trade openness, and institutional quality on environmental sustainability: Evidence from South Africa*. Multidisciplinary Digital Publishing Institute. https://doi.org/10.3390/su141610268

Zaekhan, Z., & Nachrowi, N. D. (2015). *The impact of renewable energy and GDP per capita on carbon dioxide emission in the G-20 countries*. https://doi.org/10.7454/EFI.V60I2.71

Part B

Impact on Environment, Society and Markets

Chapter 14

Exploring the Impact of Air Pollution on Female Youth Work Participation in the Light of Simultaneous Dependence Between Health Status and Their Work Participation in Rural India

Kaushiki Banerjee[a] *and Arpita Ghose*[b]

[a]*Department of Economics, Barasat Government College, West Bengal, India*
[b]*Department of Economics, Jadavpur University, West Bengal, India*

Abstract

This chapter contributes to the literature by establishing (i) the adverse impact of both outdoor and indoor air pollution on health status of the rural young females measured by female life expectancy at birth (FLE), based on major Indian state-level panel data using Baltagi's instrumental variable (IV) EC2SLS estimation method, and (ii) the interaction effect of (a) outdoor air pollution with income growth (negative) and (b) indoor air pollution with female education (positive) on FLE, implying (a) growth worsens FLE, whereas (b) rising girl education improves FLE coupled with air pollution. Though positive simultaneous dependence between FLE and female worker–population ratio (FWPR) cannot be established, the positive interaction effect of FLE and proportion of young females on FWPR suggests that given their health, a greater proportion of young females raises FWPR as being young, they can ignore their poor health caused by air pollution which increases FWPR. Another important finding is the significant 'inverted U' interaction effect of health and income growth on FWPR, that is, FWPR is high below the threshold level of the interaction term (i.e. stronger substitution effect) and low above it (i.e. dominant income effect). Importantly, given health status, further rise in growth will

Changing Dimensions in Economic Development: Theories and Empirics, 187–200

doi:10.1108/978-1-83708-384-820261017

lower young FWPR in rural India (as sample mean > critical level). Thus, worsening of FLE due to air pollution will lower FWPR as the value of the interaction term is above the critical level, reflecting higher income growth can sufficiently meet up the health damage caused by air pollution which disincentivises female work. The results of the study emphasise the need to address the problem of air pollution in rural India which may lower young FWPR further which is already poor, by worsening their health.

Keywords: Female work; life expectancy; air pollution; India; simultaneous panel model; rural

JEL Codes: J21; I19; Q59; O53; C33

1. Introduction

The depressing women's employment in India is long debated. Despite favourable demographic dynamics with blooming prospects of demographic dividend, the trend in female employment is absurd and undesirable as 96% of them are still economically inactive (i.e. NEET[1]), reflecting unsuccessful attempts to increase women's contribution in the growth process. Income per capita is expected to rise up to 20% by 2030 if female employment can be raised in tandem with men in emerging nations (Mehrotra & Sinha, 2019). Further, the scenario in rural India is grim as 80% of females are not attending any educational institutes, thus invalidating the education effect on female employment in the age group 15–24 years, and surprisingly, a majority of them are engaged in domestic duties, reflecting biased gender norms in the domestic work distribution ultimately jeopardising female employment (Sanghi et al., 2015).

There has been plethora of researches identifying different factors debarring women's paid activity. Even research documents that air pollution can produce adverse women's labour market outcomes by establishing positive simultaneous dependence between their health and employment where air pollution deteriorates female health, thereby causing a fall in their labour force participation (Banerjee & Ghose, 2022, 2023a, 2023b). Even the negative effect of air pollution on females is estimated to be stronger than males (Mishra et al., 1990; Padmavati & Arora, 1976). Though air pollution is perceived to be predominantly an urban problem, rural outdoor air quality is also deteriorating day by day due to various anthropogenic activities, like crop residue burning, increasing use of chemicals in farming activities, etc. Rural women have greater exposure to indoor air pollution due to heavy reliance on solid fuels (firewood, dung cakes, coal, crop residues) for cooking (Faizan & Thakur, 2019). Further, the working women in rural India are vulnerable due to their exposure to outdoor air pollution since majority of them

[1]Not in education, employment and training.

work as agricultural labourers or construction workers. The impact of air pollution on employment of rural working-age women given the simultaneous dependence between female work participation and their health has been explored by Banerjee and Ghose (2022). Given low youth female workforce participation and prevalence of high exposure of women to both outdoor and indoor air pollution, there is a dearth in the literature to estimate the impact of air pollution on rural young women as this may have implications on their youth employment. Though policymakers are trying to raise women's paid work, high air pollution can silently reduce their employment by weakening their health which needs to be addressed (Banerjee & Ghose, 2022, 2023a, 2023b).

Therefore, the major contributions of this chapter are summarised below: (i) it establishes the adverse impact of air pollution (both outdoor and indoor) on female health status, measured by FLE belonging to 15–29 years in rural India. Besides this, the interaction effect of air pollution with major demographic factors like (a) growth and (b) education is found to be affecting FLE significantly. This chapter uses panel dataset employing IV EC2SLS estimation method (Baltagi, 2008) based on major Indian states, spanning over 2004–2005 to 2017–2018 to explore the simultaneous relationship between FLE and youth female employment (measured by FWPR), considering the other socio-economic variables like education, growth, poverty, household size, etc. (ii) However, the positive simultaneous relation between FLE and FWPR is not obtained, implying lower FLE does not necessarily reduce FWPR. But the positive interaction effect of FLE and proportion of young females on FWPR suggests that given their health, a greater proportion of young females will raise FWPR as being young, they can ignore their poor health caused by air pollution and join work which pushes up FWPR. (iii) Another important contribution of this chapter is the interaction effect of income growth and health status on FWPR which is found to be 'inverted U', that is, the impact of FLE on FWPR actually depends on growth and vice versa. There exists a critical level of the interaction term below which FWPR rises (dominant substitution effect) and falls thereafter (stronger income effect). Thus if FLE is poor due to air pollution, given the growth level, FWPR will rise if the value of the interaction term is below the threshold level. But with high growth, given poor FLE, FWPR cannot be raised as females prefer leisure over work due to high growth of income which is sufficient to overcome the health damage caused by air pollution. Lastly, (iv) the positive interaction effect of FLE and proportion of young females on FWPR suggests that given their health, a greater proportion of young females raises FWPR as being young they can ignore their poor health caused by air pollution which increases FWPR.

The findings of this chapter indeed throw an important insight into the impact of both outdoor and indoor air pollution on FLE of young women in rural India which is often overlooked. Thus, thrust must be given to reduce outdoor air pollution in rural areas. Also, switching to cleaner cooking fuel and installing proper ventilation systems can also improve indoor air quality. Though FWPR is necessity driven as evident from the interaction effect of health and growth, a continuous effort in promoting education of women is important to raise FWPR which will motivate them.

2. Literature Survey

The literature explaining stagnant FWPR states that a dominant adverse income effect is lowering FWPR in India (Bhattacharyya & Haldar, 2020; Lahoti & Swaminathan, 2016) as against the popular feminisation-U hypothesis of Goldin (1995). Further, the anti-U feminisation hypothesis is reinstated by Banerjee and Ghose (2023b), where the interaction effect of income growth and household size is found to be rising initially but falling after a threshold level of the interaction term is achieved. Also, better education and health can augment FWPR through increased human capital formation (Barro, 1996; Cai & Kalb, 2006; Grossman, 1972). But increased educational attainment of women is often used as a status symbol and not a motivation to work. But only highly educated women are empowered enough to weaken the age-old gender norms and negative income effect which promotes FWPR. Thus, a non-linear relation between education and FWPR is also evident (Afridi et al., 2018; Dhanaraj & Mahambare, 2019; Klasen & Pieters, 2015; Olsen & Mehta, 2006).

Moreover, the literature investigating the trend in FWPR in India is not limited to these factors, but it has also explored that poverty generates acute necessity for additional income which raises FWPR (Bhalla & Kaur, 2011; Klasen & Pieters, 2015). Further, rural female employment can also be boosted by positive spillover of urbanisation in terms of increased demand for labourers due to mass male outmigration (Shrestha, 2017; Sikarwar et al., 2020). Change in household headship after separation/demise (of spouse) raises female employment as gender norms fade in female-headed households (Menon & Rodger, 2011). However, the latest debate is centred on women's prioritisation of unpaid care work often due to their caring nature and often biased gender perception heavily burdening them with household work, thus limiting their paid engagement (Dhanaraj & Mahambare, 2019; Sarkar et al., 2019). The under-reporting of unpaid care work and further limited access to employment opportunities are contributing to low FWPR (Afridi et al., 2020; Deshpande & Kabeer, 2021; Deshpande & Singh, 2021).

On other hand, promoting better health of the masses has always been in the forefront of research. Some studies focus on promoting growth, education and greater employment to boost health status (Cai & Kalb, 2006). For females, rising employment improves their bargaining position within the household which reduces unequal distribution of resources, thus promoting their health (Richards et al., 2013; Unisa & Dutta, 2005). But employment may sometimes worsen health, like occupational health hazards causing greater disease burden and early mortality (Meenakshi & Panneer, 2020). Also, along with a strong negative effect of air pollution on life expectancy, recent researches further document heterogeneous impact of it across gender. Disproportionate domestic workload (i.e. spending majority time in kitchen), concentration of women in certain occupations and difference in means of commute are causing variations in exposure to both outdoor and indoor air pollution where women are badly exposed. As a consequence, women develop blood diseases, cardiovascular and myriad respiratory complications more than men (Faizan & Thakur, 2019; Mehra et al., 2021).

Also in rural India, excessive dependence on solid fuels for cooking, improper ventilation system and use of inefficient smoke emitting stoves is further raising women's disease burden (Faizan & Thakur, 2019).

3. Gaps in the Literature and Our Contribution

The two-way interaction between health and labor force participation has been estimated earlier (Cai, 2010; Cai & Kalb, 2006), ignoring the impact of air pollution across gender. However, Banerjee and Ghose (2023a, 2023b) estimated the indirect effect of only outdoor air pollution on FWPR where pollution directly affects their health, and through positive simultaneous dependence between health and FWPR, FWPR is also adversely affected in turn for both rural and urban India for the working-age women. But given the abysmal youth FWPR and also poor rural air quality (both indoor and outdoor) in India, the present study attempts to find out the impact of both outdoor and indoor air pollution on rural young FLE and FWPR in turn which has not been attempted previously. Additionally, this chapter considers some of the interaction effects in explaining FLE and FWPR like the interaction effects between (i) growth and outdoor air pollution, (ii) indoor air pollution and education, (iii) growth and female health and (iv) proportion of young females and their health status, and the impact of those are found to be significant which has not been studied earlier. The rationale behind constructing the interaction terms is that the partial impact of one explanatory variable on the outcome variable actually depends on the other explanatory variables and vice versa.

4. Data and Methodology

4.1. Description of the Variables

To measure FWPR, female usual (principal and subsidiary) worker–population ratios in the age group 15–29 years have been taken from different rounds of NSS Employment and Unemployment Surveys (61st, 66th and 68th) and Periodic Labour Force Surveys. The data on FLE are taken from Sample Registration System, Bulletin (various issues), Office of the Registrar General and Census Commissioner. Four different pollutants are chosen to measure outdoor air pollution, viz., the concentration of (a) NO_2, (b) SO_2, (c) PM10 and (d) PM2.5 in the air which are gathered from the reports of Central Pollution Control Boards. Further, the percentage of population using solid fuel (fuel) is considered as an indicator of indoor air pollution which is obtained from different rounds of the National Family Health Survey. The data on control variables like per capita net state domestic product (PCNSDP), poverty (POV), urbanisation (Urb), sex ratio (SR), percentage of female household head (FHH), average household size (HHsz) and percentage of women completing (i) higher education (Hedu) and (ii) primary education (Pedu) are collected from Reserve Bank of India, *Handbook of Statistics on the Indian Economy* (different issues) and Census reports, Registrar General, Government of India. Here state is the unit of analysis.

4.2. Estimation Methodology

This chapter considers the following model:

$$\text{FLE} = f(\text{FWPR; Lnpcnsdp, POV, Pedu, Hedu, HHsz, FHH, SR, Pollution Variables}). \quad (1)$$

$$\text{FWPR} = \phi(\text{FLE; Lnpcnsdp, POV, Pedu, Hedu, Urb, HHsz, FHH, SR, DS}). \quad (2)$$

Simultaneously, determined equations representing FWPR and FLE for panel data containing air pollution and other above-mentioned explanatory variables are estimated for 13 Indian states for the rural sector from 2004–2005 to 2017–2018. The methodology adopted here is the IV (EC2SLS) estimators by Baltagi (2008), which is more suitable for panel data in the presence of endogeneity (Baltagi & Liu, 2009). Also a time-invariant dummy variable (DS) is incorporated in the FWPR equation as an explanatory variable as required by IV EC2SLS estimation where the states are classified according to the Gender Inequality Index (GII) scores of the states for 2017–2018 (Social Statistics Division, National Statistical Office, 2021).

Three different specifications are used to estimate FLE, where Spec 1 includes only the sole effect of the air pollutants, Spec 2 incorporates the interaction effect of air pollutants with growth and Spec 3 includes the interaction effect of education with an indicator of indoor air pollution. While estimating FWPR, two different specifications are used to estimate separately the impact of Hedu and Pedu on FWPR as they are correlated. Before estimation, two preliminary tests have been conducted, Breusch and Pagan (1980) Lagrange multiplier test and Hausman (1978) test, confirming panel regression and the presence of endogeneity. To avoid multicollinearity, different specifications are used. Both for FWPR and FLE, different combinations of the explanatory variables are tested, and the best fitted are reported in Table 14.2. Some of the included explanatory variables are not statistically significant, but keeping them in the model has improved the overall fitness and also the significance level of other explanatory variables. Those significant variables which are significant either at 10% level or less are considered. Descriptive statistics of each variable is given in Table 14.1.

5. Empirical Analysis

5.1. Analysis of FLE Equation

It is evident from Table 14.2 that FWPR positively and significantly influences FLE. Thus, a greater FWPR of rural young females will indeed improve FLE. For the air pollution variables, the sole impact of (a) outdoor air pollution, like SO_2, and (b) indoor air pollution (fuel) are found to be negative and significant. Thus, both indoor and outdoor air pollution produce an unfavourable impact on FLE in rural India. In this analysis, some of the major explanatory variables are found to be non-linearly affecting FLE. For instance, the impact of SO_2 on FLE

Table 14.1. Summary of Descriptive Statistics.

Variable	Mean	Standard Deviation (SD)	Minimum	Maximum
FWPR	29.26371	15.71285	3.38	61.967
FLE	69.74423	3.845875	62.3	77.8
PCNSDP	49,097.75	39,037.14	10,421	158,039
POV	18.82365	16.18606	2.4	73.79
Hedu	7.787962	10.1971	392	45.8
Pedu	28.425	7.585897	12.6	43.9
Urb	32.70615	11.4036	13.4	61.2
SO_2	9.521346	4.409103	3	19.59
NO_2	24.44635	10.98059	10	67.6
PM10	207.9165	87.60094	64.62	412.98
PM2.5	108.5758	60.26518	41.67	440.6
Fuel	85.90577	12.1114	44.6	97.6
FHH	12.45	4.702961	4.6	24.9
HHsz	4.45	0.5795536	3.3	5.6
SR	967.4808	68.25658	837	1,142

Source: Authors' estimation.

is non-linear, that is, there exists a threshold level of SO_2 after which further rise in SO_2 is only deleterious for FLE as the presence of certain minimum amount of these gases in the atmosphere is vital for our survival, and it is only harmful when the concentration rises above that critical level. The sample mean being greater than the estimated threshold value (critical level = 7.55 < mean = 9.52) indicates that further rise in SO_2 will shorten FLE, thus yielding a negative marginal effect (ME). Such non-linearity is also found to exist for the interaction of Lnpcsdp–SO_2 with the threshold value = 88.18 (<mean = 108.58); hence, given Lnpcsdp, further rise in SO_2 will reduce FLE. Though the sole impact of Lnpcsdp is positive, its interaction with pollution (SO_2) is negative on FLE, implying given the level of pollution, growth reduces rural FLE. Moreover, the interaction of fuel with (i) Pedu and (ii) Hedu is positive and statistically significant, implying the partial impact of fuel on FLE, in fact, depends on (i) Pedu or (ii) Hedu. As education creates knowledge and awareness regarding use of solid fuel and its role in contaminating household atmosphere, therefore, rise in the interaction terms improve FLE as with education women become aware and act accordingly to curb indoor air pollution. Therefore, the detrimental impact of outdoor as well as indoor air pollution on rural youth FLE is supported. Not only the sole impact of pollution but also the interaction effect of (i) SO_2 with Lnpcsdp and (ii) fuel with education are significantly impacting FLE.

Table 14.2. Estimated Result of FLE and FWPR (EC2SLS Estimates for Rural Sector).

Explanatory Variables	Dependent Variable: FLE			Explanatory Variables	Dependent Variable: FWPR	
	Spec 1	Spec 2	Spec 3		Spec 4	Spec 4
FWPR	0.062 (0.028)**	0.0304 (0.024)	−0.027 (0.0482)	FLE	0.752 (1.65)	0.3106 (1.649)
Lnpcsdp	3.72 (0.849)***	3.69 (0.604)***		Lnpcsdp	−325.77 (327.41)	
Pedu	0.107 (0.033)***			$(\text{Lnpcsdp})^2$	14.79 (10.04)	
Hedu			−1.18 (0.581)**	Pedu		−0.625 (1.771)
$(\text{Hedu})^2$			0.0107 (0.006)*	Hedu	−7.89 (2.97)***	
POV			−0.309 (0.125)**	$(\text{Hedu})^2$	0.447 (0.259)*	
HHsz	−1.16 (0.667)*		−2.04 (0.903)**	FHH		0.21 (0.765)
FHH		0.082 (0.018)***		Urb	0.922 (0.302)***	
SO_2	0.363 (0.124)***			Youth_fem	0.379 (0.376)	
$(SO_2)^2$	−0.026 (0.009)***			HHsz	−5.35 (3.95)	−3.05 (5.537)

(NO_2)			0.286 (0.169)*	SR	0.0153 (0.0133)	
$(NO_2)^2$			−0.003 (0.002)	(Lnpcsdp × FLE_{lagged})	1.71 (0.773)**	0.312 (0.445)
(Lnpcsdp × SO_2)		0.036 (0.015)**		(Lnpcsdp × $FLE_{lagged})^2$	−0.0012 (0.00051)**	−0.0005 (0.0003)*
(Lnpcsdp × $SO_2)^2$		−0.00023 (0.00012)*		(Youth_fem × FLE_{lagged})		0.114 (0.0334)***
(Lnpcsdp × PM2.5)		0.0008 (0.0013)		DS	−2.22 (0.885)**	−3.13 (0.855)***
(Lnpcsdp × $PM2.5)^2$		−1.97e−07 (2.25e−07)		Constant	1,184.84 (1,007.42)	98.31 (133.57)
(Lnpcsdp × PM10)		−0.0003 (0.0004)				
Fuel		−0.027 (0.029)	−0.275 (0.102)***			
(Fuel × Pedu)		0.0016 (0.0005)***				
(Fuel × Hedu)			0.0108 (0.0052)**			
Constant	1.058 (0.453)**	1.73 (0.617)***	10.58 (10.196)			

(*Continued*)

Table 14.2. (*Continued*)

Explanatory Variables		**Dependent Variable: FLE**			**Explanatory Variables**	**Dependent Variable: FWPR**	
		Spec 1	**Spec 2**	**Spec 3**		**Spec 4**	**Spec 4**
Wald chi^2		191.71	140.70	74.17	74.17	117.96	111.64
Probability > chi^2		0.0000	0.0000	0.0000	0.0000	0.0000	0.0000
R^2	Within	0.8445	0.5884	0.9145	0.8075	0.8075	0.8324
	Between	0.4148	0.7195	0.8874	0.6563	0.6563	0.2521
	overall	0.5150	0.6552	0.8869	0.7509	0.7509	0.6030

Source: Authors' estimation.

Note: Figure in the parentheses indicates the *t*-value.

***, ** and * represent significance at 1%, 5% and 10% levels, respectively.

5.2. Analysis of FWPR Equation

Table 14.2 shows that the impact of FLE on FWPR is not significant, that is, fall in FLE cannot necessarily reduce FWPR and vice versa. Thus, the positive two-way dependence between FLE and FWPR cannot be established. This phenomenon can be better explained by studying the interaction effect of FLE and proportion of young females (Youth_fem) which is positive and significant on FWPR. Since FLE is one of the endogenous variables in the model, the lagged FLE (i.e. FLE_{lagged}) is included as an explanatory variable which is uncorrelated with the error term in FWPR equation. The interaction term basically implies that the impact of FLE_{lagged} on FWPR actually depends upon Youth_age. Given the level of FLE_{lagged}, when Youth_fem rises, the interaction effect of FLE_{lagged} and Youth_fem exerts a positive impact on FWPR. Thus, if female health is worsened due to air pollution, then because of this positive interaction effect, FWPR will ultimately rise. That is, if young women are sick due to exposure to air pollution, then being young, they can easily overcome that, and thus, the rise in the proportion of youth women actually increases FWPR given their health status because of the interaction effect. Thus, Youth_fem in interaction with FLE_{lagged} is a strong driver to promote FWPR.

Another significant contribution of this chapter is the interaction effect of FLE and Lnpcsdp on FWPR. Once again lagged FLE (i.e. FLE_{lagged}) is taken into account. Given FLE_{lagged}, youth FWPR crucially depends on Lnpcsdp and vice versa. The estimated result suggests that the relationship is non-linear (*inverted U*), that is, FWPR rises when the interaction term is below the critical value and rises when it is above that critical level. Initially below the critical level, given (FLE_{lagged}), low Lnpcsdp of the states (signifies low economic development) pushes up FWPR due to extreme necessity which once again reinforces the need-driven characteristics of Indian FWPR (Banerjee & Ghose, 2023b; Bhalla & Kaur, 2011; Bhattacharyya & Halder, 2020; Klasen & Pieters, 2015). After reaching the threshold level, given (FLE_{lagged}), FWPR decreases as higher Lnpcsdp reduces the need for additional income. Thus, good health may not increase FWPR. With better FLE_{lagged}, given Lnpcsdp, women prefer to stay at home than engage in paid activity (when value of the interaction term > critical level), causing subsequent fall in FWPR. But with poor FLE_{lagged}, women are forced to work, given Lnpcsdp (when value of the interaction term < critical level). That is, a positive and dominant substitution effect in the first stage and a stronger negative income effect in the second stage explain such non-linearity in FWPR. The critical level of the interaction term is 21.655 (<sample mean = 49.75), indicating further rise in either Lnpcsdp or FLE_{lagged} will reduce FWPR. If FLE is improved due to better air quality, then, given Lnpcsdp, FWPR may decrease if the value of the interaction term lies above the critical level. The extant literature has established such non-linearity of FWPR existent with the sole effect of growth and also the interaction of growth with household size (Banerjee & Ghose, 2023b; Bhattacharyya & Haldar, 2020). The health–income nexus in explaining the *anti-U feminisation hypothesis* is the uniqueness of this chapter which helps in understanding the recent low trend in youth FWPR in India.

6. Conclusion

The empirical findings of this chapter suggests the unfavourable impact of both (i) outdoor air pollution (SO_2 and interaction of NO_2–PM2.5) and (ii) indoor air pollution (measured by percentage of rural population using solid fuel) on rural youth FLE deploying 13 state-level panel data for rural India from 2004–2005 to 2017–2018, using Baltagi's IV EC2SLS method. Though the positive simultaneous dependence between FLE and FWPR cannot be established, that is, deterioration in FLE due to air pollution cannot in turn reduce FWPR as the impact of FLE on FWPR is insignificant. This phenomenon can be better explained by exploring the significantly positive interaction effect of FLE and proportion of young females (Youth_fem) on FWPR. Since FLE is one of the endogenous variables in the model, the lagged FLE (i.e. FLE_{lagged}) is included as an explanatory variable which is uncorrelated with the error term in FWPR equation. The interaction term explains that given the level of FLE_{lagged}, rise in Youth_fem also increases FWPR. Even if air pollution adversely affects youth female health, then also FWPR will ultimately rise because of this positive interaction effect of these two. That is being young, women can easily overcome their sickness due to their exposure to air pollution, and hence, rise in the proportion of youth women actually increases FWPR given their health status. Thus, Youth_fem in interaction with FLE_{lagged} is a strong driver to promote youth FWPR.

Among the explanatory variables explaining FWPR, the interaction effect of female health status with that of growth in income is found to be significantly and non-linearly (i.e. inverted U) affecting FWPR, that is, FWPR rises below a critical value of the interaction term but reduces after that critical level. The sample mean being greater than the critical level indicates that further rise in either FLE or growth will lower FWPR, as income effect dominates, women are not joining the labour market even with good health which reveals the need-based character of female work. Thus, if air pollution deteriorates FLE, FWPR will increase only if the interaction term is below the critical level.

This chapter is crucial for the policymakers as it establishes the urgency to frame policies to mitigate rural outdoor air pollution which has gathered least attention since the concept of air pollution is wrongly apprehended to be an urban-centric phenomenon. Also, policies to encourage and provide cleaner and safe cooking fuel (like LPG), installation of smokeless *chulha*, etc. must be framed to improve indoor air quality. Rising female education can also augment rural FLE by improving indoor air quality as evident from the positive interaction effects of indoor air pollution and indicators of education. Though rural youth FWPR is necessity driven, it can be stimulated by endorsing female education, to derive the maximum benefit of the demographic dividend.

References

Afridi, F., Bishnu, M., & Mahajan, K. (2020). *Gendering technological change: Evidence from agricultural mechanization* [Discussion Paper No. 12666]. IZA.

Afridi, F., Dinkelman, T., & Mahajan, K. (2018). Why are fewer married women joining the work force in rural India? A decomposition analysis over two decades. *Journal of Population Economics*, *31*(3), 783–818.

Baltagi, B. H. (2008). *Econometric analysis of panel data* (4th ed.). Willey.

Baltagi, B. H., & Liu, L. (2009). A note on the application of EC2SLS and EC3SLS estimators in panel data models. *Statistics Probability Letters*, *79*, 2189–2192.

Banerjee, K., & Ghose, A. (2022). An analysis of the impact of environmental degradation on female health status and their labor force participation rate in urban India: A simultaneous panel approach. In C. Chakraborty & D. Pal (Eds.), *Environmental sustainability, growth trajectory and gender: Contemporary issues of developing economies* (pp. 267–279). Emerald Publishing Limited. https://doi.org/10.1108/978-1-80262-153-220221021

Banerjee, K., & Ghose, A. (2023a). Investigating the role of air quality and the nexus between female health status and their labor force participation rate: Evidence from rural India. In C. Chakraborty & D. Pal (Eds.), *Gender inequality and its implications on education and health* (pp. 125–137). Emerald Publishing Limited. https://doi.org/10.1108/978-1-83753-180-620231012

Banerjee, K., & Ghose, A. (2023b). Determinants of female labour force participation in urban India: Does outdoor air pollution matter? *The Indian Journal of Labour Economics*, *66*, 815–832. https://doi.org/10.1007/s41027-023-00451-8

Barro, R. (1996). *Three models of health and economic growth* [Unpublished manuscript]. Harvard University.

Bhalla, S. S., & Kaur, R. (2011). *Labour force participation of women in India: Some facts, some queries* [Working Paper 40]. Asia Research Centre, London School of Economics and Political Science.

Bhattacharyya, A., & Haldar, S. (2020). Does U feminisation work in female labour force participation rate? India: A case study. *The Indian Journal of Labour Economics*, *63*(1), 143–160. https://doi.org/10.1007/s41027-019-00202-8

Breusch, T. S., & Pagan, A. (1980). The Lagrange multiplier test and its application to model specification in econometrics. *Review of Economic Studies*, *47*, 239–253.

Cai, L. (2010). The relationship between health and labour force participation: Evidence from a panel data simultaneous equation model. *Labour Economics*, *17*(1), 77–90.

Cai, L., & Kalb, G. (2006). Health status and labour force participation: Evidence from Australia. *Health Economics*, *15*, 241–261.

Deshpande, A., & Kabeer, N. (2021). *Norms that matter: Exploring the distribution of women's work between income generation, expenditure-saving, and unpaid domestic responsibilities in India* [WIDER Working Paper Series wp-2021-130]. World Institute for Development Economic Research (UNU-WIDER).

Deshpande, A., & Singh, J. (2021). *Dropping out, being pushed out or can't get in? Decoding declining labour force participation of Indian women* [Discussion Paper No. 14639]. IZA.

Dhanaraj, S., & Mahambare, V. (2019). Family structure, education and women's employment in rural India. *World Development*, *115*, 17–29.

Faizan, M. A., & Thakur, R. (2019). Measuring the impact of household energy consumption on respiratory diseases in India. *Global Health Research and Policy*, *4*, 10. https://doi.org/10.1186/s41256-019-0101-7

Goldin, C. (1995). The U-shaped female labor force function in economic development and economic history. In T. P. Schultz (Ed.), *Investment in women's human capital and economic development* (pp. 61–90). University of Chicago Press.

Grossman, M. (1972). On the concept of health capital and the demand for health. *The Journal of Political Economy*, *80*(2), 223–255.

Hausman, J. (1978). Specification tests in econometrics. *Econometrica*, *46*(6), 1251–1271.

Klasen, S., & Pieters, J. (2015). What explains the stagnation of female labour force participation in urban India? *The World Bank Economic Review*, *29*(3), 449–478.

Lahoti, R., & Swaminathan, H. (2016). Economic development and women's labour force participation in India. *Feminist Economics*, *22*(2), 168–195.

Meenakshi, J. R., & Panneer, S. (2020). Occupational health of agricultural women workers in India. *Indian Journal of Community Medicine*, *45*(4), 546–549.

Mehra, R., Khan, A., & Rames, V. (2021, March 25). *USAID clean air catalyst: Gender analysis of air pollution and vehicle transport in India*. https://aqmx.org/sites/default/files/resources/Clean-Air-Catalyst-Gender-Analysis-India.pdf

Mehrotra, S., & Sinha, S. (2019). *Towards higher female work participation in India: What can be done?* [CSE Working Paper No. 2019-02]. Azim Premji University.

Menon, N., & Rodgers, Y. V. D. M. (2011). *War and women's work: Evidence from conflicting Nepal* [Policy Research Working Paper 5745]. The World Bank.

Mishra, V. N., Malhotra, M., & Gupta, S. (1990). Respiratory disorders in females of Delhi. *Journal of the Indian Medical Association*, *88*(3), 77–80.

Olsen, W., & Mehta, S. (2006). *A pluralist account of labor participation in India* [Working Paper GPRG-WPS-042]. Global Poverty Research Group, University of Oxford.

Padmavati, S., & Arora, R. (1976). Sex differences in chronic COR pulmonale in Delhi. *British Journal of Diseases in Chest*, *70*(4), 251–259.

Richards, E., Theobald, S., George, A., Kim, J. C., Rudert, C., Jehan, K., & Tolhurst, R. (2013). Going beyond the surface: Gendered intra-household bargaining as a social determinant of child health and nutrition in low and middle income countries. *Social Science & Medicine*, 95, 24–33.

Sanghi, S., Srija, A., & Vijay, S. S. (2015). Decline in rural female labour force participation in India: A relook into the causes. *VIKALPA The Journal of Decision Makers*, *40*(3), 255–268.

Sarkar, S., Sahoo, S., & Klasen, S. (2019). Employment transitions of women in India: A panel analysis. *World Development*, *115*, 291–309.

Shrestha, M. (2017). *The impact of large-scale migration on poverty, expenditures, and labor market outcomes in Nepal* [Policy Research Working Paper 8232]. World Bank.

Sikarwar, A., Chattopadhyay, A., Jaiswal, A. K., & Rani, R. (2020). Devaluation of female work participation with urbanization: A case of peri-urban Ahmedabad. *GeoJournal*, *87*, 319–331.

Social Statistics Division, National Statistical Office. (2021). *Gendering human development. A Working paper for computing HDI, GDI, and GII for states of India*. Ministry of Statistics and Programme Implementation, Government of India. http://mospi.nic.in/sites/default/files/publication_reports/Report%20on%20Gendering%20Human%20Development.pdf

Unisa, S., & Datta, N. (2005). *Female headship in India: Levels, differentials and impact* [Paper presentation]. Presented at the 25th conference of IUSSP, France.

Chapter 15

Social Dimensions of Human Development: Trends of Union Dissolution in India

Ankita Rajgarhia[a], *Zakir Husain*[b] *and Mousumi Dutta*[b]

[a]*The Heritage College, Kolkata, India*
[b]*Presidency University, Kolkata, India*

Abstract

Union dissolution, encompassing divorce and separation, is an integral aspect of social transformation, reflecting shifts in societal norms, gender roles, economic independence, and legal frameworks. In India, while marriage has traditionally been seen as a lifelong commitment, increasing urbanisation, economic independence of women, and legal reforms have contributed to shifting perceptions of marriage, leading to greater acceptance of dissolution. The incidence of divorce and separation in India has historically been low compared to Western societies. However, there has been a steady increase in marital dissolution as indicated in this exploratory study that impacts the women immensely. Women, particularly in middle age groups, are more vulnerable to dissolution, with separation rates significantly higher than divorce rates. Factors such as financial independence, domestic conflicts, changing social norms, and globalisation have influenced this trend. Union dissolution varies across regions, showing a distinct north–south divide, with southern states experiencing higher dissolution rates. Among religious groups, Christians have the highest dissolution rates, particularly in urban areas. Across all demographics, separation remains the dominant form of dissolution. While union dissolution is increasing in India, challenges such as social stigma, economic

Changing Dimensions in Economic Development: Theories and Empirics, 201–211

Published under exclusive licence by Emerald Publishing Limited
doi:10.1108/978-1-83708-384-820261018

hardship, and legal battles persist. Addressing these concerns through legal reforms, social awareness, and economic empowerment is crucial for ensuring the well-being of individuals undergoing marital dissolution.

Keywords: Dissolution; divorce; separation; social norms; empowerment

JEL Codes: J12; J16; J24; O15

1. Introduction

The different forms of union dissolution are divorce, separation, and widowhood. Divorce is an official or legal process to end a marriage. Separation is an informal break up where the couples in the marriage decide to stay separately, and widowhood is the end of marriage due to the death of either of the spouses.

The media holds the view that divorce and separation rates in India are relatively lower than the Western countries. Nevertheless, the rates have been increasing. Separation is the predominant method of marriage termination for many women in India, constituting 63% of total dissolutions. Many women do not report whether they are separated or divorced because of the stigma that is attached to the status.

Media often attributes high dissolution rates to a combination of factors. Changing societal attitudes towards marriage, increased economic independence, urbanisation, and legal reforms are frequently cited as contributors. Modern lifestyles, greater individual autonomy, and a desire for personal fulfilment can lead couples to reassess their relationships, potentially contributing to higher rates of dissolution. Increased educational attainment and economic independence, particularly among women, have empowered individuals to make independent choices, including the decision to pursue divorce.

High divorce rates entail a range of consequences at both individual and societal levels. On an individual basis, the emotional toll is significant, with divorced or separated individuals often grappling with grief, anger, and anxiety. Children of divorced parents may experience academic and emotional challenges. Economically, divorce can lead to financial strain for the parties involved, impacting the standard of living and potentially creating economic difficulties for single-parent households. The uncertain legal status and lack of rights stemming from informal breakups pose challenges for women. Moreover, when male spouses shirk their material responsibilities towards the well-being of women and children, it pushes women into poverty. The altered family structures resulting from high divorce rates, including the rise of single-parent and stepfamilies, contribute to shifts in societal norms around marriage and family. The consequences of high divorce rates are complex and multifaceted, shaped by cultural context and specific circumstances surrounding each divorce.

Hence, there is a need for a systematic study of marital dissolution based on data. The objective of this chapter is to examine the trends in union dissolution in India. The specific research questions analysed in this chapter are as follows:

1. What are the trends in divorce and separation in India?
   (a) How are the rates varying over the years 1991, 2001, and 2011?
   (b) What is the difference in divorce and separation rates in rural and urban India?
2. What are the variations in union dissolution across correlates such as state, age, and religious categories?
   (a) How are the rates differing in different states in India for the years 1991, 2001, and 2011?
   (b) What is the proportion of union dissolution due to divorce and separation for women in different age groups?
   (c) What is the variation in divorce and separation for women belonging to different religious groups?

2. Literature Review

There has been an increasing trend in union dissolution across the world since the 1970s (Bennett, 2017; Sheykhi, 2020). The crude divorce rates (the number of divorces per 1,000 people) have doubled, from 2% in the 1970s to 4% in the 2000s at the global level. Divorce rates have been increasing in developing countries since the 1980s even though the rates are lowest in such countries (Chakravorty et al., 2021; Sheykhi, 2020; Singh, 2023; Yadav et al., 2017). Asia has also witnessed rising rates of divorce due to urbanisation since the 1980s (Dommaraju & Johnes, 2011; Sheykhi, 2020). However, there is no uniform pattern for divorce trends across Asia, but they can be categorised into three major patterns: East Asian, Islamic Southeast Asian, and South Asian (Dommaraju & Johnes, 2011).

The study by Dommaraju and Johnes (2011) suggests that divorce rates in East Asia have risen since the 1980s, though patterns vary by country. China and Hong Kong, despite having the lowest divorce rates, show no signs of stabilisation or decline. Japan had the highest rates in the region from the 1970s to the mid-1980s, peaking in the early 1980s before declining and stabilising around 2009 at about 2.0 (Bennett, 2017; Dommaraju & Johnes, 2011). South Korea experienced a significant rise between 1995 and 2000 during the Asian financial crisis, peaking in 2003, and later converging with rates in other countries by 2006. Taiwan's rates followed a similar upward trend, also peaking in 2003. Overall, the region saw rising divorce rates from the 1980s to early 2000s, with most countries peaking around the early 2000s before stabilising or declining, except for China and Hong Kong.

Southeast Asian divorce patterns fall into two categories: high rates among Islamic populations, which declined in the mid-20th century, and low, stable rates among other groups. Non-Muslim populations in Thailand and the Philippines have historically had low divorce rates, while Singapore's rates increased between 1980 and 1998, dipped in the late 1990s, and stabilised by the early 2000s, resembling trends in industrialised East Asian countries like Taiwan and South Korea (Bennett, 2017; Dommaraju & Johnes, 2011).

The South Asian pattern is marked by stable and very low divorce rates (Dommaraju & Johnes, 2011; Sheykhi, 2020). Divorce is relatively rare in this region. The percentage of ever-married women who are currently divorced or separated (though not legally) was 3.2% in Bangladesh (2007), 1.8% in India (2005–2006), 1.7% in Nepal (2006), 1.5% in Pakistan (2006–2007), and 1.2% in Sri Lanka (2001).

The divorce rate in India is among the lowest in the world at less than 1% (Dommaraju & Johnes, 2011; Jacob & Chattopadhyay, 2016; Maiti, 2023). Although the divorce rates are low in India, analysis 'show a continuous increase over the last three censuses starting from 1991' (Dommaraju, 2016, p. 205; Jacob & Chattopadhyay, 2016; Maiti, 2023; Sheykhi, 2020; Singh, 2023; Yadav et al., 2017).

The study by Dommaraju (2016) shows that in the 2011 census, more than 1.5 million men and 3.2 million women were recorded as divorced or separated. Over the past two decades, the number of divorced or separated individuals in India has more than doubled. Women outnumbered men in this category in all census years since 1961, likely due to men's higher rates of remarriage. The proportion of divorced or separated individuals generally remained below 1% for both men and women in rural and urban areas, except for urban women, where it reached 1.04% in 2011. While there is a slight difference between rural and urban areas, it's not substantial. The percentages have shown a consistent increase over the last three censuses since 1991. The 2011 census distinguishes between divorced and separated individuals, with about 72% of both men and women falling into the 'separated' category among those classified as either divorced or separated (Dommaraju, 2016; Ghosh & Ranjan, 2017; Jacob & Chattopadhyay, 2016). The main reason for the same is the social stigma that is attached to divorce in India (Belliappa, 2013; Kaneez, 2015; Kumar, 2022; Ramachandrappa, 2012; Rao & Shekhar, 2002; Rathie et al., 2018; Thadathil & Sriram, 2020). The figures indicate a growing trend of marital breakdown due to divorce or separation. Nevertheless, the overall incidence of marital dissolution remains low (Dommaraju, 2016, p. 205; Jacob & Chattopadhyay, 2016; Maiti, 2023; Sheykhi, 2020; Singh, 2023; Yadav et al., 2017).

There is high variation in dissolution rates across different religious groups (Ghosh & Ranjan, 2017; Mundu & Unisa, 2018). The highest dissolution rates in the form of separation or divorce are seen among Buddhists, Christians, and 'others'[1] group (Ghosh & Ranjan, 2017; Mundu & Unisa, 2018). The lowest dissolution is seen among Sikh women (Ghosh & Ranjan, 2017). Some studies suggest that Hindu women experience lower dissolution than Muslim women and

[1]Where 'Others' refers to other religions and faiths including tribal religions, different from the six main religions of Hindus, Muslims, Christians, Sikhs, Buddhists, and Jains.

women belonging to other religious groups (Bose & South, 2003; Dommaraju, 2016; Ghosh & Ranjan, 2017; Hollander, 2004). This may be because of the greater ease of getting a divorce among Muslims. Separation is the main form of dissolution across all religious groups (Ghosh & Ranjan, 2017).

Within India, the cross-regional variation in the dissolution rates is striking. The dissolution rates are low in the northern states and high in south and north-eastern states (Ghosh & Ranjan, 2017; Hollander, 2004; Jacob & Chattopadhyay, 2016; Mundu & Unisa, 2018; Yadav et al., 2017). There is a clear north–south divide. Some studies show that Southern, Western, and North-Eastern India experienced higher dissolution in comparison to Northern, Eastern, and Central India (Dommaraju, 2016; Mundu & Unisa, 2018). Southern India like Kerala and Tamil Nadu and north-eastern states like Meghalaya, Mizoram, and Sikkim show high rates of dissolution (Ghosh & Ranjan, 2017; Jacob & Chattopadhyay, 2016; Mundu & Unisa, 2018; Yadav et al., 2017). In Central India, Chhattisgarh experiences high dissolution rates. On the other hand, northern states like Bihar, Haryana, Uttar Pradesh, and Punjab witness low dissolution rates (Bose & South, 2003; Ghosh & Ranjan, 2017; Jacob & Chattopadhyay, 2016; Mundu & Unisa, 2018). It has been mentioned in the study by Dutta and Prasad (2019) that marital dissolution is lower in socio-economically backward states like Bihar, Orissa, Jharkhand, and Uttar Pradesh. Despite this, the northern region has been experiencing an increase in divorce rates from the first two decades of the 21st century (Yadav et al., 2017).

3. Data and Method

3.1. Data

This chapter uses the census data for the years 1991, 2001, and 2011. The census provides information on the size, distribution, and other characteristics of the country's population. It collects demographic and socio-economic information through a nationwide enumeration process conducted at regular intervals by the Government of India. It captures social and cultural dimensions, including religion, language, caste, and tribal affiliations. The census of India is conducted every 10 years, and it is one of the largest administrative and statistical exercises in the world. This chapter is based on the census data that are available at the all-India and state levels along with separate data for rural and urban India for the years 1991, 2001, and 2011.

The census provides information on the marital status of an individual, that is, individuals who have never married, married, widowed, divorced, or separated. Dissolution comprises divorce and separation, and the data for divorce and separation are available separately for the year 2011. However, for the years 1991 and 2001, the census has clubbed individuals who are divorced or separated into a single category. Similarly, data are available for variations in dissolution across religious categories for the years 2001 and 2011. However, for the year 1991, data on dissolution across religious categories are not available.

3.2. Method

The study uses exploratory methods to analyse and investigate the datasets. Tabular and graphical methods are used to summarise and visually represent the data depicting variations across various correlates. Bar graphs and line plots are used to depict the trends in dissolution over the years 1991, 2001, and 2011.

The study uses box plot to depict the variations in union dissolution across various states in India over the years of 1991, 2001, and 2011. A box plot, also known as a box-and-whisker plot, is a statistical representation of the distribution of a dataset. It displays key summary statistics, including the minimum, first quartile (Q1), median, third quartile (Q3), and maximum values. The plot consists of a rectangular 'box' that spans the interquartile range (IQR) between the first and third quartiles. The line inside the box represents the median. Additionally, 'whiskers' extend from the box to the minimum and maximum values, but they do not always reach the actual minimum and maximum of the dataset. Any data points beyond the whiskers are considered outliers and are often individually plotted. Box plots are particularly useful for visualising the central tendency, spread, and skewness of a dataset. It helps in analysing and interpreting the data. They provide a concise summary of the data distribution and are valuable for comparing the distributions of different datasets.

In this study, we also make use of choropleth maps. It provides an intuitive way to visualise how union dissolution varies across different geographic areas. Choropleth maps are a type of thematic map designed to visually represent the spatial distribution of a particular variable across different geographic regions. These maps use colour gradients or shading to indicate variations in the values of the variable being mapped. The maps are associated with specific colours which have certain corresponding values or value ranges. Choropleth maps are effective for displaying spatial patterns and trends in data, making them valuable tools for conveying information about regional variations.

4. Findings

4.1. Trends in Dissolution

Union dissolution in India has been rising over the years. The analysis throughout the study has been done in the percentage of women per thousand experiencing union dissolution. The dissolution rates have increased from 6.48 in the year 1991 to 9.8 in the year 2001 and 10.01 in the year 2011. Union dissolution is higher in rural India in comparison to urban India for the years 1991 and 2001. On the other hand, for the year 2011, dissolution is higher in urban India in comparison to rural India. The dissolution rates for rural and urban India are 6.80 and 5.48, respectively, for the year 1991; 10.01 and 9.24, respectively, for the year 2001; and 9.34 and 10.36, respectively, for the year 2011.

There are two components of union dissolution, that is, separation and divorce. The overall rates of divorce are much lower in comparison to separation. The divorce rates at the all-India level are at 2.68, 2.47 in rural India, and 3.13 in urban India for the year 2011.

The separation rates at the all-India level are at 6.99, whereas for rural and urban India, it is at 6.87 and 7.23, respectively, for the year 2011. Separation rates are much higher in comparison to divorce rates which suggest that separation comprises a major part of dissolution.

Next, we show the trends in union dissolution by using box plots. State-wise census data have been used to prepare and analyse the box plots for the years 1991, 2001, and 2011. Fig. 15.1 depicts the union dissolution for the year 2011. For the year 1991, the median for total dissolution is at 7.23, whereas the mean is much higher at 9.53. Similarly, for rural India, the median is at 7.03, and the mean is higher at 9.93. The median and mean for urban India are lower in comparison to rural India at 5.28 and 8.28, respectively. The figures indicate that the distribution is positively skewed as the mean is greater than the median. The interstate variance is also high across total, rural, and urban India at around 12. There is also the presence of outliers which are seen mostly from the north-eastern states.

In the year 2001, the mean and median have increased for rural, urban, and total. The mean for rural India is at 13.14, for urban India at 11.64, and total dissolution at 12.94. The median is at 11.05 for rural India, 7.51 for urban India, and 10.43 for total dissolution. There is also the presence of outliers from the north-eastern states. The interstate variance is again high at around 13, and the distribution is positively skewed.

Fig. 15.1 shows that for the year 2011, the mean and median have increased significantly for urban India to 14.2 and 9.99, respectively. In the rural areas, the mean and median are more or less constant at 13.54 and 12.32, respectively. At the all-India level, the mean and median have increased to 14.03 and 11.14, respectively. The interstate variance is particularly high for urban India at 14.47.

Therefore, we can conclude that union dissolution has increased particularly in the urban areas, whereas in the rural areas, it is more or less constant. At the all-India level, dissolution has increased over the years as suggested by the box plots.

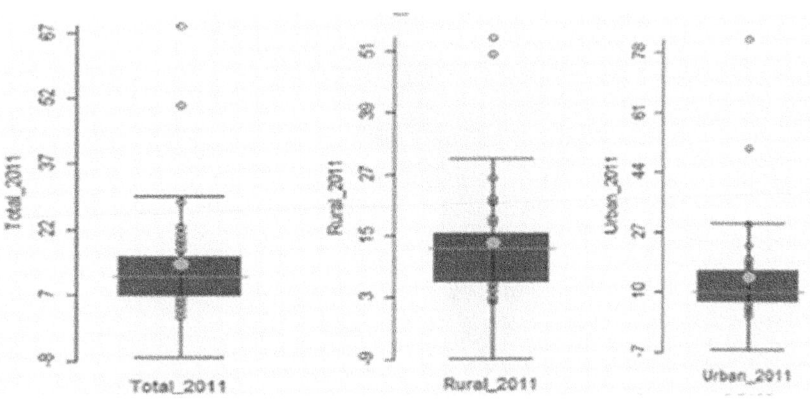

Fig. 15.1. Box Plot Depicting Union Dissolution for the Year 2011.
Source: Authors' estimate.

4.2. Spatial Patterns

The states can be divided into three groups based on the level of dissolution, that is, high, moderate, and low. This pattern can be seen by preparing the spatial maps using the state-level census data.

As we move from north to south, the dissolution rates increase for the years 1991, 2001, and 2011. As is evident from Fig. 15.2, the northern states have low dissolution rates, the central or the middle zone has moderate dissolution rates, and the southern states have high dissolution rates. The difference in dissolution rates across states suggests that there is a striking cross-regional variation. States in north India like Punjab, Haryana, Uttar Pradesh, and Rajasthan have low dissolution levels. On the other hand, southern states like Kerala and Tamil Nadu along with the north-eastern states witness high dissolution rates. The spatial patterns suggest that there is a clear north-south divide and dissolution levels increase from north to south India as can be seen in Fig. 15.2.

4.3. Age Groups

Union dissolution across different age groups of 0–9, 10–14, 15–19, 20–24, ..., 75–79, and 80+ years shows a similar pattern for total, rural, and urban. There is

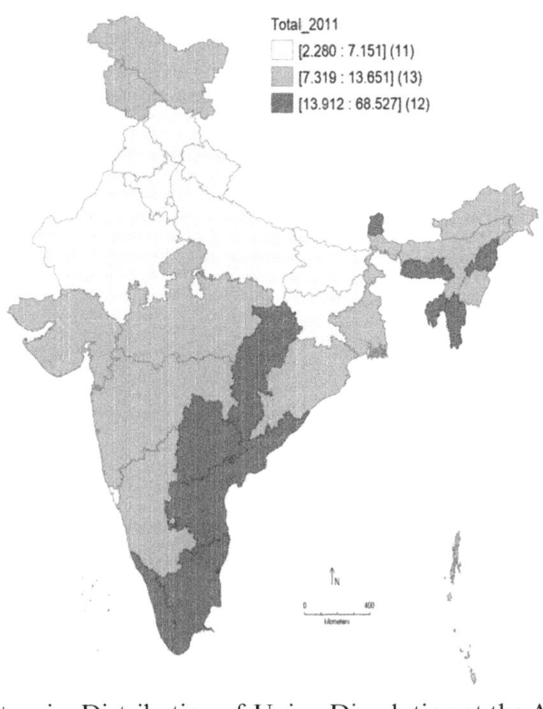

Fig. 15.2. State-wise Distribution of Union Dissolution at the All-India Level for the Year 2011. *Source*: Authors' estimate.

a sharp peak in the dissolution rates in the age category of 10–14 years and falls thereafter. From the age of 20 years, dissolution rates begin to increase, peaking for women in the middle age group. It is seen as an inverted U-shaped curve. The dissolution rate starts falling after the age of 44 years and becomes constant in the higher age groups. This pattern suggests that women in the middle age group are the most vulnerable across the years 1991, 2001, and 2011 with dissolution rates at 7.72, 9.92, and 13.18, respectively.

It can be seen from Fig. 15.3, that in the year 2011, the dissolution rates among urban women have surpassed that of rural women. The rates peak among women in the age category of 40–44 years at 13.19 for urban women and 12.17 for rural women, declining thereafter. Dissolution has increased over the years, particularly among urban women.

4.4. Religious Groups

For the years 2001 and 2011, the dissolution rates were highest for Christians at 14 and 16.63, respectively, followed by Muslims at 11 and 11.66 in general. The dissolution rate for Hindus is constant at 8 in the year 2001 with a slight variation in the year 2011.

In the year 2001, rural women experience higher dissolution in comparison to urban women across all religions, that is, Hindus, Muslims, Christians, Sikhs, Buddhists, Jains, and others. On the other hand, in the year 2011, the pattern in general changed with urban women experiencing higher dissolution in the religious groups of Christians, Muslims, and Hindus.

The census data reveal that separation is the dominant form of dissolution across the different religious groups. Divorce rates are high for Muslims and Christians at approximately 5 in comparison to Hindus and all other religious groups. The rates of separation are highest among the Christians in all the religious groups at 11.88.

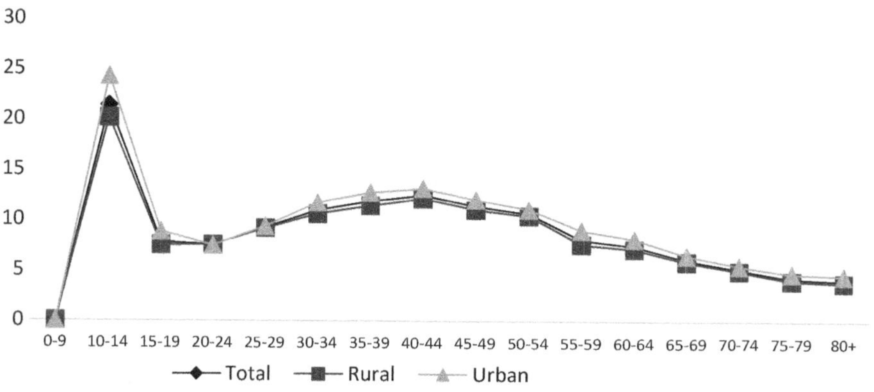

Fig. 15.3. Percentage of Women (in 000) Experiencing Union Dissolution Across Age Groups for the Year 2011. *Source*: Authors' estimate.

5. Conclusion

This chapter focuses on the trends of union dissolution in India and variations in the rates across the major correlates such as state, age, and religious categories. The exploratory study depicts that union dissolution has been rising over the years 1991, 2001, and 2011. It has been higher in rural India in comparison to urban India for the years 1991 and 2001. However, in the year 2011, union dissolution in urban India exceeded than that in rural India. The box plot depicts that dissolution has increased consistently over the years for the urban areas, whereas it remained more or less constant in the rural areas. The components of union dissolution are separation and divorce. The analysis shows that separation rates are much higher than divorce rates over the years. Thus, separation comprises the major part of dissolution.

The choropleth maps depict the variations in union dissolution across the different states in India. It clearly shows that as we move from north to south, union dissolution has increased for the years 1991, 2001, and 2011. The northern, central, and southern states depict low, moderate, and high dissolution rates, respectively. The difference in dissolution rates across states suggests that there is a striking cross-regional variation. The spatial patterns suggest that there is a clear north–south divide.

The variations in union dissolution across different age groups suggest that women in the middle age group are the most vulnerable across the years of 1991, 2001, and 2011. Dissolution rates have increased over the years, particularly among urban women across all age groups. Also, across all age groups, separation is more dominant in comparison to divorce.

The variations in union dissolution across different religious groups suggest that the dissolution rates are highest for Christians for the years 2001 and 2011. Separation has been the dominant form of dissolution across the different religious groups with the rates being highest for Christians.

The link between divorce, separation, and human development in India highlights the evolving socio-economic and cultural landscape. Rising union dissolution reflects increased gender equality, legal empowerment, and economic independence, particularly for women. While separation remains more prevalent than divorce, both indicate shifting social norms and the decline of traditional marital constraints. However, challenges persist, including social stigma, economic instability, and legal complexities, which can hinder human development. Addressing these issues through policy reforms, education, social awareness, and financial support can help mitigate adverse effects and promote personal autonomy and well-being. Recognising marital dissolution as part of broader human development is essential for creating an inclusive and progressive society.

References

Belliappa, J. (2013). *Gender, class and reflexive modernity in India*. Palgrave Macmillan.

Bennett, N. G. (2017). A reflection on the changing dynamics of union formation and dissolution. *Demographic Research*, *36*(1), 371–390. https://doi.org/10.4054/DemRes.2017.36.12

Bose, S., & South, S. J. (2003). Sex composition of children and marital disruption in India. *Journal of Marriage and Family*, *65*(4), 996–1006. https://doi.org/10.1111/j.1741-3737.2003.00996.x

Chakravorty, S., Goli, S., & James, K. S. (2021). Family demography in India: Emerging patterns and its challenges. *SAGE Open*, *11*(2). https://doi.org/10.1177/21582440211008178

Dommaraju, P. (2016). Divorce and separation in India. *Population and Development Review*, *42*(2), 195–223. https://doi.org/10.1111/j.1728-4457.2016.00127.x

Dommaraju, P., & Jones, G. (2011). Divorce trends in Asia. *Asian Journal of Social Science*, *39*(6), 727–750. https://doi.org/10.1163/156853111X619201

Dutta, M., & Prashad, L. (2019). Differential in pattern and risk factors of marital dissolution among better developed and the poorly developed states in India. *Journal of Divorce and Remarriage*, *60*(6), 436–446. https://doi.org/10.1080/10502556.2019.1586225

Ghosh, J., & Ranjan, N. (2017). *The economic effects of marriage dissolution on women: India case study*. https://doi.org/10.13140/RG.2.2.25187.86568

Hollander, D. (2004). Indian women who have daughters but no sons face an increased risk of marital dissolution. *Family Planning Perspectives*, *30*(1), 48–49.

Jacob, S., & Chattopadhyay, S. (2016). Marriage dissolution in India evidence from census 2011. *Economic & Political Weekly*, *51*(33), 25–27.

Kaneez, S. (2015). Perception of subjective well-being among divorced women: A comparative study of Hindus and Muslims. *Pakistan Journal of Social and Clinical Psychology*, *13*(2), 67–71.

Kumar, M. (2022). When love turns hate: Consequences of marital discord, marital dissolution and HCW's under risk. *Acta Scientific Women's Health*, *4*(6), 71–77. https://doi.org/10.31080/aswh.2022.04.0379

Maiti, S. N. (2023). Gaps in education and marital dissolution: Evidence from India. *International Social Science Journal*, *74*, 1–22. https://doi.org/10.1111/issj.12458

Mundu, G., & Unisa, S. (2018). Patterns of marriage dissolution in India regional, socio-economic, and religious trends. *Economic and Political Weekly*, *53*(16), 57–64.

Ramachandrappa, S. (2012). Cause and consequences of divorce in Bangalore city – A sociological approach. *IOSR Journal of Humanities and Social Sciences*, *4*(4), 6–9.

Rao, A. B. S. V. R., & Sekhar, K. (2002). Divorce: Process and correlates a cross-cultural study. *Journal of Comparative Family Studies*, *33*(4), 541–563.

Rathi, P., Pachauri, J., & Pooja Rathi, C. (2018). Problems faced by divorced women in their pre and post-divorce period: A sociological study with reference to District Meerut. *Journal of Pharmacognosy and Phytochemistry*, *7*(1), 207–212.

Sheykhi, M. (2020). Worldwide increasing divorce rates: A sociological analysis. *Konfrontasi: JurnalKultural, Ekonomi Dan Perubahan Sosial*, *7*(2), 116–123. https://doi.org/10.33258/konfrontasi2.v7i2.105

Singh, V. (2023). Exploring the recent trends of divorce in India. In N. Pandey (Ed.), *Marriages and divorces in Indian society* (pp. 193–201). The Law Brigade Publishers. https://doi.org/10.55662/book.2023MDIS.014

Thadathil, A., & Sriram, S. (2020). Divorce, families and adolescents in India: A review of research. *Journal of Divorce and Remarriage*, *61*(1), 1–21. https://doi.org/10.1080/10502556.2019.1586226

Yadav, A., Singh, T. B., & Vishwakarma, M. (2017). *Changes in the marriage patterns of northern and southern states of India, 1971-2011. Social Science Spectrum*, *3*(2), 93–103.

Chapter 16

Economic Progress of India: An Assessment Through the Lens of Financial Development Index

J. K. Das[a] *and Swapan-Kumar Pradhan*[b]

[a]*Department of Commerce, University of Calcutta, Kolkata, India*
[b]*Bank for International Settlements (BIS), Basel, Switzerland*

Abstract

The assessment of economic development across countries remains a key global concern. Development is a multidimensional concept encompassing economic growth, inequality, financial stability, and the overall prosperity of the real sector. Financial development (FD) contributes significantly to financial inclusion (FI), resource allocation efficiency, investment growth, and economic resilience. This study utilises the International Monetary Fund (IMF)'s FD Index to compare FD among BRICS nations and six other major Asian economies. The cross-country analysis shows that, as of 2021, India ranked lowest among the BRICS countries and mid-tier among the Asian economies studied. Despite improvements over past decades, India's relatively low FD score is primarily attributed to inefficiencies and limited access within its financial institutions (FIs). The findings suggest a need for targeted regulatory measures in India to enhance financial efficiency, strengthen monitoring mechanisms, enforce regulations impartially, and increase transparency within the financial system.

Keywords: Financial development; financial inclusion; financial institutions; financial markets; income inequality

JEL Codes: D31; G1; G20; G200; J31; O16

Changing Dimensions in Economic Development: Theories and Empirics, 213–229

Published under exclusive licence by Emerald Publishing Limited
doi:10.1108/978-1-83708-384-820261019

1. Introduction

There is a common misconception that FD is synonymous with FI. While related, they are distinct. FI refers to ensuring access to financial services, particularly for underserved populations, as a means to promote economic growth and reduce poverty. In contrast, FD is a broader concept encompassing access, depth, efficiency, financial literacy, regulatory strength, and financial system stability, all of which drive economic growth. Key economic development indicators include gross domestic product (GDP) per capita, poverty rates, literacy levels, and income distribution.

While FI plays a vital role in advancing FD, it does not guarantee it. A nation may exhibit broad FI yet still possess underdeveloped financial markets (FMs), or vice versa. The Alliance for Financial Inclusion (AFI) states that only 841 million people in its 84 member countries have financial access. This implies that around 75% of the population remains excluded from access to financial services. This pressing issue was underscored during the Bank for International Settlements (BIS) Global Conference in November 2023, where experts stressed the importance of striking a balance between innovation and regulation. The Chairperson of the Financial Stability Institute (FSI) remarked that FI poses a shared challenge for financial authorities, governments, inclusion-focused organisations, financial institutions (FIs), innovators, and the broader private sector. He emphasised that while innovation is key to progress, it must be supported by appropriate regulatory frameworks to mitigate unintended outcomes, particularly in areas such as consumer protection.

Barriers to FI include service costs, bureaucratic inefficiencies, and financial illiteracy. India, a key BRICS member, plays a significant role in global and regional financial dynamics. BRICS' combined GDP grew from $2.9 trillion in 2001 to $25.5 trillion in 2022, covering over 40% of the world's population. Additionally, Indonesia, Korea, Malaysia, the Philippines, Pakistan, and Thailand contribute another $5 trillion GDP and 800 million people.

This chapter assesses India's FD progress through an international comparison with BRICS and major Asian economies. The structure is as follows: Section 2 reviews literature on FI and development, Section 3 examines their relationship with economic growth, Section 4 analyses the FD Index for BRICS and selected Asian nations, and Section 5 presents conclusions.

2. Literature Review

The modern world has witnessed significant financial innovations driven by economic liberalisation and rapid technological advancements. Over the past two decades, numerous studies have assessed the impact of economic reforms in India and globally. However, financial deregulation has introduced challenges such as spillover risks, social inequality, and illicit capital flows, underscoring the need for inclusive financial policies. FI primarily aims to improve the well-being of disadvantaged communities, particularly in lower-income rural areas (Hajaj, 2002). It encompasses financial literacy, access to technology, consumer rights awareness, risk protection, and grievance redressal mechanisms.

Recognising the importance of financial sector development, Beck et al. (2000) introduced the World Bank's database on financial sector structure and development, featuring over three dozen indicators on institutional and market size, activity, and efficiency (see Table 16.1 of Beck et al., 2000). Effective outreach by mainstream financial services benefits consumers through cost-efficient products and asset-building opportunities (Dabla-Norris et al., 2015; Seidman et al., 2005). However, financial exclusion remains widespread, disproportionately affecting low-income individuals and those with poor credit (Kempson, 2006). Kempson also noted that a number of individuals, despite having bank accounts, use them minimally – often only for welfare payments – making them effectively 'underbanked'. This limited usage challenges financial service providers and deepens social exclusion and deepens social exclusion (Diniz et al., 2012).

Beyond mere account ownership, FI requires active usage and financial literacy. To track these aspects, Beck et al. (2007) compiled a comprehensive dataset measuring access to and usage of banking services, including branches, ATMs, and loan and deposit amounts. This dataset offers consistent cross-country indicators and covers 99 countries, including India.

A well-developed financial system plays a crucial role in long-term economic growth (Demirgüç-Kunt & Levine, 2008). Efforts to construct databases on financial sector structure and development have expanded over time, incorporating indicators for banks, non-bank intermediaries, and FMs. Updated versions introduced additional measures to capture broader aspects of FD (Beck et al., 2010). To facilitate cross-country comparisons, researchers such as Čihák et al. (2012), Sarma (2012), and Amidzić et al. (2014) developed multidimensional indices that summarise the status of FI in a single measure.

Several macroeconomic variables influence FI. While GDP per capita positively correlates with FI, GDP growth and interest rate spreads tend to have negative effects, whereas inflation shows no significant impact (Alber, 2019). Demirguc-Kunt and Klapper (2012) and Demirgüç-Kunt et al. (2017, 2018, 2022) and El Said et al. (2019) analysed the World Bank's Global Findex database over time and recommended it as 'an indispensable resource for financial service practitioners, policymakers, researchers, and development professionals'. While FI reduces income disparities and its marginal effect improves as inclusion progresses, empirical findings suggest that the impact depends on a range of factors, including access, usage, and the type of services offered (Inoue, 2024). Wu et al. (2023) demonstrate that financial sector development is positively correlated with remittance inflows.

Financial systems differ in their capacity to deliver key services, typically categorised into access, depth, and efficiency. Various factors – such as regulatory frameworks, reliability, security, political interference, fraud, and overall stability – influence the performance of the financial sector. Understanding these differences is essential for comparing FI and economic development across countries, particularly among BRICS nations (Brazil, Russia, India, China, and South Africa) and selected Asian economies, including Indonesia, South Korea, Malaysia, the Philippines, Pakistan, and Thailand.

3. FI Versus Economic Development of India

Over the past two decades, banking expansion and business correspondents have extended financial services to rural and unbanked areas in India. The Jan Dhan Yojana scheme accelerated bank account openings and digital payments. The National Strategy for FI (2019–2024) and Financial Education (2020–2025) focus on financial literacy and consumer protection.

Roy et al. (2021) of the Reserve Bank of India (RBI, 2020) developed a FI Index with 97 indicators covering access, usage, literacy, and consumer protection. The RBI's FI Index, based on 26 access, 52 usage, and 19 quality indicators (weighing 35%, 45%, and 20%, respectively), stood at 53.9 in 2021. The access sub-index (73.3) showed infrastructure gained by 10% over 2017, while usage (43%) and quality (50.7%) remained at a low level. However, the study lacked a full list of indicators and data sources.

While FI may expand access, inefficiencies, fraud, and low literacy can limit its impact on FD. The rise of neo-banking has increased fraud risks, as seen in the February 2024 suspension of Paytm's banking affiliate.

Economic development spans multiple factors. The World Bank's world development indicators include over 1,000 measures across six areas: poverty and inequality, demographics, economy, environment, markets, and global links. The size of GDP alone is an insufficient measure of development. By the end of 2022, global GDP reached $101 trillion, with the United States ($25.5 trillion), China ($17.9 trillion), Japan ($4.2 trillion), Germany ($4.1 trillion), and India ($3.4 trillion) among the top economies. With a world population of 8 billion, the sample of 11 emerging market and developing economies (EMDEs) comprise over $31 trillion GDP and 4 billion population.

Both China and India have nearly equal populations. Over the past decade, China's per capita GDP more than doubled, rising from $6,000 in 2012 to $12,700 in 2022. In contrast, India's per capita GDP increased from $1,400 to $2,400 during the same period. Consequently, the gap between China and India widened from over four times in 2012 to approximately six times in 2022. Additionally, India's per capita GDP in 2022 ($2,400) was recorded as the second lowest among 11 countries (Fig. 16.2), with South Korea's being the highest at $32,400. Pakistan had the lowest per capita GDP at $1,600 in 2022.

If India's GDP were equivalent to that of the United States ($25.5 trillion, which is more than 7.5 times India's level), India's per capita GDP would be approximately $18,200, still significantly lower than Korea's $32,400. Similarly, the United States ranked 15th with a per capita GDP of $80,000, while Liechtenstein ranked first with $139,000. This comparison indicates that GDP size alone cannot be treated as a measure of economic development.

Other key indicators of economic development include income distribution, inflation, unemployment, and public spending on education and health. World Bank data highlight significant income disparities between the top 10% and bottom 20% across countries. Among 11 EMDEs, Korea had the highest per capita GDP ($32,400), with its top 20% earning 24% of total income – the lowest in the group. In contrast, Brazil's top 20% held 50% of income, while India's share stood at 29%. The bottom 20% earned just 2.5% in Brazil and 8.5% in India, indicating high inequality. Inflation (6.7% in India) disproportionately affects lower earners, emphasising the need for policies to address income disparity and control inflation, as seen in China (2%) and Malaysia (3.4%).

Government spending on education, health, and employment also influences development. In 2022, Brazil allocated 8.3% of GDP to health, while India spent 4%. Education expenditure was highest in South Africa (6.2% of GDP) and 4.3% in India. Investment in human capital is essential, yet rising unemployment remains a challenge – 14.3% of highly educated individuals in India were unemployed, significantly above most other countries. While FI and development are important, they should not be the sole measures of economic progress.

A comprehensive assessment of economic development requires an index incorporating multiple indicators that reflect broader well-being and advancement. This study uses the IMF's FD Index to evaluate India's progress and compare it with other BRICS and Asian economies.

4. FD Index

A country's financial system has two main components: FIs (deposit-taking and non-deposit-taking) and FMs (capital and money markets). While financial reforms in emerging economies are widely studied, their impact on growth and stability remains complex. Traditional indicators like private credit to GDP and stock market capitalisation to GDP fail to capture the multidimensional nature of FD, including growth, inequality, and stability. Deregulation and capital openness have expanded banking, capital markets, insurance, investments, and pensions, but access, depth, and efficiency vary across countries.

International comparisons are further complicated by data limitations. While different indicators highlight specific aspects of FD, a comprehensive measure is the best achieved through an index. The IMF's FD Index incorporates 20 selected indicators from multiple sources, including World Bank FinStats, IMF Financial Access Survey, and BIS debt securities data. Indicators were chosen for their historical availability across most countries.

Despite certain limitations, the FD Index provides a standardised framework for assessing FD and comparing economies over time. Table 16.1 outlines the key indicators used in its construction.

4.1. Components of FD Index

FIs include deposit-taking and non-deposit-taking corporations, while FMs comprise stock and money markets. As defined by Čihák et al. (2012) and illustrated by the IMF, FD combines access, depth, and efficiency. Access refers to the availability of financial services, depth indicates market size and liquidity, and efficiency reflects the cost-effectiveness and sustainability of FIs and capital markets.

The FD Index follows a three-step approach, consolidating multidimensional data into a single measure. It consists of two sub-indices: the FI Index and the FM Index, each further divided into access, depth, and efficiency (Table 16.1).

Table 16.1. Components of Sub-indices of FD Index.

Indices	Indicators	
	FIs	**FMs**
Access	• Bank branches per 100,000 adults • ATMs per 100,000 adults	• Percent of market capitalisation outside of top 10 largest companies • Total number of debt issuers (domestic and external, nonfinancial and financial corporations), per 100,000 adults
Depth	• Private-sector credit to GDP • Pension fund assets to GDP • Mutual fund assets to GDP • Insurance premiums: life and non-life to GDP	• Stock market capitalisation to GDP • Stocks traded to GDP • International debt securities of the government to GDP • Total debt securities of financial corporations to GDP • Total debt securities of nonfinancial corporations to GDP
Efficiency	• Net interest margin • Lending-deposits spread • Non-interest income to total income • Overhead costs to total assets • Return on assets • Return on equity	• Stock market turnover ratio (stocks traded to capitalisation)

Source: IMF's FD Index.

The FI Index is based on twelve indicators, including bank branches and ATMs per 100,000 adults for access, private-sector credit, and insurance premiums to GDP for depth, and net interest margin and return on assets for efficiency. The FM Index uses eight indicators, measuring market liquidity and efficiency.

Constructed using principal component analysis (PCA), the FD Index assigns higher weights to indicators contributing most to variation. 'Factor loadings on the first principal component are chosen as weights. A higher weight is given to a series that contributes more to the direction of common variation. Then, sub-indices are combined into higher indices using the same procedure'. The original 0–1 scale is rescaled from 0 to 100, where 0 represents the lowest and 100 the highest level of FD.

4.2. Development Indices: BRICS and Major Asian Economies

The FD Index measures the overall FD of institutions and markets. India ranks the lowest among BRICS nations (Fig. 16.1) but has shown gradual improvement since 2013. Among seven Asian countries, India ranks mid-tier, ahead of Indonesia, the Philippines, and Pakistan (Fig. 16.2).

A score of 100 represents a fully developed financial system. Among BRICS, Brazil led with 66 in 2021, while India and Russia had the lowest at 53, indicating they are halfway (53%) towards full FD. During India's Balance of Payments (BoP) crisis in the early 1990s, its FD score was 30%. Economic reforms pushed it to 51% in 2009, but it declined to 42% by 2013. Since then, stable governance and reforms have led to a steady rise, reaching 53% with an average annual increase of 1%.

Among selected Asian countries (Fig. 16.2), South Korea ranked the highest at 82% in 2021, though slightly down from its 85% peak in 2012. Pakistan, the least developed, scored 22% and remained stagnant over the past decade. Analysing the sub-indices for FIs and FMs helps determine whether FIs or FMs drive these trends.

The FI Index (Figs. 16.3 and 16.4) and FM Index (Figs. 16.5 and 16.6) provide separate insights. Indian FIs are less developed (45%; Fig. 16.3) compared to FMs (60% in 2021). Brazil leads BRICS with 65% in both segments, while India's FI score is the lowest – 18% below Brazil and 11% behind South Africa (Fig. 16.3).

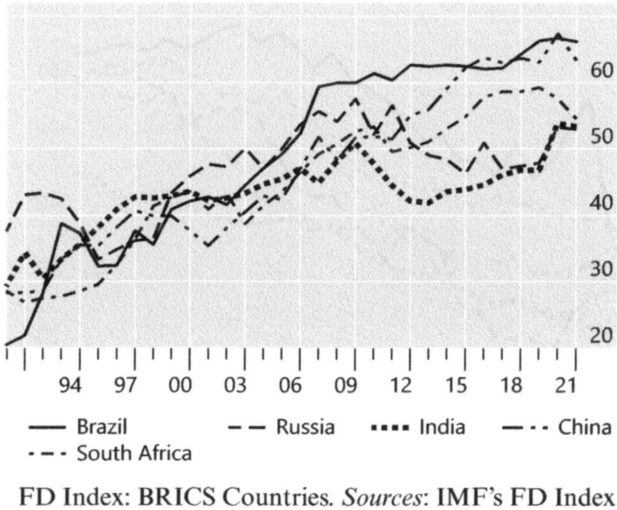

Fig. 16.1. FD Index: BRICS Countries. *Sources*: IMF's FD Index database (end-July 2023 release); authors' calculations. *Note*: The index measures a value between 0 and 100, with zero as the lowest and 100 as the highest development score. The *FD Index* presents the compositive score comprising the *FI Index* and the *FM Index*.

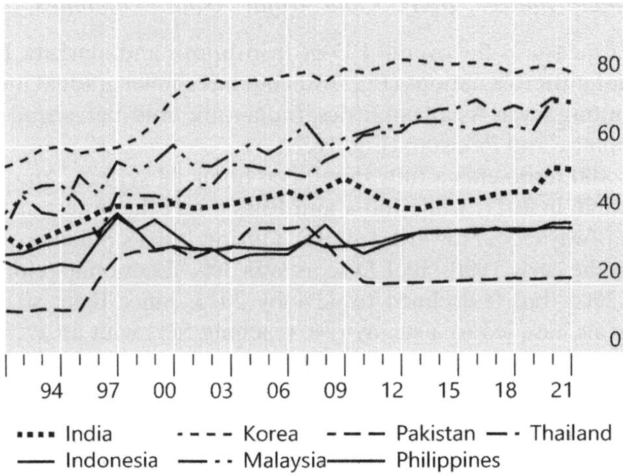

Fig. 16.2. FD Index: Major Asian Countries. *Sources*: IMF's FD Index database (end-July 2023 release); authors' calculations. *Note*: The index measures a value between 0 and 100, with zero as the lowest and 100 as the highest development score. The *FD Index* presents the compositive score comprising the *FI Index* and the *FM Index*.

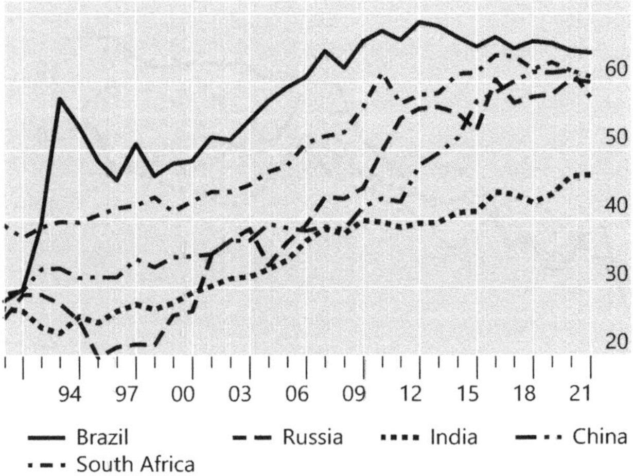

Fig. 16.3. FI Index: BRICS Countries. *Sources*: IMF's FD Index database (end-July 2023 release); authors' calculations.

Among Asian countries, India ranks mid-tier in both segments of FM Index. However, in FM Index, it stands well above Pakistan, Indonesia, and the Philippines (Fig. 16.5). Pakistan is 20% behind India in FI and 44% in FM.

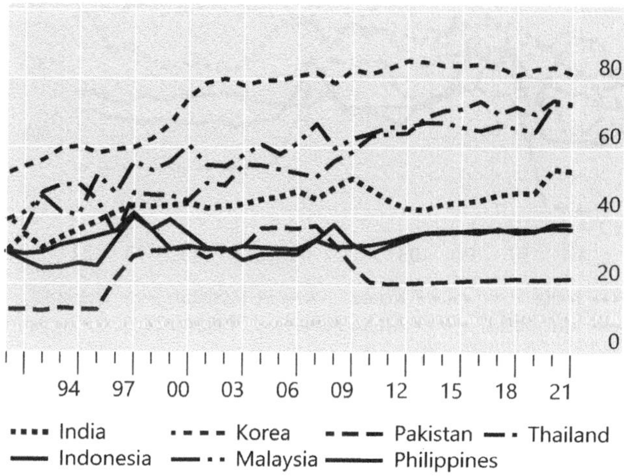

Fig. 16.4. FI Index: Major Asian Countries. *Sources*: IMF's FD Index database (end-July 2023 release); authors' calculations.

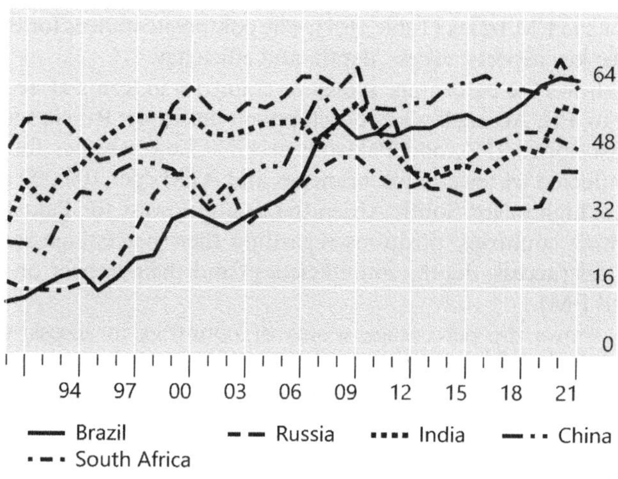

Fig. 16.5. FM Index: BRICS Countries. *Sources*: IMF's FD Index database (end-July 2023 release); authors' calculations.

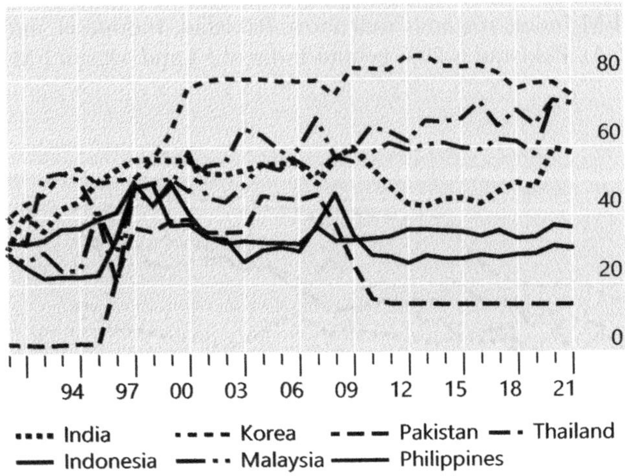

Fig. 16.6. FM Index: Major Asian Countries. *Sources*: IMF's FD Index database (end-July 2023 release); authors' calculations.

4.3. Access, Depth, and Efficiency of FIs and FMs

The FI Index and FM Index are the second-highest level of composite indexes. As stated in Section 4.1, the leaf indices are derived using 12 indicators for the FI Index and 8 for the FM Index (Table 16.1). The composite indices for both FI and FM cover three key aspects: access, depth, and efficiency.

Table 16.2 shows the percentage scores of countries in terms of access, depth, and efficiency of FIs. Access is a key development indicator: Russia scored nearly 80%, India just above 25%, and Pakistan at 17%. Lower scores for India and Pakistan are affected by fewer bank branches and ATMs per 100,000 adults. The depth of FIs is highest for South Africa (64%) and lowest for Pakistan (6.5%). The figures show countries' positions regarding their percentage scores in the three sub-indices (access, depth, and efficiency) and their impact on the parent indices (FI and FM).

Table 16.3 shows the percentage scores of countries in access, depth, and efficiency of FMs. For India, Access to the FM is low (20%) compared to depth and efficiency at 60% and 93%, respectively. Within BRICS countries, the efficiency of markets in Brazil and China is 100%, as is the case in Thailand and Korea. Among the selected countries, Malaysia's market depth is above 90%, while others are below 80%. Access to FMs in Pakistan is extremely limited, with a participation rate of only 0.1%. Furthermore, the depth of these markets is significantly shallow, scoring just 6%. In comparison, efficiency is better at 37%. Unlike FIs, India's FMs are far above the world average in all three indicators. India's overall FM Index is severely affected by access to the markets.

Table 16.2. Access, Depth, and Efficiency of Financial Institution.

Group	Countries	Access	Countries	Depth	Countries	Efficiency
BRICS	Russia	79.0	South Africa	63.9	China	73.3
	Brazil	61.6	Brazil	50.9	**India**	**66.7**
	China	46.1	China	48.6	South Africa	65.5
	South Africa	28.5	**India**	**38.9**	Russia	64.5
	India	**26.6**	Russia	19.8	Brazil	57.9
Asian	Korea	66.1	Korea	85.9	Malaysia	73.0
	Thailand	58.8	Malaysia	81.4	Korea	71.8
	Indonesia	39.7	Thailand	62.5	Pakistan	69.9
	Malaysia	34.1	**India**	**38.9**	Philippines	68.7
	India	**26.6**	Philippines	21.5	Thailand	68.7
	Philippines	23.5	Indonesia	16.2	**India**	**66.7**
	Pakistan	17.1	Pakistan	6.5	Indonesia	62.7

Sources: IMF's FD Index database (end-July 2023 release); authors' calculation.
Note: In descending order % score within each group.

Table 16.3. Access, Depth, and Efficiency of FMs.

Group	Countries	Access	Countries	Depth	Countries	Efficiency
BRICS	Russia	52.0	China	68.3	Brazil	100.0
	Brazil	42.2	S. Africa	67.2	China	100.0
	S. Africa	40.1	**India**	**59.8**	**India**	**92.5**
	India	**19.6**	Brazil	53.8	Russia	49.1
	China	18.6	Russia	31.2	S. Africa	34.5
Group	**Countries**	**Access**	**Countries**	**Depth**	**Countries**	**Efficiency**
Asian	Malaysia	47.7	Malaysia	93.0	Thailand	100.0
	Korea	44.7	Korea	77.3	Korea	100.0
	Thailand	39.0	Thailand	74.6	**India**	**92.5**
	Indonesia	34.4	**India**	**59.8**	Malaysia	70.3
	Philippines	31.9	Philippines	56.6	Pakistan	36.5
	India	**19.6**	Indonesia	24.1	Indonesia	32.6
	Pakistan	0.1	Pakistan	6.3	Philippines	14.8

Sources: IMF's FD Index database (end-July 2023 release); authors' calculations.
Note: In descending order % score within each group.

4.4. World Ranking of BRICS Countries in FD

This section provides an overview of global FD from 2011 to 2021, focusing on access, depth, and efficiency across 180+ countries (Figs. 16.7–16.11). As of 2021, the world average FD Index stands at 32.5, with its sub-indices, FI and FM, scoring 43.0 and 20.7, respectively.

FD Among BRICS Nations: Among BRICS nations, Brazil ranked the highest in the FD Index at 20, with a score of 66.2 out of 100, while Russia ranked the lowest at 33, scoring 53.0. India showed significant improvement, with its rank rising from 47 in 2011 to 31 in 2021, alongside an increase in its score from 44.5 to 53.4 over the same Period (Fig 16.7).

FI Performance: India's FI Index rank improved from 86 in 2011 to 74 in 2021; however, it still lags behind other BRICS nations, whose ranks range from 30 (Brazil) to 43 (South Africa). Notably, China made substantial progress, improving its FI rank from 75th place in 2011 to 38th in 2021 (Fig. 16.8).

India's FD has been hindered by underdeveloped FIs, with slow improvements across all three FI indicators – access (score: 26.6), depth (38.9), and efficiency 66.7) – with access being the weakest (Fig. 16.10) efficiency (66.7) – with access being the weakest. In comparison, the world averages for FI component indices in 2021 were access (35.0), depth (28.0), and efficiency (58.2).

While India's FI indicators are close to global averages, its FIs perform particularly well in efficiency, ranking among the top in the sample.

FM Performance: In the FM Index, Brazil ranked the highest among BRICS nations in 2021 at 18, with a score of 65.5 out of 100, improving from 29 in 2011 (score: 52.2). India also made considerable progress, advancing from rank 33 (score: 48.5) in 2011 to 24 (scored: 58.2) in 2021 (Fig, 16.8). China improved its rank from 25th to 21st, while South Africa and Russia trailed India at 34th and 38th.

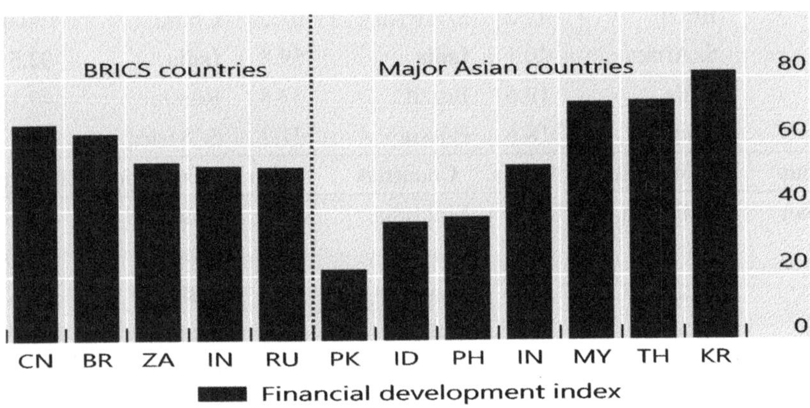

Fig. 16.7. FD indices, BRICS and Major Asian Economies, 2021 (in % Score). *Sources*: IMF's FD Index database (end-July 2023 release); authors' calculations.

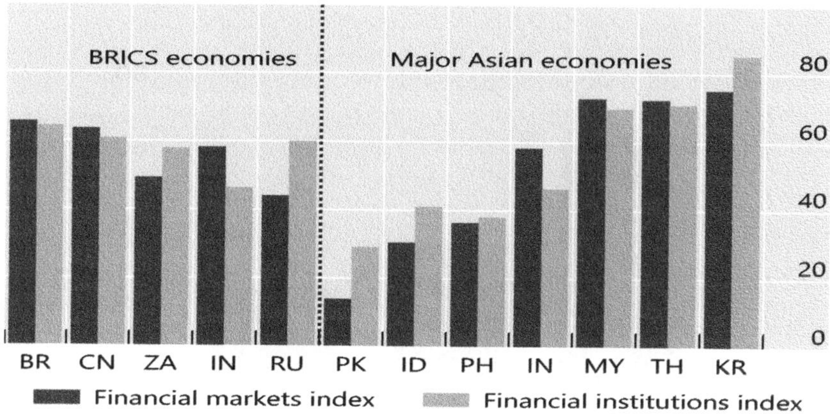

Fig. 16.8. FI and FM indices, BRICS and Major Asian Economies, 2021 (in % Score). *Sources*: IMF's FD Index database (end-July 2023 release); authors' calculations.

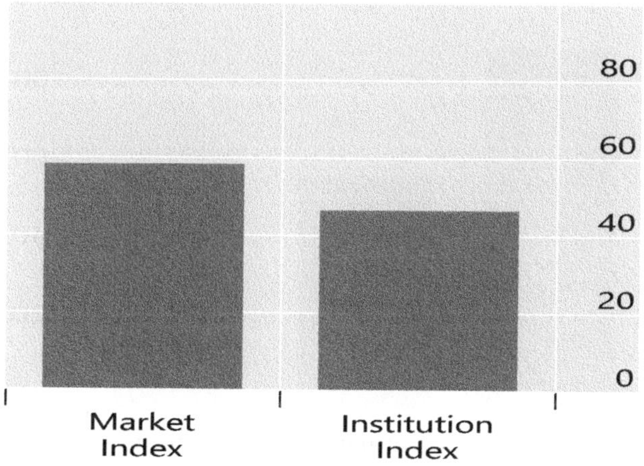

Fig. 16.9. India's FM and FI indices, 2021 (in % Score). *Sources*: IMF's FD Index database (end-July 2023 release); authors' calculations.

The world averages for the FM component indices in 2021 were access (score: 22.8), depth (21.9), and efficiency (16.5). India (19.6) and China (18.6) scored below the global average in market access, whereas Brazil (42.2), Russia (52.0), and South Africa (40.1) performed better.

However, India's FMs outperformed the global average in depth, scoring 59.8, and in efficiency, with a score of 92.5 out of 100 (Fig. 16.11).

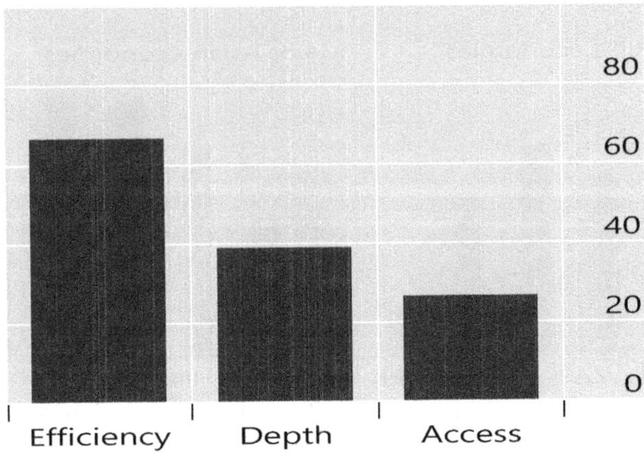

Fig. 16.10. Components of FI Index for India, 2021 (in % Score).
Sources: IMF's FD Index database (end-July 2023 release); authors' calculations.

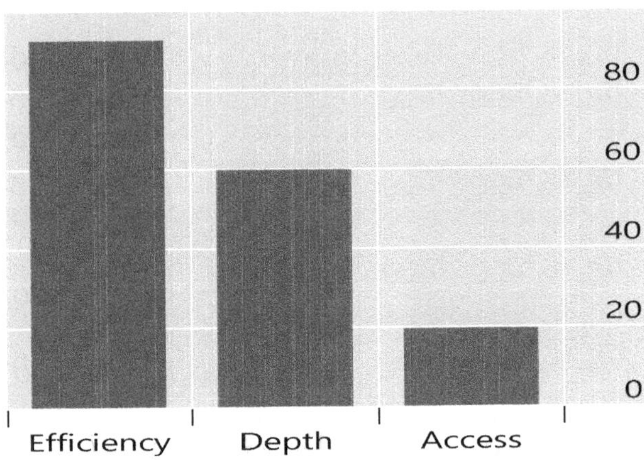

Fig. 16.11. Components of FM Index for India, 2021 (in % Score).
Sources: IMF's FD Index database (end-July 2023 release); authors' calculations.

5. Concluding Remarks

Economic liberalisation since the 1990s and continued deregulation have strengthened India's financial system. While FI ensures access to basic financial services for all, FD is broader, encompassing diverse financial products, access, depth, efficiency, literacy, regulatory strength, and stability. Extensive FI does not always translate into FD due to inefficiencies, fraud, and lack of literacy. The rise of neo-banking in India has increased fraud risks, as seen in the February 2024 suspension of Paytm's banking affiliate.

The IMF's FD Index ranks India lowest among BRICS and mid-range among seven major Asian economies, mainly due to weak performance in FIs' access and efficiency. However, the IMF notes that certain indicators may distort rankings – government controls on lending and deposit rates can inflate efficiency ratings, and a high FD score may indicate an overstretched financial system, posing risks to stability.

The FD Index has limitations, including incomplete data coverage for sub-indices (access, depth, efficiency) and exclusion of shadow banking and digital payments like credit transfers and mobile banking, which are crucial in emerging economies. Despite these challenges, the index offers a more comprehensive measure of FD than traditional indicators and aids researchers in analysing financial systems and economic growth.

In India, while economic development up to the end of 2021 showed progress, efforts are continuing (National Centre for Financial Education [NCFE], 2020), and the current status may reflect further improvements. Policymakers should prioritise financial education, transparency, and fraud prevention while ensuring efficiency, security, and stability in the financial sector. Additionally, greater investment in healthcare, education, employment, and income equality, along with effective inflation control – targeting levels similar to China's 2% or Malaysia's 3.4% – is crucial for sustainable economic growth.

Acknowledgements

We thank Sambuddha Bandyopadhyay, Prof. Soheli Ghose, Prof. Debashis Mazumdar, Prof. H. K. Pradhan, Dr Indrajit Roy, and joint seminar participants of the Heritage College, Ramakrishna Mission Vidyamandira and ICSSR at the international seminar on different dimensions of development economics and its shifting paradigms, for helpful comments and suggestions. The views expressed in this study do not necessarily reflect views of the Bank for International Settlements (BIS).

References

Alber, N. (2019). *Determinants of financial inclusion: The case of 125 countries from 2004 to 2017*. http://dx.doi.org/10.2139/ssrn.3476373

Alliance for Financial Inclusion. (2023, December). *Global standard-setting bodies and the AFI network discuss the potential and risks of digital assets*. https://www.afi-global.org/news/global-standard-setting-bodies-and-the-afi-network-discuss-the-potential-and-risks-of-digital-assets/

Amidzić, G., Massara, A., & Mialou, A. (2014). *Assessing countries' financial inclusion standing — A new composite index* [Working Paper No. 14/36]. IMF.

Beck, T., Asli Demirgüç-Kunt, A., & Levine, R. (2000). A new database on the structure and development of the financial sector. *World Bank Economic Review*, *14*(3), 597–605. https://doi.org/10.1093/wber/14.3.597

Beck, T., Demirgüç-Kunt, A., & Levine, R. (2010). Financial institutions and markets across countries and over time. *World Bank Economic Review*, *24*(1), 77–92. https://doi.org/10.1093/wber/lhp016

Beck, T., Demirguc-Kunt, A., & Martinez Peria, M. S. (2007). Reaching out: Access to and use of banking services across countries. *Journal of Financial Economics*, *85*, 234–266.

Čihák, M., Demirgüç-Kunt, A., Feyen, E. H. B., & Levine, R. E. (2012). *Benchmarking financial development around the world* [Policy Research Working Paper No. WPS 6175]. World Bank Group. https://documents.worldbank.org/en/publication/documents-reports/documentdetail/868131468326381955/benchmarking-financial-systems-around-the-world

Dabla-Norris, E., Deng, Y., Ivanova, A., Karpowicz, I., Unsal, F., VanLeemput, E., & Wong, J. (2015). *Financial inclusion: Zooming in on Latin America* [IMF Working Paper 15/206]. International Monetary Fund.

Demirguc-Kunt, A., & Klapper L. (2012). *Measuring financial inclusion: The global Findex database* [Policy Research Working Paper 6025]. The World Bank. https://ssrn.com/abstract=2043012

Demirgüç-Kunt, A., Klapper, L. F., & Singer, D. (2017). *Financial inclusion and inclusive growth – A review of recent empirical evidence* [Policy Research Working Paper 8040]. World Bank Group.

Demirgüç-Kunt, A., Klapper, L. F., Singer, D., Ansar, S., & Singer, D. (2018). *Global Findex database 2017: Measuring financial inclusion and the Fintech revolution*. The World Bank.

Demirgüç-Kunt, A., Klapper, L. F., Singer, D., Ansar, S., & Singer, D. (2022). *The global Findex database 2017: Financial inclusion, digital payments, and resilience in the age of COVID-19*. The World Bank.

Demirgüç-Kunt, A., & Levine, R. (2008). *Finance, financial sector policies, and long-run growth* [M. Spence Growth Commission Background Paper No. 11]. World Bank.

Diniz, E., Birochi, R., & Pozzebon, M. (2012). Triggers and barriers to financial inclusion: The use of ICT-based branchless banking in an Amazon County. *Electronic Commerce Research and Applications*, *11*(5), 484–494. http://dx.doi.org/10.1016/j.elerap.2011.07.006

El Said, A., Emara, N., & Pearlman, J. (2019). *On the impact of financial inclusion on financial stability and inequality: The role of macroprudential policies* [Discussion Paper Series No. 20/06]. Department of Economics. http://dx.doi.org/10.2139/ssrn.3814335

Hajaj, K. (2002). *Illiteracy, financial services and social exclusion* [Opinion Papers]. https://eric.ed.gov/?id=ED473576

Inoue, T. (2024). Financial inclusion and income distribution revisited: New findings. *Quarterly Review of Economics and Finance*, *98*, 101940. https://doi.org/10.1016/j.qref.2024.101940

International Monetary Fund. (2023, July). *Financial development index database*. https://legacydata.imf.org/?sk=f8032e80-b36c-43b1-ac26-493c5b1cd33b

Kempson, E. (2006, May 30–31). *Policy level response to financial exclusion in developed economies: Lessons for developing countries*. The Personal Finance Research Centre, University of Bristol, Paper for Access to Finance: Building Inclusive Financial Systems, World Bank.

National Centre for Financial Education. (2020). *National strategy for financial education 2020–2025*. https://ncfe.org.in/nsfe/#

Reserve Bank of India. (2020). *National strategy for financial inclusion 2019–2024*. https://shorturl.at/body

Roy, I., Phukan, S., Sengupta, S., & Sharma, A. K. (2021, September). Financial inclusion index for India. *RBI Bulletin*, 89–96.

Sarma, M. (2012). *Index of financial inclusion – A measure of financial sector inclusiveness* [Working Paper No. 07/2012]. Competence Centre on Money, Trade, Finance and Development.

Seidman, E., Hababou, M., & Kramer, J. (2005). *Getting to know underbanked consumers: A financial services analysis*. Report of the Center for Financial Services Innovation.

World Bank Group. (2022, September). *Global financial development database*. https://www.worldbank.org/en/publication/gfdr/data/global-financial-development-database

Wu, C., Nsiah, C., & Fayissa, B. (2023). Analyzing the differential impacts of financial sector development on remittance inflows. *Research in Economics*, *77*(2), 239–250. https://doi.org/10.1016/j.rie.2022.10.001

Chapter 17

India's Future Energy Consumption Scenario: A Roadmap Towards Clean Energy Transition

Bidisha Chatterjee

St. Xavier's College, Burdwan, West Bengal, India

Abstract

India being the world's most populous country is also the world's third-largest emitter of greenhouse gases (GHGs) which is found to be increasing steadily since 2010. Despite employing several energy sources, India still relies heavily on coal, its primary energy source. India's swiftly rising energy demand acts as a challenging situation for protecting the environment and preventing climate change. On the other hand, a significant rise in investments in renewables like solar and hydrogen in recent years shows the movement towards the path of sustainability and thereby reduces energy intensity across sectors of the economy. In this context, this chapter attempts to portray the energy mix in India during the recent years and in near future while examining the carbon emission trends over years as well. On the other hand, the study forecasts total primary energy consumption (TPEC) in India till 2050 using both univariate and multivariate forecasting methods. For multivariate forecasting, we have assumed two alternative possibilities for gross domestic product (GDP) growth: the business-as-usual scenario (BAUS) and the high-growth scenario. Based on these findings, this chapter recommends that Indian government policies should emphasise on expanding renewable energy resources and increasing its availability for consumption in major energy consuming sectors like manufacturing industries and households.

Changing Dimensions in Economic Development: Theories and Empirics, 231–242

Published under exclusive licence by Emerald Publishing Limited
doi:10.1108/978-1-83708-384-820261020

Keywords: Renewable energy; energy demand forecasting; economic growth; energy consumption; carbon emission; climate change

JEL Codes: Q20; Q410; Q430; Q470

1. Introduction

1.1. Background: India's Ambitious Target to Adapt Clean Energy Roadmap

In recent times, India has been the most populous country in the world and plays a pivotal role in its growth and development as an emerging nation. The journey towards the achievement of high economic growth since 1990s has also led to a significant increase in its energy consumption. We find India's TPEC has increased from 8.3 EJ in 1990 to approximately 32.2 EJ in 2020. According to the recent predictions of the International Energy Agency (IEA, 2021), over the next few decades, India's energy demand growth will be higher than in any other country. Even though in the recent times, India employs a variety of energy sources, and there is a clear shift towards non-fossil fuels, coal remains to be the most significant energy source in the country even in 2020 (close to 55% of energy coming from it), followed by oil (about 29%), which are considered to be the dirtiest sources of fossil fuel energy. Thus, the picture shows the reason for India being the world's third-largest contributor to GHG emissions, which is also steadily increasing since 2010 (Energy Statistics of India, 2023). Persistently plagued by serious environmental concerns such as severe air pollution and contaminated water supplies resulting from their heavy dependence on coal and oil, the Indian government is presently formulating policies to promote greater utilisation of carbon-free energy sources.

1.2. Significance of Renewables in the Energy Transition

In recent years, in order to scale down energy intensity and prevent climate change, India has significantly increased its investments in renewable energy production, particularly in solar and hydrogen. Renewables account for about 10% of India's total energy consumption, and it plans to increase this share to 50% by 2040 (NITI Aayog, GOI, 2017). While the commendable emphasis on renewable energy is pivotal for addressing environmental concerns, it is imperative to recognise that this alone may not be adequate to meet India's rapidly growing energy demands. Therefore, under such circumstances in the short run, India has to rely on domestic and imported fossil energy sources. However, a strong and united effort should be manifested to minimise dependence on 'dirty' fuels. As the most environmentally friendly choice among all energy alternatives, renewable energy can play a crucial role as an interim energy source in the ongoing transition process. The Indian government has established a target of raising all renewable sources in the overall energy mix to 500 Giga Watts in 2030 and reach the target of net zero emission by 2070. Besides, it has also taken a target of producing 50% energy needs through clean energy sources. To reach this ambitious objective, the government has implemented various initiatives to enhance nationwide access to renewable sources, such as implementing domestic transmission grid schemes for integration of renewable generation in several Indian states like Tamil Nadu, Karnataka, Andhra Pradesh, Madhya Pradesh, Gujrat and Rajasthan. Besides, implementation of transmission systems by identifying renewable potentialities in states like Gujrat, Rajasthan, Himachal Pradesh and Ladakh. Despite numerous government initiatives, the proportion of renewable sources in the energy mix has declined due to lack of a proper centralised regulatory authority and policy framework which differs among different states and political and regulatory barriers. Subsequently, inadequate institutional cooperation and research centres to maintain proper renewable infrastructure and lack of skilled manpower also sets challenges to the improvement targets. Besides, lack of fund allocation in the annual budget also hinders the growth process of renewable sources. It is thus imperative to examine the future growth trajectory of renewable energy needs in India in the medium run.

1.3. Existing Studies

Renewable sources of energy are still in its early stages of development. However, several researchers have studied the current trends and potential for this sector in meeting India's burgeoning energy demand while at the same time bringing down its carbon footprint and continuing with sustainable development. Some of the notable studies are those by Gupta (2021) who has analysed the trends and patterns of energy use in India and also examined the impact of economic growth on different drivers of energy use. Besides, Panwar et al. (2011) studied the role of renewables in environmental protection and how renewables help in mitigating GHG emissions and sustainable development. Dey et al. (2022) examined the present and future potentialities of renewable sources in India. Tripathi et al. (2016) studied the contribution of renewable energy in the present energy mix which helped in minimising the carbon emission and negative environmental impacts. On the other hand, Pandey et al. (2022) forecasted non-renewable and renewable energy from various sources and examined that production of renewable as well as non-renewable energy would increase in future. Studies that focus more on the policy environment related to the renewable sector in India include those by Harjanne and Korhonen (2019) who argued that renewable sources alone do not bring about sustainability and have certain negative consequences which are ignored. Therefore, they infer that proper conceptualisation of energy could be more helpful for effective climate and energy policy. Lund (2007) argues that without development in research and technological improvements, it will be a difficult task to convert energy sources into total renewables. Researchers like Kumar and Majid (2020) have also explored future prospects and challenges of renewable sources along with examining the opportunities of increasing investment and employment due to the development of this sector. However, hardly any studies attempt to forecast the renewable energy consumption scenario in India over the medium to long run and its associated policy implications.

This chapter aims to address this gap in existing research. This is especially important because India quests to be a zero-carbon economy by 2070. In this process, renewable energy sources act as an indispensable role for India during the whole transition period. Although it is costlier but cleaner than other fossil fuels which are known to increase carbon emission and thereby resulting in climate change. Thus, this sector might help Indian economy to evolve as an environmentally sustainable one, but we should examine its medium- to long-run prospects, problems, challenges and opportunities of this sector.

1.4. Research Objectives and Scope

In this chapter, we have first tried to anticipate the evolving trends in energy demand within India. We have analysed the dynamic shifts in the proportional contributions of diverse energy sources – extending both renewable and non-renewable categories – to India's overall energy consumption scenario, starting from 1990. Later, we have also tried to forecast energy consumption in India up to the year 2050. To get robust forecasting results, we have used both univariate forecasting techniques, like double exponential smoothing, as well as multivariate forecasting techniques, namely the Cochrane–Orcutt method. On the other hand, for analysing through multivariate forecasting, we have also considered two alternative scenarios for GDP growth: a BAUS which assumes a 6% growth rate and a high-growth rate scenario (assumes an 8% growth rate). We find that our univariate forecast results are very similar to that of our multivariate forecasts under the BAUS case, which highlights the robustness of our results. Considering these findings, this chapter advocates for government policies in India to prioritise augmenting renewable or clean energy production, facilitating implementation of grids across states and expanding investments and financial infrastructure in renewable energy resources.

2. Methodology and Data Sources

To forecast the future trends in total energy demand (or total energy consumption) in India, we have employed both univariate technique (using double exponential smoothing method) and multivariate technique (using Cochrane–Orcutt method) for the period 2030–2050.

2.1. Univariate Modelling

For analysing the univariate method, we have considered exponential smoothing, where forecasts are weighted averages of previous observations with exponentially decreasing weights on older terms. In particular, we have applied Holt's linear exponential smoothing technique as a process of forecasting our observation. According to Gelper et al. (2007), this method reconciles both the level or average value and trend components of the time series. Though this is a primitive technique, it is favoured because of its simplicity in understanding and computation. This method can be utilised alone or as a springboard for other methods. Some recent studies that used this technique are Tularam and Saeed (2016), Tratar et al. (2016) and De Oliveira et al. (2018). In addition, since the length of our data series is short, we refrained from using more sophisticated techniques like Autoregressive integrated moving average (ARIMA).

2.2. Multivariate Modelling

The error, trend, seasonality (ETS) approach used for Exponential Smoothing model, ignores the influence of other variables on the series to be forecasted, even if it does offer a starting point or base value for the forecast. We have employed the Cochrane–Orcutt autoregressive model for forecasting based on a multivariate model in addition to the ETS approach to account for the influence of other relevant elements. Based on recent research (e.g., Sengupta, 1993; Suganthi & Jagadeesan, 1992, for India; Hunt & Ninomiya, 2005; Intarapravich et al., 1996, for studies conducted outside of India, among others), we hypothesise that the four main factors influencing gross energy consumption are total population, energy prices, technology (or energy efficiency) and gross output or GDP from the production side. Additionally, it is also argued that in comparison to other sectors of the economy, the manufacturing sector usually has a higher energy intensity. As a result, the share of manufacturing in GDP also affects TPEC. Thus, our list of explanatory variables includes GDP (both level and per capita GDP are at constant 2011–2012 prices), population (million), gross capital formation (GCF) (both level and per capita GCF are at constant 2011–2012 prices, also acts as a proxy for technology), share of manufacturing in gross domestic product (MFGGDP) and energy prices.

Utilising a log-linear Cobb–Douglas (C–D) type functional form, we assume that the demand elasticities with respect to the components are constant and hence represent them as parameters of the equation:

$$TPEC_t = A.GDP_t^{\beta_1} . POP_t^{\beta_2} . GCF_t^{\beta_3} . MFGGDP_t^{\beta_4} . P_t^{\beta_5}; \qquad \text{(i)}$$

Applying natural log(ln)-transformation, we get the following log-linear model modifiable to Ordinary least squares (OLS) estimation:

$$\begin{aligned} \ln TPEC_t &= \ln A + \sum_i \theta_i TPEC_{t-i} + \beta_1 \ln GDP_t + \beta_2 \ln POP_t + \beta_3 \\ &\ln GCF_t + \beta_4 \ln MFGGDP_t + \beta_5 \ln P_t + u_t \ ; \end{aligned} \qquad \text{(ii)}$$

θ_i are lag parameters corresponding to lagged primary energy demand variables, and i is the lag length. This model has been analysed using the Cochrane–Orcutt method. This part of the forecasting is based on an in-sample period of 32 years, and forecasts are made for the future period of 28 years.

Although the univariate method is simple to understand, less data intensive and easy to compute, nonetheless, it lacks precision and fails to account for the influence of other associated causal variables. On the other hand, the Cochrane–Orcutt method provides more precise forecasts and allows inclusion of causal variables. But it is a relatively complex method and is much more data intensive.

2.3. Data Sources

The sources for secondary data include BP Statistical Review and IEA reports for energy consumption data; World Bank reports for population and GDP data; National Accounts Statistics of the Government of India for data on GDP, capital formation and sectoral shares in GDP; *Handbook of Statistics on Indian Economy* for data on price indices; and India Energy Outlook for details on domestic energy production and consumption. We have used annual data for the period 1990–2022. We have employed a three-year moving average for 2021 to account for the effects of the COVID-19 pandemic and lockdown on production and energy consumption. Therefore, our study consists of data for 32 periods starting from 1990 till 2022. Further, we have forecasted energy demand in India till 2050, which is a period of approximately 30 years.

3. Results and Analysis

3.1. Gross Energy Demand Pattern in India: Present and Future Scenario

3.1.1. Current Status and Trends

It is an established fact that a positive relationship exists between economic growth and energy demand. Therefore, we try to frame out the energy demand pattern and economic growth levels during 1990–2022.

From Table 17.1, we find that initially during the year 1990, India's GDP was 465.2 billion US$ (at constant 2015 prices); on the other hand, primary energy

Table 17.1. India's GDP and Energy Consumption – 1990–2022.

Year	GDP (at Constant 2015 US$ Billion)	Primary Energy Consumption (EJ)	Per Capita Energy Consumption (GJ per capita)
1990	465.2	8.3	9.5
2000	800.5	13.4	12.7
2010	1,535.9	22.6	18.1
2020	2,508.6	32.2	22.7
2022	2,954.9	36.4	25.7

Sources: BP Statistical Review (2023); World Development Indicators – World Bank Database.

consumption was 8.3 EJ and per capita energy consumption was 9.5 GJ per person. With progress in economic growth and development, GDP increased over the decades to 2,954.9 billion US$ in 2022, energy consumption increased to 36.4 EJ and per capita energy consumption increased to 0.26 EJ per 10 million persons. Therefore, we find a consistent upward trend (except for the COVID-19 pandemic period of 2020–2021).

3.1.2. Share of Coal/Oil/Nuclear/Renewables and Trends in Carbon Emission

Prior to making a prediction of the future energy demand patterns, it is very crucial to study the pattern of energy mix, which comes from different energy sources – both renewable and non-renewable or fossil energy. In India, renewables like solar and wind energy were not used until the 1980s, and coal was found to be the dominant source of energy, accounting for more than half of total energy consumption. However, during the 1990–2010 period, the share of fossil fuel increased while renewables have declined. After 2010, although the share of renewables, including hydroelectricity, has been found to be increasing steadily, we also find that the share of fossil fuels remained above 80% till 2020 (Table AI). Simultaneously, besides consumption of coal and oil, consumption of other fossil fuels has also increased in the last decade. On the other hand, we find carbon emission follows an upward trend over years for the period 1990–2022. Although the growth rate of carbon emission was maximum during 2010, it has declined during the recent years. This follows an ongoing endeavour to reduce the use of high-carbon energy sources and enhance environmental sustainability.

3.1.3. Forecast

We have tried to forecast TPEC in India over the next two decades using both univariate and multivariate methods. In this regard, we have taken into consideration exponential smoothing for the univariate approach, in which forecasts are weighted averages of prior data with exponentially decreasing weights on older terms. In particular, we used Holt's linear exponential smoothing approach for forecasting.

Using the univariate modelling technique, we find that TPEC is expected to rise to 54 EJ approximately in 2030, 75 EJ in 2040 and 99 EJ in 2050, respectively (Table 17.2). Notably, these figures are close to the predictions by IEA and BP.

However, it should be noted that the univariate forecasts depend on past trends of TPEC only and do not consider the movement of other explanatory variables on TPEC. Hence, a better estimate of the projected values would be that from the multivariate forecasting methods (Ghosh et al., 2024). For the multivariate forecasts based on the Cochrane–Orcutt method, we have assumed the following framework for the explanatory variables:

(i) GDP: two alternate scenarios – 6% per annum growth between 2020 and 2050 (BAUS, observed long-run growth rate over the 2010–2020 period) and 8% per annum growth rate (high-growth scenario).

(ii) GCF: remains unchanged at 30% of GDP.
(iii) Share of the manufacturing sector in GDP: unchanged at 16% of GDP.
(iv) Price levels: follows the IEA projections, which rises by 2.5% per annum during the period 2020–2030 and at 3% per annum thereafter.
(v) Population: follows Ministry of Health and Family Welfare (MOHFW, 2011) projections.

The multivariate model estimates or the Cochrane–Orcutt regression results are provided in Table AII. Using the calculated results and following the above outlined assumptions, TPEC is expected to reach around 50 EJ by 2030, 72 EJ by 2040 and 102 EJ by 2050 (for the BAUS scenario). Thus, if India shows a magnificent 8% per annum growth sustained over the next two decades, TPEC will touch 55 EJ in 2030, 86 EJ in 2040 and 135 EJ under the high-growth scenario.

Therefore, we find that both univariate and multivariate forecasts under the BAUS scenario are close, and the discrepancy between them is negligible, that is, less than 5% in the long run. We can thus deduce that our forecast estimates are robust. For the year 2030, the high-growth estimate is comparable to the other forecasts, but it is significantly higher for 2040 and 2050, respectively.

3.2. Roadmap of Renewables for Clean Energy Transition

Several institutions like BP have predicted that the share of coal and oil is expected to show a declining trend over the next three decades, while natural gas and renewables will show a marked rising trend, and this prediction has been proved correct through our forecasting results during the period of 2050 (Table AIII). We find that, initially, the share of fossil energy, especially that of from coal, was 52.4%, whereas the share of renewables was 4.6% of the total share during the year 2000. Eventually, with improvement in the development of renewable sources in our country, we find that in the year 2050, the share of renewables (35.1%) will surpass the share of coal (33%) which once was the dominating energy source. This trend will be accelerated if the country follows the net zero carbon policy over the 2030–2050 period. This brings us to the importance of renewable sources in India's energy transition process.

Table 17.2. Forecasted Energy Consumption in India 2030–2050.

Year	Forecasted TPEC (EJ)		
	Univariate Forecast (Holt Method)	Multivariate Forecast (Cochrane–Orcutt)	
		BAUS	High-growth Scenario
2030	54.2	50.2	55.4
2040	75.3	71.9	86.7
2050	99.4	102.7	135.3

Source: Author's calculations based on BP Statistical Review (2023).

4. Conclusion

From the above results, we find that as GDP increases over years, and per capita energy consumption also increases. India being heavily dependent on fossil energy, coal plays a dominant role in the energy sector. Besides, we also find that renewables have gained importance in the recent times, and their share has also gradually increased during the recent years.

India has the potential to follow up net zero carbon policy and prove India to be a carbon-free country with no severe environmental impacts or climate change. But these are only possible through proper investment, infrastructure and technology improvement along with skill development which can be introduced through proper channels with supportive government policies. Renewable energy cost is also a major factor which affects the transmission of grids and channels to set up renewables in every corner of the nation. Subsequently, from the multivariate forecasting analysis, we find GDP and population are the major factors affecting total energy consumption. Therefore, as India's economic growth and population both show a rising trend, they will initiate high demand for energy.

In order to help sectors to transform themselves from dirty to clean energy sources, pricing policies consisting of subsidies and soft loan facilities and proper infrastructure should be more developed. Besides, the Central Government along with the states should also look at the availability of transmission channels with a proper regulatory framework across the country such that development of renewables does not give rise to regional and sectoral imbalances.

References

BP Statistical Review. (2023). *BP statistical review of world energy, 2023*. http://bp.com/statisticalreview

De Oliveira, E. M., & Oliveira, F. L. C. (2018). Forecasting mid-long term electric energy consumption through bagging ARIMA and exponential smoothing methods. *Energy*, *144*, 776–788. https://doi.org/10.1016/j.energy.2017.12.049

Dey, S., Sreenivasulu, A., Veerendra, G. T. N., Rao, K. V., & Anjaneya Babu, P. S. S. (2022). Renewable energy present status and future potentials in India: An overview. *Innovation and Green Development*, *1*(1), 1–22. https://doi.org/10.1016/j.igd.2022.100006

Energy Statistics of India. (2023). *Ministry of Statistics and Programme Implementation, Government of India (MoSPI)*. http://www.mospi.gov.in

Gelper, S., Fried, R., & Croux, C. (2007). Robust forecasting with exponential and Holt–Winters smoothing. *SSRN*, 1–22. http://dx.doi.org/10.2139/ssrn.1089403

Ghosh, S., Majumder, R., & Chatterjee, B. (2024). Natural gas matters: LNG and India's quest for clean energy. *Gases*, *4*, 1–17. https://doi.org/10.3390/gases4010001

Gupta, S. (2021). Assessment of energy infrastructure in India: Is it sustainable .... *Journal of Global Economy*, *17*(3), 140–161.

Harjanne, A., & Korhonen, J. M. (2019). Abandoning the concept of renewable energy. *Energy Policy*, *127*, 330–340. https://doi.org/10.1016/j.enpol.2018.12.029

Hunt, L. C., & Ninomiya, Y. (2005). Primary energy demand in Japan: An empirical analysis of long-term trends and future CO2 emissions. *Energy Policy*, *33*(11), 1409–1424. https://doi.org/10.1016/j.enpol.2003.12.019

IEA. (2021). *India energy outlook 2021 special report*. http://www.iea.org

Intarapravich, D., Johnson C. J., Li, B., Long, S., & Pezeshki, S. (1996). Asia-Pacific energy supply and demand to 2010. *Energy*, *21*(11), 1017–1039. https://doi.org/10.1016/0360-5442(96)00085-0

Kumar, J., & Majid, M. A. (2020). *Energy, sustainability and society*. https://doi.org/10.1186/s13705-019-0232-1

Lund, H. (2007). Renewable energy strategies for sustainable development. *Energy*, *32*(6), 912–919.

MOHFW. (2011). *Annual report*. Ministry of Health and Family Welfare. http://main.mohfw.gov.in

NITI Aayog, GoI. (2017). *India vision 2040 (Chapter 15), draft national energy policy*. NITI Aayog, Government of India. http://www.niti.gov.in

Pandey, A. K., Singh, P. K., Nawaz, M., & Kushwaha, A. K. (2022). Forecasting of non-renewable and renewable energy production in India using optimised discrete grey model. *Environmental Science and Pollution Research*, *30*, 8188–8206. https://doi.org/10.1007/s11356-022-22739-w

Panwar, N. L., Kaushik, S. C., & Surendra, K. (2011). Role of renewable energy sources in environmental protection: A review. *Renewable and Sustainable Energy Reviews*, *15*, 1513–1524.

Sengupta, J. K. (1993). Information theory in econometrics. *Econometrics of Information and Efficiency*, *1993*, 71–105.

Suganthi, L., & Jadadeesan, T. R. (1992). A modified model for prediction of India's future energy requirement. *Energy & Environment*, *3*(4), 371–386.

Tratar, L. F., Mojškerc, B., & Toman, A. (2016). Demand forecasting with four-parameter exponential smoothing. *International Journal of Production Economics*, *181*, 162–173. https://doi.org/10.1016/j.ijpe.2016.08.004

Tripathi, L., Mishra, A. K., Dubey, A. K., Tripathy, C. B., & Baredar, P. (2016). Renewable energy: An overview on its contribution in current energy scenario of India. *Renewable and Sustainable Energy Reviews*, *60*, 226–233. http://dx.doi.org/10.1016/j.rser.2016.01.047

Tularam, G. A., & Saeed, T. (2016). The use of exponential smoothing (ES), Holts and Winter (HW) and ARIMA models in oil price analysis. *International Journal of Mathematics, Game Theory, and Algebra*, *25*(1), 13–22.

Appendix

Table AI. Energy Consumption Mix and Carbon Emission in India – 1990–2022.

Year	Total Energy Consumption (EJ) From					Shares (%) in TPEC of			Carbon Emission (MT)
	Coal	Oil	Nuclear	Other Non-renewables	Renewables (Including Hydro)	Fossil fuels	Renewables (Including Hydro)	Others	
1990	4.59	2.50	0.07	0.43	0.71	86.3	8.6	5.2	602.1
2000	6.88	4.61	0.16	0.89	0.86	86.9	6.4	6.6	959.8
2010	12.14	6.60	0.22	2.15	1.49	83.9	6.6	9.5	1,640.3
2020	17.40	9.08	0.40	2.19	3.13	83.5	9.7	6.8	2,237.5
2022	19.30	9.25	0.40	3.66	3.79	79.5	10.4	10.1	2,595.8

Source: BP Statistical Review (2023).

Table AII. Multivariate Time Series Forecasting: Cochran–Orcutt Model (Dependent Variable: TPEC).

Explanatory Variables	Coefficients (After Transformation)	p-Value
LN population	1.164* (0.830)	0.082
LN GDP	0.445*** (0.172)	<0.01
LN per capita manufacturing share in GDP	0.045 (0.099)	0.652
LN GCF	0.030 (0.034)	0.383
LN price index	0.109 (0.068)	0.124
Rho (ρ) for residuals of OLS model	0.866**	
Breusch–Godfrey test statistic for OLS model	22.183**	<0.01
Durbin Watson statistic of OLS model	0.642**	<0.01
Rho (ρ) for residuals of C–O model	0.035	
Durbin Watson statistic of C–O model	1.825	0.193
Adjusted R^2	0.928	

Source: Author's calculation.
Note: Figures in parentheses are standard errors.
***, ** and * denote significance at 1%, 5% and 10%, respectively.

Table AIII. Forecasted Energy Mix in India 2030–2050.

Year	% of TPEC Coming From				
	Coal	Oil	Natural Gas	Nuclear	Renewables (Including Hydro)
2020 (actual)	52.4	28.0	6.4	6.6	4.6
2030	43.1	23.5	13.1	4.5	15.7
2040	40.3	20.9	12.7	3.7	22.4
2050	33.0	17.0	12.1	2.8	35.1

Source: Author's calculations.

Chapter 18

Assessing Economic Trajectories: The Impact of GST on India's Fiscal Dynamics and Growth

Jagabandhu Mandal[a], *Tusar Kanti Ghorai*[b] *and Pinaki Das*[c]

[a]*Department of Economics, Subarnarekha Mahavidyalaya, West Bengal, India*
[b]*Department of Commerce, Uluberia College, West Bengal, India*
[c]*Department of Economics, Vidyasagar University, West Bengal, India*

Abstract

This study examines the long-term and short-term dynamics between tax revenues and economic growth in India, with a particular focus on the goods and services tax (GST) introduced in 2017. Using annual data from 1980–1981 to 2024–2025, the research employs advanced time series techniques including unit root tests, Johansen cointegration, Granger causality, and vector error correction models (VECMs) to explore the relationship between income tax and gross domestic product (GDP). Findings confirm a long-run equilibrium with bidirectional causality between the two variables, although short-run causality from income tax to GDP remains marginal. The GST dummy variable is statistically insignificant in the short run, indicating delayed or structural effects. A cross-sectional analysis of 27 states reveals heterogeneous outcomes, with variations in taxpayer expansion, GST collection per capita, own tax revenue, and state domestic product (SDP) growth. While states like Arunachal Pradesh and Sikkim exhibit notable improvements, others show modest or declining trends. The study concludes that while GST has enhanced tax transparency and long-run revenue alignment, its full potential is contingent on regional capacities, administrative efficiency, and targeted fiscal strategies. These insights highlight the importance of targeted reforms to enhance tax compliance,

Changing Dimensions in Economic Development: Theories and Empirics, 243–258

Published under exclusive licence by Emerald Publishing Limited
doi:10.1108/978-1-83708-384-820261021

reduce regional disparities, and foster sustainable and inclusive economic development.

Keywords: Goods and services tax; economic growth; fiscal policy reforms; tax revenue; regional economic diversity; India

1. Introduction

The architecture of a nation's tax system is fundamental to its economic fabric, serving as the backbone for government revenue generation and playing a pivotal role in shaping fiscal policy and economic development. In the intricate landscape of public finance, tax revenue occupies a central position, providing the necessary funds for government operations, public welfare initiatives, infrastructural development, and various other state responsibilities. This comprehensive exploration delves into the evolution of India's tax system, with a particular emphasis on the transformative journey from a complex web of indirect taxes to the implementation of the GST, a landmark reform aimed at streamlining tax collection and fostering a unified market.

Historically, India's reliance on indirect taxes has been significant, with these taxes forming a major chunk of the government's revenue. This dependence not only highlights the role of indirect taxes in the Indian economic milieu but also underscores the challenges posed by a complex and layered indirect tax structure. Prior to the GST era, the cascading effect of taxes – wherein taxes were levied on an already taxed value – resulted in increased product prices, distorting the market and placing an undue burden on consumers.

The introduction of the GST in July 2017 marked a paradigm shift in the Indian indirect tax landscape. Conceptualised as a comprehensive, multi-stage, destination-based tax, GST sought to amalgamate a myriad of central and state taxes into a single tax, aiming to mitigate the cascading effect, simplify the tax structure, and create a unified national market. This reform was not just a fiscal adjustment but a structural overhaul intended to facilitate ease of doing business, encourage investment, and foster economic growth by ensuring a transparent and efficient tax collection mechanism.

The concept of GST, while revolutionary in the Indian context, is not unique on the global stage. Originating in France in 1956, the GST model has been adopted by approximately 160 countries, each tailoring the tax to fit its socio-economic context. Notably, countries such as Australia, Canada, and South Africa have implemented similar reforms in pursuit of tax efficiency and equity. India's adaptation, characterised by the dual GST model, required a constitutional amendment, highlighting the monumental effort and consensus-building required to bring this reform to fruition. The journey from proposal to implementation underscores a significant policy shift aimed at economic revitalisation.

The shift to the GST regime was anticipated to catalyse economic development by streamlining tax administration, reducing the overall tax burden on consumers, and eliminating the inefficiencies of the previous indirect tax structure. By fostering a transparent and cohesive tax environment, GST has the potential to significantly boost investment and consumer spending, pivotal drivers of economic growth. Moreover, the uniform tax structure across states is expected to reduce the cost of compliance and logistics, benefiting businesses and the economy at large.

1.1. Review of Literature

The literature on GST and indirect taxation reflects a growing academic interest in understanding the fiscal and macroeconomic implications of tax reforms. In the Indian context, Mishra (2018) provides a comprehensive assessment of GST's benefits across sectors such as manufacturing, logistics, and services. The study emphasises the removal of the cascading effect of taxes, reduction in commodity prices, and improved business confidence, all of which are expected to enhance GDP growth. Vij (2018), however, offers a critical view of the GST framework, highlighting implementation challenges such as the multiplicity of tax slabs and digital compliance issues. The author recommends rationalisation of the tax structure and expansion of the GST base to improve efficiency.

Govindan (2019) examines the rising trend in GST collections, noting the reform's success in broadening the taxpayer base and fostering tax compliance. His analysis underscores the importance of GST in signalling a business-friendly environment for investors and entrepreneurs. Abhishek et al. (2019) take a forward-looking stance, discussing possible future reforms and the long-term evolution of GST in the Indian fiscal system. Using econometric tools, Pradhan (2019) evaluates the impact of tax reforms, including GST, on economic growth and finds a significant correlation between indirect tax performance and GDP.

The pandemic-induced shock and its impact on GST are analysed by Kapasi and Kurmi (2021), who report a sharp decline in tax collections during COVID-19 and call for adaptive policy mechanisms to preserve revenue buoyancy. Tiwari (2022) conducts a longitudinal study comparing pre- and post-GST periods, documenting shifts in indirect tax revenue composition and the system's contribution to improved fiscal efficiency.

Beyond the Indian context, several international studies offer valuable insights. Anokwuru and Chidinma (2023) investigate the impact of indirect taxes on inclusive growth in Nigeria using Error Correction Model (ECM) and cointegration methods. They find a positive but statistically insignificant relationship between value-added tax (VAT) and inclusive growth, whereas excise and customs duties have a significant negative impact. Nguvava and Kadenge (2024) analyse the role of GDP in driving both direct and indirect tax revenues in Tanzania, concluding that GDP positively and significantly influences tax collection.

In a broader European setting, Stoilova and Todorov (2021) examine fiscal and non-fiscal determinants of economic growth in 10 Eastern and Central European countries. Using a vector auto regression (VAR) model with data from 2007 to 2019, they find that direct taxes have a negative impact on growth, while indirect taxes and government consumption have no significant effect. Instead, economic development is positively influenced by gross capital formation and exports.

The socio-economic dimensions of indirect taxation are explored by Bogari (2020) in the context of Saudi Arabia. Using primary survey data, the study reveals that while VAT has enhanced public revenues, it has also raised concerns about social burden and implementation challenges. The author emphasises the need for administrative reform and simplification of the VAT system to improve its effectiveness.

This review highlights the need for empirical analyses grounded in time series techniques, particularly in developing economies where tax reforms continue to evolve.

1.2. Scope and Innovativeness of the Present Study

This study undertakes a comprehensive assessment of India's indirect tax system, with a focus on the transformational impact of GST on fiscal performance and economic growth. Covering the extended period from 1980–1981 to 2024–2025, it analyses trends in indirect tax revenue and GDP, comparing the pre- and post-GST periods. A unique feature of this research is its inclusion of both national-level and state-wise analyses, capturing the spatial heterogeneity in GST outcomes across India.

Methodologically, the study combines descriptive statistics with advanced time series econometrics – unit root tests, Johansen cointegration, VECM, and Granger causality – to examine the short- and long-run relationships between tax revenue and GDP. It stands apart from earlier work through its long temporal span and integrated approach, offering a deeper understanding of GST's macroeconomic implications.

The findings highlight GST's role in reducing cascading tax effects, enhancing compliance, and simplifying tax administration. However, the reform's benefits are uneven across states, underlining the importance of region-specific fiscal strategies. By offering empirical insights into both national trends and inter-state disparities, this study contributes to the literature on fiscal reform and provides policy-relevant recommendations for strengthening India's tax system.

2. Database and Methodology

This section provides a detailed roadmap of the analytical framework employed to examine the impact of India's tax structure – specifically the GST – on economic performance over a comprehensive period from 1980–1981 to 2024–2025.

2.1. Database

The study utilises both time series and cross-sectional datasets. The time series data include variables such as direct tax revenue, indirect tax revenue, total tax revenue, and GDP. These data have been sourced from official government publications, namely the Central Board of Direct Taxes (CBDT) and the Reserve Bank of India (RBI), and span the period from 1980–1981 to 2024–2025. In addition, the study incorporates cross-sectional data, including the number of GST taxpayers, GST collections, own tax revenue, and state-level GDP for the years 2016–2017 and 2021–2022. These data are obtained from the official GST portal and RBI State Finances reports.

2.2. *Methodology*

The methodological approach is structured into several analytical stages, using appropriate statistical and econometric techniques to draw meaningful inferences from the data.

2.2.1. Trend Analysis

Trend analysis is used to visualise and interpret the long-term patterns in tax collections and GDP growth. This involves plotting the time series data to detect upward, downward, or stationary trends over the study period.

2.2.2. Stationarity Tests

To ensure the reliability of time series data for further analysis, stationarity tests are employed. A stationary time series is one whose properties do not depend on the time at which the series is observed. Two common tests used are:

Augmented Dickey–Fuller (ADF) test:

$$\Delta y_t = \alpha + \beta_t + \gamma y_{(t-1)} + \Sigma \delta_i \Delta y_{(t-i)} + \varepsilon_t$$

where Δy_t is the difference in the variable at time t, α is a constant, t is the trend, $y_{(t-1)}$ is the lagged variable, δ_i are the coefficients of the lagged difference terms, and ε_t is the error term.

Phillips–Perron (PP) test:

The PP test modifies the ADF test to allow for autocorrelated and heteroskedastic residuals, making it robust to a wider range of data conditions.

2.2.3. Granger Causality Test

The Granger causality test is applied to examine the cause-and-effect relationship between tax revenue and GDP. This test assesses whether past values of one variable can predict the future values of another. The basic model for testing if X Granger causes Y is:

$$Y_t = \alpha_0 + \Sigma \alpha_i Y_{(t-i)} + \Sigma \beta_i X_{(t-i)} + \varepsilon_t$$

where Y_t and X_t are the values of the dependent and independent time series, n is the number of lags, α_0, α_i, and β_i are coefficients, and ε_t is the error term.

2.2.4. VECM Analysis

To capture both the short-run dynamics and long-run equilibrium relationship between GDP and income tax revenue, a VECM was estimated. The model incorporates a structural break due to GST implementation using a dummy variable DGTAX_t, which takes the value 1 for years 2017 onwards, and 0 otherwise. The VECM equations for the system are specified as:

$$\begin{aligned}\Delta\mathrm{LNGDP}_t = {} & \alpha_1\mathrm{ECT}_{t-1} + \beta_{11}\Delta\mathrm{LNGDP}_{t-1} + \beta_{12}\Delta\mathrm{LNGDP}_{t-2} \\ & + \gamma_{11}\Delta\mathrm{LNITAX}_{t-1} + \gamma_{12}\Delta\mathrm{LNITAX}_{t-2} + \delta_1\mathrm{DGTAX}_t + \varepsilon_{1t}\end{aligned}$$

$$\begin{aligned}\Delta\mathrm{LNITAX}_t = {} & \alpha_2\mathrm{ECT}_{t-1} + \beta_{21}\Delta\mathrm{LNGDP}_{t-1} + \beta_{22}\Delta\mathrm{LNGDP}_{t-2} \\ & + \gamma_{21}\Delta\mathrm{LNITAX}_{t-1} + \gamma_{22}\Delta\mathrm{LNITAX}_{t-2} + \delta_2\mathrm{DGTAX}_t + \varepsilon_{2t}\end{aligned}$$

where Δ indicates the first difference operator, and ECT_{t-1} is the error correction term derived from the cointegrating relationship.

3. Results and Discussions

3.1. Trends of Tax and GDP

The analysis of long-term trends in direct tax, indirect tax, and GDP at constant prices (base year 2011–2012) reveals a consistent upward movement with notable fluctuations across the four-decade period from 1980–1981 to 2024–2025 (Table 18.1). This section aims to highlight key patterns in tax collections and GDP, while also capturing the implications of structural reforms like the implementation of the GST in 2017.

The GDP of India, measured in constant prices, expanded from 14.6 lakh crore in 1980–1981 to an estimated 187.95 lakh crore in 2024–2025, indicating significant economic growth over time. Both direct and indirect taxes also grew substantially. Direct tax collection increased from 3,592 crore in 1980–1981 to 25,06,181 crore in 2024–2025, while indirect tax collection rose from 16,171 crore to 36,36,096 crore during the same period. Notably, this steady increase was interspersed with periods of sharp growth and temporary declines, particularly around economic crises and the COVID-19 pandemic.

The average growth rate of direct tax revenue was robust across most years, with the highest annual growth observed in 2006–2007 (39.3%). However, the pandemic years (2019–2020 and 2020–2021) witnessed negative or stagnant growth due to disruptions in economic activity. Similarly, indirect tax revenue recorded its highest growth in 2010–2011 (40.9%) but also experienced contractions in years such as 2001–2002, 2008–2009, and again during the pandemic in 2020–2021. Post-COVID-19 recovery was particularly strong in 2021–2022, when indirect tax grew by 30.3%.

The composition of tax revenue has shifted significantly over time. In 2000–2001, indirect taxes comprised 73% of total tax revenue, while direct taxes

Table 18.1. Tax Revenue, GDP, Their Growth Rates, and Indirect Tax–GDP Ratio in India, 1980–1981 to 2024–2025.

Year	Direct Tax (Rs. Crore)	Indirect Tax (Rs. Crore)	Total Tax (Rs. Crore)	GDP (Rs. Crore)	Growth of Indirect Tax	Growth of GDP	Indirect Tax–GDP Ratio
1980–1981	3,592	16,171	19,763	14,64,394			1.1
1990–1991	14,267	73,360	87,627	25,14,549	13.1	5.5	2.9
2000–2001	81,163	2,19,809	3,00,972	43,26,736	10.8	3.8	5.1
2001–2002	84,876	2,24,071	3,08,947	45,35,456	2.6	4.8	4.9
2002–2003	1,00,302	2,51,716	3,52,018	47,07,984	13.9	3.8	5.3
2003–2004	1,25,303	2,82,796	4,08,099	50,78,049	15.9	7.9	5.6
2004–2005	1,56,828	3,28,547	4,85,375	54,80,380	18.9	7.9	6.0
2005–2006	1,95,428	3,81,166	5,76,594	59,14,614	18.8	7.9	6.4
2006–2007	2,69,078	4,54,945	7,24,023	63,91,375	25.6	8.1	7.1
2007–2008	3,55,689	5,21,807	8,77,496	68,81,007	21.2	7.7	7.6
2008–2009	3,77,986	5,48,318	9,26,304	70,93,403	5.6	3.1	7.7
2009–2010	4,24,874	5,59,737	9,84,611	76,51,078	6.3	7.9	7.3
2010–2011	5,08,719	7,41,348	12,50,067	83,01,235	27.0	8.5	8.9
2011–2012	5,71,246	8,71,505	14,42,752	87,36,329	15.4	5.2	10.0
2012–2013	6,51,227	10,36,732	16,87,959	92,13,017	17.0	5.5	11.3
2013–2014	7,26,773	11,19,772	18,46,545	98,01,370	9.4	6.4	11.4
2014–2015	8,03,440	12,17,289	20,20,728	1,05,27,674	9.4	7.4	11.6
2015–2016	8,30,121	14,66,981	22,97,101	1,13,69,493	13.7	8.0	12.9

(*Continued*)

Table 18.1. (*Continued*)

Year	Direct Tax (Rs. Crore)	Indirect Tax (Rs. Crore)	Total Tax (Rs. Crore)	GDP (Rs. Crore)	Growth of Indirect Tax	Growth of GDP	Indirect Tax–GDP Ratio
2016–2017	9,59,627	16,62,518	26,22,145	1,23,08,193	14.2	8.3	13.5
2017–2018	11,21,189	18,56,945	29,78,134	1,31,44,582	13.6	6.8	14.1
2018–2019	12,46,083	20,32,864	32,78,947	1,39,92,914	10.1	6.5	14.5
2019–2020	12,16,203	20,15,379	32,31,582	1,45,34,641	−1.4	3.9	13.9
2020–2021	11,14,805	20,78,585	31,93,390	1,36,94,869	−1.2	−5.8	15.2
2021–2022	15,30,636	26,29,778	41,60,414	1,50,21,846	30.3	9.7	17.5
2022–2023	19,39,550	28,69,493	48,09,044	1,61,64,913	15.6	7.6	17.8
2023–2024	22,04,462	32,52,451	54,56,913	1,76,50,591	13.5	9.2	18.4
2024–2025	25,06,181	36,36,096	61,42,276	1,87,95,095	12.6	6.5	19.3

Sources: CBDT (2022); RBI.
Note: Tax revenue and GDP are in constant price (base year = 2011–2012).

accounted for only 27%. However, by 2009–2010, the share of direct taxes had increased to 60.8%, reflecting the rising contribution of income-based taxation. Post-GST, the distribution has remained more balanced; in 2024–2025, direct taxes are projected to account for 40.8% of total taxes and indirect taxes 59.2%.

The indirect tax–GDP ratio provides a useful measure of tax effort. This ratio has steadily increased from 1.1% in 1980–1981 to 19.3% in 2024–2025, showing a strengthening in the government's ability to mobilise revenue from consumption-based taxes. However, it also reflects the increasing reliance on indirect taxes, which could have regressive implications without compensatory welfare mechanisms.

Comparing the five years before and after the introduction of GST provides insights into its short-term performance. In the five years preceding GST (2012–2013 to 2016–2017), the average growth rate of indirect taxes was 17.5%, while GDP grew by 11.3% annually. In contrast, in the five years following GST (2017–2018 to 2021–2022), indirect tax growth averaged 8.6%, and GDP grew by 9.2% per year. This relative slowdown in indirect tax growth post-GST may be attributed to transition-related disruptions, compliance issues, and macroeconomic shocks such as COVID-19.

3.2. Econometric Insights into Tax Dynamics and Economic Growth

This subsection explores the intricate relationship between India's tax structure and its economic growth through a rigorous econometric analysis.

3.2.1. Stationarity Testing: Foundations for Inference

To ensure the validity of the time series analysis, both variables – log of GDP (LNGDP) and log of income tax revenue (LNITAX) – were tested for stationarity using the ADF and PP unit root tests. The results confirmed that both variables are non-stationary at levels but stationary at first differences, that is, integrated of order one (Table 18.2). These findings satisfy the preconditions for cointegration analysis and estimation of a VECM.

Table 18.2. Results of Stationary or Unit Root Test.

	***t*-Statistics and Adjusted *t*-Statistics**	**Probability****
ADF test result D(LNGDP) has a unit root	−6.37	0.00
PP test result D(LNGDP) has a unit root	−6.71	0.00
ADF test result D(LNITAX) has a unit root	−5.63	0.00
PP test result D(LNITAX) has a unit root	−5.77	0.00

Source: Author's calculation.

3.2.2. Cointegration Analysis: Unveiling Long-term Equilibrium

The Johansen cointegration test was employed to investigate the presence of a long-term relationship between GDP and income tax revenue. The trace statistic (14.73) failed to reject the null hypothesis of no cointegration at the 5% level, but the maximum eigenvalue statistic (23.45) was statistically significant, indicating the presence of at least one cointegrating equation (Table 18.3). This suggests that despite short-term fluctuations, the two variables maintain a stable long-run equilibrium relationship. Given this result, the VECM was adopted as the appropriate modelling framework to capture both short-run dynamics and long-run adjustment behaviour.

3.2.3. Granger Causality Testing: Directionality of Influence

Although the presence of cointegration necessitates the use of a VECM, pairwise Granger causality tests were conducted as a supplementary analysis to explore short-run directional influence without explicitly modelling long-run adjustments. The Granger causality test results indicate marginal evidence of short-run causality from income tax revenue to GDP ($F = 3.06$, $p = 0.058$), while no evidence of short-run causality from GDP to income tax was found ($F = 0.595$, $p = 0.557$) (Table 18.4). While these results are informative, they should be interpreted cautiously since they do not account for the cointegrating relationship. However, the VECM framework, which incorporates the long-run relationship, offers a more robust basis for inference.

3.2.4. VECM Results: Dynamic Interactions and Policy Insights

The VECM was estimated to assess both the short-run dynamics and long-run adjustment mechanisms between GDP and income tax revenue, while also incorporating the impact of the GST through a dummy variable (DGTAX_t). The cointegrating relationship was specified as:

$$\mathrm{ECT}_{t-1} = \mathrm{LNGDP}_{t-1} - 0.4074 \times \mathrm{LNITAX}_{t-1}$$

Table 18.3. Results of Johnson Cointegration Test.

Hypothesised No. of CE(s)	Eigen Value	Trace Statistics	0.05 Critical Value	Probability
None	0.181	14.73	18.39	0.1513
At most 1	0.161207	3.515835	3.841465	0.0608
Hypothesised No. of CE(s)	**Eigen Value**	**Max Eigen Statistics**	**0.05 Critical Value**	**Probability**
None	0.690425	23.45108	14.26460	0.0014
At most 1	0.161207	3.515835	3.841465	0.0608

Source: Author's calculation.
Note: CE, Co-integrating Equation.

Table 18.4. Results of Pairwise Granger Causality Tests.

Null Hypothesis	Observation	*F*-Statistic	Probability
LNITAX does not Granger Cause LNGDP	43	3.06	0.058
LNGDP does not Granger Cause LNITAX		0.595	0.557

Source: Author's calculation.

In the equation for GDP ($\Delta LNGDP_t$), the error correction term was positive and statistically significant, indicating that GDP adjusts to deviations from the long-run equilibrium. In the income tax equation ($\Delta LNITAX_t$), the error correction term was also significant, confirming that income tax revenue also responds to restore long-run equilibrium. These results demonstrate bi-directional long-run causality between the two variables.

However, none of the short-run coefficients – including those of the GST dummy – were statistically significant in either equation. The coefficient of the GST dummy was negative in both cases but insignificant, suggesting no substantial short-run effect of GST implementation on GDP or income tax revenue. The model diagnostics show no autocorrelation (Durbin–Watson statistics close to 2), and the R^2 values of 0.071 and 0.186 for the GDP and income tax equations, respectively, are within acceptable ranges for first-differenced models ((Table 18.5).

3.3. Variegated Economic and Taxation Landscapes Across Indian States Post-GST Implementation

This section scrutinises the disparate impacts on own tax revenue, GST collection, the proliferation of GST taxpayers, and SDP growth across 27 Indian states. The growth of the number of tax payers in most states was positive despite the COVID-19 pandemic, except in some states, namely Goa and Maharashtra. The average growth rate of the number of GST payers is highest in the state of Sikkim, with an average value of 20.4, followed by the state of Bihar, with an average value of 17.9. The table also discloses the GST per taxpayer; this means the strength of the taxpayer. The average strength of tax payers is highest for the state of Sikkim, with an average value of 23.14, followed by the state of Chhattisgarh, with an average value of 12.11. The average strength of the taxpayer is lowest in the state of Tripura, with an average value of 2.00, followed by the state of Bihar, with an average value of 2.12.

It also shows that the average growth rate of own tax revenue for the four years immediately preceding the introduction of GST is highest for Arunachal Pradesh, with an average value of 23.0, followed by Mizoram, with an average value of 19.2 among all states. The average growth rate of its own tax revenue in West Bengal is 8.5%. The average growth rate of own tax revenue for five years immediately following the implementation of GST is highest for the state of Arunachal Pradesh,

Table 18.5. Estimated Results of VECM.

Variable	Coefficient	Standard Error	*t*-Statistic	*p*-Value	
Equation: $\Delta LNGDP_t$					
ECT_{t-1}	0.0055	0.0016	3.56	0.0007	$R^2 = 0.17$
$\Delta LNGDP_{t-1}$	−0.1452	0.1969	−0.74	0.4632	Durbin–Watson statistics = 1.96
$\Delta LNGDP_{t-2}$	0.0101	0.2024	0.05	0.9602	
$\Delta LNITAX_{t-1}$	0.1347	0.0909	1.48	0.1426	
$\Delta LNITAX_{t-2}$	−0.0522	0.0924	−0.56	0.5739	
$DGTAX_t$	−0.0030	0.0107	−0.28	0.7817	
Equation: $\Delta LNITAX_t$					
ECT_{t-1}	0.0165	0.0032	5.11	0.0000	$R^2 = 0.29$
$\Delta LNGDP_{t-1}$	−0.4012	0.4078	−0.98	0.3285	Durbin–Watson statistics = 2.02
$\Delta LNGDP_{t-2}$	0.0247	0.4193	0.06	0.9531	
$\Delta LNITAX_{t-1}$	0.2593	0.1883	1.38	0.1727	
$\Delta LNITAX_{t-2}$	−0.3333	0.1913	−1.74	0.0858	
$DGTAX_t$	−0.0328	0.0222	−1.47	0.1448	

Source: Author's calculation.

with an average value of 38.0, followed by the state of Manipur, with an average value of 32.1, and the average growth rate of West Bengal is 10.8%.

It also discloses the growth rate of SDP in 27 states. In the years 2020–2021, most of all states had negative SDP growth due to the COVID-19 pandemic, except some states, namely Assam, Sikkim, and Tamil Nadu. The state-wise average growth rate of SDP before the GST regime is highest for the state of Mizoram, with an average value of 15.1, followed by the state of Goa, with an average value of 10.3, and the lowest for the state of Meghalaya, with an average value of 1.7, followed by the state of Jharkhand, with an average value of 4.6. The average growth rate of SDP for West Bengal is 4.8%. And the average growth rate of SDP after the GST regime is highest for Gujarat, with an average value of 7.0, followed by Mizoram, with an average value of 6.6, and the average growth rate for West Bengal is 4.0% (Table 18.6).

The heterogeneity in GST impacts across Indian states sheds light on the complex interdependencies between tax policy, administrative efficacy, and economic growth. The findings underscore the critical need for tailored fiscal and economic policies that account for regional peculiarities and challenges. Moreover, the differential growth rates in taxpayer bases and revenue collections post-GST signal the reform's transformative potential, while also highlighting areas for further administrative refinement and capacity building.

Table 18.6. Taxpayers, GST Collection, Own Tax, SDP Across States of India.

State/ Union Territory	Tax Payer		GST Collection		Pre-GST				Post-GST			
					Own Tax		GDP		Own Tax		GDP	
	2021–2022	Average[a]	2021–2022 (Amount)	Average[a]	2016–2017 (Amount)	Average[b]	2016–2017 (Amount)	Average[b]	2021–2022 (RE)	Average[b]	2021–2022 (Amount)	Average[b]
Andhra Pradesh	3,05,535	8.1	23,424	6.85	44,181	−5.5	5,40,21,177	9.2	73,632	11.3	7,04,88,945	5.6
Arunachal Pradesh	13,618	14.6	535	3.17	709	23.0	1,48,92,66	7.3	2,258	38.0	19,80,053	6.0
Assam	1,72,738	9.8	9,121	4.70	12,080	10.1	2,02,08,084	8.3	21,985	13.4	2,62,52,252	5.4
Bihar	4,56,786	17.9	8,842	2.12	23,742	10.7	3,18,79,745	5.6	35,050	8.6	3,99,92,978	4.8
Chhattisgarh	1,29,555	8.3	17,567	12.11	18,945	9.8	2,13,70,477	6.6	27,500	8.1	2,67,68,086	4.7
Goa	37,269	8.1	3,462	8.98	4,261	10.0	51,24,924	10.3	5,720	7.3	55,54,765	1.7
Gujarat	9,86,775	7.9	70,286	6.32	64,443	4.6	9,81,34,196	9.5	1,05,300	12.1	13,72,20,362	7.0
Haryana	4,69,904	8.4	49,117	9.84	34,026	9.6	45,67,0911	9.2	64,992	15.6	56,808,606	4.7
Himachal Pradesh	97,423	10.1	6,186	6.84	7,039	11.1	1,03,05,499	7.4	9,770	7.0	1,26,43,325	4.2
Jharkhand	1,67,253	9.7	16,935	9.33	13,299	12.8	1,93,17,392	4.6	20,711	9.6	2,43,34,844	4.9
Karnataka	8,30,528	9.1	67,602	7.48	82,956	11.5	9,41,77,405	10.0	1,11,498	6.3	12,29,71,294	5.6
Kerala	3,35,514	8.3	17,588	4.65	42,176	8.8	4,85,30,154	5.8	58,868	7.4	5,72,74,734	3.6
Madhya Pradesh	4,10,654	7.8	19,470	4.60	44,194	9.6	4,70,66,916	7.6	64,297	8.0	6,00,68,910	5.1
Maharashtra	14,68,416	6.7	1,57,625	9.33	1,36,592	7.2	18,07,04,575	7.4	2,27,237	12.2	20,27,97,104	2.5

(Continued)

Table 18.6. (*Continued*)

State/ Union Territory	Tax Payer		GST Collection		Pre-GST				Post-GST			
					Own Tax		GDP		Own Tax		GDP	
	2021–2022	Average[a]	2021–2022 (Amount)	Average[a]	2016–2017 (Amount)	Average[b]	2016–2017 (Amount)	Average[b]	2021–2022 (RE)	Average[b]	2021–2022 (Amount)	Average[b]
Manipur	10,711	6.3	404	2.70	587	16.1	17,08,192	7.1	1,903	32.1	20,51,458	4.0
Meghalaya	26,642	14.5	1,321	4.25	1,186	8.9	21,73,023	1.7	2,579	18.7	24,26,676	2.4
Mizoram	7,097	15.5	226	2.95	442	19.2	13,59,521	15.1	787	17.8	18,49,372	6.6
Nagaland	7,214	10.6	296	3.37	511	11.0	15,64,992	5.0	1,335	25.3	18,36,336	3.3
Odisha	2,70,589	10.3	28,202	7.95	22,852	11.2	33,734,806	8.6	41,467	13.4	4,32,95,967	5.2
Punjab	3,36,608	6.3	13,942	3.66	27,747	5.3	3,52,72,056	5.9	38,062	7.1	4,33,76,898	4.3
Rajasthan	6,51,560	9.6	28,557	4.16	44,372	9.9	5,96,74,551	7.0	82,803	14.1	7,38,92,163	4.5
Sikkim	8,941	20.4	2,091	23.14	653	11.0	15,39,727	7.8	1,195	14.1	20,72,805	6.2
Tamil Nadu	9,86,817	7.2	61,007	5.80	85,941	4.8	10,36,76,212	7.0	1,21,858	7.4	13,43,28,684	5.4
Tripura	26,131	11.1	583	2.00	1,422	9.1	30,53,759	10.2	2,251	10.2	39,48,668	5.4
Uttar Pradesh	13,19,511	9.9	47,475	3.37	85,966	10.3	10,11,50,027	7.5	1,60,350	14.2	12,04,65,992	3.7
Uttarakhand	1,51,377	9.1	10,604	8.23	10,897	14.2	1,67,70,325	7.9	14,122	5.7	1,93,41,230	3.0
West Bengal	6,22,234	7.5	33,869	4.87		8.5	6,53,41,593	4.8	73,905	10.8	7,87,75,806	4.0
Average	–	10.19	45,466	6.42	10.1	10.1	–	7.6	0.0	13.2	–	4.6

Sources: Authors calculated from GST government data (https://www.gst.gov.in/) and of RBI.
Note: RE, Revised Estimate.
[a]Taxpayer averages span 2018–2019 to 2021–2022, with per capita GST collections calculated from 2017–2018 to 2021–2022.
[b]Pre-GST averages are calculated from 2013–2014 to 2016–2017, and post-GST from 2017–2018 to 2021–2022.

Strategically, the insights gathered from this analysis advocate for a nuanced approach to fiscal federalism in India, emphasising the importance of state-specific strategies to leverage GST for economic revitalisation and enhanced tax compliance. Additionally, the resilience exhibited by certain states amid economic downturns underscores the value of diversifying economic bases and investing in robust fiscal management practices to navigate future uncertainties.

4. Conclusion

The period from 1980–1981 to 2024–2025 captures key phases in India's economic evolution, marked by major reforms like the introduction of GST and challenges such as the global financial crisis and the COVID-19 pandemic. This study examined the dynamic relationship between GDP and tax revenues using advanced time series techniques and state-level data. Econometric results confirm a stable long-run equilibrium between GDP and income tax revenue, with bidirectional long-run causality. However, short-run Granger causality from tax to GDP is only marginal. The GST dummy showed no significant short-run effect, suggesting the reform's economic impact may be more structural or delayed. At the state level, GST's effects vary widely. While states like Arunachal Pradesh and Sikkim show strong growth in tax revenue and taxpayer expansion, others lag behind, indicating the need for region-specific strategies. GST has contributed to long-run tax-GDP alignment, but realising its full potential depends on administrative strengthening, digital adoption, and adaptive, inclusive policy measures. Regional disparities highlight the need for tailored fiscal approaches to ensure equitable growth and sustainable revenue generation.

References

Abhishek, N., Kaikamba, S., & Dibyashree, M. S. (2019). An analysis of future road map of goods and services tax in Indian scenario. *IOSR Journal of Business and Management (IOSR-JBM)*, *21*(1), 12–17.

Anokwuru, G., & Chidinma, C. (2023). Indirect tax and inclusive growth in Nigeria. *European Journal of Economic and Financial Research*, *7*(2), 33–49.

Bogari, A. (2020). The economic and social impact of the adoption of value-added tax in Saudi Arabia. *International Journal of Economics, Business and Accounting Research (IJEBAR)*, *4*(2), 62–74.

Central Board of Direct Taxes (CBDT). (2022). *Annual report 2021–22*. Ministry of Finance, Government of India.

Govindan, P. (2019). A study on growth of goods and services tax (GST) in India – An innovative instrument for Indian corporate sectors. *UNNAYAN: International Bulletin of Management and Economics*, *11*, 14–29.

Kapasi, B., & Kurmi, M. K. (2021). A knock around the economic impact of Covid-19 with reference to the quantum of goods and service tax collection in India. *EPRA International Journal of Multidisciplinary Research*, *7*(5), 121–126.

Mishra, N. (2018). Impact of GST on Indian economy. *International Journal of Basic and Applied Research*, *8*(11), 385–389.

Nguvava, H. E., & Kadenge, S. K. (2024). Gross domestic product (GDP) determinant of direct and indirect tax revenue collection in Tanzania. *International Journal of Economics, Business and Management Research*, *8*(12), 80–90.

Pradhan, P. K. (2019). Tax reforms and economic growth: An empirical analysis in Indian context. *Orissa Journal of Commerce*, *40*(II), 33–44.
Stoilova, D., & Todorov, I. (2021). Fiscal policy and economic growth: Evidence from Central and Eastern Europe. *Journal of Tax Reform*, *7*(2), 146–159.
Tiwari, N. K. (2022). Impact of tax reforms in government India's indirect tax collections with special reference to year 2000–2020. *International Journal for Research in Applied Science & Engineering Technology (IJRASET)*, *10*(1), 139–147.
Vij, D. (2018). A study on GST (goods and service tax): The way forward. *IJAR&D*, *4*(1), 13–18.

Chapter 19

Association Between Maternal Issues and Malnutrition of the Children of Tribal and Non-tribal Categories in Purulia District of West Bengal, India

Uttam Haldar[a], Swati Dutta[b] and Santanu Bisai[b]

[a]*Department of Economics, Serampore Girls' College, West Bengal, India*
[b]*Department of Economics, Sidho-Kanhu-Birsha University, West Bengal, India*

Abstract

The aim of the study is to understand the association between child malnutrition and maternal issues across tribal and non-tribal households in Purulia district, West Bengal. The study is based on primary data collected by face-to-face interview methods and stratified random sampling procedures. We calculated z-scores for anthropometric measures of malnutrition like stunting, wasting, underweight, and mother's body mass index (BMI) following World Health Organization (WHO) guidelines. The percentage method and linear regression model were used to determine the association between child malnutrition and maternal issues. About two-thirds of children were suffering from malnourishment with one or two types of malnutrition. The prevalence of malnutrition was higher among children of working mothers compared to non-working mothers and undernourished mothers with low BMI compared to nourished mothers. Child malnutrition decreases with an increase in a mother's education. The prevalence of low-age marriage and low-age pregnancy was observed more among tribal women compared to non-tribal women. There was a negative association between a child's underweight and their mother's marriage age, but a positive association between a child's stunting and their mother's marriage age. The regression result shows that the probability of underweight among children declined with the increase in mother's education, BMI, and first

Changing Dimensions in Economic Development: Theories and Empirics, 259–271

Published under exclusive licence by Emerald Publishing Limited
doi:10.1108/978-1-83708-384-820261022

pregnancy of the mother at a higher age, increasing the gap between births of two babies, and the chances of stunting among children declined with the increase in mother's age, mother's marriage age, and mother's higher socio-economic status.

Keywords: Anthropometric measures; child malnutrition; Global Hunger Index; maternal issues; National Family Health Survey; public health; Purulia district; scheduled tribe; sustainable development goals; undernutrition

JEL Codes: I10; I15; I18; J13; J15

Introduction

Malnutrition is a matter of grave concern in the globe. Sustainable development goals (SDGs 2.1 and 2.2) target to end hunger and malnutrition by 2030 from all corners of the world; however, more than 700 million people (9% of the global population) remain undernourished in 2023 (FAO, 2024). The prevalence of malnutrition was maximum in Africa (20.4%) and is followed by Asia (8.1%), and Latin America (6.2%). In terms of number of populations, Asia is the home to the largest number of malnourished populations. About half of the world's malnourished population resides in Asia. Malnutrition, particularly among children, is the most serious problem. It was estimated that 22.3%, 6.8%, and 5.6% of children under five years were stunted, wasted, and underweight, respectively, in the world in 2022. The main concern is that the rate of decline of undernourishment is either very slow or stagnant. These three estimates were 19.5%, 7.5%, and 5.6% in 2012. Similarly, the prevalence of low birth weight among newborn babies in the globe declined at a very slow rate from 15% to 14.7% in eight-year periods (2012–2020). The prevalence of undernourished children below five years was found at higher levels in less developed countries.

India occupies the second-highest position in South Asia in terms of child malnutrition. According to the Global Hunger Index (GHI), India ranks 105th out of 127 countries with a score of 27.3 in 2024 and marked as serious (GHI, 2024). The GHI score in India is gradually decreasing over the years but at a very slow rate. In India, 13.7% of population is undernourished in 2024. Despite the different initiatives (such as the National Food Security Act, Integrated Child Development Centres (ICDS), PM POSHAN, Pradhan Mantri Matru Vandana Yojana, scheme for adolescent girls, etc. (MWCD, 2023) taken by the Government of India to reduce hunger and malnutrition, the prevalence of undernourishment in India has increased from 11.5% in 2016 to 13.7% in 2024. The prevalence of undernourishment among children under five was estimated as 35.5% stunted and 18.7% wasted. The child-wasting rate in India is the highest in the world. Both these indicators of wasting and stunting showed very slow progress of nutritional status among children in India during the eight years of 2016–2024.

The prevalence of underweight children declined slowly from 35.8% in National Family Health Survey (NFSH-4) (2015–2016) to 32.1% in NFSH-5 (2019–2021) in India.

Child malnutrition has a long-term negative impact on child growth as well as growth of future human capital. Physical and mental growth and maturity of children will be halted if the child is suffering from malnutrition. Many life-threatening diseases easily crop up in a malnourished child. A significant proportion of child deaths occurred in India due to severe malnutrition (Tebeje et al., 2017). The problem of child malnutrition is a complex and multidimensional issue. The prime reason is the socio-economic background of the family to which children belong. Occupation and income play a pivotal role in the intake of a nutritious, balanced diet. The ill-health of a child is one of the main reasons behind his/her low absorption of nutrition from food intake and leads to malnutrition (Hakim & Rahman, 2016). Health status, demographic characteristics, and socio-economic empowerment are also important indicators of child malnutrition.

Above all maternal issues like the health of the mothers, the prevalence of malnutrition among mothers, anaemia among mothers, the practice of breastfeeding, mother's education, knowledge, occupation, birth order, multiple children, etc. are important factors that determine the nutritional status of children under-five aged (Kofi Amegah et al., 2024; Teshale et al., 2025; Waghode et al., 2025). We observe a slow progress in maternal issues related to child malnutrition in India in NFSH-5 (2019–2021) over NFSH-4 (2015–2016) (NFHS 5, 2022). For example, the practice of breastfeeding within one hour of birth increases from 41.6% in NFSH-4 to 41.8% in NFSH-5. The percentage of women with malnourishment (BMI < 18.5) decreased from 22.9% in 2015–2016 to 18.7% in 2019–2021. To date, about 28.5% of women are illiterate, and only 41% of women above 10 years of age are attending school. The early marriage rate (before 18 years) declined from 26.8% in NFSH-4 to 23.3% in NFSH-5. Pregnancy of women in age groups 15–19 years reduced from 7.9% to 6.8% in the same period.

A significant proportion (8.6% in census 2011) of India's population is scheduled tribes (indigenous people). They have distinct cultures, languages, customs, livelihood practices, social systems, and self-governance. They are the most disadvantageous section of our society with poor socio-economic development. Owing to the most vulnerable groups, the tribal population in India is at high risk in most of the healthcare indicators (Biswas et al., 2022). Analysing NFHS data (Subramanian & Joe, 2024) showed that tribal people remain disadvantageous compared to non-tribal people in terms of 81 indicators out of 129 such as women status, public health facilities, nutritional status of children, child mortality rate, vaccination completion, and fertility rate. The prevalence of undernourishment among children belonging to scheduled tribes is much higher compared to the national average. According to NFSH-5, the rate of stunting, wasting, and underweight among tribal children under five years of age was 40.9%, 23.2%, and 39.5%, respectively, in 2019–2021. The positive sign is that the rate is slowly decreasing because the above indicators of malnourishment were 43.8%, 27.4%, and 45.3% in 2015–2016 (MWCD, 2023). By analysing the latest three rounds of NFHS data, it is observed that the prevalence of malnutrition among tribal children was much higher than the non-tribal children under five in India (Rekha et al., 2023).

Purulia is one of the backward districts of West Bengal, India. More than 18% of the population in this district are tribal. They are poor and belong to socially disadvantaged groups. They are being excluded socially and economically. Their culture and customs are different from those of other populations. The health status of children in Purulia district is basically poor. According to the NFHS, malnutrition among children aged below five years in Purulia has decreased from NFHS-4 in 2015–2016 to NFHS-5 in 2019–2020. During this period, the percentage of stunting children declined from 45.5 to 36.9. Anaemic children aged 6–59 months have decreased from 77.9% in 2015–2016 to 66.8% in 2019–2020. Though malnutrition in terms of major indicators such as stunting, wasting, and underweight has decreased in Purulia district from 2015–2016 to 2019–2020, it remains high above the West Bengal state average. Even the percentage of underweight children was highest in Purulia among the districts of West Bengal (Das et al., 2021). Beside child malnutrition, malnutrition among mothers in terms of BMI also decreased from 47.5% in 2015–2016 (NFHS-4) to 33.7% in 2019–2020 (NFHS-5) in Purulia district of West Bengal. Obesity among mothers in Purulia district has been increasing during that period.

In this background, the objective of the study is to determine the association of child malnutrition with different maternal issues in Purulia district. The study also tries to find out the differences in this regard among tribal and non-tribal populations.

Material and Methods

The study is based on primary data collected from extensive field surveys following a face-to-face interview method and stratified random sampling procedure during 2022–2023. The basis of stratification is the higher tribal concentration in population. Two blocks with a higher tribal concentration were selected purposefully from each sub-division of this district. The sample blocks are Hura, Balarampur, Bandawan, Manbazar-II, Jhalda-II, Bagmundi, Kashipur, and Santuri. Randomly, four sample villages with a higher tribal concentration were selected from each block. Among four villages in each block, tribal concentrations in two villages were 60%–90% and 30%–60% in the other two villages. We have collected lists of children under five years old from the registers of Angan Wari Centres (AWC) and ICDS. At first, we have collected 640 tribal households and 224 households from non-tribal category randomly, and from these selected households, we got a total sample children consisting of 997 children (714 tribal and 283 non-tribal). We interrogated the mother of each selected child to know the socio-economic, demographic, and maternal issues. We record the age, height, and weight of mothers and children. Using these variables, we calculated z-scores for anthropometric measures of malnutrition like stunting, wasting, and underweight and mother's BMI following WHO guidelines. The z-score or standard deviation (SD) unit is defined as the difference between the value for an individual and the median value of the reference population for the same age or height, divided by the standard deviation of the reference population.

$$z\text{-score} = \frac{(\text{observed value}) - (\text{median reference value})}{\text{standard deviation of reference population}}$$

z-score greater than −2SD is treated as nourishment, z-score less than −2SD is treated as moderate malnourishment, and z-score less than −3SD is treated as severe malnourishment. We incorporated a range of maternal issues like mother's education, occupation, mother's BMI, fertility rate, marriage age, and age of first pregnancy for examining malnutrition of the children. To know the association between child malnutrition and maternal issues, we estimated three linear regression models corresponding to stunting, wasting, and underweight.

Results

Patterns of Child Malnutrition Across Age Groups

The study estimated that 69% of tribal children under five years of age were malnourished compared to 66% of non-tribal children (Table 19.1). The prevalence of malnourished children was higher among tribal children compared to non-tribal children in all age groups except 12–35 months of age. Very few children suffered from three anthropometric measures: stunting, wasting, and underweight, both among tribal and non-tribal children. About one-third of children suffered from any one of the three anthropometric measures. The prevalence of one anthropometric measure was higher among tribal children compared to non-tribal children, except in the age group of 24–47 months. Another one-third children were suffering from two of the three anthropometric measures. The prevalence of two anthropometric measures was higher among non-tribal children compared to tribal children, except in the age groups below six months and 36–47 months.

Child Malnutrition and Maternal Issues

Mother's Education

In the present study, literacy rate among tribal mothers (90.7%) was higher compared to non-tribal mothers (88.8%). Most of the mothers were passed in primary education. The percentage of mothers passed in the upper primary level was higher among non-tribal mothers (39.9%) compared to tribal mothers (35.9%). Analysing the relationship between mother's education level and child malnutrition, it is observed that mothers of the highest percentage (more than half) of malnourished children (in all categories stunting, wasting, and underweight) were illiterate. Mothers of the second-highest percentage of malnourished children were primary-level passed. Mothers of the least percentage of malnourished children were upper-primary-level passed. That implies the percentage of children suffering from malnourishment decreases with the increase

Table 19.1. Percentage Distribution of Malnourished Children by Their Age Groups in Purulia District.

Age Group of the Children	Children Suffering From Any One of the Anthropometric Issues		Children Suffering From Any Two of the Anthropometric Issues		Children Suffering From All of the Three Anthropometric Issues		Nourished Children	
	Tribal	**Non-tribal**	**Tribal**	**Non-tribal**	**Tribal**	**Non-tribal**	**Tribal**	**Non-tribal**
<6 months	41.9	23.1	45.2	38.5	0.0	7.7	12.9	30.8
6–11 months	32.6	27.3	16.3	27.3	4.7	0.0	46.5	45.5
12–23 months	35.6	35.1	26.7	33.3	3.3	0.0	34.4	31.6
24–35 months	35.1	42.3	30.5	35.2	4.6	2.8	29.8	19.7
36–47 months	31.2	37.5	39.5	26.8	5.1	5.4	24.2	30.4
48–59 months	32.2	25.0	23.7	28.1	5.3	3.1	38.8	43.8
All	34.8	31.7	30.3	31.5	3.8	3.2	31.1	33.6

Source: Computed by authors from primary field survey (2022–2023).

in mother's educational attainment. The pattern is observed for both tribal and non-tribal communities. In a study of Africa, it was found that mother's knowledge plays a very important role in boosting a child's nutritional status (Teshale et al., 2025).

Mother's Occupation

The study estimated that about one-sixth of mothers were working outside, and the rest were homemakers. Percentages of working women were higher among non-tribal mothers (16.6%) compared to tribal mothers (15.8%). It is observed that the percentage of children suffering from malnourishment of any type (stunted, wasted, or underweight) was higher among working mothers compared to non-working mothers for both tribal and non-tribal categories. The prevalence of wasted children among tribal (34%) and non-tribal (28.9%) working mothers was higher than the tribal (23.7%) and non-tribal (20.4%) children of non-working mothers. The prevalence of stunted children among tribal (54%) and non-tribal (64.9%) working mothers was greater than the tribal (45.5%) and non-tribal (45.1%) children of non-working mothers. The prevalence of underweight children among tribal (42%) and non-tribal (35.1%) working mothers was greater than tribal (34.4%) and non-tribal (34.4%) children of non-working mothers. Therefore, it is observed that prevalence of wasted and underweight children was higher among tribal children compared to non-tribal children, whereas prevalence of stunted children was higher among non-tribal population compared to tribal population. A similar result was found in a study that reveals an adverse impact of mother's occupation in unskilled low-paid jobs on a child's nutritional status (Waghode et al., 2025). The contradictory result is that the prevalence of malnutrition among children increased with the number of mothers who were unemployed (Shahid et al., 2022).

Fertility Rate of the Sample Mother

The total fertility rate is defined as the average number of children to be born per woman during their entire reproductive period. On the other hand, age-specific fertility rate (ASFR) is important as it helps understand the likelihood of a particular population bearing children by age. The study estimated that the total fertility rate among non-tribal mothers was higher compared to tribal mothers (Table 19.2). A similar pattern also followed in the case of ASFRs. It was also observed that the ASFR gradually increases with the increase in age groups for both tribal and non-tribal categories. Again, the ASFR for tribal mothers is lower than that of non-tribal mothers in each age group.

BMI of the Sample Mother

In this section, we try to understand the association between a mother's nutritional status (in terms of BMI) and their children's nutritional status. A BMI below 18.5 indicates that the mother was undernourished. A BMI above 25 indicates the

Table 19.2. ASFR of the Sample Mother in Purulia District of West Bengal.

Age Group of Mothers (Measured in Years)	Tribal				Non-tribal			
	Number of Mothers	Number of Live Births	Still Birth	ASFR	Number of Mothers	Number of Live Births	Still Birth	ASFR
Below 18 years	13	14	0	1.08	3	3	0	1.0
18–25 years	343	471	31	1.37	132	206	5	1.6
26 and above	284	554	10	1.95	89	187	6	2.1
Total fertility rate		1.62				1.76		

Source: Computed by authors from primary field survey (2022–2023).

obesity of the mother, which is also one type of malnourishment. BMI between 18.5 and 25 indicates the normal health of the mother. Here, we categorised children into three categories: moderate malnourishment, severe malnourishment, and normal health. The estimated result shows that the percentage of malnourished children (both severe and moderate) was highest among mothers suffering from undernutrition with a BMI less than 18.5 compared to nourished mothers in both tribal and non-tribal categories. Again, the percentage of malnourished children was found to be higher among non-tribal malnourished mothers compared to tribal malnourished mothers for both severe and moderate malnourishment. In a study of Africa, it was observed that undernutrition among children was high whose mothers were undernourished compared to nourished mothers (Kofi Amegah et al., 2024). Another study conducted by Maitra and Ray (2013) showed that a newborn baby of a malnourished mother has a higher possibility of dying due to being underweight.

Marriage Age and Age of First Pregnancy of the Sample Mother

Early marriage for a woman leads to early pregnancy. It will hamper the mother's health physically and biologically. Pregnancy before the physical and mental maturity of women leads to undernutrition of the mother and child malnutrition from the womb. Thereby, early marriage (before 18 years of age) of the mother and first pregnancy at an early age (before 20 years) are two important factors behind child undernourishment. Not only early marriage but also lack of access to healthcare services was another factor responsible for adolescent pregnancy (Nguyen et al., 2019). In a case study from South Africa, it was observed that 44% of children were hospitalised with severe malnutrition whose mothers were less than 20 years old (Mokwena & Kachabe, 2022). Children of the mother aged between 21 and 25 were less likely (32%) to suffer from severe malnutrition.

In the present study, we observed that 19% of tribal women got married before the age of 18, and 7% of tribal women become pregnant prior to reaching 18 years of age. Furthermore, 82% of tribal women got married before the age of 20, and about 61% experience their first pregnancy before the age of 20; 22% and 12% of non-tribal women got married and experience their first pregnancy before reaching the age of 18. Again, 84% and 68% of non-tribal women got married and experienced their first pregnancy before reaching the age of 20. This fact is deeply troubling. These disparities indicate that both marriage and the occurrence of a first pregnancy are more frequent at younger ages among non-tribal women compared to their tribal counterparts. Insights from interviews conducted during the field study revealed that tribal girls receive greater concessions and additional support to pursue their education, resulting in them marrying after completing their studies. Conversely, non-tribal adolescents often find themselves compelled to marry due to cultural taboos.

In a study of Gadchiroli, many tribal women got married at an age below 18 years, resulting in early pregnancy (Sonowal, 2010). This is also evident from the study of Singh et al. (2024). They showed that the age at first pregnancy of the mother (<19 years) was negatively associated with the underweight among the tribal children in Meghalaya state.

The field survey observation shows a clear negative association between children suffering from severe underweight and their mother's marriage age (Table 19.3). The prevalence of severe underweight among children declined with the higher marriage age of the mother, both in the tribal and non-tribal categories. But in the case of moderately underweight children, there was no such relationship. The association between stunting among children and the marriage age of their mother was also found to be positive both for moderate and severe types and for tribal and non-tribal categories. It implies that the prevalence of stunting among children increased with the increase in marriage age of the mother. Those non-tribal women got married before 15 years of age, and two-thirds of their children were suffering from severe wasting. Thereby, we found a mixed picture about the association between mother's marriage age and the malnutrition of their children.

Linear Regression Model

In the regression model, we have taken WAZ WHO (underweight), HAZ WHO (stunting), and WHZ WHO (wasting) as dependent variables (Y) in model 1, model 2, and model 3, respectively. There were 12 explanatory variables. These are:

Category dummy (X_1): Whether children is non-tribal, yes = 1, '0' = otherwise (tribal).
Age of the children (X_2): Age is measured in months (0–59 months).
Gender of the children (X_3): Whether child is male, yes = 1, otherwise = 0.
Present age of the mother (X_4): Present age of the mother is measured by year.

Mother's education (X_5): '0' for illiterate, '1' for primary level, and '2' above primary level of education.
Marriage age (X_6): Age at which mother got married.
First pregnancy (X_7): Age at first pregnancy of the mother.
Mother's occupation (X_8): Whether mother is working? Yes = 1, otherwise = 0.
Socio-economic status (X_9): '1' = lower, '2' = lower middle, '3' = middle, and '4' = upper middle class.
Birth order (X_{10}): Number of living children born per mother.
Birth weight (X_{11}): Weight of the children at the time of birth.
BMI (X_{12}): BMI of the mother.

Interpretation of Regression Result

The estimated result of the regression model is displayed in Table 19.3.

Model 1: In this model, the dependent variable is the *z*-score of weight for age. A decreasing *z*-score implies an increase in malnutrition. Probability > *F* of the model is zero, which indicates the model is overall significant. Except for mother occupation and the tribal-non-tribal category, all explanatory variables are significant. There is a positive association between the *z*-score of weight for age and a mother's education. It implies a negative association between the underweight of children and their mother's education. The probability of underweight children is reduced with an increase in mother's education. Using similar logic, we observed that the chances of being underweight among children declined with the increase in the mother's BMI and the first pregnancy of the mother at a higher age, increasing the gap between the births of two babies.

Model 2: In this model, the dependent variable is the *z*-score of height for age. Probability > *F* of the model is zero, which indicates the model is overall significant. There is a significant positive association between the *z*-score of height for age and the marriage age of the mother. It implies a negative association between child stunting and the marriage age of the mother. The probability of child stunting decreased with the increase in marriage age of the mother. Using a similar logic, we observed that the chances of stunting among children declined with the increase in mother's age and mother's socio-economic status. There were no significant differences in stunting children among tribal and non-tribal mothers.

Model 3: In this model, the dependent variable is the *z*-score of weight for height. Probability > *F* of the model is zero, which indicates the model is overall significant. There is a significant positive association between the *z*-score of weight for height (wasting) and the marriage age of the mother. It implies a negative association between child wasting and the marriage age of the mother. The probability of child wasting is reduced with the increase in marriage age of the mother. Using a similar logic, we observed that chances of wasting among children declined with the increase in mother's BMI, mother's socio-economic status, and mother's education. There were no significant differences in wasting children among tribal and non-tribal mothers.

Table 19.3. Regression Result.

Explanatory Variables	WAZ WHO (Underweight)		HAZ WHO (Stunting)		WHZ WHO (Wasting)	
	Coefficient	$p > t$	Coefficient	$p > t$	Coefficient	$p > t$
Category dummy	0.0417	0.605	0.0352	0.841	−0.0291	0.853
Socio-economic status			0.3099	0.015	0.2262	0.045
Mother's occupation	0.0719	0.562	−0.1236	0.645	0.1973	0.409
Mother's education	0.4620	0.000	0.0185	0.878	0.6151	0.000
Present age of mother			0.0392	0.097	−0.0274	0.192
Marriage age			0.0878	0.094	0.0890	0.056
Age at first pregnancy	0.0759	0.003	0.0088	0.86	−0.0071	0.874
Mother's BMI	0.0414	0.000	0.0052	0.826	0.0793	0.000
Gender	−0.1686	0.017	−0.1447	0.361	−0.1694	0.229
Birth order	0.1090	0.062	−0.0824	0.571	−0.1077	0.405
Birth weight	0.4672	0.000	0.5765	0.003	0.1301	0.449
Age of the children	−0.0083	0.000	−0.0052	0.327	−0.0207	0.000
_cons	−3.5905	0.000	−2.7654	0.002	−3.1338	0.000
Number of observations	997		997		997	
Probability > F	0.000		0.024		0.000	
R^2	0.0588		0.0234		0.0808	
Adjusted R^2	0.0521		0.0115		0.0695	

Source: Authors' calculation from primary data (2022–2023).

Conclusion

The present study analysed the association between child malnutrition and maternal issues across tribal and non-tribal households in Purulia district, West Bengal, using anthropometric measures. Results show that about two-thirds of children were suffering from malnourishment due to one or two types of malnutrition. The prevalence of malnourishment was found to be higher among tribal children compared to non-tribal children. We found child malnutrition, and particularly child undernutrition, is highly related with maternal characteristics. It is urgent need of the hour to empower mothers in all aspects (demographically, educationally, socially, and financially) along with improvement of health and nutritional status of mothers to reduce undernutrition among children across both tribal and non-tribal communities in backward Purulia district. This policy prescription will be applicable in the Indian context as well as in the global perspective.

References

Biswas, S., Hansda, C. K., Singh, N., Malla, V. R., & Pal, A. K. (2022). Determinants of nutritional status among scheduled tribe women in India. *Clinical Epidemiology and Global Health*, *17*, 101119. https://doi.org/10.1016/j.cegh.2022.101119

Das, P., Roy, R., Das, T., & Roy, T. B. (2021). Prevalence and change detection of child growth failure phenomena among under-5 children: A comparative scrutiny from NFHS-4 and NFHS-5 in West Bengal, India. *Clinical Epidemiology and Global Health*, *12*, 100857. https://doi.org/10.1016/j.cegh.2021.100857

FAO. (2024). *The state of food security and nutrition in the world 2024*. https://doi.org/10.4060/cd1254en

GHI. (2024). *Global Hunger Index – India, 2024*. https://www.globalhungerindex.org/india.html

Hakim, M. A., & Rahman, A. (2016). Health and nutritional condition of street children of Dhaka City: An empirical study in Bangladesh. *Science Journal of Public Health. Special Issue: Childhood Malnutrition in Developing Countries*, *4*(1), 6–9. https://doi.org/10.11648/j.sjph.s.2016040101.12

Kofi Amegah, A., Ayinemi, R., Sewor, C., Fenta, H. M., Yeboah, K., Mohammed, S. A., Dwomoh, D., Annim, S. K., Stranges, S., & Kandala, N.-B. (2024). Birth weight mediates the association of maternal undernutrition with child undernutrition prevalence in West Africa. *European Journal of Clinical Nutrition*, *78*(9), 772–781. https://doi.org/10.1038/s41430-024-01453-5

Maitra, P., & Ray, R. (2013). Child health in West Bengal comparison with other regions in India. *Economic and Political Weekly*, *48*(49), 5–58.

Mokwena, K., & Kachabe, J. (2022). Profile of mothers whose children are treated for malnutrition at a rural district hospital in the North West province, South Africa. *South African Journal of Clinical Nutrition*, *35*(1), 17–22. https://doi.org/10.1080/16070658.2021.1921899

MWCD. (2023). *Malnourishment in tribal children shows a declining trend*. https://pib.gov.in/PressReleaseIframePage.aspx?PRID=1945843

NFHS 5. (2022). *National Family Health Survey (NFHS-5): India report*. International Institute of Population Sciences (IIPS).

Nguyen, P. H., Scott, S., Neupane, S., Tran, L. M., & Menon, P. (2019). Social, biological, and programmatic factors linking adolescent pregnancy and early childhood undernutrition: A path analysis of India's 2016 National Family and Health Survey. *The Lancet Child & Adolescent Health*, *3*(7), 463–473. https://doi.org/10.1016/S2352-4642(19)30110-5

Rekha, S., Shirisha, P., Muraleedharan, V. R., Vaidyanathan, G., & Dash, U. (2023). Wealth inequalities in nutritional status among the tribal under-5 children in India: A temporal trend analysis using NFHS data of Jharkhand and Odisha states – 2006–21. *Dialogues in Health*, *2*, 100135. https://doi.org/10.1016/j.dialog.2023.100135

Shahid, M., Cao, Y., Ahmed, F., Raza, S., Guo, J., Malik, N. I., Rauf, U., Qureshi, M. G., Saheed, R., & Maryam, R. (2022). Does mothers' awareness of health and nutrition matter? A case study of child malnutrition in marginalized rural community of Punjab, Pakistan. *Frontiers in Public Health*, *10*. https://doi.org/10.3389/fpubh.2022.792164

Singh, A., Sundaram, S. P., & Ningombam, J. D. (2024). Undernutrition and its determinants among under-five children in a tribal community of Meghalaya. *Journal of Family Medicine and Primary Care*, *13*(1), 340–347. https://doi.org/10.4103/jfmpc.jfmpc_1095_23

Sonowal, C. J. (2010). Factors affecting the nutritional health of tribal children in Maharashtra. *Studies on Ethno-Medicine*, *4*(1), 21 36. https://doi.org/10.1080/09735070.2010.11886359

Subramanian, S. V., & Joe, W. (2024). Population, health and nutrition profile of the scheduled tribes in India: A comparative perspective, 2016–2021. *The Lancet Regional Health - Southeast Asia*, *20*, 100266. https://doi.org/10.1016/j.lansea.2023.100266

Tebeje, N., Bikes, G., Abebe, S., & Yesuf, M. (2017). Prevalence and major contributors of child malnutrition in developing countries: Systematic review and meta-analysis. *Journal of Childhood Obesity*, *2*(4). https://doi.org/10.21767/2572-5394.100037

Teshale, A. B., Biney, G. K., Sarfo, M., Ameyaw, E. K., & Yaya, S. (2025). What do mothers know about nutrition? Impacts on childhood nutrition outcomes in Sub-Saharan Africa. *Maternal and Child Health Journal*, *29*(3), 349–360. https://doi.org/10.1007/s10995-025-04052-3

Waghode, R. T., Yadav, S. S., Ghooi, R., Razak, S. A., & Menon, K. C. (2025). Work, motherhood, and nutrition: Investigating the association of maternal employment on child nutritional status in South Asia – A systematic review. *Nutrients*, *17*(6), 1059. https://doi.org/10.3390/nu17061059

Chapter 20

Social Discrimination and Inclusive Development in India: An Empirical Analysis

Jhumur Sengupta

Dinabandhu Andrews College, Kolkata, India

Abstract

The sustainable development goals (SDGs) call for equality of opportunity and the elimination of any form of discrimination and socio-economic inclusion of all. The International Labour Organization's (ILO) Discrimination (Employment and Occupation) Convention, 1958 (No. 111) calls for a national policy to eliminate discrimination based on race, colour, sex, religion, political opinion, national extraction, or social origin. In this context, we can argue that sustainable development is difficult to achieve in a socially fragmented society because consensus on the demand from the government is impossible to obtain in the presence of differentiation in tastes and preferences of the groups. In a democracy, politicians often get motivated to do interest group politics, leading to less provision of public service delivery. Social heterogeneity encourages governments in interest group politics, which contradicts the spirit of inclusive development. Using panel data on Indian states, the relationship between social discrimination and public goods provision is tested along three measures of diversity: caste, religion, and language. The results show that social discrimination along these lines is negatively associated with public goods provision. This chapter concludes that social discrimination hampers the economic development of society.

Keywords: Public goods; economic development; economics of minorities; races; indigenous peoples; immigrants; non-labour discrimination; public policy; state and local governments: other expenditure categories

JEL Codes: H41; O1; J15; J18; H760

Changing Dimensions in Economic Development: Theories and Empirics, 273–287

Published under exclusive licence by Emerald Publishing Limited
doi:10.1108/978-1-83708-384-820261023

1. Introduction

The SDGs call for equality of opportunity and the elimination of any form of discrimination and socio-economic inclusion of all. The ILO's Discrimination (Employment and Occupation) Convention, 1958 (No. 111) calls for a national policy to eliminate discrimination based on race, colour, sex, religion, political opinion, national extraction, or social origin. The enactment of discriminating laws and the provision of unequal public services have often represented the exploitation of groups with some political power in history. It is argued that all discriminations by race or ethnic group can be traced to such a dynamic in which a group mobilises political and economic resources to further their material interests. The goal of such actions excludes minority groups from the labour market and provides the dominant group preferential treatment (Bonacich, 1972). The government often has a role in fulfilling the dominant group's interests. In a democratic setup, voting is a means of facilitating the fulfilment of the dominant group's interests. Voting sets a rule for making a collective decision on public goods provision. Majority voting is one such rule that indicates how a collective decision is to be made. It can be shown that the majority voting outcome of public spending coincides with the point most preferred by the median voter. Moreover, it can also be shown that majority voting might not lead to a collective decision on the public goods outcome, which is stable. When preferences over public goods of all voters are single-peaked, then one of the alternative quantities of public goods will be a Condorcet winner. But when the preferences of at least one voter are not single-peaked, then instability occurs. In such a case, there is no Condorcet winner, and any alternative can be defeated by another alternative.

Habyarimana et al. (2007) analyse mechanisms through which diversity may undermine public goods provision and how it motivates the government to do interest group politics. The 'preference' mechanism explains that preferences are correlated with group membership, and ethnic diversity implies a diversity of tastes, which may cause disagreements over public goods. Under the 'strategy selection' mechanism, ethnicity determines the selection of strategies by individuals. Under this mechanism, co-ethnics believe that cooperation with others of the same ethnic group is reciprocated under the threat of sanctioning. Hence, public goods provision will be higher in homogeneous societies. Ake (1993) argues that conflicts among nationalities, ethnic groups, and communal and interest groups that broke out after the independence of African nations were so absorbing that everything else, including development, was marginalised. To examine the influence of ethnic diversity on public goods provision in the Indian context, social discrimination along caste, language, and religion is considered, and it is shown that discrimination hampers inclusive development because of the unequal distribution of public goods to different communities. In Section 2, the theoretical framework is explained. In the next section, the previous literature is documented. The data and the methodology are explained in Sections 4 and 5, respectively. The findings are summarised in Section 6, and Section 7 concludes.

2. Theoretical Framework

Under the assumptions of identical preferences over public goods, same pre-tax income, and same perception over taxation policy in a pure majority voting setup, we consider that each extra unit of public goods costs Rs. $1/P$, where P is the population, and utility depends on government expenditure on public goods and disposable income. In such a society where every individual has the same preference, the same pre-tax income, and the same perception of tax, the utility function is represented by $U = (1-\lambda)\ ln\ (Y^i - T^i) + \lambda\ ln\ (G),\ \lambda \in [0,1]$, where G: government spending, T^i: tax paid by i, Y^i: pre-tax income of i. Hence, the optimisation problem is $MAX(1-\lambda)\ln(Y^i - T^i) + \lambda \ln G$ subject to $Y^i = \frac{G}{P} + (Y^i - T^i)$. The most preferred point of i will be identical to the most preferred point of the median.

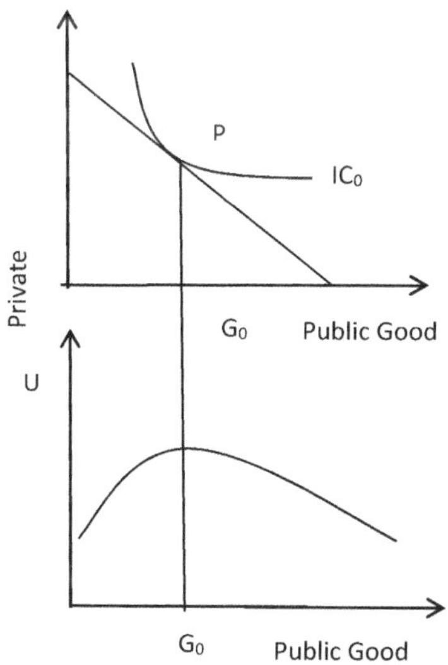

Fig. 20.1 Public Goods Provision in Homogeneous Society.

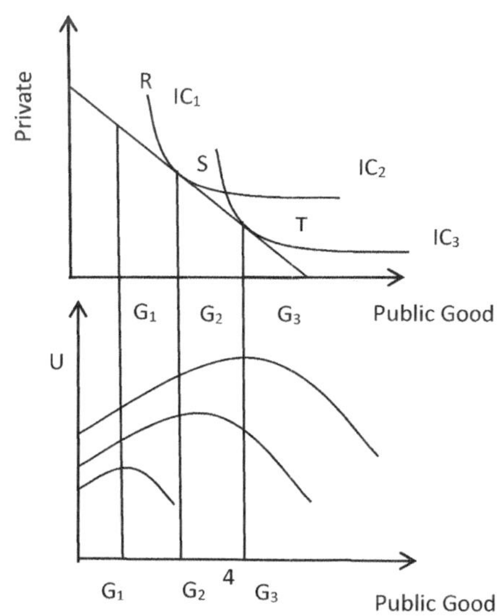

Fig. 20.2 Public Goods Provision in Heterogeneous Society.

Panels A and B consider a homogeneous society where everyone has identical preferences and a heterogeneous society where individuals have different preferences for the public goods, respectively. In panel A, the equilibrium is at the point of tangency between IC_0 and the budget line AB. The optimal public goods level is G_0, where the individual's utility level will be maximised. In panel B, the utility levels of three individuals are represented by three different indifference curves, IC_1, IC_2, and IC_3, with the same budget constraint. So, the equilibrium point for the three individuals are *R*, *S*, and *T*. Therefore, in a heterogeneous society, there is no consensus for providing public goods.

3. Literature Review

During the current years, social scientists increasingly pay attention to social diversity as an important determinant of economic outcomes. Alesina et al. (1999) study the effect of ethnic diversity on local government spending. Using US data for cities, metropolitan areas, and countries, they find that ethnic diversity reduces government spending on education, roads, sewerage trash pickup, and police spending. Miguel and Gugerty (2005) examine the relationship between ethnic diversity and school funding in local schools in Kenya. It is observed in the paper that higher ethnic diversity leads to lower local school funding and less provision of infrastructure facilities in schools, like desks, latrines, and classrooms per pupil. Collier and Garg (1999) study the effect of ethnic diversity on the Ghanaian labour market. They find that the largest tribe has disproportionate power and influence to share a substantial wage premium compared to the other tribes. They have done the analysis separately for private and public sectors and find that the wage premium for the locally largest tribe is 25% in the public sector, whereas it is nil in the private sector. Hence, they suggest that ethnic diversity tends to be a public sector-specific problem. Kain (1968) suggests that Ghettos are bad for society. It creates a physical separation between the places where blacks live and the location of jobs. This tends to lower the public goods outcomes in areas where blacks reside. Manski (2001) argues that public policy should ideally treat all uniformly. But in practice, the American legal system allows for many forms of discriminatory treatment (including racial discrimination) of the US population. Vigdor (2004) examines the effect of country-level ethnic composition on 2000 US Census postal response rates and finds a negative relationship. It assumes that people will pay taxes for financing public goods if these public goods are enjoyed only by the members of their communities. Khwaja (2009) shows that ethnically heterogeneous societies face difficulties in maintaining community projects in Northern Pakistan since returns from the projects are unequally distributed among the members of a diverse community. The study of Shleifer and Vishny (1993) suggests that more ethnically diverse societies have higher rates of corruption than ethnically homogeneous societies. Barro (1999) argues that ethnic diversity makes it more difficult to sustain a democracy due to ethnic competition for control over limited resources. The ultimate effect of such competition is ethnic conflict, which may cause it to become more violent into civil war. Svensson (1998) suggests that a possible consequence of ethnic polarisation is to cause governments to under-invest in the legal infrastructure. Some studies (Wilson, 1987, 1996) reveal that poor minorities in highly segregated cities have low public goods provision because of ethnic conflict. It is argued that they need good public schools to improve their skills, but the relative skill level of minorities in ghettos does not improve. As a result, their poverty level and unemployment increase, and ethnic conflicts become more acute. The implication of this fact is a vicious circle.

Efendic and Pugh (2018) analyse how ethnic diversity affects household and individual economic performance in Bosnia and Herzegovina (BiH) by examining nationally representative cross-sectional survey data. They examine household sector responses to a cross-sectional survey carried out between June and

October 2012. The targeted sample consisted of 2,017 people, and each person was chosen at random. They discovered that ethnic diversity benefits households and individuals economically. The authors estimate that personal and family income is about 10% greater in ethnically diverse areas than in ethnically homogeneous areas after adjusting for other factors.

Using data from Indonesia, Ananta et al. (2023) discuss how ethnic variety functions as a mediating factor in the connection between economic growth and internal migration. The study assesses whether the residences of the respondents in 2005 and 2010 are different, and information on economic growth from 2009 to 2010 is considered to determine whether there may be a connection between migration in 2005–2010 and economic growth in 2009–2010. The report finds that ethnic diversity is an intermediary element in the relationship between migration and economic growth. According to the study, migration may not always be bad for the economy; in some cases, it may spur it by increasing ethnic diversity in Indonesia.

In the present chapter, the empirical findings of the panel data analysis match the standard theoretical prediction that the heterogeneity of the population concerning caste, language, and religion reduces the efficiency of resource allocation and public service delivery.

4. The Panel Data

In the present study, panel data are considered for the analysis because panel data consist of many observations and capture state-specific and time-specific unobserved heterogeneity that are relevant for explaining the variation in public goods supply in different states and times. It spans the financial years from 1981–1982 to 2015–2016 for analysing the outcome based on caste, religion, and language-based discrimination in the state of India. A few control variables (see Appendix), such as literacy rate, state domestic product, and proportion of rural population to total population, are considered along with the social discrimination measures to examine the impact of social discrimination in influencing public goods provision. The data on public goods variables and the control variables are obtained from the Central Statistical Organisation, Ministry of Statistics and Program Implementation under the Government of India. Literacy rate and state domestic product have a favourable influence on public goods supply because education makes individuals more conscious about their requirements and expectations from governments. Furthermore, a higher proportion of the urban population motivates the government to supply public goods equitably as people in urban areas are mainly engaged in the industrial sector and politically more conscious about their demand for public goods. In the present chapter, the public goods variables (see Appendix) considered are government expenditures per capita in highways, power capacity installed, post offices, beds in hospitals, schools, and law and order. The incidence of crime acts as a proxy for the law and order situation, and it seems obvious that the rate of crime rises when the law and order situation gets worse in a society. Moreover, it is assumed that higher social fragmentation leads to more incidence of crimes.

To compute the diversity among the population, a social discrimination measure is constructed, and it is calculated as, $Index = 1 - \sum_{i=1}^{K} \left(\frac{n_{ist}}{N_{st}} \right)^2$, where i represents an ethnic group, n_{ist} is the number of people in group i in the state s during the financial year t, and N_{st} is the total population for the given state year. Here, the population is assumed to be divided into K groups. The index measures the probability that two randomly drawn individuals from a given state year belong to different ethnic groups. As the value of the index increases, heterogeneity rises. First, a measure of discrimination based on three caste groups, scheduled caste, scheduled tribe, and general is considered for a given state year. Second, the religious discrimination measure is constructed based on six religious groups as per the Census of India 2011. Third, a linguistic fractionalisation measure is computed by the same formula based on 14 linguistic groups as per the Census of India 2011 (see Appendix).

5. Methodology

To check the stationarity of the variables in the panel data set, a panel unit root test called the Levin–Lin–Chu (LLC) test is undertaken where the null hypothesis and the alternative hypotheses of the LLC unit root test are specified as follows:

$$\Delta y_{it} = \alpha_i + \beta y_{i,t-1} + \varepsilon_{it}$$

In this case, $H_0 : \beta = 0$ and $H_A : \beta < 0$

In the LLC panel unit root test, homogeneous dynamic panels are considered where the coefficient of $y_{i,t-1}$ is assumed to be the same for all i. A variable in the panel data set is non-stationary if the null hypothesis is not rejected.

After that, the Hodrick–Prescott filter is used for the non-stationary variables to decompose the original series into its trend and cyclical components. Then, the cyclical component is considered to examine the impact of the social discrimination index along with the control variables on the expenditure of public goods by the government.

The LLC test reveals that the public goods variables possess unit roots. Therefore, the cyclical components are considered for further analysis. Let y_{st} denote a public goods supplied in state s during the financial year t. Let τ_{st} and denote, respectively, the trend and cyclical components of y_{st}.

To see whether state-specific heterogeneity shocks can account for the cyclical component, $(y_{st} - \tau_{st})$ of the public goods variable y_{st}, the regression model is specified as follows:

$$(y_{st} - \tau_{st}) = \alpha_s + \delta_t + \theta x_{st} + \gamma h_{st} + \varepsilon_{st} \, (s = 1,\ldots,S; t = 1,2,\ldots,T)$$

where α_s captures the state-specific unobserved heterogeneity, δ_t represents the year-specific unobserved heterogeneity, x_{st} is a ($k$xl) vector of explanatory variables that capture economic and demographic characteristics, and h_{st} is a variable that ranges from 0 to 1 and measures the heterogeneity in state s during year t and is the error term. The estimation of the above equation is performed by using fixed-effect and random-effect regression models. The estimate γ indicates the amount by which the expenditure on the public goods will change going from zero social discrimination ($h_{st} = 0$) to complete social discrimination ($h_{st} = 1$). In the model, if α_s and δ_t are assumed to be correlated with the explanatory variables, fixed-effect estimators will be efficient. But in case the state-specific and time-specific unobserved heterogeneity is not correlated with the explanatory variables, the random-effect Generalised least squares (GLS) estimators will be more efficient.

After estimating the within-effect (fixed-effect model) and random-effect regression, Hausman specification tests are performed to decide the appropriate model. The Hausman specification test is performed for each regression model specifying a public goods supply variable. The test is performed as follows:

The null hypothesis is: The unobserved individual specific effects are not correlated with the explanatory variables.

The Hausman specification test statistic is

$$H = (\beta_{\text{fixed}} - \beta_{\text{random}})(V_{\text{fixed}} - V_{\text{random}})^{-1}(\beta_{fixed} - \beta_{\text{random}})$$

where β_{fixed} is the coefficient obtained from the fixed effect and β_{random} is the coefficient obtained from the random effect models. The measures V_{fixed} and V_{random} are the covariance matrix of the fixed and the random effect model, respectively.

The test statistic follows χ^2 distribution with k degrees of freedom, where k is the dimension of β. Under the null hypothesis, the random effect estimator is consistent and efficient. If the null hypothesis is rejected, then the fixed effect is appropriate, and the random effect is a suitable model if the null hypothesis is not rejected.

If all the explanatory variables are treated as exogenous, the one-stage within estimation and GLS random-effect models are relevant for the analysis. In the next analysis stage, it is assumed that the fractionalisation index h_{st} is endogenous because the expenditure on public goods may influence it. Therefore, the two-stage within-effect (2SLS) and the two-stage GLS random-effect models (RE2SLS) are considered in the subsequent analysis using instruments for the fractionalisation index.

6. Results

We study the relationship between public goods provision and heterogeneity using three different dimensions: caste-based, religion-based, and language-based heterogeneity.

6.1. Fixed Effects and Random Effects Results

Table 20.1 presents the regression estimates for local government expenditure per capita at the state level. Only the coefficients of the heterogeneity index are

Table 20.1. Effects of Discrimination Based on Caste, Religion, and Language on Expenditure on Public Goods (Fixed-effect and Random-effect Results).

	Expenditure on Roads		Incidence of Crime		Expenditure on Schools		Expenditure on Installed Capacity		Expenditure on Post Office		Expenditure on Hospital Beds	
	FE	RE	FE	RE	FE	RE	FE	RE	FE	RE	FE	RE
CASTE	−1.09 (−3.75)***	−1.14 (−3.41)***	1.10 (4.26)***	1.18 (4.32)***	−1.00 (−3.19)***	−1.34 (−3.22)***	−1.42 (−4.44)***	−1.64 (−4.49)***	−1.57 (−3.22)***	−1.18 (−3.29)***	2.25 (1.00)	1.12 (0.91)
RELIGION	−1.12 (−2.39)*	−1.11 (−2.29)*	1.00 (1.00)	1.04 (1.01)	−1.18 (−2.11)*	−1.35 (−2.00)*	−1.08 (−2.56)**	−1.10 (−2.51)**	−0.03 (−1.18)	−0.13 (−1.22)	−0.27 (−0.52)	−0.24 (−0.69)
LANGUAGE	−1.16 (−3.49)***	−1.18 (−3.47)***	1.89 (3.38)***	1.88 (3.42)***	−1.11 (−1.00)	−1.01 (−1.09)	−1.12 (−4.42)***	−1.11 (−4.35)***	−0.04 (−3.26)**	−0.09 (−3.42)**	−1.67 (−2.45)*	−1.71 (−2.41)**
No. of observation	396	396	396	396	418	418	418	418	288	288	528	528
Hausman test	0.0021 (fixed effect)		0.2315 (random effect)		0.0003 (fixed effect)		0.0009 (fixed effect)		0.0000 (fixed effect)		0.3219 (random effect)	

Source: The figures are based on the author's calculations.

Note: The *p*-values for the Hausman test are reported in the last row displaying the appropriateness of the model. FE, Fixed effect; RE, Random effect.

*, **, and *** represent the statistical significance at 10%, 5%, and 1% levels, respectively.

reported in the table. The results show that higher social fragmentation negatively impacts the public goods supply. The values in the parenthesis represent the z statistic value. The left entry under each of the columns representing a public goods supply variable reports the fixed-effect estimation results and the right entry reports the random-effect estimation results.

In Table 20.1, the coefficients of the caste-based discrimination index in all cases are negative in both the fixed- and random-effect model except in the provision of hospital beds where the expenditure increases with caste-based fragmentation although the positive association is statistically insignificant. The discrimination based on religion has negative impacts on all the public goods variables, and the coefficients are statistically significant for the expenditure on roads, schools, and installed capacity. The linguistic differences among the population are negatively associated with the provision of all public goods, and the adverse relationships are statistically significant in the case of roads, law and order, installed capacity, post offices, and hospitals. The last row of each table implies that the fixed-effect model is a more appropriate model for the analysis which aligns with the fact that state and year-specific unobserved heterogeneity are relevant to explain the relationship between social fragmentation and the public goods supply. The coefficients of the control variables (not reported here in Table 20.1) reveal the favourable impacts of literacy and the state domestic product on the public goods supply by the government, whereas the effects of the greater proportions of the rural population in the total population are negative in motivating the government for higher public goods supply. Moreover, the adverse influences of social fragmentation among the population remain unaffected after considering other factors, such as literacy rates, state domestic products, and the proportions of the rural population in the total population. The findings of the present chapter do match up with the theory in most cases when we consider the impact of caste, religion, and language-based diversity on the public goods supply.

6.2. Instrumental Variable Regression Results

The heterogeneity index, h_{st}, and the error terms, ε_{st}, may be correlated. For example, if people migrate from one state to another that offers more of the local public goods they desire, the composition of the population in terms of caste, religion, and language would change over time, and an endogeneity problem may arise in the regression model. Hence, the instrumental variable regression is considered. To address the possible endogeneity and to construct the instrument, each state's initial year's diversity index is considered. This initial heterogeneity acts as a set of weights that show how each state is expected to be impacted by the national rise of heterogeneity. Hence, the index changes over time in accordance with the average growth of the population. The actual heterogeneity index is modified by this anticipated heterogeneity index. In the instrumental variable regression, the pooled two-stage least square estimator and the random effects two-stage least square models are estimated.

Before running the 2SLS regression, the instrument's validity has been checked by looking at the extent of significant relationship between the instrument and the heterogeneity index, h_{st}, which is an endogenous variable. The coefficients of the regression of heterogeneity index, h_{st}, on the instrument which is the index changes over time in accordance with the average growth of the population along with the other exogenous variables that capture economic and demographic characteristics such as male literacy rate, female literacy rate, per capita Gross state domestic product (GSDP), and proportion of rural population to total population are found to be significant, and the F statistics are also significant implying the joint significance of the instrument and the exogenous variables. Hence, it is evident that the instrument is valid for the 2SLS regression.

During the 2SLS estimation process, it was discovered that heterogeneity had negative impacts on most of the public goods expenditure variables for all types of discrimination. Moreover, the 2SLS estimates (Table 20.2) are similar to the error component model estimates (Table 20.1).

This suggests that the error component model estimates (Table 20.1) are not influenced by reverse causation, meaning that the movement of groups between the states was due to changes in heterogeneity nationally over the years and not due to the changes in expenditure on public goods in the states.

Relocating to other states could have been another significant factor contributing to the shift away from local government services. Our 2SLS results rule out the possibility of endogenous group sorting across the states.

6.3. Controlling for Income Levels and Robustness Checks

Another source of substitution of public services is income which acts as a greater barrier to relocation. For example, compared to the rich states, the population of the poorer states had a higher incidence of residence mobility in search of jobs. Therefore, it may be argued that rather than racial heterogeneity, economic disparities among the states influence the spending patterns among states. In Table 20.3, the relationship between social fragmentation and expenditure on public goods for the rich states and the poorer states is taken into consideration separately. The results of Table 20.3 indicate that the nature of the impact of social fragmentation on expenditure on public goods variables is similar to the results obtained in Tables 20.1 and 20.2. According to these findings, the provision of public goods is determined by factors other than income disparities across states.

7. Conclusion

This work aims to theorise the fundamental mechanism of the connection between public goods provision and social heterogeneity. The results indicate that the socially fragmented states have less provision of public goods even after controlling for factors such as GSDP, literacy rates, and proportion of rural population. The results show that the effect of social discrimination is negative for expenditure on roads, hospital beds, schools, installed capacity, and provision of

Table 20.2. Effects of Discrimination Based on Caste, Religion, and Language on Expenditure on Public Goods (2SLS Results).

	Expenditure on Roads		Incidence of Crime		Expenditure on Schools		Expenditure on Installed Capacity		Expenditure on Post Office		Expenditure on Hospital Beds	
	2SLS	RE2SLS	2SLS	RE2SLS	2SLS	RE2SLS	2SLS	RE2SLS	2SLS	RE2SLS	2SLS	RE2SLS
CASTE	−1.32	−1.35	1.17	1.19	−1.11	−1.10	−1.46	−1.79	−1.31	−1.46	2.37	1.45
	(−4.49)***	(−4.56)***	(4.75)***	(4.82)***	(−3.21)***	(−3.23)***	(−4.33)***	(−4.46)***	(−3.59)***	(−3.70)***	(0.33)	(0.40)
RELIGION	−1.25	−1.24	1.12	1.29	−1.18	−1.11	−1.24	−1.29	−0.11	−0.10	−0.42	−0.43
	(−2.29)*	(−2.45)*	(1.02)	(1.04)	(−2.43)*	(−2.44)*	(−2.48)**	(−2.45)**	(−1.46)	(−1.72)	(−0.79)	(−0.98)
LANGUAGE	−1.05	−1.09	1.84	1.89	−1.21	−1.19	−1.11	−1.13	−0.13	−0.10	−1.84	−1.91
	(−3.79)***	(−3.88)***	(3.27)***	(3.45)***	(−1.19)	(−1.27)	(−3.92)***	(−3.98)***	(3.36)**	(−3.34)**	(−2.57)*	(−2.61)**
No. of observation	396	396	396	396	418	418	418	418	288	288	528	528

Source: The figures are based on the author's calculations.

*, **, and *** represent the statistical significance at 10%, 5%, and 1% levels, respectively.

Table 20.3. Effects of Discrimination Based on Caste, Religion, and Language on Expenditure on Public Goods by Income Levels.

	Expenditure on Roads		Incidence of Crime		Expenditure on Schools		Expenditure on Installed Capacity		Expenditure on Post Office		Expenditure on Hospital Beds	
	Rich States	Poor States	Rich States	Poor States	Rich States	Poor States	Rich States	Poor States	Rich States	Poor States	Rich States	Poor States
CASTE	−1.01	−1.06	1.09	1.10	−1.07	−1.09	−1.34	−1.37	−1.21	−1.24	1.45	1.41
	(−3.28)***	(−3.32)***	(3.47)***	(3.82)***	(−3.78)***	(−3.80)***	(−4.29)***	(−4.35)***	(−2.14)***	(−2.21)***	(0.19)	(0.23)
RELIGION	−1.19	−1.23	1.31	1.34	−1.09	−1.10	−1.15	−1.19	−0.14	−0.12	−0.33	−0.38
	(−3.34)*	(−3.37)*	(1.00)	(1.01)	(−2.78)*	(−2.82)*	(−2.67)**	(−2.35)**	(−1.27)	(−1.31)	(−0.28)	(−0.21)
LANGUAGE	−1.19	−1.14	1.84	1.89	−1.21	−1.19	−1.11	−1.13	−0.13	−0.10	−1.84	−1.91
	(−4.11)***	(−4.23)***	(3.33)***	(3.37)***	(−1.01)	(−1.00)	(−3.34)***	(−3.38)***	(4.52)**	(−4.45)**	(−2.82)*	(−2.89)**
No. of observation	180	216	180	216	190	228	190	228	180	108	240	288

Source: The figures are based on the author's calculations.

Note: The rich states include Andhra Pradesh, Gujarat, Haryana, Karnataka, Kerala, Maharashtra, Orissa, Tamil Nadu, Goa, and Punjab based on the GSDP data. The poor states are Arunachal Pradesh, Assam, Bihar, Himachal Pradesh, Madhya Pradesh, Mizoram, Tripura, Uttar Pradesh, West Bengal, Rajasthan, and Sikkim based on GSDP data.

*, **, and *** represent the statistical significance at 10%, 5%, and 1% levels, respectively.

post offices, but the impact is positive on the incidence of crime implying that the government will spend more on police to maintain the law and order situation. Therefore, the results suggest that the expenditure on public goods and services is rebalanced as states become more socially diverse.

Economic development scholars today are increasingly sensitive to the role of ethnicity in influencing the potential to erupt into incessant social conflict, which continues to remain a strong retardation to economic development. A successful economic development agenda today in many developing countries characterised by extreme ethnic fragmentation depends not only on identifying and stabilising traditional macroeconomic targets but also on recognising the benefits of ethnic diversity in economic organisation and the threat that ethnic diversity can lead to the sustainability of political and economic structures.

This chapter reports the impact of heterogeneity among the population on public goods provision using state-level data on India. It is found that there is a negative association between ethnic diversity and public goods supply. The implications of both theoretical and empirical discussions, however, suggest that ethnically fragmented societies have significant problems in achieving development patterns. To counter this problem, more accurate policy measures using executing equal development goals to both ethnically homogeneous and heterogeneous localities are needed.

References

Ake, C. (1993). What is the problem of ethnicity in Africa? *Transformation*, *22*, 14–22.

Alesina, A., Reza, B., & Easterly, W. (1999). Public goods and ethnic divisions. *Quarterly Journal of Economics*, *114*, 1243–1284.

Ananta, A., Arifin, E., Purbowati, A., & Carnegie, P. J. (2023). Does diversity matter for development? New evidence of ethnic diversity's mediation between internal migration and economic growth across Indonesia's regions. *Journal of Population Research*, *40*(3), 1–21.

Barro, R. J. (1999). Determinants of democracy. *Journal of Political Economy*, *107*(2), 158–183.

Bonacich, E. (1972). A theory of ethnic antagonism: The split labor market. *American Sociological Review*, *37*, 547–559.

Collier, P., & Garg, A. (1999). On kin groups and wages in the Ghanaian labour market. *Oxford Bulletin of Economics and Statistics*, *61*(2), 133–151.

Efendic, A., & Pugh, G. (2018). The effect of ethnic diversity on income – An empirical investigation using survey data from a post-conflict environment. *Economics: The Open-Access, Open-Assessment E-Journal*, *12*, 1–34.

Habyarimana, J., Humphreys, M., Posner, D. N., & Weinstein, J. (2007). Why does ethnic diversity undermine public goods provision? *American Political Science Review*, *101*(4), 709–724.

Kain, J. (1968). Housing segregation, Negro employment, and metropolitan decentralization. *Quarterly Journal of Economics*, *82*(2), 175–197.

Khwaja, A. (2009). Can good projects succeed in bad communities? *Journal of Public Economics*, *93*, 899–916.

Manski, C. F. (2001). Designing programs for heterogeneous populations: The value of covariate information. *AER Papers and Proceedings*, *91*(2), 103–106.

Miguel, E., & Gugerty, M. K. (2005). Ethnic diversity, social sanctions, and public goods in Kenya. *Journal of Public Economics*, *89*(11–12), 2325–2368.

Shleifer, A., & Vishny, R. (1993). Corruption. *Quarterly Journal of Economics*, *108*(3), 599–618.

Svensson, J. (1998). Investment, property rights and political instability: Theory and evidence. *European Economic Review*, *42*(7), 1317–1342.

Vigdor, J. (2004). Community composition and collective action: Analyzing initial mail response to the 2000 census. *Review of Economics and Statistics*, *86*(1), 303–312.

Wilson, W. (1987). *The truly disadvantaged: The inner city, the underclass, and public policy* (2nd ed.). University of Chicago Press.

Wilson, W. (1996). *When work disappears: The world of new urban poor* (1st ed.). Knopf.

Appendix

1. *Public goods variables*:

- Expenditure on length of national highways in km per capita.
- Expenditure on total installed capacity in 1000 kWh per capita.
- Expenditure on post offices per capita.
- Expenditure on beds in government hospitals per capita.
- Expenditure on government schools for general education per capita.
- Incidence of total crimes under the Indian Penal Code per capita.

2. *Social discrimination index*:

- Caste-based discrimination index:
  $CASTE = 1 - \sum_{i=1}^{3}\left(\frac{n_i}{N}\right)^2$ is the number of people in group i and N is the population of the state.
- Religious discrimination index:
  $RELI = 1 - \sum_{i=1}^{6}\left(\frac{n_i}{N}\right)^2$, where n_i is the number of people in group i and N is the population of the state.
- Linguistic discrimination index:
  $LANG = 1 - \sum_{i=1}^{14}\left(\frac{n_i}{N}\right)^2$, where n_i is the number of people in group i and N is the population of the state.

3. *Control variables:*

- Per capita net state domestic product at constant prices (SDPPC).
- Proportion of population in the rural area to total state population (RURALPOP).
- Literacy rate (LITERACY).

Chapter 21

Inter-state Disparity in the Growth of Women SHG Savings in India

Dyuti Chatterjee[a] *and Soovankar Das*[b]

[a]*Department of Economics, St. Xavier's University, Kolkata, India*
[b]*Department of Economics, University of Calcutta, Kolkata, India*

Abstract

The women population of India is almost equal to its male population. However, when it comes to their position in society, women lag far behind their male counterparts in terms of parameters like economic freedom, decision-making, and bargaining power. Despite an increase in the education level, there has not been a concomitant rise in the employment of women. Women self-help groups (WSHGs) were created with the main objective of offering some employment opportunities to women to make them self-reliant. It was thought that financial inclusion would serve the dual purpose of reducing poverty and at the same time empower these women. However, despite several years passing by, the performance of self-help groups (SHGs) shows mixed results. While some states show a fair number of active SHG-bank linkage programmes (SHG-BLPs) with promising savings, there are states where the number of dormant SHGs is alarming. Unlike most literature, this chapter tries to analyse the patterns of within-region (intra-region), across-region (inter-region), and across-state (inter-state) inequalities in WSHG savings for the period 2013–2014 to 2022–2023 using the Theil index and the Gini coefficient and has presented some mixed results. It also seeks to trace out the possibility of conditional convergence in the savings of WSHGs for the same period. This chapter finds significant beta (β) and sigma (σ) convergence in WSHG savings over the years. However, the fact remains that unless and until the outreach of WSHGs is evenly spread across the country, the concept of

Changing Dimensions in Economic Development: Theories and Empirics, 289–302

doi:10.1108/978-1-83708-384-820261024

women empowerment and inclusive growth may remain an elusive dream forever.

Keywords: Women SHGs; savings; convergence; inequality; Theil index; Gini coefficient

JEL Codes: J16; R11; G21; O16

Introduction

SHGs are small, informal groups, ranging from 10 to 20 individuals from the same socio-economic background who come together and enhance their standard of living. They are formed with the main objective of access to finance so that individuals can start any entrepreneurial activities on their own. A key reason for encouraging women to save through SHGs is that women unlike men tend to use their savings for investing it in productive purposes like the health and education of the members of the household.

Before the SHG model in India, Self-Employed Women's Association (SEWA) was a trade union for women in the unorganised sector. The SHG model was pioneered by MYRADA in the 1980s to improve livelihoods. In 1992, NABARD and MYRADA established the Self-Help Group–Bank Linkage Programme (SHG-BLP) to reach families without formal financial institutions. Commercial, Regional Rural, and Cooperative banks have since partnered with SHGs, with non-governmental organisations (NGOs) serving as intermediaries between banks and the poor.

India's financial exclusion ranks fourth globally, with 135 million people living in poverty. The SHG-bank linkage aims to provide sustainable financial credit to low-income individuals. The SHG-BLP is the world's largest microfinance programme, with a focus on WSHGs due to their higher repayment rates. This has led to employment generation, as women can start businesses and create secondary employment in rural and semi-urban areas. Since 2011–2012, NABARD has sanctioned grants for the promotion and financing of SHG-BLP in backward regions, with approximately 1.29 lakh women linked with the bank through this scheme. This microfinance serves both poverty removal and women empowerment. The government has also conducted various schemes for the promotion of SHGs. Programmes like Deendayal Antyodaya Yojana – National Rural Livelihoods Mission (DAY-NRLM) aims to mobilise rural women into SHGs, providing them with financial support and promoting economic activities. As of December 2024, approximately 10.05 crores of households have been organised into 90.87 lakh SHGs across India (available at: https://rural.gov.in/en/press-release/under-deendayal-antyodaya-yojana-national-rural-livelihoods-mission-all-eligible-rural). The Pradhan Mantri Jan Dhan Yojna (PMJDY) scheme has also benefitted SHGs by integrating them as business correspondents, promoting their involvement through convergence with NRLM for bank account openings, engaging them in financial literacy and financial inclusion at the grassroot level (available at: https://pmjdy.gov.in/files/E-Documents/PMJDY_BROCHURE_ENG.pdf). Some state-level initiatives like the YSR Aasara Scheme by the Andhra Pradesh government aim to uplift rural and urban women of SHGs by clearing their existing bank loans and supporting them in production, manufacturing, and marketing of their future establishments (available at: https://gramawardsachivalayam.ap.gov.in/GSWS/AdsandGos/assets/go/G.O.Ms.No.655-RD.I-YSR-AASARA-guidelines.PDF).

This chapter is divided into the following sections: Section I deals with the existing literature, Section II points out the research gap and the objective of the study, while Section III is about the data collection and methodology. Section IV analyses the findings, whereas Section V concludes and prescribes policies. Finally, the last section, Section VI, deals with the limitations of this study.

Section I: Review of the Existing Literature

A common conjecture among researchers is that microfinance helps in the alleviation of poverty and leads to women empowerment. Swain and Wallentin (2009) validated this hypothesis using household data from five Indian states for 2000–2003. They found a significant increase in women's empowerment in SHG members, but unevenness, with some women being more empowered than others. Empowerment also increased over longer periods of women's membership in SHGs. Ghosh and Banerjee (2010) found that self-employed SHGs outperform wage-earning ones in terms of employment continuity. They also highlighted the significant impact of training on SHG members' performance, with trained members more likely to be empowered and employed. Midya et al. (2021) in their primary survey claims lack of credit support from financial institutions and lack of family support as the two major problems faced by WSHG members. Deshmukh-Ranadive (2004) chooses the state of Andhra Pradesh to point out the correlation between poverty reduction and improvement in women's social and economic condition. They point out that SHGs have allowed women to either expand their existing occupational activities or venture outside agriculture. Similarly, Sarania (2015) takes a sample of 100 SHG members from Assam and comes up with the conclusion that there is a significant difference between the annual income of SHG members before and after joining the SHGs. Ravindra and Tiwari (2016) also highlight the relationship between poverty and growth of SHGs. This is evident from the fact that the growth of SHGs is slow in states like Bihar, Uttar Pradesh, etc., which are also very poor in nature. Again, the southern states which are relatively better off like Karnataka and Tamil Nadu are also the ones where the SHG movement has been very successful.

Another important strand of literature highlights the variation in the performance of SHGs. Sinha and Navin (2021) demonstrate that as of 2018–2019, the southern region scored highest in terms of the total number of SHGs and their financial resources. The eastern region stands next to the southern region in terms of both parameters. There was a substantial reduction in the disbursement of loans in both the northeastern region and the central region, two of the most backward regions of the country. Bhansali (2019) has shown that the SHG-BLP has increased over the years 2013–2014 to 2017–2018. However, this growth has been uneven across different states in India. This growth of linkage was mostly concentrated in the southern part, while in the north-eastern region, the growth was significantly low. Venkatesh (2017) also corroborates that the southern region outweighs the eastern and the central regions in terms of the progress and dominance of SHG activities and points out that the north and north-eastern regions have shown slow catching up in the last few years. Similarly, the findings of Kadir et al. (2024) agree to the view that from 2013–2014 to 2015–2016, the north-east region has shown significant growth in SHG-BLP. They further claimed that there is substantial intra-regional disparity even within the north-east region. Tabassum (2024) in her very recent study explored the key factors for the success of SHGs. She states that the southern states like Kerala, Tamil Nadu, and Andhra Pradesh have dominated the northern and eastern states like Bihar and Rajasthan through robust institutional support, efficient financial linkages, and integration with welfare programmes. Moreover, the northern and eastern states face severe hindrances in forms of poor infrastructure, improper training, and other socio-economic barriers that limit women's participation in SHGs. Parida and Sinha (2010) in their paper claim that since income-generating activities and other characteristics vary with the gender composition of SHGs, their sustainability also varies based on their primary survey covering six states of the country which covered approximately almost 80% of India's bank-linked SHGs; they showed that it was the all WSHGs which performed the best in terms of recovery of loans and per capita saving.

Section II: Research Gap and Objectives

The present study is a departure from the other studies involving SHGs in many ways. Most studies involving SHGs are usually primary surveys that focus on women empowerment. There is not much work done regarding the pattern of savings of SHGs. Savings are essential for the smooth functioning of any SHG, as they can go a long way in eradicating poverty in the country. Yet few studies have established the inequality of WSHG savings and tried to check their convergence over time. Most studies have paid limited attention to the importance of crucial factors like training and capacity building, the amount of grants received on the savings of the SHGs, which are examined in this chapter.

Objectives

(1) To analyse the pattern of within-region (intra-region), across-region (inter-region), and across-state (inter-state) inequalities in WSHG savings over the period 2013–2014 to 2022–2023.
(2) To study whether the growth of WSHG savings of each state tends to converge to its own steady-state contingent upon the amount of grants and the number of participants of SHG members in training and capacity building for the given period.

Section III: Data Source and Methodology

This chapter relies on secondary data. We extract the information regarding SHGs from the NABARD Microfinance Reports of the period 2013–2014 to 2022–2023 (available at: https://www.nabard.org/content.aspx?id=651). We particularly select this time period because of the restricted availability of data regarding the variables concerned. The data for the net state gross domestic product (NSGDP) at constant prices having 2011–2012 as base year have been taken from the *Handbook of Indian Statistics* published by the Reserve Bank of India (RBI) (https://www.rbi.org.in/scripts/AnnualPublications.aspx?head=Handbook±of±Statistics±on±Indian±States). And the data for size of the respective states (in sq.km.) are collected from census report, 2011 (https://www.mospi.gov.in/sites/default/files/statistical_year_book_india_2015/Table%202.1_5.xls). The pattern of inequality in WSHG savings present within the selected regions, across the regions, and across the states has been analysed with the help of Theil's index and Gini coefficient.

Theil's index is computed by the formula provided by Johnston (1969):

$$T_X = \frac{1}{n}\sum_{i=1}^{n}\left(\frac{X_i}{\overline{X}}\right)\log\left(\frac{X_i}{\overline{X}}\right) \tag{1}$$

While to construct the Gini coefficient for individual-level data, we have followed Allison (1978):

$$G_X = \frac{2}{n^2\overline{X}}\sum_{i=1}^{n} i.X_i - \frac{n+1}{n}, \quad X_1 \le X_2 \le \ldots \le X_n \tag{2}$$

where:

X = concerned variable.

$\overline{X}$ = mean of X.

n = number of observations.

In the context of prevalent inequality in WSHG savings over the studied period, it was attempted to find out whether there exists convergence in the aggregated savings of WSHGs across 24 states in India over the period 2013–2014 to 2022–2023. To check the convergence, tests for beta (β) and sigma (σ) convergence have been performed in this study. Each state in the country possesses dissimilar characteristics in terms of geography and size, amount of grants received, and number of active participants in productive training programmes. This leads all the states to converge to 'different steady-states' in terms of WSHG savings. Therefore, under the assumption of 'relative homogeneity', this chapter checks for the absolute convergence of the states in terms of WSHG savings and then tests for relative convergence, conditioned upon the possible significant determinants of growth of WSHG savings, in the form of the factors mentioned above.

Beta Convergence

To test the β-convergence, conventional Baumol (1986) approach of absolute convergence (model of specification 1) is used. In the next step, the panel generalised least squares (GLS) is used to check the effect and significance of the hypothesised parameters on the WSHG savings growth (model of specification 2). In the final step, Mankiw et al. (1992) approach to relative convergence, conditioned upon the hypothesised parameters (model of specification 3), has been used.

Model of specification 1:

$$\frac{1}{T}\ln\left(\frac{S_{n,T}}{S_{n,t_0}}\right)=\alpha_1+\beta_{11}\ln\left(S_{n,t_0}\right)+\theta_{i1} \tag{3.1}$$

Model of specification 2:

$$\ln\left(S_{n,t}\right)=\alpha_2+\beta_{12}\ln\left(\text{SGDP}_{n,t}\right)+\beta_{22}\ln\left(\text{GT}_{n,t}\right)+\beta_{32}\text{NP}_{n,t}+\theta_{i2} \tag{3.2}$$

Model of specification 3:

$$\begin{aligned}\frac{1}{T}\ln\left(\frac{S_{n,T}}{S_{n,t_0}}\right)=\alpha_3+\beta_{13}\ln\left(S_{i,t_0}\right)+\beta_{23}(\ln\left(S_{i,t_0}\right))^2+\beta_{33}\ln\left(\text{SGDP}_n\right)\\+\beta_{43}\ln\left(\text{GT}_n\right)+\beta_{53}\text{NP}_n+\beta_{63}\ln\left(\text{SSZ}_n\right)+\theta_{i3}\end{aligned} \tag{3.3}$$

where:
α_j = level constant (intercept term) of jth model.
β_{kj} = slope parameter of kth variable of jth model.
t_0, T = initial and current time periods.
n = index of different states, $n = 1,\ldots,N$.
$S_{n,t_0}, S_{n,T}$ = aggregated WSHG savings of the nth state at respective time periods.
SGDP_n = net GDP of the nth state.
GT_n = amount of grant released.
SSZ_n = geographical size.
NP_n = number of participations of SHG members in training and capacity building of a state.
ln = natural logarithmic transformation.
θ_{ij} = random error of jth model.

In Equations (3.1) and (3.3), significant negative values of β_{1j} confirm convergence (Baumol, 1986; Mankiw et al., 1992).

Sigma Convergence

Barro et al. (1991) defined sigma convergence as reduction in cross-sectional dispersion of the concerned variable (in their model, per capita income) over time.

To capture this cross-sectional dispersion, they had analysed standard deviation (sd_t here on) of different cross-sections over time periods. However, this chapter uses coefficient of variation for different periods (CV_t here on) as a measure of dispersion in the analysis of sigma convergence (following de la Fuente, 1997; Giannetti, 2002; Sala-i-Martin, 2006).

Standard deviation of logarithmic aggregated WSHG savings is given by,

$$sd_t = \sqrt{\frac{1}{N}\sum_{i}^{N}[\ln(S_{n,t}) - \overline{\ln(S_{n,t})}]^2}, \overline{\ln(S_{n,t})} = \text{Mean of log of WSHG savings}$$

for period t

And CV_t is defined by the formula:

$$CV_t = \frac{sd_t}{\overline{\ln(S_{n,t})}} \times 100 \tag{4}$$

The sigma convergence requires,

$$CV_t > CV_{t+1} \tag{5}$$

Section IV: Empirical Findings

The performance of the SHGs is skewed across different regions. Around 70% of the SHGs are found to be concentrated in the southern part of the country. The southern and eastern regions both dominate the overall credit flow.

Panels (A) and (B) of Fig. 21.1 show the distributions of the number of SHGs and aggregate SHG savings across different regions for the financial year (FY) 2022–2023. From the figures, it is obvious that there is a high concentration of SHGs, both in terms of their absolute number and aggregated savings in the southern and eastern regions whereas the northern and north-eastern regions lag by far. The number of SHGs in southern and eastern regions is 8 times higher than that in northern and north-eastern states, and the aggregated SHG savings is almost 14 times larger in the southern and eastern regions than in north-eastern and northern regions. This clearly depicts the picture of alarming inequality among the regions in terms of the progress of SHGs. In panels (C) and (D), the respective GRs of existing SHGs and aggregated SHG savings for the FY 2020–2021 to 2021–2022 and FY 2021–2022 to 2022–2023 are plotted. Interestingly, it is evident from the figures that the GRs of the number of existing SHGs and aggregate savings had declined. It has reached negative in the case of southern regions, whereas the northern and north-eastern regions show increasing GRs in terms of the number of SHGs and a fall in the GR of SHG savings (still the difference being lower than the southern part). Central and western regions, however, show mixed results. Being moderately endowed with the number of SHG formations and amount of total savings in the FY 2022–2023, the central region has experienced significant growth in the number of SHG formations, while on the savings count, it has declined slightly. The western part with almost similar endowments as in the central region has shown positive progress in the GRs from

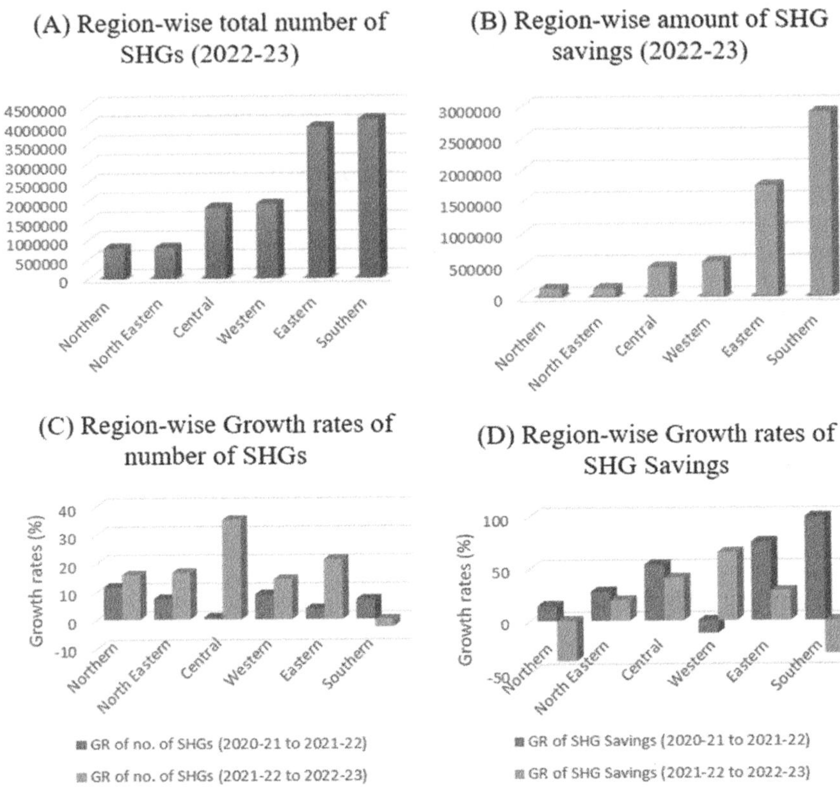

Fig. 21.1. Region-wise Volume and Growth Rate (GR) of SHGs and SHG Savings. *Source*: Authors' computation from data.

both fronts. This depicts that the picture of inequality is not only present in terms of the endowments of SHG savings and the number of SHG formations but is also quite evident in their respective GRs.

After 2019, while regional inequality in SHG savings declined, state-wise disparities consistently climbed up. This indicates that despite regional convergence, significant variations persist across states in WSHG savings endowments. Table 21.1 shows the values of both the Gini coefficient and the Theil's index, revealing that the northern and western regions have maintained consistently medium inequality level in WSHG savings. A key factor of some of the northern and the western states is their patriarchal structure that restricts the mobility of women. The average years of education for a woman from the north are also much less than her southern counterparts. All these ensure that the effectiveness of WSHGs is less in these areas.

Both the Gini coefficient and the Theil's index clearly shows that inequality in WSHG savings is the highest in the north-eastern region. Several reasons contribute to this such as geographical isolation, limited access to education, and lack of supportive policies and programmes by the government. For example, states like

Table 21.1. Within-region, Across-region, and Across-state Inequality in WSHG Savings Measured by Theil's Index and Gini Coefficient.

		Within-region Inequality						Across-region Inequality	Across-state Inequality
	Year	Northern	North-eastern	Eastern	Central	Western	Southern		
Theil's index	2014	0.674	1.41	0.307	0.227	0.553	0.273	0.706	1.09
	2015	0.539	1.09	0.281	0.058	0.598	0.152	0.619	0.927
	2016	0.304	1.02	0.351	0.165	0.563	0.292	0.551	1.05
	2017	0.644	0.632	0.308	0.581	0.526	0.396	0.572	1.04
	2018	0.551	0.91	0.132	0.129	0.449	0.5	0.708	1.15
	2019	0.699	0.794	0.195	0.154	0.521	0.44	0.583	1.01
	2020	0.56	0.849	0.231	0.175	0.512	0.293	0.577	0.933
	2021	0.562	0.936	0.245	0.223	0.679	0.348	0.55	0.978
	2022	0.636	1.06	0.239	0.17	0.595	0.333	0.532	0.913
	2023	0.624	0.901	0.218	0.202	0.704	0.628	0.506	1.03
Gini coefficient	2014	0.586	0.778	0.416	0.357	0.531	0.189	0.741	0.734
	2015	0.536	0.699	0.403	0.176	0.547	0.291	0.713	0.699
	2016	0.403	0.675	0.443	0.268	0.535	0.399	0.731	0.727
	2017	0.548	0.56	0.407	0.551	0.519	0.457	0.692	0.724
	2018	0.516	0.642	0.269	0.228	0.482	0.502	0.744	0.74
	2019	0.587	0.604	0.315	0.26	0.514	0.475	0.698	0.713
	2020	0.537	0.627	0.357	0.307	0.514	0.385	0.695	0.696
	2021	0.543	0.667	0.37	0.339	0.577	0.315	0.686	0.706
	2022	0.576	0.701	0.349	0.303	0.548	0.334	0.666	0.697
	2023	0.571	0.661	0.329	0.332	0.585	0.485	0.662	0.728

Source: Authors' computation from data.

Mizoram and Nagaland from the north-east are quite isolated and cut off from the rest of the country. They do not have adequate schools and colleges which limits their education. They therefore lack the necessary skills and confidence to actively participate in SHG savings and decision-making processes. Moreover, some of these regions have limited infrastructure which can restrict women's access to financial services, markets, etc. Limited access to education, employment opportunities, infrastructure, and connectivity further marginalise women in these communities. Unless the government comes up with supportive policies to increase awareness and build up the necessary infrastructure, the north-east states shall lag in WSHGs. The central states on the other hand have exhibited a fluctuating trend. Absence of strong backup from the local Panchayats often allows the WSHGs to stop functioning properly. A strong government is a prerequisite as a stable government helps the local administration work freely. Inequality of the WSHG savings was lowest in the southern states in 2014. This is because southern states like Andhra Pradesh, Telangana, Tamil Nadu, and Kerala have a robust history of SHG movements. These states have implemented effective programmes to promote SHGs, providing them with institutional support, training, and access to credit. The southern states mostly have a matriarchal society, and the women are far more educated. This cultural acceptance leads to higher participation and contribution from women in SHGs. However, the recent variations in market structure and dynamics have affected the SHGs clearly which is reflected in their savings. Continuous monitoring and evaluation of SHG programmes is required to reduce the drop in savings of WSHGs.

The test for absolute convergence indicates β-convergence, having a significant (1%) value of −0.04 (Table 21.2, specification 1) with respect to the initial endowment. This means that the GR of the initially lower endowed states will 'catch-up' with the states with higher initial endowment. Interestingly, the Ramsey regression equation specification error (RESET) test of a mis-specified model rejects the null hypothesis of the no-omitted variable at 1% level of significance.

In the model of specification 2, the importance of two government-aided treatment variables in the form of amount of grant released and number of programmes was conducted along with the control variable of NSGDP in explaining the GR of WSHG savings over the prescribed years. Panel GLS estimation has been used (panels are controlled for heteroskedasticity) which shows that apart from the number of participations of SHG members in training and capacity building, other variables are positive and significant at 1% level of significance.

The value of the estimated slope coefficient of the β-convergence test, conditioned upon the amount of grant released and the number of participants is −0.11and is significant at 1% level of significance (Table 21.2, specification 3), which confirms the hypothesis of convergence over the defined period. The treatment variables apart from one of the control variables, NSGDP, are significant at 1% level of significance. Unlike the other specifications, here a non-linear term of initial WSHG savings was introduced. The coefficient of this variable is found to be positive and significant at 1% level of significance. This represents that the states eventually approach to their own 'Steady state', defined by the chosen parameters at different paces over time. Also, this model could not reject the null

Table 21.2. Beta Convergence Test.

Specification	1	2	3
$\ln(S_{i,t0})$	−0.0407063*** (0.006809)		−0.1136297*** (0.0207299)
$(\ln(S_{i,t0}))^2$			0.004751*** (0.001128)
$\ln(SGDP_i)$		0.7117374*** (0.035269)	−0.0272002 (0.0215717)
$\ln(GT_i)$		0.7136625*** (0.0367666)	0.0489083*** (0.0159297)
$\ln(SSZ_i)$		−0.0000227 (0.0000173)	0.0315021* (0.0105493)
NP_i		2.709913*** (0.4486624)	0.0000115*** (3.59e−06)
Constant	0.596273*** (0.0591625)		1.058661*** (0.210683)
R^2	0.6190		0.8784
F-statistics	$F(1, 22) = 35.74$***		$F(6, 17) = 60.83$***
Wald chi^2		$chi^2(3) = 1{,}107.96$***	
Ramsey RESET test	$F(3, 19) = 5.22$***		$F(3, 14) = 0.49$

Source: Authors' computation from data.

***$p < 0.01$, ** $p < 0.05$, *$p < 0.1$.

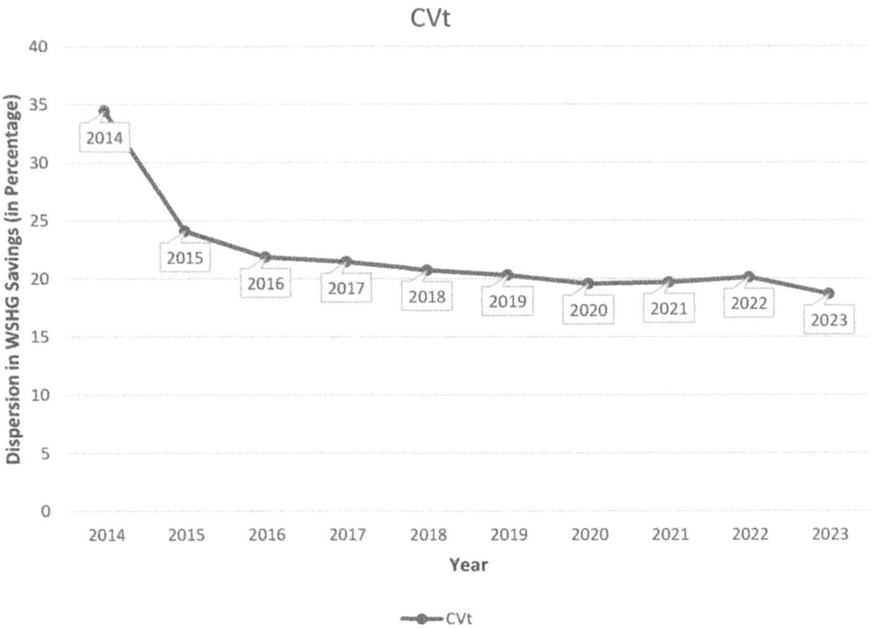

Fig. 21.2. Sigma Convergence Result. *Source*: Authors' computation from data.

hypothesis of no-omitted variables in the Ramsey RESET test. The comparison of the results tabulated above indicates the importance of relative convergence over absolute convergence in this study. In reality, it is true that the states facing different financial and socio-economical constraints can never converge to a common steady state, and therefore, the undergoing convergence should effectively take place with respect to their own ideals.

The plot of cross-states WSHG saving dispersion (measured by CV_t) against different time periods (Fig. 21.2) shows that apart from 2022, the dispersion in WSHG savings has declined over time, indicating σ-convergence. The dispersion has dropped significantly from the year 2014 to 2015 almost by 10%. But after 2015 up to 2023, the CVt has consistently declined at an average rate of 6.07% Year-On-Year (YOY) (except a slight increase in 2022). Since a relative measure such as CV_t has been introduced, the results become mean independent of each year and therefore can be safely compared across the periods.

Section V: Conclusion and Policy Prescription

SHGs have the potential to generate both income and employment for the poor. They have encouraged women of rural and semi-urban areas to initiate savings in banks. Women from different states have come forward with the idea of new job opportunities as well as the expansion of existing businesses. Thus, the SHGs have been able to satisfy to some extent the twin objectives of poverty removal and financial empowerment of women involved in SHGs. However, while the

SHG-BLP has experienced exponential growth over the past decade, there remain large regional disparities in the growth of the SHG movement with limited progress in certain regions. For example, almost 70% of the SHGs are concentrated in the southern regions. The present chapter has a twofold objective. First, it tries to analyse the inequality pattern in savings of WSHGs with the help of Theil's index and Gini coefficient. The results show that the inequality in the WSHG savings remains highest for north-eastern states. This may be attributed to factors like lack of education and skills, geographical isolation of the states, absence of appropriate infrastructure, etc. The eastern and the western states show moderate level of inequality. While inequality was found to be the lowest in southern states in 2014, it has been found to be increasing thereafter. The inequality across states and across regions were much higher than the within-region counterpart over the periods. For the second objective, the conditional convergence of the growth of WSHG savings was tested. The panel GLS estimation shows that apart from the number of participants for training and capacity-building programmes, the amount of grant released and NSGDP were found to be significant in explaining the growth of WSHG savings over the period of time across states. The findings showed that both conditional beta and sigma convergence have taken place with respect to the savings of WSHGs (2013–2014 to 2022–2023). If the disparity in savings has to be reduced, it is essential to know the factors that are important for the convergence of growth of WSHGs. Here, the fact that both the amount of grant released and the number of participants for training and capacity-building programmes are found to be highly significant proves that a continuous inflow of funds along with effective participation in government-aided programmes are required for the smooth operation of the SHGs. In other words, the activities of the SHGs can flourish further with the supply of sufficient financial support and productive training. Thus, it is expected that the backward states will eventually catch up to their ideal steady states in terms of WSHG savings and that the fruits of WSHG formation will be shared equally by all the states. The following recommendations can be considered for reducing the inter-state disparity in WSHG savings.

First, more resources must be spent on training and capacity building in the backward areas to enhance the entrepreneurial skill of the members of the SHGs effectively. Second, the SHG-BLP must be intensified in parts of the country where bank networking is poor. The total amount of grants sanctioned and grants released must also be scaled up for these backward areas. Lastly, organisations must also come forward to teach the SHG members the utilisation of funds appropriately. The financial sustainability of any SHG ultimately depends on the generation of further income from the loans taken from banks and the maintenance of savings.

Section VI: Limitations of the Study

Due to the unavailability of data, the time for studying the convergence of savings has been restricted to 2014–2023 though the SHG project by NABARD was started long back in the 1990s. For the same reason, some states could not be incorporated to match the consistency of the data taken.

References

Allison, P. D. (1978). Measures of inequality. *American Sociological Review*, *43*(6), 865–880.

Barro, R. J., Sala-i-Martin, X., Blanchard, O. J., & Hall, R. E. (1991). Convergence across states and regions. *Brookings Papers on Economic Activity*, *1991*(1), 107–182.

Baumol, W. J. (1986). Productivity growth, convergence, and welfare: What the long-run data show. *The American Economic Review*, *76*(5), 1072–1085.

Bhansali, P. (2019). Growth of SHG-bank linkage program in India [comparative study-region wise. *International Journal of Advance Research, Ideas and Innovations in Technology*, *5*(6), 4–13. www.IJARIIT.com

De la Fuente, A. (1997). The empirics of growth and convergence: A selective review. *Journal of Economic Dynamics and Control*, *21*(1), 23–73.

Deshmukh-Ranadive, J. (2004). *Women's self-help groups in Andhra Pradesh: Participatory poverty alleviation in action*. World Bank.

Ghosh, C., & Banerjee, T. (2010). Self help group participation and employment of the women: Myths and the reality. In L. Áron Kóczy (Ed.), *Proceedings of FIKUSZ 2010* (pp. 55–78). Óbuda University.

Giannetti, M. (2002). The effects of integration on regional disparities: Convergence, divergence or both? *European Economic Review*, *46*(3), 539–567.

Johnston, J. (1969). H. Theil economics and information theory. *The Economic Journal*, *79*(315), 601–602. https://doi.org/10.2307/2230396

Kadir, A., Majumder, S. H., & Mondal, B. (2024). Analyzing self-help group-bank linkages through volume of savings and credit: Insights from the northeastern states of India. *Agricultural Research Journal*, *61*(1), 75–85.

Mankiw, N. G., Romer, D., & Weil, D. N. (1992). A contribution to the empirics of economic growth. *The Quarterly Journal of Economics*, *107*(2), 407–437.

Midya, D. K., Hota, A., & Das, A. (2021). Empowerment of women through self help group: SHG participants' perception about enhancement of their capacity. *Journal of the Indian Anthropological Society/the Indian Anthropological Society*, *56*, 109–126.

Parida, P. C., & Sinha, A. (2010). Performance and sustainability of self-help groups in India: A gender perspective. *Asian Development Review*, *27*(01), 80–103.

Ravindra, K., & Tiwari, A. K. (2016). Relationship between poverty, women empowerment and SHGs: A study of Indian states. *International Journal of Managerial Studies and Research*, *4*(3), 1–10.

Sala-i-Martin, X. (2006). The world distribution of income: Falling poverty and … convergence, period. *The Quarterly Journal of Economics*, *121*(2), 351–397.

Sarania, R. (2015). Impact of self-help groups on economic empowerment of women in Assam. *International Research Journal of Interdisciplinary & Multidisciplinary Studies*, *1*(1), 148–159.

Sinha, P., & Navin, N. (2021). Performance of self-help groups in India. *Economic and Political Weekly*, *56*(5), 36–43.

Swain, R. B., & Wallentin, F. Y. (2009). Does microfinance empower women? Evidence from self-help groups in India. *International Review of Applied Economics*, *23*(5), 541–556.

Tabassum, K. (2024). Comparative roles and functioning of SHGs in different states of India. *International Journal of Financial Management and Economics*, *7*(2), 539–544. https://doi.org/10.33545/26179210.2024.v7.i2.413

Venkatesh, P. (2017). Revival of responsible cooperative movement through self help groups in India: A regional and agent wise analysis. *EPRA International Journal of Economic and Business Review(JEBR)*, *5*(12), 123–128. https://eprajournals.com/IJES/article/8165

Chapter 22

Impact of Alcohol Ban on Crime and Regional Development in India: The Case of Bihar

Rishabh Mukherjee[a] *and Rajeshwari Kumari*[b]

[a]*Public Policy and Tax, Ernst & Young, India*
[b]*Economic Advisory, Deloitte, UK*

Abstract

The World Health Organization (WHO) noted that alcohol consumption directly contributes to 2.6 million deaths per year globally. However, its indirect effect is far worse, resulting in about 3 million violent crimes each year, in the United States alone. Under such circumstances, considering a ban on alcohol consumption seems an obvious conclusion, possibly leading to lower crime rates, improved workplace productivity and reduced healthcare costs. However, due to a variety of social, cultural and economic consequences, global instances of alcohol ban are scarce and remote. Bihar is an Indian state, infamous for the widespread prevalence of crime. The state government identified high alcohol consumption as one of the main reasons behind it and implemented an Alcohol Ban in 2016. Our objective is to study the impact of the policy on crime in Bihar and analyse whether it has served its purpose. We have used a difference-in-difference (DiD) approach with Bihar being our treatment group and other Indian states as the control group. The DiD coefficient was positive (4.06) and significant, implying that crime, in fact, increased in the state. Subsequent regressions corroborated the robustness of our results. We identified that the absence of alcohol ban in neighbouring states, rampant corruption and poor enforcement of laws as key reasons behind the counterintuitive results. Poverty and income inequality are perhaps bigger factors behind

Changing Dimensions in Economic Development: Theories and Empirics, 303–315

doi:10.1108/978-1-83708-384-820261025

the high incidence of crime, and it is only through education, economic upliftment and social awareness that the government shall be able to reduce both consumption of alcohol and incidence of crime in the state.

Keywords: Alcohol ban; income inequality; crime; corruption; education

JEL Codes: I180; I320; K420; I280

1. Introduction

India has a long history of alcohol prohibition. In the directive principles of state policy in the Indian Constitution, Article 47 states that:

> The State shall regard the raising of the level of nutrition and the standard of living of its people and the improvement of public health as among its primary duties and, in particular, the State shall endeavour to bring about prohibition of the consumption except for medicinal purposes of intoxicating drinks and of drugs which are injurious to health.

Alcohol policy is a state subject in India, and therefore, state governments have the power to decide all policies related to alcohol. Total alcohol prohibition has existed in the Indian state of Gujarat since independence, and several other states have had prohibition at different points in time.

Bihar, one of India's most populous states with a population of around 125 million as of 2019, has been notorious for its crime since the pre-independence days. The state has perpetually remained poor, with its per capita income being at almost one-third of the national average (Mukherji & Mukherji, 2012). Additionally, it ranks the lowest in India for a number of development indicators. Bihar is also known to be a state where crime of all kinds is commonplace. Poverty, inequality in income, caste-based class division, rampant corruption, poor implementation of government policies, lack of employment opportunities and lack of infrastructure and industry have all played their parts in Bihar's state of affairs.

In 2016, the state government of Bihar passed the Bihar Prohibition and Excise Act 2016 which banned the sale and consumption of alcohol in the state. The main purpose of the law, as stated by the state government, was to reduce crime and violence in the state. This chapter aims to study the impact of the policy on crime in Bihar.

2. Literature Review

Kanbur (2007) noted that while there exists a causal link between poverty and conflict, the same cannot be said for economic inequality. Rapid economic growth naturally becomes an antidote to curb conflict of all kinds. Kang (2016) confirmed the conclusion and added that the perception about income inequality being considered a determinant of crime was mostly based on inadequately aggregated data sets, making its interpretation complex. Shah (2016) said that eliminating poverty in Bihar requires a holistic range of efforts with a focus on the agriculture sector and the need for industrialisation.

However, numerous studies in the past tried to estimate the relation between alcohol consumption and violent behaviour and found a definite correlation. A study was conducted to estimate the association between murder and alcohol in Sweden. It concluded that alcohol abuse and alcoholism were prevalent among 30% of the offenders of criminal homicide (Lindqvist, 1986). Another study (Welte & Wieczorek, 1998) suggested that 'heavy drinking and lower intelligence was a dangerous combination' and that lower intelligence showed a surprising 'booster effect' on violent offending when combined with high average alcohol consumption. The study used data from the first wave and second wave of the BLSYM (a five-year panel study of adolescent substance use and delinquency, from Buffalo, New York). In this study, the effect of low intelligence and high consumption of alcohol on violent behaviour was conducted through two tests of covariance. Bromley and Nelson (2002) showed that alcohol was noted as a contributory factor in 8% of recorded crime, but that the recorded role of alcohol was far higher for certain crime types: 48% of all harassment crimes; 36% of violent crime and 16% of criminal damage (other).

Another research that aimed to estimate the success of the alcohol ban in Bihar, used a DiD model and suggested that the policy was ineffective and found a significant increase in violent crimes post the policy implementation (Dar et al., n.d.). The paper also concluded that the ban was implemented more because of 'political considerations' than true welfare concerns. A major limitation of this chapter is the fact that it concentrated only on the impact along a singular-dimension crime. However, first-order impacts like incidents of public nuisance and spousal violence haven't been considered at all.

3. Global History of Alcohol Bans

Alcohol has been a part of human culture for centuries. Be it through ancient rituals or modern social gatherings, it has always found a central place in society. However, the laws that govern its consumption and sale vary widely across the globe. While countries like Sweden, Denmark and Finland have relaxed their alcohol policies since the mid-1990s, the Nordic countries continue to have some of the most stringent alcohol-related policies in Europe (der Velde et al., 2025).

Norway, especially, has had a fair tussle with liquor over the years. Between 1916 and 1926, the government prohibited sale of distilled spirits, while fortified wines were banned from 1917 to 1923. It came at a time, when Europe was war-torn and ensuring food security was far bigger a priority than diverting resources to produce alcohol (Johansen, 2013). However, problems like illegal production of alcohol, smuggling, prescription swindle, organised crime, questionable police practices and burgeoning corruption ensured that the programme failed (Johansen, 2013). But almost half a decade later, a total ban on alcohol advertising in 1975 led to a noticeable decline in liquor sales, thereby indicating a definite reduction in its consumption.

Today, while some countries discourage alcohol consumption to maintain social harmony and promote public health through their policy initiatives, many have outright banned its consumption and sale. This mainly includes Islamic countries like Afghanistan, Brunei, Iran, Kuwait, Saudi Arabia, among others, whose adherence to Islamic law and traditions prohibits alcohol consumption (Mamchii, 2024).

In 2020, the South African government imposed a five-week ban on liquor sales to 'ease pressure on the healthcare system and reduce deaths and injuries from alcohol-related incidents' in the wake of the Covid-19 pandemic. This quasi-natural experiment showed a startling result – the ban reduced injury-induced mortality by at least 14%, while reported instances of violent crimes decreased significantly. Homicides fell by 21%, assaults by 33% and reported rapes by 19% (Barron, 2024). The experiment served as good evidence about the causal relationship between alcohol consumption and incidence of crime. In the following section, we have decided to analyse this relation further through a case study of a similar ban introduced in Bihar, India.

4. Case Study: Impact of Alcohol Ban on Crime in Bihar, India

4.1. Data

In our analysis, we first look at how the consumption of alcohol (as a percentage of the population has changed) during our study period. For this, we have used data from the National Family Health Survey (NFHS). NFHS is a large-scale survey conducted in multiple rounds across the country on various social indicators.

Our primary objective is to investigate whether the alcohol ban enforced by the state government in 2016 has indeed led to a reduction in crime in Bihar. For this, we have used data from the National Crime Records Bureau (NCRB) from the years 2010–2019. The NCRB is an agency that has been established to collect and analyse crime data by the Government of India. In our analysis, we have considered the major Indian states in which the crime trends were similar to Bihar prior to the implementation of the ban. One problem that we faced was the unavailability of data for some states for certain years, and hence, we had to omit those from our analysis. Moreover, we decided not to include the Union Territories in our study as the structure of their governance and operations is very different from Indian states.

The data collected took into account all types of serious and violent crimes like murder, dacoity, robbery, burglary, theft, riots, kidnapping, rape, to name a few. It includes all cognisable crimes reported under both the Indian Penal Code (IPC) and the Special and Local Laws (SLL).

The Government of India conducts a census every 10 years where it collects detailed information about the population and various other socio-economic and demographic characteristics. In order to normalise our data and avoid any scale effects, we calculated 'crime per 10,000 people' and used that as a variable in our analysis. Since there was no census in 2021 because of the ongoing pandemic, we used population data from the 2011 census in order to do this as it is the latest data available.

4.2. Empirical Strategy

4.2.1. Methodology: DiD

To study the causal impact of banning alcohol on crime, we used a DiD approach. The DiD estimator measures the difference between the difference in the crime in Bihar before and after the Bihar Prohibition and Excise Act 2016 came into effect and in the average crime in other Indian states before and after the law. We decided to use a DiD approach because it allows us to establish causality, and it eliminates the issue of unobserved elements confounding the results. The treatment group is Bihar, and the control group consists of other Indian states, namely Arunachal Pradesh, Assam, Himachal Pradesh, Jammu and Kashmir, Jharkhand, Maharashtra, Manipur, Meghalaya, Odisha, Punjab, Rajasthan, Sikkim and Tripura. The treatment is the prohibition of alcohol. Since we are using a DiD approach, any difference in the crime rate can be attributed to the alcohol ban. Our regression equation is as follows:

$$Y_{it} = \beta_0 + \beta_1 * \text{treatment} + \beta_2 * \text{post} + \beta_3 * \text{treatment} * \text{post} + \varepsilon_{it}$$

where:

Y is the crime rate in state i in time t.

β_0 is the average crime in other Indian states before the treatment.

β_1 is the difference in crime between other Indian states and Bihar before treatment.

β_2 is the change in crime in other Indian states between the pre- and post-treatment.

β_3 is the DiD estimator.

ε_{it} is the error term.

We used the bootstrapping method with all our regression. Since our sample size is very small we cannot assume that our sample distribution would be normal. Therefore, using the bootstrapping method, we were able to resample our dataset 500 times and derive a better estimate of our data. This method helped us to reduce our standard errors significantly, thereby achieving a better and more accurate estimate of the standard errors.

4.3. Descriptive Statistics

In this part of our analysis, we look at how the consumption of alcohol (as a percentage of the population) has changed during our study period. We have considered data for both men and women from the NFHS report for two years 2015 (a year before the implementation of the ban) and 2019 (the first available report after the ban) (Fig. 22.1).

We observe that consumption of alcohol among men in the control group has reduced from 38.4% in 2015 to 28.7% in 2019. While in the treatment group (Bihar), we see a more drastic reduction in alcohol consumption among men, which goes down from 28.9% in 2015 to 15.5% in 2019. However, among the women, consumption of alcohol has reduced (from 5.9% in 2015 to 5.3% in 2019) but has marginally increased (from 0.2% to 0.4%) in the treatment group. Because the increase in consumption among women is negligible, we do not think that would affect our results.

Fig. A1 shows the evolution of crime in all the states in the treatment and control groups. Apart from a few fluctuations during some years, crimes in the states have maintained a steady upward trend during the time of our study.

4.4. Results

4.4.1. Parallel Trend Assumption

To confirm our parallel trend assumption and our results, we plot our before and after treatment in the 14 states graphically:

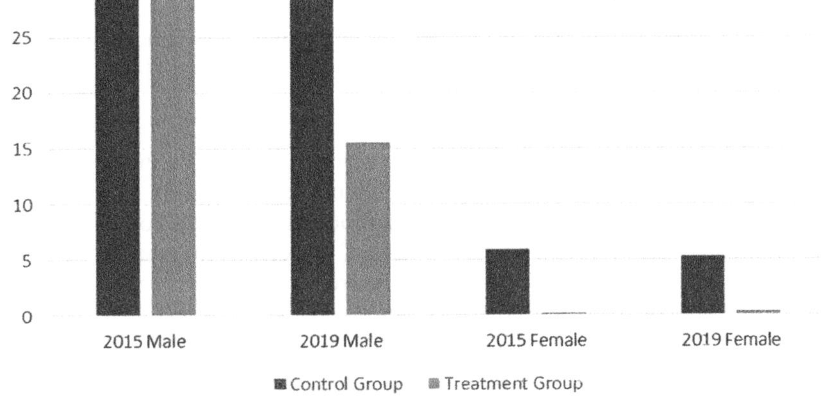

Fig. 22.1. Alcohol Consumption as a Percentage of Population. *Source*: Authors' own calculations based on NCRB data.

Fig. 22.2 shows the trends in crimes in the treatment and control groups before and after the treatment. The observed means in the treatment group and the control group move parallelly before the treatment kicks in. After the treatment, crime has increased in both the treatment group and the control group. The increase in crime is more substantial in the treatment group than in the control group.

To validate our assumption even further we do the *p-trends test* to formally assess the parallel trajectory:

Parallel-trends test (pretreatment time period).
H0: Linear trends are parallel.
$chi^2(1) = 1.22$.
Prob > $chi^2 = 0.2687$.

We cannot reject the null hypothesis of parallel linear trends. Therefore, we can conclude that the linear trends are parallel in this case.

Table 22.1 shows the results from initial regression with a total of 140 observations of crime clustered at the state level. Our treatment group is the state of Bihar that banned the consumption of alcohol in 2016. The control group consists of the remaining 13 states where alcohol is sold and consumed. Nearly all the covariates' coefficients are significant at either 5% or 10% significance level, including the interaction time*treated, that is, DiD. The DiD coefficient is 4.06 which is positive and significant, indicating that alcohol ban increased crimes. The findings suggest that the ban led to a significant increase in crime to the tune of 21 per 10,000 population.

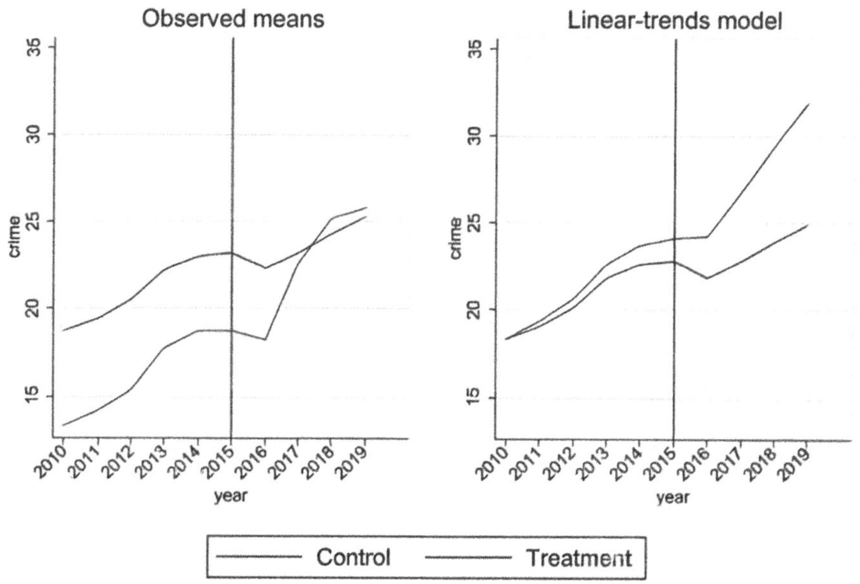

Fig. 22.2. Graphical Diagnostics for Parallel Trends. *Source*: Based on authors' own calculations.

Table 22.1. Primary Regression Estimates.

Variables	(1) Crime
Time	2.591** (1.230)
Treated	4.862** (2.365)
DiD	4.064*** (1.230)
Constant	21.21*** (2.365)
Observations	140
R^2	0.042

Source: Based on authors' own calculations.
Note: Standard errors in parentheses.
***$p < 0.01$, **$p < 0.05$.

Table 22.2 reports our DiD estimates of the impact of alcohol prohibition on crime. The estimates control for time and state-fixed effects. In column (1), the Average Treatment Effect on the Treated (ATET) estimate is 4.06, which is positive and significant, indicating that there is a 4-point increase in crime per 10,000 population in the treatment states, that is, Bihar as compared to the rest of the 13 control states. In other words, if the policy of alcohol ban was not implemented, the crime per 10,000 population would be lower by 4 points. Each result in column (2) shows how much the crime has increased in that year in comparison to 2010 (base year). We can see that crime increases every year, falls a little in the

Table 22.2. DiD Estimates of the Impact of Alcohol Ban on Crime.

Variables	(1) ATET	(2) Controls
2011.year		0.713** (0.308)
2012.year		1.767*** (0.599)
2013.year		3.528*** (0.775)
2014.year		4.367*** (0.912)
2015.year		4.554*** (1.114)
2016.year		3.359** (1.447)
2017.year		4.498*** (1.494)
2018.year		5.709*** (1.705)
2019.year		6.748*** (1.871)
r1vs0.DiD	4.064*** (1.230)	
Constant		18.37*** (2.010)
Observations	140	140

Source: Based on authors' own calculations.
Note: Standard errors in parentheses.
***$p < 0.01$, **$p < 0.05$.

year 2016 but then starts rising in the consecutive years. This suggests that the ban on alcohol in fact led to an increase in crime which again indicates that the policy has no effect.

To examine these results further, we conducted a regression with 'i.year*i.treated' to investigate the yearly effect of the policy (Table AI). We study the *p*-value and find that although the policy was implemented from 1 April, we do not see any results till 2017. This might be due to the reason that on 2 October 2016, the Bihar government formulated the Bihar Prohibition and Excise Act, 2016, which reacted the all penal provisions associated with violation of the ban, that is, minimum 10 years of jail term which may extend to life imprisonment. But the effectiveness of this Act didn't last long as we noticed that from 2019, the crime started increasing again.

4.4.2. Explaining the Anomalies

The results of our analysis might come across to be a little startling. The ban on alcohol was imposed to ensure a reduction in crime in the state. However, our results show that crime has in fact increased in the state of Bihar after the alcohol ban. This could be attributed to a variety of factors.

1. No ban on alcohol in neighbouring states – Because the sale and purchase of liquor is illegal in Bihar, local people often bring alcohol from other neighbouring states like Uttar Pradesh, West Bengal, Jharkhand and Madhya Pradesh, where it is available cheaply and in abundance. The ease of interstate travelling in India only aggravates the situation. Travelling to other regions to meet their addiction leads to the average Bihari spending more and thus lowering his welfare.
2. Corruption and poor implementation of laws – Bihar has a reputation for being one of the most corrupt states in the country. Rampant corruption in the state has ensured that some shops continue to sell liquor by bribing the local authorities, including the police. Moreover, the laws haven't been implemented in full measure across the state due to political and bureaucratic bottlenecks, inefficiency of the people and corruption, again.
3. Other bigger reasons behind the incidence of crime – It is important to recognise that poverty and income inequality are possibly two bigger factors contributing to the incidence of crime in Bihar. The stark disparity between the wealthy and the poor creates a fertile ground for criminal activities. Individuals often turn to crime out of desperation or as a perceived shortcut to financial security. The lack of access to education and employment for the lower-income population exacerbates the situation, potentially leading to higher crime rates as people struggle to survive and improve their circumstances in an unequal society.

5. Conclusion and Discussion

Our results clearly show that the alcohol ban had no impact on the reduction of crime in Bihar. Crime, in fact, increased in the state. The Bihar government, however, claims that the ban was successful, but there have been continuous relaxations on the ban. Discussions to revoke it all together are also doing rounds. Though there are political reasons for it, such as the ruling party fears losing a large percentage of their vote share ahead of the elections, the prohibition on the sale of alcohol also has resulted in massive revenue losses for the government (through the duties).

If reducing crime is the primary objective, the government must take other measures to curb it. More stringent implementation of laws, proper policing and ensuring that the social and economic divide between the rich and the poor is reduced would help solve the problem. Empowering people through better education, adequate employment opportunities and improved social inclusivity is bound to improve peoples' lives, making them less likely to engage in criminal activities.

When it comes to tackling alcohol consumption, the best way is to spend more on education and awareness drives, which would discourage people from consuming alcohol by educating people about the harm of liquor consumption. The entire problem is a demand-driven one, as alcohol, being an addiction for most people, has a pretty inelastic demand. The policy implemented by the state focused on breaking the supply chain, but till the time the authorities are able to reduce the demand of the commodity, people will find ways to peddle alcohol legally or illegally, and crimes would therefore not decrease.

Acknowledgements

The completion of this chapter would not have been possible without the support and guidance of Professor Manuel Bagues, University of Warwick. His encouragement and insightful feedback were instrumental in accomplishing this task. We thank all the staff of the Department of Economics, University of Warwick, for their cooperation and kind support throughout our research period. Special thanks to the University of Warwick for equipping us with all the necessary tools and resources to conduct such research. Words cannot express our gratitude to Professor Dr Debashis Mazumdar, Head of Department of Economics, The Heritage College, Kolkata, India, for his invaluable support and continuous motivation. We express our sincere gratitude to our batchmate at Warwick, Sharvari Rajadhyaksha, whose constant help has been instrumental in refining the methodology and scope of this research. Finally, we would like to express our sincere thanks to our parents, friends, well-wishers and the Divine power whose encouragement kept us focused and helped us overcome numerous challenges during our research journey.

References

Barron, K. (2024). *Lessons from South Africa's alcohol ban*. WZB Berlin Social Science Center. https://www.wzb.eu/en/news/lessons-from-south-africas-alcohol-ban

Bromley, R. D. F., & Nelson, A. L. (2002). Alcohol-related crime and disorder across urban space and time: Evidence from a British city. *Geoforum*, *33*(2), 239–254. Retrieved

March 20, 2022, from https://www.academia.edu/10902630/Alcohol_related_crime_and_disorder_across_urban_space_and_time_evidence_from_a_British_city

Dar, A., Sahay, A., Malik, A., Stuart, B., Barnwal, P., Kumar, C., Mantri, P., Verma, R., & Gupta, P. (n.d.). *Designing policy in weak states: Unintended consequences of alcohol prohibition in Bihar*. Retrieved November 6, 2020, from http://barrett.dyson.cornell.edu/NEUDC/paper_586.pdf

Der Velde, L., Shabaan, A. N., Månsson, A., Wennberg, P., Allebeck, P., Karlsson, T. G., Flodin, P., Eikemo, T. A., Knudsen, A. K. S., de Soysa, I., Skogen, J. C., GBD 2019 Nordic Alcohol Collaborators, Gissler, M., McGrath, J. J., Sigfusdottir, I. D., Sigurvinsdottir, R., Pasovic. M., Danielsson A.-K., & Agardh, E. E. (2025). Alcohol-attributed disease burden and formal alcohol policies in the Nordic countries (1990–2019): An analysis using the Global Burden of Disease Study 2019. *European Journal of Public Health*, *35*(1), 52–59. https://academic.oup.com/eurpub/article/35/1/52/7915047

Johansen, P. O. (2013). The Norwegian alcohol prohibition: A failure. *Journal of Scandinavian Studies in Criminology and Crime Prevention*, *14*(1), 46–63. https://www.scup.com/doi/full/10.1080/14043858.2013.771909#:~:text=The%20prohibition%20was%20based%20on,not%20considered%20in%20the%20reckoning

Kanbur, R. (2007). *Poverty, inequality, and conflict* (pp. 3–5). International Peace Institute. http://www.jstor.com/stable/resrep09599.6

Kang, S. (2016). Inequality and crime revisited: Effects of local inequality and economic segregation on crime. *Journal of Population Economics*, *29*(2), 593–626. http://www.jstor.com/stable/44280406

Lindqvist, P. (1986). Criminal homicide in Northern Sweden 1970–1981: Alcohol intoxication, alcohol abuse and mental disease. *International Journal of Law and Psychiatry*, *8*(1), 19–37.

Mamchii, O. (2024). *13 Countries where alcohol is banned and why*. Best Diplomats. https://bestdiplomats.org/countries-where-alcohol-is-banned/

Mukherji, A., & Mukherji, A. (2012). *Bihar: What went wrong? And what changed?* Retrieved March 20, 2022, from https://repository.iimb.ac.in/handle/2074/13747

Shah, M. (2016). Eliminating poverty in Bihar: Paradoxes, bottlenecks and solutions. *Economic and Political Weekly*, *51*(6), 56–65. https://www.jstor.org/stable/44004355

Welte, J. W., & Wieczorek, W. F. (1998). Alcohol, intelligence, and violent crime in young males. *Journal of Substance Abuse*, *10*(3), 309–319.

Appendix

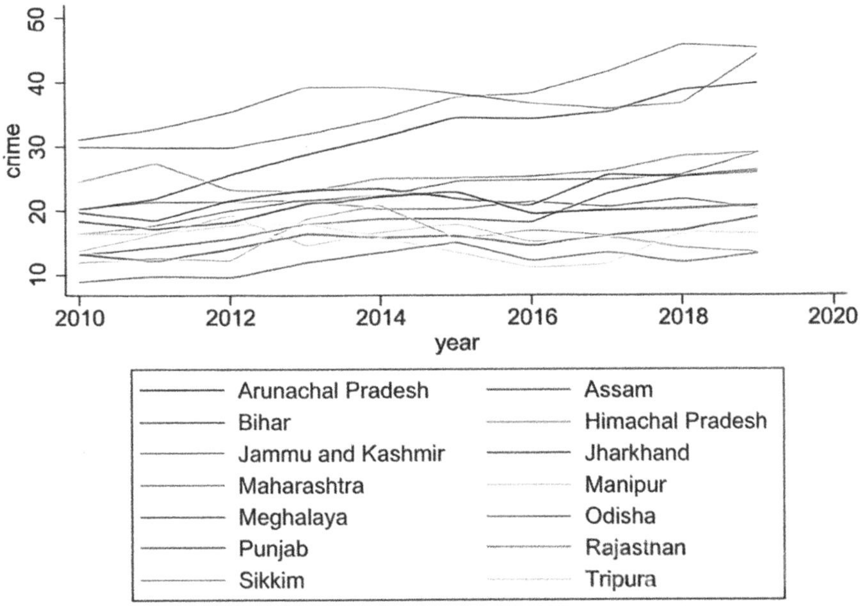

Fig. A1. Evolution of Crime in all the States Under Study. *Source*: Authors' own calculations based on NCRB data.

Table AI. Secondary Regression Estimates.

Variables	**(1) Crime**	**(2) *p*-Value**
_Iyear_2011	0.693** (0.350)	0.048
_Iyear_2012	1.735*** (0.661)	0.009
_Iyear_2013	3.449*** (0.849)	0.000
_Iyear_2014	4.279*** (1.006)	0.000
_Iyear_2015	4.477*** (1.245)	0.000
_Iyear_2016	3.545** (1.465)	0.016
_Iyear_2017	4.429*** (1.539)	0.004
_Iyear_2018	5.535*** (1.767)	0.002
_Iyear_2019	6.608*** (1.968)	0.001
_Itreated_1	−5.552** (2.211)	0.012
_IyeaXtre_2011_1	0.273 (0.350)	0.435
_IyeaXtre_2012_1	0.445 (0.661)	0.501
_IyeaXtre_2013_1	1.104 (0.849)	0.194
_IyeaXtre_2014_1	1.242 (1.006)	0.217
_IyeaXtre_2015_1	1.079 (1.245)	0.386
_IyeaXtre_2016_1	1.462 (1.465)	0.318
_IyeaXtre_2017_1	5.031*** (1.539)	0.001
_IyeaXtre_2018_1	6.496***(1.767)	0.000
_IyeaXtre_2019_1	6.028*** (1.968)	0.002
Constant	18.77*** (2.211)	0.000
Observations	140	140
R^2	0.080	0.080

Source: Based on authors' own calculations.
Note: Standard errors in parentheses.
***$p < 0.01$, **$p < 0.05$.

Chapter 23

Gender Differences in Occupation: A Sector-wise Analysis with PLFS Data in West Bengal

Madhurima Saha

Department of Economics, University of Calcutta, India
Department of Economics, South Calcutta Girls' College, India

Abstract

The present study aims to examine the age-wise occupational disparity in West Bengal using National Classification of Occupation (NCO) classifications between working age male and female workers by different occupation status using the latest Periodic Labour Force Survey (PLFS) data 2022–2023 separately for the rural and urban sectors. Three different age cohorts that are (15–24) as young, (25–44) as middle and (45–65) as old are considered here to examine the age-wise contribution in each occupation of both the workers. The substantial differences in occupations have been observed by not only gender but also sectors. Occupations in urban West Bengal are mainly semi-skilled and high-skilled types, whereas in the rural sector, the predominance of agricultural activity and elementary occupations led the workers to perform mainly low-skilled occupations. The contribution of youth female workers in professional occupations is notable in both the sectors. An ordered logit model is performed to determine the possible personal and household factors for the participation of different ranks of occupations for separate gender of both the sectors where marital status, number of children and dependency ratio are found to be potential obstacles for the females to engage in high-rank occupations. Finally, this chapter concludes with some policy suggestions.

Keywords: Occupation; gender; sector; age; logit; PLFS

JEL Codes: C10; J21; J24; J71

Changing Dimensions in Economic Development: Theories and Empirics, 317–328

doi:10.1108/978-1-83708-384-820261026

1. Introduction

The status of female employment has been the subject of research interest in the present Indian context. The absence of women in the workforce has a severe economic impact as the development of an economy depends on the joint contribution of both men and women. Discrimination in employment is defined as the difference in share of types of activities and quality of jobs between males and females, given the same level of effort. Several survey reports are claiming that the labour force participation rate of women has been increasing in India during the past few years, but the main concern is that whether the status of women has improved by performing high-paid skilled jobs or whether the majority of them are engaged in low-paid unskilled activities. This study mainly tries to look at this matter by the distributional analysis of female workers compared to male workers by the occupation categories at NCO one-digit level. The study examines the employment gap between working age male and female workers by the distribution of different occupation categories using the latest PLFS 2022–2023 data to analyse the prevailing occupational discrimination by gender in work status at present context. This study only focuses on West Bengal, motivated by the fact that in the past few years, the female worker population ratio (FWPR) of West Bengal has been found to have increased, creating a more balanced workforce. Moreover, according to the Employment Exchange Statistics Report (GOI, 2023), Tamil Nadu had the highest number of women jobseekers (36.1 lakh) on the live register of employment exchanges, followed by West Bengal (24.6 lakh) among the major states in India. In this background, the study examines the employment disparity in West Bengal by principal occupation categories at NCO one-digit level of working age male and female workers using the latest PLFS 2023 data for the period July 2022–June 2023. The analysis has been done separately for rural and urban West Bengal as the job characteristics of workers differ between sectors.

2. Review of Literature

The literature mentioned above mainly focused on the pattern of occupational segregation by gender into the differences in human capital accumulation and examined the incidence of discrimination across occupations. Bertrand (2011) used gender differences in cognitive skills and analysed the differences in occupations and wages between men and women, whereas according to another study (Welch, 2000), the women have a comparative advantage in cognitive skills relative to manual skills, and these facts are likely to explain why women are absorbed more in cognitive-intensive jobs. The occupational segregation is lower among educated persons and the permanent workers (Chattopadhyay et al., 2013) and higher in urban sectors as compared to rural sectors (Agrawal & Agrawal, 2015). Occupational segregation by different social groups has been empirically analysed in some other studies: Agrawal (2016), Rammohan et al. (2017), Madheswaran and Attewell (2007). A state-level analysis of occupational segregation using NCO classifications (Sharma, 2018) indicates that West Bengal has low occupational segregation in terms of main urban workers, whereas high values of segregation are found in Gujarat, Haryana and Punjab, which calls for immediate action. Chakraborty and Chakraborty (2010) explored that limited opportunities in agriculture force the women to seek non-farm work with very little formal education in generally low-paying jobs like beedi-rolling, tailoring, zari work (a kind of embroidery) and production of fireworks in Murshidabad and South 24 parganas. Rathee and Sarkar (2023), using primary data of Paschim Bardhaman, attempted to look at various aspects of the problem of gender inequality among the Santhal tribes and found significant gender inequality.

3. Objective

The above literature extensively studied the occupational segregation, but the major limitations of the existing literature are that they mainly focused on gender- or caste-based occupational segregation in the Indian context. Our study will fill this gap in the literature by analysing the employment gap in occupation between male and female workers by quality of occupations across different ages, and in this sense, it is a unique contribution to the literature.

The main objective of the present study is to examine the relative position of working age females in the labour market of West Bengal compared to the position of their male counterparts by their contribution of each occupation using the PLFS 2022–2023 data. The scenario has been analysed in different occupations by NCO classification separately in rural and urban West Bengal as the demographic features vary between sectors. The study wants to locate whether the major concentration of female workers is towards high-ranking occupations or low-ranking occupations and how it differs from the male counterparts to find out the prevailing occupation gap. For the entire analysis, the working age (15–65) is divided into three separate age cohorts, which are '15–24 years' as the young age group, '25–44 years' as the middle age group and '45–65 years' as the old age group.

4. Methodology

The study has applied a discrete choice model with the ordered logit specification to consider different alternative and mutually exclusive situations of performing occupations of different ranks. Here, the model is used to investigate and determine the effect of descriptive variables of age, age squared, education and social groups and impact of each of these variables on the likelihood of individuals to be placed at one of three types of occupation categories. Ordered logit in our study produces predictions about the probability of participation of male and female workers in different ranks of occupations. We have regrouped the dependent variable in three different categories and put the ranks according to their nature of work, so the best way to express the numerical relationships between this dependent variable and a set of explanatory variables is by ordered logit model as the rank ordering of the dependent variable is defensible.

5. Employment Distribution by Occupation Categories

Table 23.1 describes the distribution of the workforce of West Bengal by occupation categories separately for male and female workers in rural and urban India. The distribution has been performed for three different age cohorts which can be defined as 15–24 years as the young age group, 25–44 years as the middle age group and 45–65 years as the old age group. The reason for consideration of different age cohorts is due to the fact that participation in different economic activities differs with the difference in ages. An old-aged worker seems to be engaged in the work which can be different from the young-aged worker. The occupations are ranked as high, middle and low according to their nature of work.

The comparison of occupations between the sectors reveals that in urban sectors, the occupations are mainly high-skilled and semi-skilled types, whereas in the rural sectors, the workers are mainly engaged in low-skilled occupations. This is because of the predominance of primary activities in the rural economy where most of the workers are dependent, followed by the elementary activities or craft-related works as a second choice of livelihood. In the urban sectors, however, the main dominating activities for both of the male and female workers are professionals and service work which are mainly identified as skilled activities by their nature of work. In the rural economy, the share of professionals and service activities is low compared to the share in the urban sectors, among all other high-status occupations for both the genders. In the urban economy, among several low-graded occupations, the contributions are notably observed from craft-related works and elementary activities.

A detailed analysis by gender reveals that most of the high- and semi-skilled occupations have been dominated by the male workers though there are substantial differences between the rural and urban West Bengal during 2022–2023. It is observed that among high-skilled occupations, females are only dominating the professional occupations in both the rural and urban West Bengal during the mentioned period. This is mainly due to the increasing participation of females in teaching and health professionals as women employment in teaching in both primary and secondary levels has changed substantially and has been increasing over the years, and in health sector, they are mainly engaged as nursing professionals, including midwives which are also increasing substantially because of the employment created by public programmes in health, especially the National Rural Health Mission (NRHM). Among the semi-skilled activities, the participations of both male and female workers are higher in service work activities compared to clerical jobs in both the sectors. Notably, the share of female workers in service work activities is higher than their male counterparts only in urban West Bengal during our study period. Among the low-skilled occupations, the participation of females is mostly higher in agriculture and allied activities and craft-related trade activities only in rural West Bengal, whereas plant and machinery operators' occupation is completely dominated by the male workers reflecting the highest occupation gap in both rural and urban sectors. In case of elementary occupations, the share of female workers is marginally higher than their male counterparts though only for old-aged workers in both the sectors.

Table 23.1. Distribution (in Percentage) of Workforce by Occupation Categories for the Age Cohorts 15–24, 25–44 and 45–65 During 2022–2023.

Occupations	Rural						Urban					
	15–24		25–44		45–65		15–24		25–44		45–65	
	Male	Female	Male	Female	Male	Female	Male	Female	Male	Female	Male	Female
Managers	1	0	2	1	1	0.3	3	1	7	1	7	2
Professionals	2	16	4	6	2	4	7	34	10	26	8	11
Technicians	1	0	2	1	1	1	4	4	6	5	5	5
Clerks	1	2	2	1	1	0	3	5	6	5	6	2
Service workers	11	9	17	9	13	9	18	26	24	29	29	34
Skilled workers in agriculture	14	24	22	28	44	37	0.2	0	1	2	3	3
Craft-related trade activities	22	39	17	26	12	22	27	27	19	17	16	19
Plant operators	6	0	9	1	5	1	9	0	12	1	9	2
Elementary occupations	43	10	26	27	22	27	28	4	15	14	15	22

Source: Author's own calculation from PLFS 2022–2023 data.

The age-wise analysis reveals the substantial differences in the contribution between male and female workers towards each occupation for different age groups. Considering the young age group (15–29 years), the study explored that the male workers from this age group are mainly engaged in elementary activities in the rural economy followed by craft-related activities, whereas female workers of rural economy from this age cohort are mainly concentrated in craft-related trade activities followed by agricultural activities. The female workers from this age group have a notable contribution in professional work among the high-skilled occupations in rural West Bengal, whereas the contributions of males are found in the service work to a little extent. The distribution of the middle age group (25–44 years) in the rural economy infers the major concentration of both the workers in agriculture, craft and elementary activities, and notably, in all these three activities, the share of female workers dominates the share of their male counterparts. Among the high-skilled occupations, the notable contribution is only found in service activities where the share of male workers increases as their age increases, whereas the share of female workers remains the same. Analysis of old age cohort (45–65 years) in the rural economy infers the highest concentration of workers in the agriculture and related activities where male workers are dominating with share more than 40%, whereas the female workers from this age groups are leading the craft and elementary occupations with the share a little above 20%. The scenario of urban economy is somehow different due to its demographic characteristics. The distribution of young age group reveals the major concentration of urban male workers in craft and elementary activities followed by service activities, whereas the females from this age groups are mainly concentrated in high-skilled professional activities with more than 30% share followed by low-skilled craft and semi-skilled service activities with the share around 26%. The distribution of the middle age group reveals that both male and female workers of urban West Bengal have the highest share in service works which is mainly dominated by the females. In case of the old age group, both the workers are found to be mainly concentrated in service works with around 30% share followed by craft-related trade activities with share near around 20%, and surprisingly, both of these activities have been dominated by the female workers of urban West Bengal.

6. Econometric Model

In this study, we apply ordered logit regression. The ordered logit model estimates one equation over all levels of the dependent variable. In the ordered logit model, there is an observed ordinal variable, Y. This Y, in turn, is a function of another variable, Y^*, that is not measured. The probability of participation of male and female workers in different ranks of occupations has been predicted by dividing up the domain of a logistic distribution into three categories defined by two cut points, $c1$ and $c2$. We assume that the extent of participation of a person in different skilled occupations, y^*, depends on household and personal characteristics:

In terms of occupation categories,

$$y_i^* = \alpha + \Sigma_k \beta_k X_{ik} + \varepsilon_i \tag{1}$$

where

$$E(\varepsilon_i) = 0$$

$$V(\varepsilon_i) = \sigma^2.$$

Equation (1) is used to find out the probability of participation in different ranks of occupation of a person. Here, α is the intercept term, x includes all the explanatory variables and β is the corresponding coefficient. We assume that ε has standard logistic distribution. The mean of the error terms is zero and variance is σ^2.

In this model, y_i*is a non-observable latent variable. What is observed is the ordinal variable y related to y^* defined in terms of occupation categories:

$y = 0$ if a person is engaged in low-skilled occupations which comprise of skilled labour in agriculture and forestry and fishery works, craft-related trade activities, plant operators, elementary occupations;

$y = 1$ if a person is engaged in semi-skilled occupations which comprise clerk and service workers;

$y = 2$ if a person is engaged in high-skilled occupations which comprise managers, professionals and technicians.

7. Construction of Variables

A number of explanatory variables have been considered to predict the outcome of the ordinal dependent variable. Age is used as a proxy to the experience of the workers. As we have considered the three different age groups in the study, the best way to capture the effects of age increment in the regression model is by creating an age dummy. This can predict how experience matters as a person moves to the higher-order skilled occupations. The variable 'age' takes the value 1 if the workers are from an old-aged group, that is, 45–65 years, and 0 otherwise. Social status and education among the person specific factors are also used as regressors in the model as they have some significant reflections in the labour market. As the education and social groups data are provided as a categorical form in the PLFS schedule, so we have created a dummy for different levels of education and different social groups. To capture the effect of marriage and religion on the participation of different ranks of occupations, the study has constructed 'Marriage' and 'Religion' dummy variables, respectively. To understand whether any formal training provides any positive impact on the workers to engage in high-rank occupations, a 'formal training' variable has been created as a dummy. Finally, among the household -specific factors, the study has considered the number of children in a household and dependency ratio of a worker. Children of a household are considered below 15 years of age as defined in PLFS schedule, and dependency ratio is the ratio between the dependent person of a household that is persons below 15 years of age and above 65 years of age as a proportion of the household size.

8. Empirical Results

The age-wise distributional change in occupational categories as described in the above is analysed in Table 23.2 in terms of estimated coefficients of ordered logit model separately for male and female workers. From the estimated coefficients, we can locate the effects of household specific and personal factors on the status of occupation types to assess how the factors are affecting their degree of employment in both rural and urban economy of West Bengal during 2022–2023.

The lower panel of the table provides the value of χ^2 statistic and pseudo R^2 that are used to test the overall significance of the model. As can be seen in Table 23.2, the variable age dummy is positively significant for rural female

Table 23.2. Ordered Logit Model of Participation in Different Ranks of Occupation in Both Rural and Urban West Bengal During 2022–2023.

	Rural		Urban	
Explanatory Variables	**Male**	**Female**	**Male**	**Female**
Age	−0.005	0.76**	0.52***	0.33*
Education				
Primary	0.79***	0.88***	0.38***	0.42***
Middle	1.35***	1.55***	0.70***	0.93***
Secondary	1.73***	2.30***	1.15***	1.44***
Higher secondary	2.29***	3.06***	1.66***	3.21***
Diploma	2.76***	4.34***	2.80***	4.45***
Graduate	3.67***	4.59***	3.09***	4.54***
Postgraduate	4.63***	5.56***	3.96***	4.93***
Caste and religion				
SC	0.03	−0.03	−0.29***	−0.18*
OBC	0.20***	−0.08	0.09**	−0.18**
General	0.39***	−0.17**	0.45***	0.22***
Religion	−0.40***	−0.40***	0.07***	0.03
Other factors				
Marriage	0.90**	−0.56***	0.01	−0.11*
Formal training	0.29***	0.22***	0.50***	0.35***

Table 23.2. (*Continued*)

	Rural		Urban	
Explanatory Variables	**Male**	**Female**	**Male**	**Female**
Children	−0.09***	−0.14***	0.03	0.04
Dependency ratio	0.24***	−0.13	0.06	−0.23*
Cut 1	3.03	2.77	1.64	1.23
Cut 2	4.42	3.94	3.38	3.18
No. of observations	56,838	27,725	42,402	12,826
LR (chi^2)	10,122.4	6,542.67	15,124.7	7,310.02
Prob. > F	0.0000	0.0000	0.0000	0.0000
Pseudo R^2	0.134	0.2021	0.1672	0.2665

Source: Author's own calculation from PLFS 2022–2023 data.
Note: Age, religion, marriage and formal training are dummy variables; LR: Long Run.
$*p < 0.05$, $**p < 0.01$, $***p < 0.001$.

workers and in the urban area for both male and female workers, which infers that as age increases, the workers are getting more likely to be placed on high-skilled jobs may be due to their experience by working in practical fields. The positive coefficients for different levels of education predict that compared to illiterate workers, the probability of engagement in high-skilled jobs is higher for the highly educated workers which are quite obvious. As the level of education increases, both the male and female workers from the rural and urban areas are likely to get placed on high-paid skilled occupations. Surprisingly, the coefficients suggest that in rural areas, the probability of higher educated (that is above graduate level) workers of both the genders are more likely to involve in high-skilled jobs than their urban counterparts. Notably, the analysis reveals that almost for all education categories, the return to education is higher for female workers than male workers in both rural and urban sectors in regard to the participation of skilled activities.

Analysis by caste and religion shows the substantial differences among the participation of male and female workers between rural and urban sectors. The Other Backward Community (OBC) and general category male workers are more likely to perform skilled work in both rural and urban sectors of West Bengal during 2022–2023, whereas female workers of general category from the rural sector are less likely to engage in skilled activities compared to Scheduled Tribe (ST) category female workers. In the urban sectors, both Scheduled Caste (SC) category male and female workers and OBC category female workers are less likely to engage in skilled occupations during the mentioned study period. It is found that both male and female Hindu workers of rural West Bengal are less likely to participate in skilled work compared to other religious workers, whereas in the urban sector, Hindu male workers are more likely to perform skilled activities.

However, we have failed to capture any significant effect for female workers in the urban sector in this regard.

Marital status of a female worker reduces the likelihood to engage in any skilled occupation both in rural and urban West Bengal during 2022–2023 though the effect is stronger in the rural sector which indicates that being married, the rural females are less likely to engage in skilled works than their urban counterparts. On the other hand, married male workers have a higher chance to engage in any skilled activities, though it is only found to be significant for the workers in rural areas for the considered study period. Any kind of formal training provides a better opportunity for both the male and female workers to occupy in skilled works, and effects are stronger for the male workers than females especially in the urban areas.

The number of children and household dependency burden are the important household-specific labour market indicators which matter for the choice of a person regarding their type of occupation. Analysis reveals that as the number of children in the household increases, not only rural females but surprisingly also the rural males are less likely to engage in high-skilled occupations. This may be due to that as they have to provide some extra time for the children for their caring, so they fail to devote the required time and follow the time-bound rules which are essential for high-skilled occupations. However, the study has failed to capture any significant impact of children on the engagement in skilled activities for the urban male and female workers. In case of dependency burden, it is positively significant for the rural males and negatively significant for the urban females which infer that as the number of dependent households increases, rural males are more likely to choose skilled occupations, whereas urban females are less likely to enter into the skilled occupations. This might be due to the fact that they are to provide time for taking care of children and elderly persons in the family, and hence, they are not able to join in skilled work. For the rest, results are not significant.

9. Conclusion

This study analyses the age-wise occupational segregation by gender after considering the distribution of workers by their occupation status using the PLFS 2023–2024 data in West Bengal both in rural and urban sectors. Occupations of urban areas are mostly high-skilled types due to the provision of professional occupations, whereas in the rural areas, most of the occupations are low-skilled types due to the provision of agriculture and elementary activities. Analysis reveals that most of the occupations have been dominated by the male workers both in rural and urban sectors of West Bengal during the considered period, though it differs for the different age cohorts. The study explored the notable contribution of female workers in high-skilled professional occupations in both the sectors, mainly by young groups, whereas male workers totally dominate the low-skilled plant operators' activity. The major contribution in agriculture and related activities in the rural sector of Bengal is found among the old-aged group of workers, though it is also male dominated. Among the household and person-specific factors, level of education provides the workers of both the sectors to engage in higher rank of occupations, whereas marriage and the number of children acts as the barriers for the female workers of both the sectors to engage in higher rank of occupations, especially the women from rural areas. Any kind of formal training insists the females to engage in high-skilled occupations, and the effects are stronger towards the urban females. General caste female workers from rural areas have lesser chance to engage in high-skilled occupations compared to reserved category female workers, but the opposite happens in the urban sector of West Bengal.

10. Policy Implications

The work participation of women has increased over the years as pointed out by different survey reports, but that participation remains mostly in unskilled low -graded activities as pointed out by this study. So, it is clear that the rising work participation of women is likely to be driven by distress especially in the rural sector. In this regard, some policies have been suggested to promote inclusive growth and job creation which can benefit the female workforce. Vocational training needs to be given as this can expand the occupational choices for women. A conditional cash transfer scheme like 'Kanyashree Prakalpa' to keep the girls in school rather than using that money for their marriage at young ages can be considered as an effective step in this direction as marriage creates a social barrier to engage in high-skilled decent jobs as observed in this study. Along with this, different social security benefits (including maternity benefit and child care leave) should be properly implemented in every sector to remove the occupational discrimination and enhance the participation of females in high-rank jobs.

Note: Kanyashree Prakalpa is an initiative by the government of West Bengal to remain the girl child on education by cash transfers rather than marrying off at a young age.

References

Agrawal, T. (2016). Occupational segregation in the Indian labour market. *The European Journal of Development Research, 28*(2), 330–351. http://www.palgrave-journals.com/ejdr/journal/v28/n2/pdf/ejdr201510a.pdf

Agrawal, T., & Agrawal, A. (2015). Trends in occupational gender segregation in India. *International Journal of Gender Studies in Developing Societies, 1*, 4–24. https://doi.org/10.1504/IJGSDS.2015.067919

Bertrand, M. (2011). New perspectives on gender. *Handbook of Labor Economics, 4*(B), 1543–1590. https://doi.org/10.1016/S0169-7218(11)02415-4

Chakraborty, I., & Chakraborty, A. (2010). Female work participation and gender differential in earning in West Bengal, India. *Journal of Quantitative Economics, 8*(2), 98–114. http://www.jqe.co.in/journals/JQE_v8_n2_2010_p7.pdf

Chattopadhyay, M., Chakraborty, S., & Anker, R. (2013). Sex segregation in India's formal manufacturing sector. *International Labour Review, 152*(1), 43–58. https://doi.org/10.1111/j.1564-913X.2013.00168.x

GOI. (2023). *Employment exchange statistics*. Ministry of Labour & Employment. https://labour.gov.in/employment-exchange-statistics

Madheswaran, S., & Attewell, P. (2007). Caste discrimination in the Indian urban labour market: Evidence from the National Sample Survey. *Economic and Political Weekly*, *42*(41), 4146–4153. https://www.epw.in/journal/2007/41/caste-and-economic-discrimination-special-issues-specials/caste-discrimination

Rathee, N., & Sarkar, C. (2023). Gender Inequality in West Bengal, with special reference to the Salanpur CD block, Paschim Bardhaman. *International Journal for Research Trend and Innovation*, *8*(6), 323–332. https://www.ijrti.org/viewpaperforall?paper=IJRTI2306052

Rammohan, A., Goli, S., & Reddy, A. B. (2017). *Occupational segregation by caste and gender in India* (Munich Personal RePEc Archive Paper 101969). MPRA. https://mpra.ub.uni-muenchen.de/101969/

Sharma, H. (2018). A state level analysis of gender occupational segregation in India. *International Journal of Social Science and Economic Research*, *3*(6), 2688–2702. https://ijsser.org/more2018.php?id=182

Welch, F. (2000). Growth in women's relative wages and inequality among men: One phenomenon or two? *American Economic Review*, *90*(2), 444–449. http://dx.doi.org/10.1257/aer.90.2.444

Printed and bound by CPI Group (UK) Ltd, Croydon, CR0 4YY

20/08/2026

14946493-0006